HOYLE'S MODERN ENCYCLOPEDIA OF CARD GAMES

Others Books by Walter B. Gibson

HOYLE'S MODERN ENCYCLOPEDIA OF CARD GAMES

Rules of All the Basic Games
and Popular Variations

BY WALTER B. GIBSON

Broadway Books
New York

First Broadway Books trade paperback edition published 2001.

The Library of Congress has catalogued the previous edition as:
ISBN 0-385-07680-0
Library of Congress Catalog Card Number 73–163085

39   38   37   36   35   34   33

How to Use This Book

This concise encyclopedia of modern card games and their variations is arranged alphabetically according to the name of each specific game. To assist the reader further, all games and their variations are cross-referenced so that complete explanations may be found easily and quickly. Illustrations of certain games and hands are also provided in their appropriate places.

All variations of any particular game may be found in this general alphabetical listing excepting those included under the broad headings of pinochle, poker, and solitaire. Since these three categories encompass such a wide variety of variations, all are listed alphabetically under the general divisions of pinochle, poker, and solitaire in an effort to ensure utmost organization in the book.

For even further assistance in locating a game or other information, a complete Glossary-Index featuring definitions and page references is found in the back of the book.

INTRODUCTION: FACTS ABOUT CARD GAMES
Including General Rules and Procedure

The term "Hoyle" has been used to signify a rule book of card games ever since the first such volume written by Edmond Hoyle appeared in 1746. There were only five games described in that modest work, but although the total has increased a hundredfold and more during the intervening years, many of them follow the old original patterns, and distinct traces of earlier games are found in most of the rest. Hence a preliminary description of playing cards and features applicable to games in general will prove valuable when discussing them under individual heads.

Formation of Packs Used in Various Games

Today's standard pack remains unchanged since the time of the original Hoyle. It consists of fifty-two cards, composed of four suits, spades (♠), hearts (♡), diamonds (◇), clubs (♣), each with thirteen values, ace, king, queen, jack, ten, nine, eight, seven, six, five, four, three (or trey), two (or deuce). They are usually ranked in descending order: **A, K, Q, J, 10, 9, 8, 7, 6, 5, 4, 3, 2;** but in a few games, the order runs: **K, Q, J, 10, 9, 8, 7, 6, 5, 4, 3, 2, A,** with ace low instead of high. There are also a few games in which the ace is either high or low.

In other games, most notably solitaires or one-person games, an ascending sequence is common: **A, 2, 3, 4, 5, 6, 7, 8, 9, 10, J, Q, K.** In some of the time-honored games, certain cards are given special valuation, and such rules may apply to suits, or even to colors; namely, red (♡ and ◇) or black (♠ and ♣). All these variations are covered in descriptions of the games in which they occur.

Modern packs, or "decks," as they are frequently called, contain two extra cards known as "jokers." For many years, a single joker has been used in certain games, commonly ranking higher than the other cards; and there are now games, most notably canasta, in which both jokers are used. This makes a quota of fifty-four cards for a single pack, 108 for a double pack, and 162 for a triple pack. Here, again, individual rules apply in evaluation of the cards.

Worthy of mention is a special sixty-three-card pack, including a single joker, which is used in the game of five hundred when six players are involved. This pack includes four elevens, four twelves, and two thirteens (in red suits only), which rank higher than the tens of their respective suits.

Special Packs for Special Games

In various games, the size of the pack is reduced by removing some of the cards beforehand. Such instances are cited in descriptions of the games themselves, along with the reasons for using a depleted pack. There are, however, certain famous games in which less than fifty-two cards represent the standard pack, hence they deserve preliminary descriptions as follows:

The Piquet Pack: Used in the French game of the same name, this pack consists of thirty-two cards ranking A, K, Q, J, 10, 9, 8, 7 in each of the four suits. The same pack is used in the now outmoded game of écarté, but with the curious ranking of K, Q, J, A, 10, 9, 8, 7. Games of the skat family also use the thirty-two-card pack; and it is standard in most forms of euchre, so other peculiarities in ranking will be found under those heads. French packs of only thirty-two cards are available, but in America it is customary to use a standard fifty-two-card pack and simply remove the cards of lower values. In two-handed euchre, the pack is further reduced to twenty-four cards by removing the eights and sevens.

Bezique and Pinochle Packs

In the game of bezique, played extensively in Europe, two piquet packs are combined to form a total of sixty-four cards, with those of each suit ranking A, A, 10, 10, K, K, Q, Q, J, J, 9, 9, 8, 8, 7, 7. In America, such a pack is made up from two standard fifty-two-card packs, from which all below the sevens have been discarded. However, bezique is seldom played in the United States, as it has been heavily overshadowed by the kindred game of pinochle, which uses a pack reduced to forty-eight cards: A, A, 10, 10, K, K, Q, Q, J, J, 9, 9. Such packs are sold extensively and are very desirable for special forms of pinochle in which two or more packs are combined.

Other Data on Playing Cards

Various types of playing cards have enjoyed brief periods of popularity. One innovation was a five-suit pack of sixty-five cards, the fifth suit either being termed "royals" and represented by a crown, or "eagles," with a bird. Special games or variants of existing games were devised for such packs, but none took permanent hold. More important to the average card player are the sizes of the standard packs. For years, the accepted measurement of an American playing card was three and one half by two and one half inches; and packs of those dimensions are sometimes sold as "poker" decks, as they are preferred by poker players. Since bridge players like narrower cards, other packs have been reduced to three and one half by two and one fourth inches and are popularly known as "bridge" decks. But the two styles have the same component of fifty-two cards plus two jokers, so all the usual games can be played with either pack.

The first cards to be printed with indexes in the upper left and lower right corners were advertised as "squeezers," because they could be identified by spreading them very slightly apart. Today, all American cards have such indexes and some English cards have them in all four corners, though that is generally superfluous. More practical are cards with "jumbo" indexes, which are oversized and therefore easier to read, making them excellent on television programs.

The term "jumbo" was originally applied to oversized cards, four times as large as the common variety and proportionately thicker, which made them suitable for outdoor play, where breezes might blow away ordinary cards. In striking contrast, there are miniature cards, half the size of standard packs. These are specially adapted to games of solitaire, in which a lone player spreads a pack over a limited area, where space is at a premium.

Customary Procedure in Card Games

The opening procedure in most card games is the shuffling or mixing of the pack. This may be done in various ways. One is to divide the pack and bend the ends of each section upward, with each thumb, then release them gradually so that they interweave as they fall. This is called the "riffle" or "dovetail" shuffle. The sections are then pushed together, the pack is squared, divided, and the process is repeated.

Less spectacular, but equally effective is the "overhand shuffle" in which the right hand holds the pack lengthwise, with the fingers at the outer end, the thumb at the inner. The left thumb then pulls away clusters of cards from the top of the face-down pack, letting them fall on those already drawn away, until the shuffle is completed. It can then be repeated in the same fashion as often as desired.

Before starting a game, anyone may shuffle the pack and spread it face down on the table. Players then draw cards from the spread to determine who will be the first dealer in the game. Whoever draws the highest card becomes the dealer, unless the participants specify that the lowest card should decide. Another way is for anyone to shuffle the pack, then start dealing cards face up to each player in turn, saying, "The first jack will be the dealer." Or some other value may be named at random, rather than the jack.

The dealer then shuffles the pack for himself and then allows another player to cut the cards. This consists of lifting off an upper portion of the pack and placing the lower portion upon it. In a two-player game, the dealer's opponent naturally is called upon to cut the pack; with more players, the privilege is customarily assigned to the player on the dealer's right, though others may demand and exert the same privilege.

Usually, in dealing, the pack is held face down in the left hand

and the left thumb pushes cards toward the right so that the right thumb and fingers can draw them off and place them on the table in front of the players, beginning at the dealer's left and continuing to the right in clockwise fashion, finishing with himself. Always, the cards are dealt face down unless otherwise specified. In some games of foreign origin, cards are dealt counterclockwise, but those are comparatively rare. Cards may be dealt singly or in clusters; any accepted procedure is specified with individual games.

Deals, Hands, and Play

This distribution of the cards is termed a "deal." When a player picks up his cards and holds their faces toward himself, they become his "hand." Each hand is then "played" by showing its cards, according to the rules of the particular game, though in some cases, hands may be simply discarded, or "thrown in" as worthless or unplayable.

The entire process from start to finish is known as a "deal," since it is not really finished until another deal supplants it. However, as it involves the play of the hands, it is also called a "hand," the two terms being interchangeable. In most games, each new deal moves to the player on the left, and after all have dealt and played out the hands, it is termed a "round."

In certain games, extra cards are dealt face down as a "widow," which may be claimed later by one of the players. A similar type of hand is known as the "crib" in the game of cribbage. Sometimes the extras represent "dead cards" or a "dead hand" that is out of play. In a few instances, an extra hand may be dealt to an imaginary player, or "dummy." In cassino extra cards are dealt face up as a "layout" in the center of the table. All these factors are discussed under game headings.

In dealing, any violation of an accepted pattern constitutes a misdeal. It is also a misdeal if the face of a card is exposed during the deal, except in games where certain cards are dealt face up, as with the central layout in cassino, or in blackjack and stud poker. However, if the dealer can correct that by dealing another card face down, he may do so if the other players agree. It is a misdeal to give too few or too many cards to a player, or to deal the wrong number of hands. Here, too, corrections are allowable; and if the mistake is ignored, the deal stands.

When a misdeal is confirmed, the cards are gathered, shuffled, and dealt again, usually by the same dealer, except in cases where dealing gives a player a definite advantage, in which case the others may insist that it move along to the next player. In social play, this presents few problems, if any; but players who take their card games seriously should decide beforehand how misdeals should be handled. If the pack itself is found to be incomplete, the deal should be immediately nullified, regardless of how far play has progressed.

Basic Facts on Games and Players

In certain popular games involving three or more players, as whist, bridge, pinochle, and hearts, the entire pack is dealt in every hand. In a multitude of others, including poker, cribbage, euchre, and pitch, only a limited number of cards are dealt; hence these are known as "short" games. Most games involving only two players fall into the "short" category, because if the entire pack were divided between them, each would know exactly what the other held.

However, some games begin with a "short" deal, and during the play more cards are dealt or drawn from the pack, so that one player is not aware of his opponent's exact holdings until near the end of the hand. This applies to two-handed forms of cassino, pinochle, and rummy. But short games are not limited to two players; many may include three, four, five, or even more participants. Games in which three or more players operate strictly on their own are known as "round games," but here, circumstances frequently introduce the new element of partnership play. For example:

When playing for score, whereby a player gaining a specified total becomes the winner (as 500 in the game of five hundred), a player in a three-handed game will naturally favor an opponent with a lower score rather than one whose score is higher. So keen can the competition become that these are commonly termed "cutthroat" games. In other three-handed games, where one player, as a bidder, stands to win or lose a big amount in a single hand, his opponents openly team against him, sharing whatever they make. Hence they become actual partners for that deal only.

In full-fledged partnership games, four players are usually involved and maintain their partnership throughout. Terming players *A, B, C,* and *D* in rotation, those seated opposite are usually partners, so that Team *A–C* would oppose Team *B–D*. In bridge, the players are designated South, West, North, East, with North and South forming one side or partnership, East and West the other. In such games, each team scores as a unit, so it becomes the equivalent of a two-player game, with opposing sides instead of individuals.

Occasionally, six players may participate in a partnership game. Terming the players *A, B, C, D, E, F,* two plans are available. Alternate players may form two teams of three each, *A–C–E* versus *B–D–F*, playing accordingly; or those seated opposite, *A–D, B–E, C–F* may form three teams of two each, so that it becomes practically a three-player game, in terms of sides or teams. (*Note:* This is specially applicable to five hundred, which even has a five-handed version involving temporary partnerships, as described under that head.)

Tricks, Counters, and Trumps

By far the largest category of card games is those in which each player, in turn, takes a card from his hand and lays it face up in the center of the table. The card of highest value wins all the rest, and the fortunate player gathers them, turns them face down in front of him, and is credited with a "trick." Usually that gives him the privilege of leading to the next trick, by being the first to place a card face up while the other players follow in order, as before.

In games like bridge, whist, euchre, and many others, the whole aim is to take tricks, as they go toward the score of the player or team. In games like pinochle, taking tricks is important only when they contain "counters" in the form of cards that alone count toward the player's score (as aces, tens, and kings). In pitch and its offshoots, there are premium cards that players go after; while the game of hearts is so named because cards of that suit count against a player who takes them in his tricks.

These factors are covered in detail under the headings of the various games, but there is another vital feature that characterizes practically all trick-taking games, with the notable exception of hearts. That is the inclusion of a "trump suit," which takes precedence over the three other suits during play. The name was derived from the old and now obsolete French game of triomphe, which later became anglicized as "trumps," but although the pattern has persisted, the modern derivations have striking points of individuality, which explains why each has its own coterie of enthusiastic followers.

General Procedure in Trump Games

Among modern card games, whist dates back to the triomphe era, and therefore has the simplest of rules where a trump is concerned. Since bridge, the most popular game today, follows practically the same rules, they make the best introduction to the trump games. Prior to play, one suit—say, spades—is named as trump; in whist, this is done by turning up the final card of the dealer's hand. Play then proceeds thus:

The player to the dealer's left leads any card to the first trick; and the others must play cards of the same suit if they can. This is called "following suit" and if all players comply, the one who played the highest card wins the trick. If a player is unable to follow suit, he may play a card from any nontrump suit—these are called "plain" or "ordinary" suits—and a card thus discarded or "thrown off" has no taking power, hence it simply goes to the winner of the trick.

That rule applies when any suit—including trumps—is led. However, if an ordinary suit is led, and a player is out of it, he has an added privilege. Instead of discarding from a plain suit, he may play a card of the trump suit, which is called "trumping the trick," thereby winning it, since any trump is higher than a card of a plain suit; unless another player "overtrumps" by playing a higher trump card; in which case, he naturally wins the trick.

A few simple examples will clarify all this. Assuming that spades are the trump suit, with players *A, B, C, D:*

Example 1: *A* leads ♡ **Q;** *B* plays ♡ **7;** *C* discards ◊ **3;** *D* plays ♡ **K.** Player *D* wins with ♡ **K.**

Example 2: *D* leads ♣ **A;** *A* plays ♣ **J;** *B* plays ♣ **10;** *C* trumps with ♠ **2.** *C* wins with ♠ **2.**

Example 3: *C* leads with ♡ **8;** *D* trumps with ♠ **J;** *A* discards ◊ **10;** *B* overtrumps with ♠ **K** and wins.

In bridge, players bid for the privilege of naming trumps; and "no-trump" is allowable, which simply means that there will be no-trump suit during that hand; otherwise, the play is the same, with cards in each suit ranking in the customary order: **A, K, Q, J, 10, 9, 8, 7, 6; 5, 4, 3, 2.**

In euchre, the highest trump is the jack, hence with spades as trumps, the ♠ **J,** as top card, is termed the "right bower." Next in value is the other jack of the same color, in this case the ♣ **J,** known as the "left bower," followed by the remaining cards of the trump suit, from ace down. Play follows the same rules as in whist. In five hundred, there are bowers, as in euchre; but the joker is also used and ranks as the highest card, or "best bower," no matter what suit is trumps.

In pitch, whatever card the bidder leads to the first trick represents the trump suit. Players must follow suit when a trump is led; but when a plain suit is led, he may trump it instead of following suit. If out of the suit, he may either discard or trump. In skat, the four jacks are the highest trumps, in the order ♣, ♠, ♡, ◊, regardless of what suit is named as trumps.

In pinochle, with its duplicated values, **A, A, 10, 10, K, K, Q, Q, J, J, 9, 9,** the first of two identical cards played on a trick takes precedence over the next. Players must follow suit when able, but when out of suit, a player must trump the trick if he can. Whenever a trump is led, a player must play a higher trump if he has one. Other games have special rules regarding trumps and trumping, which should be carefully checked by the participants, as they have important bearing on the play of the hand.

Irregularities and Penalties

Along with misdeals, which have already been discussed, there are other irregularities that can mar the smooth progress of a card game. In social play, these are generally condoned, unless they give a player or a team an unfair advantage, which naturally should be offset. In betting or bidding, each player should await his turn; otherwise, his opponents may decide whether it should be nullified or forced to stand. In bidding, this applies strictly to team play, as an irregular bid may tip off facts to the player's partner; but in round games, such bids can be ignored.

Similarly, if a player shows a card that would be helpful to his partner, it must be placed face up on the table and the opponents can call upon its owner to play it at the first opportunity. In the case of two or more exposed cards, the opponents may choose between them when all are playable. In bridge, these are termed "penalty cards," and the rule is often rigidly enforced; but only against the defending team, as the high bidder, or declarer, plays a lone hand and therefore can gain nothing by showing a card. Hence the same should apply in any game where a similar situation arises.

In trump games, failure to follow suit may cause complications. This is termed a "revoke," and the offender can correct it before the next trick is played by taking back the wrong card and replacing it with a proper card. The wrong card is then treated as an exposed or "penalty" card. The other players may take back any cards played following the revoke, as it may have had a bearing on their play. In bridge, when a revoke has been established, there is a penalty of two tricks, which are transferred from the offender's team to the opponents, provided those tricks were taken following the revoke. If the offending team took only one such trick, it is transferred; if none, there is no transfer.

In most trump games, if the bidding player or team revokes, the penalty is the loss of the bid or the full score that the hand might have brought. Conversely, if a defending player or team revokes, the bidder scores the full amount that he might have made if he had played the hand successfully. In games where there is no bidding, the offender is generally charged with a full loss; for example, in hearts, where every card of that suit counts against the player who takes it, a player who revokes would be saddled with all such points, just as though he had actually taken the tricks containing them.

In social play, an established revoke may be disregarded if it has no real bearing on the outcome. This sometimes happens when a player is throwing worthless cards on tricks toward the end of a deal. Similarly, if a revoke occurs during the last few tricks, when play is almost automatic, it is often easy to reconstruct those tricks as they should have been played and score them accordingly. This is generally the preferable procedure, as friendly card players seldom care to win hands by default.

However, an early revoke sometimes goes undetected until the play is practically completed, thus making it impossible to go back trick by trick to learn what might have happened, as some of those tricks might have been played differently except for the revoke. In that case, the penalty is the only answer. A revoke is not limited just to failure to follow suit. In games where a player is forced to trump when out of suit, or to "head" a trick by playing a higher card than the one led, infraction of such rules is also a revoke.

The term "renege" is similar to "revoke" but was formerly applied in games like spoil five, where specific high trumps do not have to be played when a lower trump is led. A player was said to renege when he exerted that privilege, so a renege, though actually a revoke, was legitimate. But the term soon was used in connection with more popular games that had no such privilege, and renege became synonymous with revoke. The term "renounce" has also been given the same connotation, though originally it meant "to disclaim having a card of the suit led by playing a card of another suit." That is quite legitimate, if the player actually has no card of the suit led.

Other irregularities are mostly of a minor nature, or the sort that rarely occur. When they do, they can usually be decided by good judgment; and the average circle of friendly card players can often agree beforehand as to the penalties to be invoked when such rules are infracted. Indeed, the real decision makers in the great majority of card games are the local groups whose time-tested modes of play spread so rapidly and widely that they become innovations elsewhere.

In a strict sense, there are no absolute rules for card games; if there were, very few new games would be developed, yet the number of variants and offshoots is legion and shows a continued increase. Often, some new trend takes such strong or rapid hold that some of the most time-honored customs become obsolete. Hence the rules listed in the games that follow may be regarded chiefly as accepted procedures that players are free to modify or amend as they see fit, even if it means coining an identifying name for what is practically a new game. That has been happening constantly with poker and canasta, which accounts for the ever-increasing popularity of those games.

Hence, being rule makers in their own right, social players should not hesitate to settle irregularities and other minor problems as they deem best. By concentrating on the more important features of a game, they will qualify for more serious circles, where players are already familiar with special procedures and conventions. Thus the newcomers can acquaint themselves with the finer or exacting points that can properly be learned only through actual experience.

When a game becomes so established that it is widely played in clubs or tournaments, special rules are adopted for such purposes and are sometimes codified under the more definitive title of "laws." Inveterate card players frequently refer to these as their guides for regular play.

ACCORDION: A type of *Solitaire*. See page 323.

ACEPOTS: In *Draw Poker*, a game with a pair of aces or better as an opening requirement. See page 241.

ACES UP: A type of *Solitaire*. See page 323.

AIRPLANE: A form of *Partnership Pinochle* (described under that head, page 189), in which four cards are exchanged by partners winning the bid. Also termed *Racehorse*.

ALL FIVES: A two-player variant of *All Fours* (see below), in which extra points are scored during play by the player taking the following trump cards: ace, 4; king, 3; queen, 2; jack, 1; ten, 10; five, 5. The usual scores of 1 each for high, low, jack, and game are added at the conclusion of the hand, but in the usual "count" for "game" involving honor cards of all suits (**A, 4; K, 3; Q, 2; J, 1; 10, 10**) the five of trumps is valued as 5. The *All Fives* method of scoring is also adapted to various forms of *Pitch*, most notably *California Jack* and *Shasta Sam*, in which the entire pack is played out during each hand. For convenience, such scores may be pegged on a cribbage board, with 61 points the winning total.

ALL FOURS: Known variously as *Seven Up, Old Sledge,* and *High-Low Jack,* this is preferably a two-player game, so will first be described as such. With more players, a modern version, *Pitch,* is more popular. A fifty-two-card pack is used, with each suit ranking **A, K, Q, J, 10, 9, 8, 7, 6, 5, 4, 3, 2** in descending order, with a trump suit taking precedence. The term "all fours," originally used in England, refers directly to the principal points that can be scored: high, for holding the highest trump; low, for holding the lowest trump; jack, for turning up or taking the jack of trump; and game, for taking, during play, the greatest total in certain cards, which count as follows: An ace, 4; king, 3; queen, 2; jack, 1; ten, 10.

Six cards are dealt to each player, and the next is turned up as a trump. If a jack, the dealer scores 1 point. The opponent, after examining his hand, decides whether or not he wants that suit for trump. If he does, he states, "I stand," and play begins. If not, he says, "I beg," and puts the next step up to the dealer, who also has two choices: to accept the turned-up trump by telling the opponent, "I give you one"—this being a special point for the opponent—or to state, "I refuse the gift."

In that case, he lays the turned-up card aside and deals three cards to his opponent and three more to himself, turning up the next card as a trump. If it is the suit already rejected, he turns it down and deals three more cards to his opponent and three more to himself until a new suit is turned up and is definitely established, with the dealer scoring 1 point if it is a jack. If no new suit turns up, the cards are gathered and shuffled, and the dealer deals again. Such deals are called "running the cards," and if they prove futile, the cards are "bunched" for the new deal. Indeed, if neither the opponent nor the dealer likes a new trump that turns up, they can agree to "bunch" the cards and start all over. Generally, however, either the original trump or the next is accepted; and play proceeds as follows:

The opponent leads any card he wants. If a trump, the dealer must follow suit if he can; otherwise, he must play from another suit. If an ordinary suit is led by the opponent, the dealer can follow suit or trump, as he prefers; if he can do neither, he may discard from a side suit. The higher card of the suit led wins the trick unless trumped, then trump wins. The winner of the trick leads to the next, and so on. After any preliminary scoring, points are scored in the order high, low, jack (if it appears in play), and game (unless the count is tied). The deal moves on, and the first player to score 7 points wins, though 11 or 12 are sometimes agreed upon.

With three or four players, only the first can "beg." With

three, each is on his own, and if two tie for "game," that point is not counted. With four, those opposite are partners and pool whatever tricks they take. Other rules follow those of modern *Pitch,* page 214. See *All Fives,* page 13, for an older variant.

ALSOS: A game closely resembling *Klaberjass* or *Klob,* page 151.

AMBIGU: A French forerunner of *Poker,* with two to six players using a forty-card pack (each **K, Q, J** eliminated), with cards ranking in descending order, **10, 9, 8, 7, 6, 5, 4, 3, 2, A.** Each player antes a set number of chips and is dealt two cards face down. He may keep them or reject either or both, drawing the needed replacement. Two more cards are then dealt to each player, making four in all. Each in turn passes or bets within a set limit, with successive players calling, raising, or dropping as in poker.

If no one calls the last raiser, he wins the pool or pot and shows his hand face up. If anyone calls, so that two or more players have equalized their bets, each has the privilege of another draw, replacing one to four cards, unless he prefers to stand pat. Hands are then shown and the highest takes the pool. In addition, he receives a bonus from each loser, according to the value of his hand, as follows:

Point: Total number of spots on two cards of one suit. If a tie, two cards in sequence win (example: ♡ **6,** ♡ **5** wins over ♠ **9,** ♠ **2**). Bonus: 1 token.
Prime: Four cards of different suits. Bonus: 2 tokens.
Grand prime: Same, with more than thirty spots. Bonus: 3 tokens.
Sequence: Three cards of one suit in numerical order. Higher wins (as ♠ **6, 5, 4** over ♢ **4, 3, 2**). Bonus: 3 tokens.
Tricon: Three of the same value (as **8, 8, 8**). Bonus: 4 tokens.
Flush: Four of the same suit (as ♠ **9, 7, 5, 2**). Bonus: 5 tokens.

Doublet: These are double combinations, each a prime or better, and are ranked accordingly, as:

Prime and *tricon* (♠ 6, ♡ 6, ♣ 6, ◇ 2). Bonus: 2+4=6 tokens.

With *grand prime* (♠ 9, ♡ 9, ♣ 9, ◇ 5). Bonus: 3+4=7 tokens.

Sequence and *flush* (♣ 9, 8, 7, 3). Bonus: 3+5=8 tokens.

Fredon: Four of a kind (♠ 4, ♣ 4, ♡ 4, ◇ 4). Bonus: 2+8=10 tokens.

With *grand prime* (♡ 10, ♠ 10, ♣ 10, ◇ 3). Bonus: 2+9= 11 tokens.

There can be no ties in ambigu because when identical hands occur (as ♠ 9, ♣ 7, ◇ 5, ♡ A vs. ♣ 9, ◇ 7, ♡ 5, ♠ A) the player nearest to the dealer's right becomes the winner. That is because in ambigu, as in other French games, hands are dealt counterclockwise, to the right instead of left.

AMERICAN BRAG: See *Brag,* page 39.

AMERICAN PINOCHLE: Another name for modern forty-eight-card *Pinochle,* page 174.

AMERICAN SKAT: A modernized form of the old German game. See page 314.

AMERICAN WHIST: *Whist* with 7 points for game, no other points being scored. See page 375.

ANACONDA: *Poker,* a form of *Dealer's Choice,* 241.

ANIMALS: See *Menagerie,* page 160.

ANY CARD WILD: *Poker,* 242.

ANY SUIT WILD: *Poker,* 242.

ANYTHING OPENS: *Poker,* 242.

ANY VALUE WILD: *Poker,* 242.

ARLINGTON: An advanced form of *Rummy,* also known as Oklahoma, but the term Arlington is preferable, as it avoids confusion between this game and *Oklahoma Gin.* It is played with a double pack of 104 cards, or 105 if a joker is included. The cards rank: **A, K, Q, J, 10, 9, 8, 7, 6, 5, 4, 3, 2, A,** the ace being either high or low, while a deuce ranks either as itself (2) or as a wild card, representing any card in the pack. The joker, when used, is wild.

The game is played by two, three, four, or five persons, each being dealt thirteen cards, with the next turned up beside the pack as starter for a discard pile. Each player in turn has the option of taking the upcard into his hand and discarding another in its stead; but after it has been taken up by one or refused by all, the next player may draw from the top of the pack if he prefers. Play continues thus, but from then on, anyone taking the upcard must pick up the entire discard pile with it.

Before discarding, a player may meld sets of three or four cards of the same value (as **J–J–J** or **9–9–9–9**) regardless of suit; or sequences of three or more cards of the same suit, which, thanks to the double pack, can be extended to fourteen cards, with an ace at each end. Odd cards can be laid off on a player's own melds; not on melds of others. If a deuce is melded as a wild card, its value must be stated, as with ♡ **2**, ♠ **2**, ♠ **9**, which could represent 9–9–9 or ♠ J 10 9. Once specified, the deuce's value must stand, and the same applies to a wild joker. However, the joker can be reclaimed by a player who melded it by replacing it with a card that it represents, which then leaves him free to use the joker in another meld. The player can take the upcard for that purpose, also picking up the discard pile with it, as usual. In all other cases, a player taking the discard pile must use the upcard in a meld or layoff.

The ♠ Q plays a special part in Arlington, in that it cannot be discarded unless it is the only card left in the player's hand. He can, however, meld the ♠ Q or lay it off on one of his previous melds. Play ends when a player "goes rummy" by disposing of all his cards by melding them, either with or without the need of discarding his final card. Melds are then reckoned thus:

Joker	100 points	Any eight or above	10 points
Spade queen	50	Any seven or below	5
Each ace	20	Bonus for going out	100

Each deuce is valued according to the card it represents.

From the total of his meld, each player then deducts for each unmelded card remaining in his hand, but the joker and ♠ Q count double against him (200 and 100 respectively) and each deuce counts 20 points against him. If play ends with no one going rummy, there is no bonus score. Scores of each deal are added, and the first player to go over 1000 with a higher total than any other gets a bonus of 200 points. If two tie above 1000, they split the bonus.

If a player goes out in one meld, keeping his hand concealed until then, he gains a special 250 bonus, which does not count in his running score but is added to his total after the game. This rule applies to each deal.

ARMY AND NAVY PINOCHLE: A popular name for *Double Pack Pinochle,* described in the section on *Pinochle.* See *Army and Navy Pinochle,* page 204.

AROUND THE WORLD: *Poker.* See page 242.

AS or AS NAS: A Persian progenitor of *Poker.*

AUCTION BID WHIST: A form of *Bid Whist,* described under *Whist.* See page 375.

AUCTION BRIDGE: The predecessor of *Contract Bridge,* page 72, this game is played by the same rules but with a different scoring schedule, which runs:

	♣	◇	♡	♠	No-trump
For each trick won over six	6	7	8	9	10
The same, if doubled	12	14	16	18	20
The same, if redoubled	24	28	32	36	40

A team making its bid scores for all tricks it takes. These are entered "below the line," which runs across the score sheet, and count toward game, which is 30 points. A new game is then started, and when a team wins two, it wins the rubber and scores 250 bonus points, which go "above the line," as do the following:

Winning contract when doubled	50	When redoubled	100
Each extra trick when doubled	50	When redoubled	100
For each trick under contract, the opposing team scores	50		
If doubled	100	If redoubled	200
Small slam (taking 12 tricks)	50	Grand slam (13)	100

A team also scores a bonus for holding a majority of honors —A K Q J 10 of trump or A A A A in no-trump—above the line:

For 3 honors (trump or no-trump)	30	For 4 trump honors in one hand	80
For 4 honors divided by partners	40	Same with fifth in partner's	90
For 5 trump honors, divided	50	All honors in one hand	100

At the conclusion of a rubber, each team's points are added (both above and below the line) and the lower score is subtracted from the higher to determine the latter's margin of victory. In auction, bidding is much less exacting than in contract, as strong hands often win bids at low levels. Hence auction bridge is still a good game for beginners.

AUCTION CINCH: Also called *Razzle Dazzle*. See page 67.

AUCTION EUCHRE: An elaboration of *Euchre,* described in that section. See page 113.

AUCTION FORTY-FIVE: See *Forty-five,* page 123.

AUCTION HEARTS: A game similar to *Hearts,* in which the players bid for the privilege of naming the suit whose cards are to be avoided during play. See *Hearts,* page 140.

AUCTION HIGH FIVE: Another name for *Auction Cinch.* See page 67.

AUCTION PINOCHLE: A three-handed form of *Pinochle* with a widow, long the most popular form of the game. See page 177.

AUCTION PITCH: Commonly termed *Pitch,* as it is the most popular form of that game, which in turn is derived from *All Fours* or *High-Low Jack.* Known also as *Setback, Auction Pitch* is described in the section on *Pitch,* page 214.

AUCTION SHEEPSHEAD: See page 306.

AUCTION SIXTY-SIX: See page 313.

AULD LANG SYNE: A type of *Solitaire.* See page 324.

AUSTRALIAN POKER: Another term for *English Poker* and *Blind Opening.* See latter under *Poker,* page 245.

AUTHORS: A card-matching game in which the fifty-two cards of a standard pack are dealt singly to any number of players from three to seven, in clockwise fashion. Player on dealer's left notes a card in his hand (say the ◇ 5) and asks another player for a specific card of that same value, as the ♣ 5. Thus with five players, Alf, Bob, Cal, Don, and Ed, assume that Alf put the request to Don. If Don has the ♣ 5, he must give it to Alf, who then can ask for another card (provided he has one of its value) from any player. But as soon as Alf misses, the calling privilege moves along to Bob on the same basis, and continues thus around the board. Upon completing any set of cards (as all four jacks) a player lays it face up in front of him as a book, and calls for another card to match any that he holds. When a player runs out of cards, the call moves along until all cards are gone.

The player with the most books wins unless a specific number of deals has been agreed upon; or a grand total of books has been set (say ten, twelve, or more) to constitute the game. In any case, each new deal moves to the left. The title "authors" comes from a proprietary game in which each set of specially printed cards is represented by four works of some famous author.

AUTOMATIC LOWBALL: A form of *Draw Poker,* page 243.

AUXILIARY SEQUENCES: An early form of *Storehouse.* See page 348.

BACCARA or BACCARAT: Chiefly a gambling casino game played with three packs of cards, values running from ace, as 1, up to 9, with tens and face cards rating 0. The banker sets a betting limit, and two players stake wagers against him individually. The banker deals cards alternately to the player on his right, then on his left, finally to himself, twice around, each getting two, face down. These are noted and if anyone has a total of 8 or 9, he turns up his cards as a "natural." Example: $2+6=8$, or $8+J=8$. $4+5=9$, or $9+Q=9$. If the total comes to more than 9, the first figure is dropped; thus $9+9=18$ would be a natural 8.

The banker pays off or collects from each player separately; and in the case of two naturals, 9 wins over 8, while with a tie, bets are off. If no one has a natural, cards remain face down, and each person can "stand" on those he has or call for one more card, which is dealt face up, his purpose being to come closest to 9 and thus become the winner. Example: Player A stands with $5+2=7$. Player B, holding $3+J$, draws a 6, making $3+0+6=9$. Dealer, holding $8+4$, draws a 6, making $8+4+6=18=8$. Dealer collects from A and pays off B.

Other players may participate, betting along with A or B, as they prefer. Or they may place bets on a middle line, winning if both players win and losing if both lose. These bets, termed *à cheval,* are called off if one player wins and the other loses. Before the deal, a player may announce "Banco," thereby betting the full amount of the bank and playing both hands for himself, with no other players allowed.

BANGO: A card game resembling "bingo," utilizing a fifty-two-card pack, or preferably a double pack (104 cards) when up to a dozen players participate. Each contributes a specified number of chips to a pool or pot and is then dealt five cards in a face-up row. Cards are turned up singly from the pack, and whenever a player can match one in value (as nine for nine), he turns down his corresponding card or cards. The first player to turn down his entire row calls, "Bango" and wins the pot. With a tie, the pool is split; if no one wins, it is carried into the next pool.

Note: Instead of turning down cards, markers (such as odd chips) can be placed upon them.

BANKER AND BROKER: Also known as *Blind Hookey, Dutch Bank,* and *Honest John.*

The pack: The standard fifty-two cards running in descending values, **A, K, Q, J, 10, 9, 8, 7, 6, 5, 4, 3, 2.** Suits play no part.

Number of players: Up to a dozen.

Deal and Play: The dealer, as "banker," cuts the pack into four, five, or six piles. Players place tokens alongside whatever piles they want, leaving one vacant for the banker, who turns the piles face up, beginning with his own, showing the bottom cards. For every card of higher value, the banker pays off chip for chip. He collects from all that his card matches or exceeds in value. By rotating the deal after each hand, the banker's advantage can be spread equally among the players.

BANK NIGHT: See page 243.

BARNYARD: A variant of *Menagerie,* using names of fowls and domestic animals. See page 160.

BASEBALL: A form of wild-card *Poker*. See page 243.

BASSET: An early form of *Faro*, popular in Venice in 1700. See *Faro*, page 116.

BATTLE ROYAL: Three-handed *Gin Rummy* (page 130) allowing each player to take up either of the two previous discards. When a player knocks, the others, in turn, lay off on his hand.

BEAST: A now obsolete forerunner of *Loo* and *Nap*.

BEAT YOUR NEIGHBOR: A form of *Stud Poker*. See page 243.

BEDSPRINGS: A modern variant of *Poker*, page 243.

BEER PLAY: Another name for *Bierspiel*. See *Rams*, page 287.

BEGGAR MY NEIGHBOR: An automatic but exciting two-player game with each holding half a fifty-two-card pack in a face-down pile. They deal cards alternately from the top of their respective piles into a center heap, face up, as long as only spot cards appear. But when one turns up a picture card (or ace), it calls for his opponent to deal cards as follows: jack, 1; queen, 2; king, 3; ace, 4. If all are spots, the original player wins the center heap, gathering it as it stands and placing it face down beneath his pile. But if the opponent turns up a picture card (or ace), it takes precedence and the original player must meet the new demand on the same terms; and so on.

(Example: *A* deals a queen, calling for two cards. *B* deals a spot, then an ace, calling for four. *A* deals spot, spot, jack, calling for one. *B* deals a spot and *A* wins the center heap.)

The winner starts the play anew, and it continues until one player has "beggared" his opponent by taking all his cards, thus winning the game. As many as six players can participate, all being given nearly equal piles; or still more, if a double pack of 104 cards is used. All deal in rotation to the center pile, and when one runs out of cards, he drops from the game and the next player continues where he left off. This eventually narrows the game to two players, as in its simple form.

BELEAGUERED CASTLE: A type of *Solitaire*. See page 324.

BELOTTE: A French game similar to *Klaberjass,* described under that head. See page 151.

BEST FLUSH: A form of *Poker* in which only flushes or partial flushes count. See page 244.

BET OR DROP: *Draw Poker,* with the rule that a player must bet or pass up the hand. See pages 226 and 244.

BETROTHAL: A form of *Solitaire,* page 325.

BETTY HUTTON: A form of *Poker,* page 244.

BEZIQUE: This forerunner of *Pinochle* requires a sixty-four-card pack with two of each value in each suit, ranking A, A, 10, 10, K, K, Q, Q, J, J, 9, 9, 8, 8, 7, 7, with each seven of trump serving as a dix, with a value of 10 points. In the original two-handed game, the play and melds are as follows:

Only eight cards are dealt to each player (usually three, three, two) with the next turned up beneath the pack to represent trump. In play, the leads and draws are the same as in two-handed pinochle, with no need to follow suit or trump until the last eight tricks. However, in bezique, only aces and tens—called brisques—are counters, at 10 points each, with 10 for the last trick, making 170 points taken in play.

In melds, there is a marked difference from pinochle, namely:

A trump sequence (**A, 10, K, Q, J**) scores 250		
Royal marriage (**K, Q** of trump) 40. Plain marriage		20
Any four aces	100	*Any* four kings	80
Any four queens	60	*Any* four jacks	40
Bezique (♠ **Q,** ◊ **J**)	40	Double bezique	500
Each dix (exchangeable for turned-up trump)		10

With each player starting with a hand of eight cards, the opponent leads any card and the dealer plays whatever he wants. The highest card of the suit led takes the trick unless a plain suit lead is trumped. The winner of each trick may lay his melds face up in front of him, but can score only for one. Others must wait until he wins later tricks. For example, a player lays down:

♠ K Q ◊ J ♡ J ♣ J ♣ J

He declares four jacks for 40 points and is free to play any jack except the ◊ J, which he retains in order to meld a bezique (◊ J ♠ Q) after winning another trick. After winning a third trick, he can declare the spade marriage (♠ K Q) for a further score.

The winner of each trick adds the top card of the pack to his hand and the loser takes the next. The winner leads either from his hand or his meld, and the loser plays accordingly. When all the pack has been drawn, a player must follow suit and take the trick if possible; if out of suit, he must take the trick with a trump if he has one; otherwise, he plays from an odd suit. At the finish, brisques and last trick are counted at 10 points each and added to each player's individual melds.

As in pinochle, a player can meld a royal marriage for 40 points and later add the A, 10, J for a trump sequence at 250. But once a meld is made, none of its cards may be used toward another meld in the same class. Thus, after melding four aces for 100, the remaining four aces would have to be melded as a group to score 100; and so on.

A player melding a bezique (♠ Q, ◊ J) for 40 points can add another such combination to score 500 for double bezique (♠ Q Q, ◊ J J), but if forced to declare both simultaneously, he would not score 40, but only the 500 for double bezique. Similarly, he might lose 40 for a royal marriage if forced to meld it as part of a sequence.

Otherwise, the melding rules of bezique are more liberal than in pinochle. A player does not have to add a card from his hand in making a fresh meld, but may, on occasion, declare a combination already showing on his board. Example: A player melds ◊ J, ♠ J, ♣ J, ♡ J for 40. He retains the

◇ J while playing other jacks. Later, he melds ♠ Q, ♣ Q, ♡ Q, ◇ Q for 60. He wins a trick a few plays later and points to the ◇ J, ♠ Q combination still on the board, announcing it as a 40-point meld for bezique.

Each hand in bezique can constitute a game, but it is preferable to set a cumulative total for game, such as 1000 points; or better, 1500, due to the fact that a player scoring a double bezique (500) would have too great an advantage in a 1000-point game.

Note: Since bezique is seldom played today, it has been described as though it were an offshoot of the more popular pinochle, rather than as the parent game. Bezique itself has variants, the simplest being to disregard the dix as a scoring factor and to begin the play without turning up a trump. All suits are plain until one player melds a marriage, which is declared a royal, thereby making its suit trump.

Bezique is sometimes confused with sixty-four-card pinochle, which utilizes the sixty-four-card bezique pack but is played and scored exactly like pinochle, except that each player is dealt sixteen cards and the seven of trump serves as the dix, instead of the nine.

RUBICON BEZIQUE: This introduces some radical and intriguing departures from the original two-handed game. A 128-card pack is used with four of each kind, ranked A, 10, K, Q, J, 9, 8, 7 as usual. Nine cards are dealt to each player, but no trump is turned up, hence there is no dix. Instead, the first marriage declared by either player establishes the trump suit.

As a preliminary, if either hand is entirely devoid of court cards (K, Q, J), the player displays it face up and scores 50 points for a carte blanche. If he fails to draw a court card after the first trick, he scores another; and the same applies to successive tricks until a court card does appear, after which the player can make no more such declarations.

Other declarations or melds are as follows:

Royal marriage	40	Plain marriage	20
Trump sequence	250	Any sequence	150
Bezique (♠ Q, ◊ J)	40	Double bezique	500
Triple bezique	1500	Quadruple	4500
Any four jacks	40	Any four queens	60
Any four kings	80	Any four aces	100

Playing and drawing proceed as in the standard game of bezique, but brisques (each A or 10) do not count, unless the score is tied, in which case the brisques are counted to determine the winner. The player taking the last trick scores 50 points; but earlier in the game, however, we encounter the somewhat fantastic departure from the normal that gives rubicon bezique its decisive individuality:

After playing a card from a meld, the player may add another card to form a new meld, with another score. Example: From a meld of ♣ Q, ♠ Q, ♠ Q, ◊ Q, for 60 points, he plays the ♣ Q and wins the trick. He promptly lays down a ♡ Q for another 60 points and plays a ♠ Q, winning that trick also. So he lays down a ◊ Q and calls it another 60 points.

Even more wonderful, he can meld a ♣ K Q as a marriage for 20 points; then another ♣ K Q for 20 points; and following that, he can interchange the kings and queens, scoring 20 points for the first ♣ K and the second ♣ Q; then 20 points again for the second ♣ K and the first ♣ Q. However, once a king and queen have been declared and scored as part of a sequence (A, 10, K, Q, J), neither can be used toward a new marriage.

With a bezique, a player can meld a ◊ J and ♠ Q for 40 points, then later play a member of the pair (as the ◊ J) and form another 40-point bezique by adding another, identical card, in this case, a ◊ J. This can be repeated with either member of the pair. However, unless nearly all the cards have been drawn from the pack, or needed cards have already been played, a player melding ◊ J, ♠ Q would do better to hold another ◊ J on the chance of drawing a ♠ Q, when he could add them to

those already melded, forming a double bezique (◊ **J J, ♠ Q Q),**
for 500 points.

Similarly, he could go for triple bezique (1500) and quadruple bezique (4500) by adding new combinations to those
still on the board, making a total of 40+500+1500+4500=
6540. But such an opportunity would be rare indeed. So many
combinations are possible in this game that a player usually
must choose those that are most profitable or most expedient,
rather than try to cash all his holdings or bank on potentials.

Since rubicon bezique is essentially a high scoring game, care-
ful score must be kept throughout the hand, which is regarded as
a complete game. In declaring a meld, a player may announce a
future meld by laying down the necessary cards; but they serve
only as a reminder, as the future meld cannot be scored until he
has taken another trick.

Example: A player can lay down four queens, including
♠ **Q,** and with them a ◊ **J** and ♠ **K,** declaring, "Sixty for
queens," then adding, "With forty to score for bezique [♠ **Q,**
◊ **J]** and twenty to score for a marriage [♠ **K Q]."** The three
cards thus involved would have to remain on the board until
the player takes another trick, then the bezique could be
counted and he could play the ◊ **J.** But he would have to retain the ♠ **K Q** until after taking another trick, in order to count
the marriage.

A player should continue to announce such futures after
each trick, until he actually scores them, just to keep the
record straight; but he can abandon any futures if need be.
Players are also allowed to count the remaining cards in the
pack, as the draw nears the end, as after that no more melds
can be declared. During the play of the last nine tricks, a player
must follow suit and take the trick if he can; if out of suit, he
must trump if possible.

Scoring follows a special pattern in rubicon bezique. Each
deal is regarded as a game in itself, and the player with the
higher score wins the game, but brisques are not usually
counted. Scores are reckoned in hundreds, so if the dealer
should total 1420 and the opponent 1150, the final scores
would be 1400 and 1100, giving the dealer a margin of 300

points, to which he adds 500 as a bonus for winning the game, for a final margin of 800 points. If the difference is less than 100 points, the winner is credited with 100 plus 500 for game, or 600 points in all.

However, if a loser fails to reach the 1000 mark, he is said to be "rubiconed" and the winner adds the loser's points to his score, as though he had taken all the tricks, and is credited with 320 for the brisques that they contain (sixteen aces and sixteen tens at 10 points each). Also, the winner is given a double bonus, scoring 1000 for winning the game. As an example: Opponent scores 1120 and dealer scores 470. Opponent counts his 1100 plus dealer's 400, with 320 for brisques and 1000 for game: 1100+400+320+1000=2820, or 2800, as customarily reckoned.

If a loser's score is close to 1000, he is allowed to count his own brisques to avoid being rubiconed. Assuming that his meld comes to 860, and he finds that he has taken sixteen brisques for 160 points, his total would be 1020, giving him the needed 1000. That would be deducted from the winner's score, which in this case would include the winner's brisques, since the loser was allowed to count his own.

Similarly, brisques should be checked when scores are close enough for them to decide the issue. Example: Dealer scores 1160; opponent, 1070. Brisques are counted and dealer has only ten against opponent's twenty-two. Final score: Dealer 1160+100=1260. Opponent 1070+220=1290. Opponent becomes the winner.

SIX-PACK BEZIQUE: This is the modernized form of rubicon bezique, played with three bezique packs of sixty-four cards each, making a total of 192 cards. This is the equivalent of six piquet packs of thirty-two cards each—valued A, 10, K, Q, J, 9, 8, 7—hence the term "six-pack bezique." The original version was called "Chinese bezique" and was simply rubicon bezique with more cards, which made it somewhat unwieldy, but new features were added later, bringing the game up to its present standard.

There are two players, as in rubicon bezique, but each is

dealt twelve cards. This makes it more difficult to receive a hand devoid of kings, queens, and jacks; hence a carte blanche, as such a hand is called, scores 250 and can be repeated as long as the player continues to draw cards of other values. In addition to the melds listed under rubicon bezique, the following are included in the six-handed game:

Four trump aces	1000	Four trump kings	800
Four trump tens	900	Four trump queens	600
	Four trump jacks	400	

Play proceeds exactly as in rubicon bezique, with the first marriage melded establishing the trump suit, a very important feature, because of the bonus counts just listed. There is no count whatever for any brisques—aces and tens—that are taken during play, but the player taking the last trick scores 250 points in this game. A dix (seven of trump) has no meld value. Each deal is a game, as in rubicon bezique, but the winner scores 1000 points in six-pack play. That is added to the winner's high score, and the loser's low score is deducted to determine the margin of victory in terms of hundreds, just as in rubicon bezique.

Also, the loser can be rubiconed if he fails to score 3000 or more. In that case, the winner adds the loser's score to his own to determine the winning total. There is no bonus for brisques as in rubicon bezique, because, as already mentioned, they do not figure at all.

An interesting preliminary may be introduced in six-pack bezique, namely: Before dealing, the dealer tries to lift exactly twenty-four cards from the top of the pack; while his opponent, watching the action, tries to guess the actual number lifted. If the dealer is right, he scores 250 points; if the opponent is right, he scores 150. This is not recommended, as it has nothing to do with the actual play of the game.

Another optional rule is that the same trump cannot be declared in two successive deals; hence a marriage in the old trump, if melded first, is scored as an ordinary marriage. This rule, too, is dubious, since each deal constitutes a game in itself, and therefore it is hard to see why one should have a bearing on the next.

In some circles, a meld of the ♠ Q ◇ J is scored as a bezique only when spades are trump. Instead, the ◇ Q ♠ J is used when diamonds are trump; the ♣ Q ♡ J when clubs are trump; and the ♡ Q ♣ J when hearts are trump. This means that beziques cannot be melded in any form until a trump has been declared, which at times can have a very marked effect upon the play. This rule, too, is of questionable value, as it tends to complicate the game; hence like the other options, it should be decided upon beforehand.

EIGHT-PACK BEZIQUE: Almost identical with the six-pack game, this requires a fourth bezique pack of sixty-four cards, or in other terms two more piquet packs of thirty-two cards each. In all, this means a total of 256 cards, so the two players are each dealt fifteen cards each. All scoring is the same as in six-pack bezique, but with these additions to the schedule:

Quintuple pinochle	9000	Five trump kings	1600
Five trump aces	2000	Five trump queens	1200
Five trump tens	1800	Five trump jacks	800

Scores are much greater due to more cards in the hands as well as in the pack, so the loser is rubiconed unless he scores 5000 points or more. As in all forms of rubicon bezique, the winner does not have to reach that level, the whole burden being on the loser.

Summarizing games of the rubicon type, the big feature is that of "repeating" melds or declarations by simply playing one card and adding another such card to the existing meld. This can be done with any form of meld, including beziques; but in that case, particularly, good judgment must be exercised. A player can meld a ♠ Q and ◇ J for 40 points; then play the ♠ Q and put a second ♠ Q with the ◇ J for another 40; then play the ◇ J and put a second ◇ J with the ♠ Q for still another 40. But all those would be "single" beziques, so he would do far better to hold onto his second ♠ Q until he acquires the second ◊ J, when he could lay both with the "single" bezique on the board and declare a "double" bezique for 500 points. The same applies to triple, quadruple, and quintuple beziques.

BID EUCHRE: A name originally applied to the game of *Five Hundred*. See page 117.

BID WHIST: A fast-moving form of *Whist* dependent on a special bidding feature. Described under *Whist*, page 375.

BIERSPIEL: A variation of *Rams*, described under that head. See page 287.

BIG FORTY: A variant of *Lucas*. See page 339.

BIMBO: *Double-handed High-Low Poker*. See page 248.

BINOCHLE: A former term for *Pinochle*, applicable to the old-style game; not the more modern versions. See page 174.

BISLEY: A type of *Solitaire*. See page 328.

BLACK JACK: A name given the game of *Hearts* when the ♠ J is counted as a 13-point penalty card instead of the ♠ Q. See *Hearts*, page 140.

BLACKJACK: This highly popular game is basically the same as Twenty-one, but the term blackjack usually applies to the sociable or private form, with twenty-one referring to variations played at gambling casinos. In sociable blackjack, a standard fifty-two-card pack is used with suits disregarded and each card valued numerically only: ace, 1 or 11; face cards (K, Q, J), 10 each; others according to their spots, 10 down to 2.

One player acts as banker and deals a single card face down to each player, including himself. Each looks at his card and bets up to an agreed limit. The dealer does not bet but may double the amounts; if he does, any other player may redouble individually, but if any player is unwilling to go double, the dealer wins that player's original stake. Each player is then dealt a second card face up, dealer included. If a player holds an ace (11) and a face card or a ten (10), it is a "natural" 21 and he collects twice the amount of his bet from the dealer, unless the dealer also has a natural. In that case, the dealer collects the amount bet by that player, or twice the amount bet from any player who does not have a natural.

If the dealer has no natural, he pays off any players who do have, then, beginning with the remaining players at his left, he deals cards face up, one by one, as that player calls for them. The player's aim is to hit a total as close to 21 as possible without going over, so he declares that he will "stand" when he thinks he has enough cards, or if he wants more, he says, "Hit me." If he goes over 21, his hand is a "bust" and he must turn it down, while the dealer collects the bet.

The dealer does the same with the next remaining player and so on, with up to a dozen in the game. Any who stand wait while the dealer draws cards for himself; if he goes bust, he pays each standing player the amount he bet. But if the dealer stands, all cards are turned up and the dealer pays off all players with totals higher than his own, but collects from any that are less or the same. The rule is that ties favor the dealer, exactly as with naturals.

Despite this advantage, a dealer risks heavy losses if he goes bust a few times in a row. So in some circles the deal simply moves around the board hand by hand, as in other card games, each new dealer shuffling the pack and having it cut before he deals. But the more popular rule is for all players to "cut for low" to determine the original dealer, who retains that privilege but with the option of selling it to the highest bidder before or after any hand. However, if he deals a natural to another player and is unable to match it, the dealing privilege goes to that player beginning with the next hand. With more than one claimant, the player nearest the dealer's left takes precedence.

Under that rule, a standard procedure is for the new dealer to shuffle the pack, have it cut, then turn up the top card—say the ◇ 8—and "burn" it by placing it face up at the bottom of the pack. He then deals a regular round of blackjack, but in gathering up the dealt cards, he places them face up beneath the burnt card and deals another round from the top of the pack, as is. He continues thus with the next round until he comes to the burnt card (◇ 8), when he pauses in the deal to turn the pack face down, shuffle it, have it cut, burn another card, and continue the deal from the point where it was interrupted. However, at the beginning of any round in which the burnt card is soon due to appear, the dealer may turn all cards of the pack face down and shuffle as with the original deal.

Here is a typical hand in a blackjack game with six players.

1st Player: Down ♣ Q. Up ♠ K. Stands at 20.
2nd: Down ♡ 4. Up ◇ 8. Dealt ♠ 2, ◇ 7. Stands at 21.
3rd: Down ♠ 10. Up ♣ 6. Dealt ♣ 8. Busts (24).
4th: Down ♠ 5. Up ♣ A. Dealt ♠ 6, ♡ 6. Stands at 18.
5th: Down ♡ 3. Up ♠ 7. Dealt ♡ 5, ♣ 3. Stands at 18.
Dealer: Down ◇ 5. Up ♡ 8. Dealt ◇ 3, ♡ 2. Stands at 18.

If the fourth player had counted ace=11, he would have gone bust on the ♠ 6, so he counted ace=1 and with 5+1+6=12 called for another card.

The dealer, after drawing the ◇ 3, had only 16 (5+8+3). He figured the first player for 18, 19, or 20. The second player has 17 showing in face-up cards (8+2+7); the fourth, 13 (1+6+6); the fifth, 15 (7+5+3), making the dealer's 16 a very probable loss on all three counts. So the dealer drew one more, the ♡ 2, and banked on his 18 (5+8+3+2) to match at least two of the rival hands, which it did. So the dealer paid off the first and second, while he collected from the fourth and fifth.

Certain special hands are customarily played in blackjack. These include:

Splitting Pairs: If a player's first two cards, down and up, are of the same denomination, as two kings, or any other pair down to two deuces, he can turn the first card up and call each member of the pair the upcard of a separate hand, betting equally on each. The dealer then gives him two downcards, one for each hand; and the player draws or stands on each, playing them on their individual merits. With a pair of cards valued at 10 each, or better still a pair of aces, the lucky player has twice the usual chance of making a natural.

Doubling Down: If a player's first two cards total exactly 11, as **9–2, 8–3, 7–4, 6–5,** he can turn up his first card and call for another downcard to replace it, provided he also doubles his bet. He must then stand on those three cards, playing them as a regular hand. Since there is about one out of three chances of making 21 by this procedure, many players regard it as an ideal opportunity to double a bet. By agreement, players may be allowed to double down on a total of 10 (as **2–8, 3–7, 4–6, 5–5**) or a total of 9 (as **7–2, 6–3, 5–4**). In the case of 9, if the player is dealt a 2 as his new downcard, he can turn it up, add it to his total, making 11, and demand another downcard.

Payoff Hands: By agreement, a player holding any of the following combinations may turn up his downcard and demand an instant payoff, regardless of whether the dealer can later match or exceed his total:

Any five cards that do not exceed 21 (as **3–3–4–A–9** or **6–2–3–4–5**). Player receives double the amount of his bet. For each additional card, another double (as **3–5–2–2–3–4**, four times). (Or **5–3–3–A–A–2–6**, eight times.) (Or **2–3–2–4–4–2–A–3**, sixteen times.) A total of 21 composed of a **6, 7,** and **8** pays double the bet. A total of 21 composed of three **7**'s pays triple the bet.

BLACK LADY: A form of *Hearts* in which the ♠ Q (or Black Lady) counts 13 points against the player taking it. Known also as *Black Maria, Black Widow* and by other names. See pages 140–41.

BLACK MARIA or BLACK WIDOW: Other names for *Black Lady*. See pages 140–41.

BLACKOUT: Another name for the game of *Oh, Hell!* See page 165.

BLIND ALL FOURS: A name originally given to the game of *Pitch*. See page 214.

BLIND AND STRADDLE: The early form of *Blind Opening*. See page 245.

BLIND CINCH: A variation of *Cinch*, page 67.

BLIND EUCHRE: Simple *Euchre* with a two-card widow. See page 113.

BLIND HOOKEY: A popular name for *Banker and Broker*, page 22.

BLIND OPENING: A form of *Poker* in which players make opening bets before looking at their hands. See page 245.

BLIND STUD: See page 245.

BLIND TIGER: A modern form of *Blind Opening*. See page 245.

BLOCK RUMMY: A form of *Rummy*, page 293, in which a player must make a final discard to go out; and play is blocked after all cards have been drawn from the pack, hand with lowest count becoming winner.

BLUCHER: *Napoleon*, with two extra bids. See *Napoleon*, page 163.

BLUFF: The original and now obsolete form of *Poker*, using a twenty-card pack, ranking in descending order, **A, K, Q, J, 10,** with four players each being dealt a five-card hand. Bets, raises, and calls follow, each trying to outbluff the others, with the highest hand winning in the case of a showdown. The term "bluff" also applies to *Straight Poker*, page 269.

BOATHOUSE RUMMY: Regular *Rummy*, page 293, but with the rule that, if a player takes the top card of the discard pile, he must also take the card below it or the top card of the pack. Though he takes up two, he can discard only one. Play ends only when a player can lay down his entire hand, with an ace counting high or low; or both, as **2, A, K.** Other players can match their own combinations but cannot lay off on other hands. The winner collects the value of each card left in an opposing hand, or simply one point for each card, whichever is agreed.

BOBTAIL OPENER: *Poker*. See page 245.

BOBTAIL STUD: *Poker*. See page 245.

BOLIVIA: This is an extension of *Samba,* page 300, that has become a game in its own right. It is played with the triple pack (162 cards including jokers), and it follows the basic rules of samba, including the scoring of sequences of three to seven cards in the same suit, with a run of seven being termed an "escalera" (instead of a "samba") and counting the customary 1500 points. However, a meld of three to seven "wild cards" is also allowed, as in certain forms of *Canasta,* and this is termed a "bolivia," counting 2500. A "natural canasta" scores 500; a "mixed canasta," 300, as in the parent games.

To go out, a team must meld at least one escalera (or sequence), plus either another escalera, a bolivia, or a canasta. The opening meld requirements are exactly as in samba, but with the greater scoring possibilities, game is 15,000 points.

Bolivia has been stepped up with the following rules applied to opening melds: At the 5000 level, 150 points; at 7000, still 150, but the player must lay down a mixed canasta or higher; at 8000, an opening meld of 200, with the player laying down a mixed canasta or better; at 9000, still 200, but the player must lay down a natural canasta or better. Game, however, is set at 10,000 (as in samba). In this version, a bolivia only counts

2000, but in going out it is allowable to add to the ends of an escalera. Thus played, this game is also termed *Brazilian Canasta*.

As a penalty rule, a team caught with a melded three- or four-card sequence has 1000 points taken from its score. Red threes double in value from 500 to 1000 when a team holds five of them; with 200 more points for the sixth. But unless a team manages to meld a canasta or better, its red threes are deducted from its score. Black threes can be rated on the same basis if so desired.

BOODLE: Technically, this is a transitional game between *New Market* and *Michigan,* but it is also applied to any form of Michigan in which additional "boodle cards" are added to the layout. See *Michigan,* pages 161–62.

BOSTON: A complex and now obsolete variation of *Whist,* page 375, introduced at the time of the American Revolution and incorporating features of other games that were popular at the same period, including the turnup of a card from another pack to designate a preferred trump suit.

BOSTON DE FONTAINEBLEAU: A variant of *Boston,* with no turnup of a "preference card" from another pack. Instead, bidders can name their suits, with ◊ ranking over ♡, ♣, ♠ in the order given, when bids are for the same number of tricks. See *Whist,* page 375.

BOUILLOTTE: A famous French antecedent of *Poker,* usually played by four players with a twenty-card pack ranking **A, K, Q, 9, 8.** Three cards are dealt to each player, and the next is turned up as a common card for all hands, termed the *retourne.* Hands are bet somewhat as in poker, the highest being a *brelan carre,* or four of a kind including the wild card; next a *simple brelan,* or three of a kind in hand; with a special bonus for a *brelan favori,* or three of a kind including the *retourne.* If no one holds a *brelan,* all dealt cards are shown along with the *retourne* and those of each suit valued as ace, 11;

face cards, 10 each; others according to their spots. The active player holding the highest card in the *winning suit* is credited for *point* and wins the pool. With three players, queens are eliminated to leave only twelve cards; with five players, they are retained and sevens are added to make twenty-four cards.

BOURRE: A modern adaptation of *Écarté*, page 105, with two to seven players using a full pack of fifty-two cards, ranking **A, K, Q, J, 10, 9, 8, 7, 6, 5, 4, 3, 2**. Each player contributes an equal number of chips to a pool or pot. Five cards are dealt to each player, and the next card is turned up to designate the trump suit. Any player may then turn down his hand and drop out; those who remain or "stay" can "stand pat" with their holdings, or discard one to five cards, drawing others to replace them.

The player at the dealer's left leads to the first trick, and the rest must follow suit, each playing a higher card if he has one. If out of suit, a player must play any trump he holds. If unable to do either, he can discard from an odd suit. Highest card of suit led wins the trick unless trumped, and winner of each trick leads to the next.

However, there is one *special rule:* Any player holding any of the three top trumps **(A, K, Q)** must lead his highest trump at the first opportunity, thus drawing out or forcing out others, a unique feature of this game. Whoever wins the most tricks takes the pool; in case of a tie, it is split equally. But if any player *stays* and *takes no tricks* whatever, he must contribute the *full amount* of the pool (or pot) toward the *next* deal's pool. That, perhaps, is the game's great feature, encouraging players to "stay" when they really should "drop" but depend on the hope of cashing in the double pot on the next round.

BRAG: An English antecedent of *Poker,* page 219, in which three cards are dealt to each player from a fifty-two-card pack. After betting, hands are compared to determine the winner. Three aces are the highest, followed by three kings and so on down, then pairs from aces down, with the odd card breaking a tie; then simply high card, with the same ranking, **A, K, Q, J, 10, 9, 8, 7, 6, 5, 4, 3, 2.** There are, however, three wild cards called "braggers," each representing any card in the pack, including itself. They are the ◊ **A,** ♣ **J,** ◊ **9** and are ranked in that order. A "natural" combination takes precedence over one containing a "bragger"; hence three fives composed of ♠ **5,** ◊ **5,** ♡ **5** would beat one formed by ♣ **5,** ◊ **A,** ◊ **9.** Similarly, a pair such as ♣ **10,** ♡ **10** would defeat ♠ **10,** ◊ **A,** which in turn would beat ◊ **10,** ♣ **J.** In case of an absolute tie, the player nearest the dealer's left is winner.

In *American Brag,* there are eight braggers, consisting of the four jacks and the four nines. All are equal in value, and a combination containing a bragger outranks a natural hand of the same value, making three braggers the highest possible hand (over three aces) with tie hands fairly frequent.

BRAZILIAN CANASTA: A name given to *Bolivia* with stepped-up rules. See page 37.

BRELAN: Another name for *Bouillotte.* See page 38.

BRIDGE: See *Auction Bridge,* page 18, and *Contract Bridge,* page 72, now universal games.

BRIDGE WHIST: A once highly popular game representing the transition from *Whist* to *Bridge.* See pages 375 and 72.

BUILD-UP: *Double Dummy Bridge* (see page 103) with nine-card dummies. Players bid, two cards are dealt to each hand, then two moved from hand to dummy. This is repeated and play follows.

BUTCHER BOY: A form of *Five-Card Stud Poker.* See page 245.

CALABRASELLA: A fast but simple three-player game with a pack from which the eights, nines, and tens are removed, leaving forty cards ranking **3, 2, A, K, Q, J, 7, 6, 5, 3,** all suits plain; never any trump. The aim is to take tricks containing counter cards, aces being valued at 3 points; the **3, 2, K, Q, J** at 1 each; and last trick 3 points—a total of 35. Each player is dealt twelve cards, and four go in a face-down widow. Player at dealer's left can "stand," meaning he will take on the other two; or he can "pass," putting the choice on the next player. If all three pass, the hand is abandoned and the deal moves along.

The player who stands must discard one to four cards from his hand, laying them face down. He then turns up the widow and selects cards from it to replace his discards. The player at his left leads any card to the first trick, and the others must follow suit if they can. High card of the suit led wins the trick, and the winner leads to the next, with the discards and remaining widow cards going to the player who takes the last trick.

Counters are added at the end of play, and the single player scores plus or minus according to the difference between his count and that of the combined opponents. *Example:* Taking 25, he would lose 10, giving him +15. He would then collect that amount in points or chips from each opponent, making 30 in all. Conversely, if he takes only 14 and loses 21, he would be —7, and each would collect that amount from him. To take all counters doubles the score to +70; to lose all is —70. In playing for points, game is usually 100.

CALABRELLA: An old Italian game like *Cassino,* page 57.

CALCULATION: A type of *Solitaire,* page 328.

CALIFORNIA JACK: A development of *Pitch,* usually limited to two players, in which the entire pack is used in each deal. The pack is cut and the bottom card of the upper half is shown to designate the trump suit. The pack is then shuffled, six cards are dealt singly to each player, and the pack is squared and turned face up on the table. The opponent leads any card, and the dealer either follows suit or trumps; or if out of suit, he may either trump or play a side suit.

The winner of the first trick draws the card showing on the face-up pack and adds it to his hand; the other player takes the next face-up card. The winner then leads to the next trick, and play continues thus until the entire pack has been drawn and all cards played from each player's hand. Each goes through the cards he took and scores 1 point each for high (ace of trump), low (two of trump), jack (of trump), and game, the highest total of counter cards in which each ten=10; each ace=4; each king=3; each queen=2; each jack=1.

The original opponent then deals, and deal is alternated until one player reaches 7 points (or 10 points, if so agreed) and becomes the winner. If both go out in the same hand, points are scored in the order high, low, jack, game. With three or four players, the deal rotates to the left, and each player is on his own. With three players, a three-spot is removed from the pack; with four, the full pack is used.

Note: Some go by the rule that when a player is out of a suit he must trump if he can; others, that if he can follow suit, he must do so. Any such options should be specified beforehand.

Additional points can be included, as described under *All Fives* (page 13) and any of the pedro games (page 172) can be played like California Jack. See also *Shasta Sam* (page 304).

CALIFORNIA LOO: Another name for *California Jack*. See page 41.

CALIFORNIA LOWBALL: A game played according to the accepted rules for *Lowball* in the poker clubs of California. See page 237.

CALL-ACE EUCHRE: A special form of *Euchre* with temporary partners. See page 113.

CALL RUMMY: See page 293.

CANADIAN STUD: A variant of *Five-Card Stud Poker*. See page 246.

CANASTA: A highly elaborated development of *Rummy* orig-
inated in South America, with further elaborations to be described under individual heads. Primarily a four-handed game,
with players seated opposite operating as partners, canasta requires two standard fifty-two-card packs, each with two jokers
in addition, for a total of 108 cards. Suits are disregarded, the
cards being considered in terms of their rank or denomination,
with jokers and deuces wild.

In play, the following values are given to individual cards:
jokers, each 50 points, deuces, each 20; aces, each 20; K, Q,
J, 10, 9, 8, each 10; 7, 6, 5, 4, each 5 points. Red and black
threes are special cards, both in purpose and in values.

The Deal: Eleven cards are dealt singly to each player, beginning at dealer's left. The bulk of the pack is placed in the
center of the table, and the top card is turned up beside it, to
represent *el pozo* or the "pot." The first player draws a card
from the top of the pack and adds it to his hand, or, as play
develops, he may, under specified conditions, pick up the pot
instead. Either way, he completes his turn by discarding a
single card from his hand, placing it face up on the pot as a new
upcard. The next player takes a similar turn, and so on, in
continuous rotation.

During each turn, however, a player may lay down sets of
cards of the same denomination, scoring whatever points they
represent. These are commonly termed "melds" as in rummy.
The cards are melded face up, and there must be at least three
in a set, with one wild card allowable (as **8–8–2** instead of
8–8–8). Two wild cards are permissible in a set of four (as
K–K–2–2), and three in a set of five or more (as **joker–7–7–2–2**
or **joker–joker–Q–Q–Q–2**). But no more than three wild cards
are allowable.

New cards can be added to existing melds during later turns,
and a player melding a set of seven or more cards is credited
with a *natural canasta,* if the cards are all alike (as **9–9–9–9–9–9
–9**), for a bonus of 500 points; while a *mixed canasta,* containing
wild cards (as **joker–J–J–J–J–J–J–2**), scores 300 points. These
bonuses are in addition to the point count of the individual

cards; hence a natural canasta such as **10–10–10–10–10–10–10** would score 70+500=570. The addition of another ten would make it 80+500=580. However, if instead a player added a joker and a deuce, forming **joker–10–10–10–10–10–10–10–2,** he would reduce the status of the natural canasta to that of a mixed canasta, scoring 70+50+20+300=440. This is allowable and sometimes even advisable, as play will prove, one reason being that any number of wild cards can be added to a canasta, which means "basket" and is therefore flexible.

Partners can add to each other's melds but not to those of the opposing team. For convenience, all melds of a team may be placed in front of one partner. The cards of a canasta are squared up, with a red card put on top to signify a natural and a black on top for a mixed. When a player melds or discards his last card, he "goes out," ending the play and scoring special bonus points for his team. But a team must first meld a canasta before a member is permitted to go out. This means that a player may often need more than his original eleven-card quota. To gain that, he must take the upcard because the entire pot, consisting of all discards, comes with it. The more the better, as more cards mean more melds and therefore a larger score, which is the great aim in canasta.

However, at the start of the hand, the pot is "frozen" against each team, which means that the upcard cannot be taken until one member of the partnership has made an opening meld of 50 points or more. If, as part of such an opening meld, he can match the upcard with two or more of the same rank, as **Q–Q** with a **Q,** he can take the frozen pot then and there. But no wild card can be used in such a match while the pot is still frozen (as **joker–Q** with a **Q**).

Some examples of possible hands will clarify this:

(a) Player holds: **2 K K K Q 10 9 8 8 7 6.** Upcard: **7.** He can meld **2 K K K** for 20+10+10+10=50. Or even **K K K** (30) along with **2–8–8** (40) for a total of 70, so that he or his partner could take the pot later. But he cannot meld **K K K** (30) along with **2–7--7** (30) because the upcard can only be matched by a natural pair (as **7–7**).

(b) Player holds: **2 A K K Q 10 9 8 7 7 6.** Upcard: **7.** Here he can make it with **2–K–K** (40) and **7–7–7** (15) as 40+15=55, meeting minimum, and the **7–7–7** is a natural.

(c) Player holds: **A A K K J J 9 9 8 8 7.** Upcard: **A.** Match **A–A** with **A,** for 20+20+20=60 and a natural as well.

(d) Player holds: **A A K K 8 6 6 6 6 6 6.** Upcard: **6.** Matching sixes with upcard would produce a canasta but won't do for opening, as it only adds to 35. (Bonus points cannot be counted.)

Upon successfully matching an upcard and thus taking the pot, a player may immediately continue melding cards he finds in it before making his customary discard, which starts a new pot. As long as it stays unfrozen, either partner can take the pot by matching its upcard with two naturals (as when it was frozen), or by matching the upcard with a card of the same rank and a wild card (as using **K–2** to match a **K**); or by simply adding the upcard to a meld already made (as picking up a **9** and placing it with an existing meld of **Joker–9–9** or **9–9–9**). It is also allowable to add such an upcard to an already closed canasta (as placing a **Q** with a melded **joker–2–2–Q–Q–Q–Q**).

However, as play continues, it is often advisable to freeze the pot again, particularly when it contains some much needed cards that a member of the opposing team might acquire by taking the pot himself. The pot can be refrozen by simply discarding a wild card, such as a joker or preferably a deuce, as a player may need the joker for himself. Once the pot is refrozen, the rule again applies that it can be taken only by matching the upcard with a natural pair, though the count does not matter. (Example: Placing **8–8** from the hand with an upcard **8** will suffice. No need to meld 50 points or more.)

When some player does that, he acquires a *pozo premiado,* or "prize pot," so termed because of the wild card that it contains. As a team's melds increase, it is often wise to end the play before the opponents can meld heavily; and, to do that, one member of the team must "go out" by disposing of the last card in his hand either by a meld or as a discard. All hands are then shown and are scored as follows:

Each side adds its bonus scores for canastas (300 for mixed; 500 for natural) along with other bonus scores, which include 100 points for going out. Sometimes a player can go out "concealed" by melding his entire hand at once, without making any previous meld. In that case, his team scores double for going out; namely, 200. Following that, points are counted for melded cards, as already listed, these being added to each team's score. Unmelded cards are then counted and their points subtracted from the score.

Special bonus points are scored for red threes, which as already stated have a special purpose. They do not figure in the play at all. If a player is dealt a red three, he lays it face up in front of him and draws another card from the pack as a replacement for his hand. Similarly, if he draws a red three during play, he lays it face up and draws another card. When scores are added, a team receives 100 for each red three; and if it holds all four, its bonus (400) is doubled, making 800. However, if a team is unable to make a meld during play, the count for red threes is subtracted from its score instead of being added to it.

Black threes form part of the regular hand and are valued at 5 points each but cannot be melded except by a player who is going out; and even then, he must put down three or four of them for a count of a mere 15 or 20, as it is not permissible to meld a wild card with them. So if a player is left with a black three in his hand, it counts 5 points against him. However, black threes are useful, because if a player discards one, which is allowable, it becomes the upcard; and the next player —an opponent—cannot match it and thereby acquire the pot. That is, the black three serves as a temporary "stopper" giving the player's partner a chance to take the pot after the in-between opponent has his turn.

After each team's total is entered on the score sheet, the deal moves to the left. The packs are shuffled and dealt as already specified, and play proceeds accordingly but with this proviso: If a team's score has reached 1500 or higher, its requirement for an opening meld is advanced to 90 points. Once a score reaches 3000, the opening requirement becomes 120 points. This makes it harder for a team once it begins to pile up a score, thus favoring the underdog. Also, if a team's score falls below 0, as it may at the conclusion of the opening hand, it is allowed to play the next hand with an opening requirement of only 15 points, instead of the usual 50.

Game is 5000 points or more. When one team attains that goal, the smaller score is subtracted from the larger to establish the winning margin. For convenience, scores are usually figured to the nearest hundred; thus if Team A should total 5175 and Team B 2830 they would be rated as A, 52 and B, 28, so that 52—28=24 would establish A's margin as 24, with settlements being made accordingly.

The following special rules are important:

During the deal, if the original upcard is a wild card (joker or deuce), a red three, or a black three, another card must be turned up and placed upon it. If the new upcard is also one of those types, still another must be turned up and placed upon it; and so on, until a playable card (A down to 4) is turned as upcard.

With a wild card or a red three in the pot, its very presence there keeps the pot frozen, even after a team has met the minimum requirement of 50, 90, or 120, as the case may be. The minimum must still be met; but in meeting it, or during a later turn either by the player or his partner, it is necessary to meld a natural pair (as 9–9) with an upcard of the same rank (9) to take the pot. Even then, if a red three is in the frozen pot, the player taking it must remember to place it in front of him face up and draw another card to replace it.

During play, reasonable information may be asked or given, as asking or reminding a partner as to the minimum required for an initial meld; reminding him to lay down his red threes and draw other cards instead; or asking how many cards another player holds or how many cards are still in the undrawn pack. Such courtesies help the game generally and can be limited or expanded as agreed upon. However, there is one phase of information that is covered by a set rule, namely:

When ready to go out by melding all his cards, a player can ask his partner, "Can I go out?" either before or after drawing from the pack. His partner, after due consideration, must answer yes or no, and the player must act accordingly. A player does not have to ask this question, but if he does so after starting to meld, or indicating that he might take the pot instead, his opponents can decide whether or not he is to go out on that turn.

If he is unable to go out after asking and receiving permission, the player's team is penalized 100 points. Conversely, if he receives a negative reply and then proceeds to go out, his opponents can demand that he revise his meld so that he can take one or more cards back into his hand; and his team is penalized 100 points.

Other penalties include failure to show and lay down a red three after the player has taken his first turn. This costs his team 500 points, provided he is still holding the card when play ends and hands are shown. Usually, a player notices the offending red three during one of his turns and announces it as if he had just drawn it.

Making an opening meld short of the required count can be rectified if the player is able to meld enough extra cards to meet the minimum. Or he can take back the insufficient meld, and 10 points will be added to his team's opening requirement for that hand. But if increasing an insufficient meld to the required count means taking back some of the cards already melded, his team is penalized 100 points.

If a player starts to take the pot illegally, either by an improper meld or by playing out of turn, he can be stopped without penalty; but once he has added the discard pile to his hand, opponents can demand that he lay his hand face up so that they can restore his hand and replace the discards as far as possible. His team is penalized 100 points, but he can draw from the pack and resume his proper play.

If a player starts to meld his entire hand in order to go out, before his team has made its required canasta, his team is penalized 100 points and he must take back one or more cards. Similarly, any illegal meld, notably one containing too many wild cards (as 8–2–2 in a set of three, or adding a fourth wild card to a set), must be taken back into the hand, with a 100-point penalty. This would apply to any miscalled meld, such as counting a jack as a third king. However:

If any such illegal meld is not noticed until the next player has started his turn, there is no penalty. An opening meld with a short count stands as valid, because it was condoned. So does a meld containing too many wild cards, but in that case, any wild cards are checked for future reference and are subtracted from the team's score in the final reckoning, as if they had remained in the hand where they properly belonged. Minor mistakes, when noted later, are simply rectified by having the player take back the cards involved.

There is no point penalty for lesser infractions, such as a player drawing more than one card from the pack. He must either show and replace such extras on the pack, giving the next players the right to draw in turn or shuffle before making a draw; or if he has already put the cards in his hand, he keeps it as is but passes the draw on his next turn or turns. Any card shown inadvertently or as part of a wrong meld is classed as a "penalty card" and must be placed face up on the table, where it still belongs to his hand. He can meld one or more penalty cards during each successive turn, but if unable to meld them all at once, he must finish a turn by discarding a penalty card, instead of a card from his hand. At the end of play any penalty card that has not been melded goes back into the player's hand and is therefore subtracted from his score.

Canasta can be played with varied numbers of players, with the following rules pertaining to the different games:

Two-handed Canasta: Excellent because of its simplicity. Each player is dealt fifteen cards to make up for the lack of a partner to help establish an opening meld, but the usual minimum requirements apply. To increase the scoring potential, a player must meld two canastas before going out. To simplify the game further, practically all penalties are eliminated, as there is no partner who might gain valued information through a player's mistake, intentional or otherwise. To increase scoring further, an optional rule may be introduced; that of having each player draw two cards from the face-down pack but discard only one from his hand, so that his quota automatically grows larger even when he does not take the pot. Scoring is the same as in the four-handed game.

Three-handed Canasta: In simple form, this is very similar to the four-handed game, but instead of having a partner, each player is on his own. Each player is dealt either eleven or thirteen cards, but the latter is preferable. As another option, either one canasta or two may be required to go out. In a popular variant styled "cutthroat canasta," the first player who takes the pot must play a lone hand against the other two, who act as partners during that deal; or if no one takes the pot, a player who goes out is regarded as a lone hand.

Either way, the lone player scores what he makes, while each of his opponents is credited with the full amount that they scored as a temporary team, with this exception: A red three shown by a player counts only for or against his own score, depending on whether or not he and his temporary partner went out. If nobody takes the discard pile, each player scores individually; and in any case, if nobody goes out, play is concluded by the player who draws the last card. Game is 7500 points.

Note: In as much as partners may change in successive hands, their scores may vary where amounts required for an opening meld are concerned. Hence, each must be governed by his own individual score.

Six-handed Canasta: This is similar to the four-handed game, but with special provisions for the accommodation of the two additional players. The six form two partnerships, each formed of three players seated alternately; and a third pack—containing fifty-two cards and two jokers—is added to the double pack ordinarily used, making a total of 162 cards, including six jokers.

Each player is dealt thirteen cards and play proceeds as usual, but continues on beyond the 5000 mark. When the score reaches 7000, an initial meld of 150 is required; and game itself is set at 10,000. In each hand a team must meld two canastas to go out. Red threes are valued at 100 each, up to five, which are worth 1000, while a team scores 1200 for all six.

This game can be played like three-handed canasta, with three teams composed of partners seated opposite each other.

Special Penalties in Canasta: Since high scoring is a great feature in all forms of canasta, infractions of the rules, intentional or otherwise, are apt to work to a player's advantage and therefore should be offset by corresponding penalties. All can be modified by agreement, and any enforcement should be immediate, as they are nullified if play is allowed to go on.

If a player draws too many cards, the only penalty is to wait for other turns to discard without a draw. If he picks up too many, he can replace the extras but must show them to other players if he saw them himself. In partnership play, if he lets cards in his hand be seen, he can be required to lay them face up and discard them after each ensuing draw, as the preview might be turned to profit by his partner.

A card drawn out of turn must be given to the player who should have drawn it. His partner must keep it, but an opponent can keep it or bury it in the pack, drawing another instead. If he puts it in his own hand before the mistake is noted, he must keep it there and make a discard when his turn comes to draw. In that case, he is penalized 100 points.

There is no penalty for a mistake in an opening meld if the offender is able to add to it and complete it. If he takes back his cards without melding, 10 points are added to his team's requirement for an opening meld; while if he uses other cards for the opening meld, he is penalized 100 points.

This applies to similar mistakes in melds. If a player uses too many wild cards or lays down wrong cards, he can add others from his hand to alter or expand the meld and complete the discard; but if forced to retract and take back cards already shown, the player—or his team—is penalized the customary 100 points. If he picks up the discard pile and adds it to his hand after an illegal meld, or out of turn, he must replace it as it was, showing his own hand if opponents demand it. Again, the customary penalty is 100 points.

When a player asks his partner, "Can I go out?" and receives "Yes" as a reply, he must meld out his entire hand or take a 100-point penalty. If he starts to meld out before putting the question or receiving an answer, or after the reply is "No," the same 100-point penalty can be invoked. Also, if he tries to go out before his team has formed a canasta—or two canastas or whatever else may be required—the 100-point penalty is in order.

Wild-Card Canasta (page 378) allows the formation of canastas composed entirely of wild cards—jokers and deuces—which led to the development of the following games:

Three-Pack Canasta: As wild-card canasta gained in vogue, it became apparent that the more cards in the pack the greater the melding opportunities. Since players were already familiar with the triple pack of 162 cards used in the six-handed game, the obvious course was to adapt it to four-handed play. Instead of dealing eleven cards to each player, fifteen became the rule; and other measures were added to speed the game.

One device is to note the value of the upcard and deal that many cards face down from the top of the pack—from 3 to 13, with a jack counting 11, a queen 12, a king 13; while an ace, deuce, or joker counts 20. The upcard is placed upon them, and the first player to pick up the discard pile gets the face-down group with it. This is used in a popular variant termed *Italian Canasta,* which includes these rules:

A canasta of wild cards scores a bonus of 2000; if deuces

only, 3000, but only for the team that goes out. The other team is credited only with the points represented by its melded cards; and, to make things still harder, once a team begins a wild-card meld, it must complete its seven-card canasta before using deuces in any other meld. To go out, a team must meld two standard canastas—either mixed or natural—gaining a bonus of 300 points.

The discard pile is always frozen, and game is 12,000 points, with opening melds as follows: from 0 to 1500, 50 points; to 3000, 90 points; to 5000, 120 points; to 7500, 160 points; to 10,000, 180 points; above that, 200 points. Sometimes a bonus of 1000 points is given for holding five canastas; with 2000 points if all are natural. Red threes score 100 points each, doubling to 200 if a team holds four or more.

Four-Pack Canasta: In the continued effort to increase the scope and scoring of canasta, the size of the pack is obviously a helpful factor, so from the triple pack, used in the games just described, the addition of a fourth pack became a logical and almost inevitable step. Along with utilizing a 216-card pack, including eight jokers, the new forms of wild-card canasta that developed also borrowed two features from the related game of *Mexicana*, a canasta-offshoot described under its own head.

Those two features are a special bonus in the form of extra cards for melding the first canasta; and special scores for melding a canasta composed of sevens. With the quadruple pack, those opportunities are expanded, along with others, resulting in many minor variations, all following a general pattern. A typical four-player version runs:

The partners, seated opposite, are each dealt fifteen cards in the usual rotation. Play proceeds as in standard canasta, but with each drawing two cards and discarding only one. A canasta is limited to seven cards; and the first player to meld a canasta of any type draws eleven cards from the top of the pack and adds them to his hand after the completion of his turn.

Only two wild cards are allowed in a mixed canasta, which scores the usual 300 points, while a natural canasta scores 500, except for canastas composed of sevens; in their case, a mixed canasta counts 1000; a natural of sevens, 1500. A wild canasta scores 2000. In a lesser meld, a seven counts 5 points, but if a player is caught with any sevens in his hand, they count 200 points against his team.

A natural pair is needed to take the discard pile, which is always frozen in this game. A seven may be discarded, like any other card, but the discard pile cannot be taken when a seven is showing there. A team needs three canastas to go out; and one of those must be either wild or composed of sevens.

Game is usually 15,000 points, with opening meld requirements running: from 0 to 3000, 50 points; to 6000, 90 points; to 10,000, 120 points; above that, 150 points.

The game as just described can be played by six persons, with alternate players forming two teams of three players each. In this case, only thirteen cards are dealt to each player, instead of fifteen, but otherwise the same rules apply. However:

Among the numerous variants of four-pack canasta, the following are both applicable and appropriate in the six-player game: Instead of an eleven-card bonus for melding the first canasta, a player receives only seven; and any of the other players receive the same bonus for melding a canasta. But in that case, a meld of a mixed canasta of sevens is not allowed; it must be a natural. This makes it riskier to hold a seven, and thereby adds to the action.

Game is boosted to 20,000 points, with opening melds as follows: from 0 to 5000, 50 points; to 10,000, 90 points; to 15,000, 120 points; above that, 150 points.

Red threes score 100 points each for the team that holds them, with a score of 2000 for all eight, which happens very rarely. If a team fails to make a canasta of sevens, or a wild-card canasta—and that can happen fairly often!—it loses 100 points for each red three it holds. So red threes may be more of a liability than an asset.

Summary of Canasta: From the original game, so many others have developed that it is difficult to classify them in detail, because they have so much in common, with one blending into another. Those just given in this section on canasta include:

Four-handed canasta, two-handed, three-handed, six-handed, wild-card canasta, three-pack canasta, Italian canasta, four-pack canasta, in the order listed.

Other related games and their developments will be found under the following heads:

Brazilian Canasta, page 37, *Bolivia,* page 37, *Chile* (or *Chilean Canasta*), page 64, *Hollywood Canasta,* page 146, *Mexicana,* page 161, *Quinella,* page 286, *Samba,* page 300, *Tampa,* page 365, *Uruguay* (or *Uruguayan Canasta*), page 372, and *Cuban Canasta,* page 101.

CANCELLATION HEARTS: An elaboration of *Hearts,* page 140, with seven to ten individual players using two standard fifty-two-card packs that are dealt out equally. Any leftovers form a widow that goes to the player taking the first trick, as in *Omnibus Hearts,* and any other features of that game can be included as agreed upon. If two players top a trick with the same card, as ♣ A, and ♣ A, the two cancel out and the trick goes to the next highest, as ♣ K. If all cancel out, or there is no high card of the suit led, the trick is laid aside like a widow and goes to the winner of the next. Also called *Draw Hearts.*

CANFIELD: A name frequently applied to the highly popular form of solitaire called *Klondike,* described under that head. See page 388.

CANS: A nickname for *Quinze.* See page 286.

CARD DOMINOES: Another name for *Fan-Tan,* page 115, in which cards are "built" in domino fashion.

CAROUSEL: Primarily a two-person game combining older forms of *Rummy* with modern *Gin* along with its own distinctive features, using a fifty-three-card pack, valued in descending order K, Q, J, 10, 9, 8, 7, 6, 5, 4, 3, 2, A, with the joker as a wild card. Each player is dealt a hand of ten cards, and his purpose is to meld them in sets of three or four of the same value (as Q–Q–Q or 6–6–6–6) or in sequences of three or more of the same suit (as ♡ J 10 9 8 7) exactly as in rummy.

The opponent begins by drawing one card from the top of the pack and making whatever melds he can or wants to make. If he does not meld, he must draw a second card; failing to meld then, he must draw a third, with his turn ending then, whether or not he melds. There is no discard. The dealer now draws a card and follows the same procedure, but he can lay off one or more cards on any melded by the opponent, that counting as a meld; otherwise, he must draw twice if necessary. It is then the opponent's turn again and play continues thus, with all melds being open to each.

A player can borrow an extra card from a meld and use it toward forming another. For example, if Q–Q–Q–Q has been melded, he could take the ♡ Q and add it to the ♡ J 10 from his hand to form a sequence of ♡ Q J 10, but he could not do that if only Q–Q–Q had been melded. With an existing meld of ♠ 9 8 7 6, he could take either the ♠ 9 for a meld of 9–9–9 or the ♠ 6 for 6–6–6, but he could not take the ♠ 8 or ♠ 7. However with ♠ 10 9 8 7 6 5 4 already melded, he could take the ♠ 7 toward 7–7–7, because he would leave ♠ 10 9 8 and ♠ 6 5 4, each a three-card sequence in its own right.

The **joker,** being wild, can be used as part of any meld, as ♣ 7 6 **joker,** with the **joker** representing the ♣ 5; but once given that value it cannot be changed, as from ♣ 5 to ♣ 8. However, if a player holds or draws the actual card thus represented—in this case the ♣ 5—he can exchange it for the **joker,** which must be used as part of another meld and cannot be taken up into the player's hand.

Any rearrangement of melded cards is allowable whenever a player makes a meld; and the **joker** can figure in such switches. For example, assume that the board shows ♡ K ◇ K **joker,** with the **joker** named as ♠ K; and two sequences, as ♡ 8 7 6 and ♡ 3 2 A. A player holding the ♣ K and the ♡ 4 could meld the ♣ K, forming K–K–K–K; then remove the **joker** (no longer needed as the ♠ K) and call it the ♡ 5, so the **joker** and ♡ 4 could be inserted between the two heart sequences to form ♡ 8 7 6 5 4 3 2 A, with the **joker** as ♡ 5.

As in gin, face cards count 10 each, others according to numerical value, with each ace 1. When a player's count is down to 5 or less, following a first or second draw, he can knock, ending the play. Hands are shown and low hand credited with the difference between its count and high. If the knocker is tied or beaten for low, the other player scores a bonus of 10 points. If the knocker goes "gin" by melding all his cards, he scores a bonus of 25. If a player is caught with the joker in his hand, it adds 25 points to his count. The deal moves to the opponent and continues alternately until one player wins game with 150 points, scoring a bonus of 100, with each player getting 25 for each deal he won. Winner of the game scores double if he shuts out or "skunks" his rival.

This game can be played by three to five players with a double pack of 106 cards. No duplicates can be used in the same combination.

CASSINO: A simple but unique game, in which the strategy may vary greatly in the course of a single deal, cassino demands skill as well as wits. Most of all, the pack must be thoroughly shuffled between deals to prevent the recurrence of certain card combinations on which the game hinges.

The pack: The standard fifty-two cards, which are valued numerically, as ace=1, two=2, and so on up to ten=10. This applies to playing, not to scoring, which is treated separately. Face cards (**J, Q, K**) have no numerical value.

Number of Players: Two, three, or four, each on his own; or four, with players seated opposite acting as partners.

The Deal: Four cards are dealt singly to each player, all face down; but another four cards are dealt in a face-up row in the center of the table, preferably just before the dealer deals each card to himself. The pack is temporarily laid aside, face down, for further use. Thus, in the two-handed game (which is simplest to describe), the opponent and the dealer would each be holding a hand of four cards, with a layout of four face-up cards between them.

The Play: The opponent tries to take up a card (or combination of cards) from the layout, by matching its value with a card in his hand. Example: He could take up the ◊ **7** from the board with the ♠ **7** from his hand, turning both cards face down in front of him; or if the ♡ **4** and ♠ **3** were showing in the layout, he could count them as "seven" and take up both with the ♠ **7.**

When more than one choice is available, a player may take up all with a single card. Thus, if the ◊ **7,** ♡ **4,** ♠ **3,** ♣ **7** composed the original layout, the opponent could place the ♡ **4** and ♠ **3** on the ◊ **7,** declaring them as "Sevens," and add the ♣ **7** to the pile, repeating "Sevens," then take up the lot with the ♠ **7** from his hand.

Instead of merely *combining* values, a player may *build* on a layout card (or cards) with the intent of taking up the pile on a future play, provided he holds a card that can fulfill that purpose. Example: Layout shows ♠ **3,** ◊ **2,** ♣ **8,** ♡ **K.** The player holds ♠ **4,** ◊ **9,** ♣ **A,** ♡ **J.** He can combine ♠ **3** and ◊ **2** on the board, calling it "Five" and immediately adding the ♠ **4** from his hand, saying "—and four makes nine."

In this case, on the player's next turn, instead of taking up his build (♠ **3,** ◊ **2,** ♠ **4**) with the ◊ **9,** he could make another build by placing the ♣ **A** from his hand on the ♣ **8** on the board, saying "Nine," then dropping one build on the other and declaring "Nines," to be taken up on the next turn.

In building, a player runs a calculated risk, as his adversary may take up the build if he has a suitable card. Assuming that the opponent begins the hand by building a nine as described, the dealer could take up the build with the ♡ **9.** Or, if the dealer happened to hold the ♡ **A** and the ♠ **10,** he could add the ♡ **A** to the opponent's build of nine (♠ **3,** ◊ **2,** ♠ **4**) and raise the build to "Ten," taking it on his next turn with the ♠ **10.**

However, once two combinations have been "doubled up" —as with "Sevens" or "Nines" as described—they cannot be built higher. This even applies when cards of a single value

are involved. Suppose that the opponent holds ♣ 3 and ◊ 3,
while the ♠ 3 is showing in the layout. He places the ♣ 3
on the ♠ 3, announcing "Threes," which he intends to take up
with the ◊ 3. The dealer happens to hold the ◊ A and ♣ 7,
so he would like to count the two "Threes" as "Six," add
"One" (the ◊ A), making seven, and take up the build on his
next turn with the ♣ 7. But he can't, as the ♣ 3 and ♠ 3 have
been declared "Threes" and can be taken up only by a card of
that value.

If a player has made a build that stands until his next turn,
he must either take up the build, add to it, or take up some
other card or combination. If he has made no build, or cannot
take up any cards, or does not care to do so, he simply plays a
card directly from his hand face up on the table, where it becomes part of the layout. This is called "trailing" and happens
frequently during a cassino hand, generally because a player
has no other choice. It brings up another point regarding building; namely, that the value of a build can be increased only by
adding a card from a player's hand, without using any odd
card from the layout.

The following example not only illustrates that point, but
shows exactly how a two-handed game of cassino might proceed, immediately following the original deal:

Opponent holds:	◊ A	♡ A	♠ 3	♣ 10
Layout shows:	♡ 2	♣ 2	◊ 4	♠ Q
Dealer holds:	♣ 4	♣ 7	◊ 7	◊ 8

Play proceeds: Opponent builds ◊ A on ♡ 2, calling it
"Three." He intends to build ♡ A on ♣ 2 on his next turn,
putting the two builds together and terming it "Threes," but he
doesn't get that far because:

Dealer increases the "Three" build to "Seven." He would
like to put the ◊ 4 from the layout on the opponent's build
(◊ A and ♡ 2), add the ♣ 7, and call it "Sevens." But that is
not allowable, as the additional card must come from the

dealer's hand. However, he holds the ♣ 4, so he adds that to the build, announcing "Seven."

Opponent takes immediate advantage of that, as the single "Seven," like the "Three," is unprotected. Opponent would like to add the ♡ A to the ♣ 2 and put them on the build, saying "—and three makes ten." But he can't use the ♣ 2 as part of the addition, because it comes from the layout. So instead, he retains the ♡ A and puts the ♠ 3 on the build, saying, "Ten."

Dealer now must trail, having no possible build and nothing he can take up. He lays down the ♣ 7 for two good reasons: First, he can take it up with the ♢ 7 on his next turn; while if he should lay down the ♢ 8, the opponent would simply combine it with the ♣ 2, terming it another "Ten" and place the combination with the build, taking both with the ten spot (♣ 10), which he must be holding in order to build.

Opponent takes advantage of that, too. He combines the ♡ A from his hand with the ♣ 2 and ♣ 7 in the layout, calls it "Ten," and puts it with the existing build, announcing "Tens."

Dealer is forced to trail with either ♢ 7 or ♢ 8.

Opponent takes double build with ♣ 10.

Dealer trails with his remaining card.

At this point, the opponent has taken up eight cards; the dealer, none. The layout now consists of the following cards:

$$\diamond\ 4 \qquad \diamond\ 7 \qquad \diamond\ 8 \qquad \spadesuit\ Q$$

Taking the pack, the dealer now deals four cards each to the opponent and himself, but no more are added to the layout. Play continues until that round of four is exhausted; then another round of four each is dealt; and so on, until no cards remain. In the final round, whoever takes up the last trick also takes up any cards remaining in the layout.

Face cards, having no numerical value, are taken up only by those of their own denomination: king takes up king; queen takes up queen; jack takes up jack. However, if there are two (or even three) jacks in the layout, one jack can take them all. If a king is in the layout and a player holds two kings, he can put one king on the other and announce "Kings," taking them later with the third king—unless his adversary holds the fourth king and takes them up ahead of him! In that case, he must trail later with his frustrated king.

Quite often, a player clears the board by taking any or all cards remaining in the layout. This is termed a "sweep," and the opposing player is thereby forced to "trail" on his next play, as there is nothing left for him to "take up" or make a "build."

At the end of the hand, each player goes through the cards that he has taken and points are scored as follows:

Cards: For the most cards taken	3 points
Spades: For the most spades taken	1 point
Big Cassino: For taking the ◇ **10**	2 points
Little Cassino: For taking the ♠ **2**	1 point
Aces: Each counting 1 point	4 points
Total points in each deal	11
Sweeps: Each counts an additional	1 point

(Since "sweeps" often depend on sheer luck, they may be disregarded if it is so agreed.)

In *two-handed cassino,* the hands are totaled up, and if there is a tie in "cards," neither player scores the 3 points under that head. The pack is shuffled and the original opponent becomes the dealer, continuing this until one reaches 21 points, which represents game.

In *three-handed cassino,* if two players tie for the greatest number of "cards," neither scores, which is a good break for the third player, who gets by with a lesser number. The same applies to a tie in "spades," with nobody scoring the single point. The deal moves to the player on the left, who deals, in clockwise order, four cards to each player and four to the original layout. Game is 21 points.

In *four-handed cassino,* with players on their own, the same rules apply. The only difference in the play is that building becomes more dangerous than in the two-handed game, because there are more players in between. However:

In *partnership cassino,* with four players, *A* and *C* vs. *B* and *D,* the players seated opposite pool the cards that they take up, so it is often possible for one player to take up his partner's build and later trail with cards that will prove helpful toward another build with the same total. But the individual rule still applies, that a player must hold a card totaling whatever amount he builds. In partnership play, the teams may occasionally tie for "cards" as in two-handed cassino.

In case two players or two teams both go over 21, there are various ways of deciding the winner, so one should be agreed upon before the start of play. The simplest method is to declare the player with the highest score to be the winner, as 24 to 22. In case of a tie (as 23 to 23) another hand is played; and still more, if need be. This is helpful to a third player, who stays in the game and sometimes may win.

Another system is for a player to declare "out" when he thinks he is over 21. Play stops, a count is made, and if the player is right, he wins; if wrong, he loses. If no one declares out in a close game, points are counted in the order: cards, spades, big cassino, little cassino, ♠ A, ♣ A, ♡ A, ◊ A, sweeps. The first player to reach 21 wins.

Some groups prefer to set a higher total for game, such as 49, which is very good in three-handed play, where one unlucky hand may put a player out of the running, if game is only 21. Others treat each deal, with its complete set of rounds, as a single game, sometimes setting a total number to be played in order to determine the winner.

See descriptions under: *Draw Cassino,* page 104, *Royal Cassino,* page 290, *Royal Spade Cassino,* page 291, *Spade Cassino,* page 356, and *Spades Royal,* page 356.

CATCH THE TEN: A popular name for *Scotch Whist.* See page 302.

CAYENNE or CAYENNE WHIST: A now obsolete development of *Whist* in which the final card is turned up, not to determine trump, but to fix the values of the suits for that deal.

The dealer may then name a trump suit, or no-trump; or he can "bridge" that privilege over the heads of his opponents to his partner. Hence cayenne is historically important as it anticipated the modern game of *Bridge* by (a) fixing suit values (b) establishing no-trump (c) passing the bid to the partner, from which the modern game bridge gained its name. But it also included nullo, a later feature of *Bridge Whist,* which in its turn enjoyed popularity and became appropriately obsolete.

CEDARHURST: A name for *Oklahoma Gin,* page 134.

CENT: An old form of the French game of *Piquet,* in which a hundred (*cent*) points established the winner. See page 211.

CHASE THE ACE: A modern name for a variant of *Ranter-Go-Round.* See page 288.

CHECK PINOCHLE: Under *Pinochle.* See page 199.

CHEMIN-DE-FER: A popular development of *Baccarat,* page 21, suited to social as well as casino play. Three to six packs are used, cards valued from ace, 1, up to 9, with tens and face cards 0, but the banker deals only to the player who makes the largest bet, with others betting along with the opponent, up to the limit of the bank. Two cards are dealt face down to opponent and banker, with a "natural" 9 (as **6+3**) winning over a "natural" 8 (as **8+10**), which wins over anything else. As in baccarat, when cards add to more than 10, only the last figure is used. Thus, $8+10=18=8$. If there are no naturals, each can take or refuse an extra face-up card, and the total closest to 9 wins. As an example, $6+7+2=15=5$, would beat $7+8+9=24=4$, the first figures being dropped. With ties, bets are off. As in old-style baccarat, a player may announce "Banco" and monopolize the betting for himself. In social play, the banker keeps on dealing until he loses, when the deal moves in rotation.

In both baccarat and chemin-de-fer, the banker has the advantage of being the last to "stand" or "draw" a card for himself. Chemin-de-fer is faster, as there is only one opponent and therefore no "line bets." The pack is dealt straight through, passing along to the new banker without shuffling, until only a few cards remain, when a shuffle is in order.

Gambling casinos provide their own dealer in baccarat, but the deal moves along in chemin-de-fer. There is a set rule that a player must take a third card if no higher than **4**, can do as he pleases with **5**, and must stand on **6** or **7**, in justice to those who are betting along with him, unless he "goes banco," which puts him on his own. In gambling casinos, the dealer as well as the players must conform to house rules that apply to such totals.

CHICAGO: A popular name formerly applied to *Michigan.* It now refers chiefly to the modern game of *Four-Deal Bridge,* page 124, which was first introduced in Chicago. Also, a form of *Seven-Card Stud Poker,* page 229, in which the player holding the highest spade splits the pot with the highest hand.

CHILE or CHILEAN CANASTA: Three-pack *Canasta* (168 cards) including sequence melds, which are scored as in *Samba;* or with wild-card melds allowed instead, a wild-card canasta scoring 2000 bonus points. See *Canasta,* page 43.

CHINESE BEZIQUE: A popular name for *Six-Pack Bezique.* See page 29.

CHINESE BRIDGE: A variation of *Double Dummy Bridge.* See page 103.

CHINESE FAN-TAN: A large rectangular card is placed on a table, with its corners numbered:

$$3 \quad\quad 2$$
$$4 \quad\quad 1$$

Players put chips on the corners or along the edges as they prefer. A dealer, acting as banker, cuts a batch of cards from a pack and counts them off by fours. Any left over determine the winning number, as 1, 2, or 3; with an exact count signifying 4. A winning corner bet receives three chips. An edge bet collects one if the winning number is on an adjacent corner, as 1–2, 2–3, 3–4, 4–1. This is a direct adaptation of the original Chinese game in which a handful of beans is used instead of a pack of cards.

CHINESE WHIST: An old but intriguing form of *Whist,* page 375, in which each player is dealt a row of six face-down cards, then six face-up cards upon them, and finally an odd card as his hand. Dealer names trump and player at his left leads any upcard. Others must follow suit if possible with an upcard, or the card held in hand. All downcards are turned up as soon as uncovered, thus becoming upcards. Winner of each trick leads to the next, with play and scoring as in whist. This can be played *three-handed,* with eight downcards and eight upcards, each player on his own and an odd card for his hand. A player must take one trick more than his opponents combined in order to score. In the *two-handed* game, each player is dealt twelve downcards covered by twelve upcards, with two cards for his hand.

CHOUETTE or RUBICON BEZIQUE: A mode of play in *Rubicon Bezique,* page 26 (or *Six-Pack,* page 29 and *Eight-Pack Bezique,* page 31), involving a group of players. All cut cards and the highest becomes banker, with the next high as his opponent, others waiting their turn, as third high and so on. The banker has the choice of deal, and if he wins he collects from all the others and continues as banker. If he loses, he pays all and his opponent becomes banker, while the next player in line becomes the new opponent. As loser, the original banker goes to the bottom of the list.

CIENTOS: A Spanish antecedent of *Piquet.* See page 211.

CINCH: Known also as "double pedro" and "high five"—both very appropriate terms, by the way—this game is actually an elaboration of *Auction Pitch* (page 214), including features of *Pedro,* with additional features that characterize it as a game in its own right. It is a four-player game, with two teams of partners seated opposite, using a fifty-two-card pack, with cards ranking from ace down to two, but with a special feature, namely, that the trump suit includes the five of the other suit of the same color, which ranks just below the five of trump.

As an example, with hearts as trump, the suits would be valued as follows:

Trumps: ♡ A, K, Q, J, 10, 9, 8, 7, 6, 5, ♢ 5, ♡ 4, 3, 2
       ♢ A, K, Q, J, 10, 9, 8, 7, 6, 4, 3, 2
       ♠ A, K, Q, J, 10, 9, 8, 7, 6, 5, 4, 3, 2
       ♣ A, K, Q, J, 10, 9, 8, 7, 6, 5, 4, 3, 2

Nine cards are dealt three at a time to each player, making thirty-six in all, and the remaining sixteen cards are laid aside. Beginning at the dealer's left, players make single bids for the privilege of naming the trump suit. Bids can run as high as fourteen, which is the greatest number of points that a team can take during play, according to the following schedule, which pertains strictly to trump cards:

High, the ace, 1; low, the deuce, 1; jack, 1; game, the ten, 1; right pedro, the five, 5; left pedro, the five of the same color, 5.

The highest bidder names the trump of his choice, and each player in turn discards at least three cards, to reduce his hand to a playing quota of six. He can discard as many more as he wants, provided they are not trumps, and then draw enough cards from the pack to bring his hand up to the required six. All discards are made face up; and after the dealer discards, he is allowed to look through the remainder of the pack and take whatever cards he wants, instead of merely drawing from the top, this privilege being termed "robbing the pack."

High bidder leads to the first trick, and other players can either follow suit or trump the trick. Highest card of suit led wins the trick, unless trumped, when highest trump wins. If a player is unable to follow suit, he can play from another suit instead of trumping. If a player should violate such rules by revoking, play continues, but his team cannot score and an opposing bid is automatically regarded as made.

At the end of play, each team counts its points according to the schedule already given. If any are still in the pack, they go to the bidding team's score. The simplest way of scoring is to deduct the lower score from the higher and credit the winning team with the difference. Example: Team *A* bids 8 and makes 10 points, with team *B* making only 4. Team *A* scores 10—4=6. However, if a team falls short of its bid, it scores nothing, and the opposing team scores the amount bid plus its own points. Thus if Team *A* bids 8 but takes only 7 points, with Team *B* taking the other 7, Team *B* would score 8+7=15 for that hand. Game is usually set at 51 points.

Though primarily a four-player partnership game, cinch can be played by two to six players, each on his own; but with five or six, only six cards are dealt to each and they frequently prefer a form of the game called:

Auction Cinch, Auction High Five, or *Razzle Dazzle:* Six cards each are dealt to five or six players, who bid entirely on their own, proceeding as usual until ready to play. Then the high bidder calls upon the player holding some specific card (often the ace of trump) to be his partner for that hand only. No one knows who the secret partner is until he reveals himself by playing the card named.

Blind Cinch: A four-player game, with each being dealt a nine-card hand plus a packet of four cards, which is kept face down. The highest bidder adds his packet to his hand before naming trump, then, after naming it, he discards seven of his thirteen cards, reducing his hand to six. Other players then pick up their packets and do the same. Play follows as in regular cinch.

Widow Cinch: A six-player game, with those seated opposite acting as partners, thus forming three teams of two players each. The deal consists of eight cards to each player, the remaining four cards being laid aside as a face-down widow, which goes to the high bidder, who then names trump and discards six cards, reducing his hand to the usual six. Other players do the same by discarding two cards each and play proceeds as in cinch.

Sixty-three: A game similar to cinch, but with additional trump points as follows: king, 25; three, 15; nine, 9. This makes a total of 63, hence the name of the game. Players can outbid one another as often as they want, until all pass but one, with 63 the highest possible bid. Playing and scoring follow the usual pattern but with 150 points as game.

CINCINNATI and **CINCINNATI LIZ:** Wild forms of *Poker*. See page 246.

CINQ-CENT: A form of *Bezique,* page 24, with a pack of thirty-two cards, ranking **A, 10, K, Q, J, 9, 8, 7,** one of each value in all four suits. Melds are counted as in bezique, but in addition, a player scores 120 for a sequence in an ordinary suit. A meld of ♠ **Q** and ◊ **J** is the usual 40, but is called binage instead of bezique. A pinochle count is used; ace, 11; ten, 10; king, 4; queen, 3; jack, 2, with 10 for taking last trick, 120 points in all. Game is 500 points.

CITADEL: A variant of *Beleaguered Castle.* See page 324.

CLABBER, or CLOB, CLOBBER, CLOBBERYASH, CLUBBY: Names for the game now call *Klaberjass.* See page 151.

CLOSED POKER: See page 246.

COLD HANDS or COLD-HAND POKER: See page 246.

COLD HANDS WITH DRAW: See page 246.

COMET or COMMIT: A game of the "stops" type introduced when Halley's comet appeared in 1759. It is played with a standard pack from which the ◊ **8** is removed, leaving fifty-one cards. From three to eight players are dealt hands of equal numbers, but at least three cards are left over and laid aside face down. Cards are rated in ascending value, A, 2, 3, 4, 5, 6, 7, 8, 9, 10, J, Q, K, according to suits. Player at dealer's left places any card from his hand face up on the table (as ♡ 5) and continues to add more (as ♡ 6, ♡ 7, etc.) to represent the tail of a comet, until he is stopped, say at ♡ 10, because he lacks the next in sequence, in this case the ♡ J. Whoever holds that card plays it and continues on from there until he too is stopped.

Upon reaching a king, however, a player can begin another sequence, representing a new comet's tail. If play is completely blocked because a needed card is among the extras, whoever made the last play can begin a new sequence. The ◊ 9 can either be used to start a sequence as itself or can be played as a "wild card" without disturbing the order of a sequence. Example: A player could play the ◊ 9 following the ♠ 4, but then he or another player would have to follow with the ♠ 5 or begin a new tail.

Before play starts, all contribute equally to a pool or pot, which goes to the player who first disposes of all his cards. Whoever plays the ◊ 9 collects two chips from everyone else, but must pay them two chips each if caught with the ◊ 9 at the finish. As a general rule, anyone playing a king collects one chip from each, but must pay one each for any king left in his hand. As an option, a player beginning a sequence with an ace collects one chip from each, but with no penalty if left with an ace.

COMMERCE: An old English progenitor of poker. Up to a dozen players put an equal number of chips in a pool or pot. The dealer gives each three cards singly, and, beginning at his left, each may "trade" by giving a card to the dealer, who places it face down beneath the pack and deals the player another instead, receiving one chip from the player for this service. Or, the player may "barter" with the player on his left, giving him a face-down card and receiving one in exchange, no payment being involved.

This continues indefinitely around the table, each player trying to form a combination in the following order: *Tricon,* three of the same value, these ranking **A, K, Q, J, 10** down to **2.** *Sequence* (later called *Sequence Flush*), with three cards of one suit in descending order, ace high (as ♡ **A, K, Q**) or low (as ♣ **3, 2, A**). *Point:* The lowest total of spots on three cards of the same suit: Ace counting 11, face cards (king, queen, jack, 10 each). (Example: ♡ **J, 7, 2**=10+7+2=19, beats ♠ **A, 6, 5**=11+6+5=22.)

Later, these values were introduced: *Flush,* just below sequence, any three cards of one suit (as ♡ **J, 7, 3**), and *Pair,* two cards of the same value (as ♡ **J,** ♠ **J**) rating just below that. This reduced *Point* to the status of only two cards of one suit, with the highest total of spots being winner (as ♠ **A,** ♡ **K**=11+10=21, beating ♡ **9, 8**=17). This makes a much better game.

In all cases, however, play ends when a player decides to stand on what he has. When his turn comes to trade or barter or even accept the barter offered by the player just ahead of him, he knocks on the table instead. Then all hands must be shown and the highest takes the pot. The dealer, having collected from the traders, must pay the others one chip each unless he is the winner, provided he holds a pair or better.

COMMERCIAL PITCH: Another name for *Sellout*. See page 303.

CONCENTRATION: A memory game in which a fifty-two-card pack is dealt face down in half a dozen rows of eight or nine cards each. A player turns up any pair of cards, and if they match in color and value (as ♠ **8** and ♣ **8,** or ◇ **Q** ♡ **Q**), he removes them and tries to turn up another matching pair. When he fails, he turns the two cards face down and another player makes a try. This continues with from two to six players, who make mental note of any cards turned down. Thus if Player *A* should turn down the ♡ **8** and the ♠ **K,**

Player *B* might later turn up either the ◊ 8 or the ♣ K and immediately be able to match it, provided he remembers where its mate happens to be. The player pairing the most cards wins the game. As a variant, the game is easier if dependent on values only, as any two aces being accepted as a pair regardless of color, and so on. Half-sized playing cards can be used to accommodate the layout in less space.

CONQUIAN: A Mexican predecessor of *Rummy*, with two players using a forty-card pack ranking in descending order: **K, Q, J, 7, 6, 5, 4, 3, 2, A.** Each is dealt a hand of ten cards, and his aim is to meld or lay down three or four cards of the same value (as **J–J–J** or **6–6–6–6**) and sequences of three or more in one suit (as ♡ **5 4 3**). Opponent begins by turning up top card of the undealt pack and melding whatever he can from his hand, using the turned-up card if it is suitable. In that case, following his meld, he discards an odd card from his hand, laying it face up beside the pack to start a discard pile. Otherwise, he must use the turned-up card to start the discard pile, as he cannot take it into his hand (as in rummy).

In his turn, the dealer may use the top card of the discard pile toward a meld if possible; otherwise, he must turn up the top card of the pack and proceed as the opponent did. Alternate play continues until one player has melded his entire hand, plus an extra card, making eleven in all. Thus sometimes, with ten cards already melded, a player must continue to turn up cards or wait for a discard that can be added to his existing meld. Besides "laying off" on his own meld, a player may "borrow" from one toward another, if both are kept valid. Example: Having melded ♠ **K Q J 7**, he could put the ♠ **K** with two other kings, for **K–K–K**. Or having melded **3–3–3–3** and ◊ **6 5 4**, he could take the ◊ **3** from the "set" and attach it to the "run" in order to add ◊ **2 A** for a sequence of ◊ **6 5 4 3 2 A**. At any time one player may insist that the other use a turned-up card toward a meld that he has already made, as that may hinder his further play.

Each hand is regarded as a separate game, and if the pack

is exhausted before either player melds out, the next game counts double. The deal changes after each hand or game.

CONSOLATION: A name given to the final hand or "game" in *Five in One*. See page 122.

CONTINENTAL RUMMY: A multiple type of *Rummy*, using two packs (each with one or two jokers) for up to six players; three such packs for up to nine; four such packs for up to twelve. Cards rank **A, K, Q, J, 10, 9, 8, 7, 6, 5, 4, 3, 2, A,** the ace being both high and low. Each player is dealt fifteen cards (preferably by threes). Play follows the standard rummy pattern, page 291, but with these provisos:

No sets (as **K–K–K**) can be melded; only sequences of three or more cards in the same suit (as ♡ **9 8 7**). The entire hand must be melded at once to go out; and it must be composed exactly of five sequences of three cards each; three of four cards and one of three; or one five, one four, and two threes. A joker is wild, representing any card a player may require. Winner collects 1 point from every other player, plus 2 points for each joker that he holds.

With deuces wild as well as jokers, the cards rank **A, K, Q, J, 10, 9, 8, 7, 6, 5, 4, 3, A** and the winner collects 1 point for each deuce he holds. Various bonus counts may be included, as 10 points for going out without a wild card and 15 points for going out with all cards in one suit.

CONTRACT BRIDGE: By far the most popular of modern card games, contract bridge is a high-powered extension of *Auction Bridge,* the leader of its day. The games follow the same bidding procedure, but contract is more exacting because of its advanced mode of scoring. In play, both follow the rules of *Whist,* see page 375. The standard fifty-two-card pack is used, with each suit ranking **A, K, Q, J, 10, 9, 8, 7, 6, 5, 4, 3, 2** in descending order.

There are four players, commonly called South, North, East, and West because of their positions at the table. Those seated opposite play as partners against the other pair (*E* and *W* vs. *N* and *S*). The entire pack is dealt singly in clockwise order, giving each player thirteen cards. While only a single pack is used in playing each hand, convention requires a second pack, which is shuffled by the dealer's partner and laid at the partner's right, in readiness for the next dealer. In each deal, the dealer has the pack cut by the player on his right.

The bidding begins with the dealer, who may either "pass" or specify how many tricks he will contract to take, with his partner's aid, either with a certain suit as trump, or in no-trump. The lowest bid is "one," meaning that the team must take one trick over a "book" of six, making seven tricks in all; and the bids run in ascending order: clubs, diamonds, hearts, spades, and no-trump. A bid of two clubs is higher than one no-trump; three clubs is higher than two no-trump; and so upward, with the highest bid of all seven no-trump.

The bidding is started by the dealer and proceeds in clockwise rotation. If all pass, the hands are turned in and the deal moves to the left. If a bid is made, a succeeding player may raise it (as from one heart to two hearts), bid higher (as two NT over two diamonds), or "pass," but with the privilege of re-entering the bidding, unless three players pass in succession, in which case the last actual bid stands.

A player may "double" a bid made by the opposing team, which enables the bidder to score double in trick points, plus an extra bonus count, if he makes his bid. But if the bidder should fail, the team that doubled scores an additional bonus. A double has the status of a regular bid; hence the next player can either "pass" or "overcall" it with a higher bid. Instead, he can also "redouble," which again doubles the trick points and also increases the bonus points for one team or the other. Naturally, a player can only double a bid made by an opponent; never his partner's bid. Similarly, he can only redouble an opposing double.

When the bidding ends, the player who made the final bid becomes the "declarer," unless his partner originally named the suit (or no-trump). In that case, the partner becomes the declarer. It is the declarer who plays the hands for the bidding team.

Example: *S* bids one spade; *N* bids one NT; *S* bids two diamonds; *N* bids three hearts. If the bidding stops there, *North* becomes declarer with a contract of three hearts. But if *North* had bid three spades, *South* would be declarer at three spades, since he initiated the suit. However, if *South* should continue the bidding to three NT, *North* would become declarer at three no-trump, since he was the first to name no-trump.

When bidding is completed, the play starts with the opponent on the declarer's left, who leads any card. Immediately, the declarer's partner lays his hand face up on the table, arranging it in suits from ace down, so that the declarer can play it as a "dummy" hand while playing his own hand in the usual fashion. Play proceeds to the left, or clockwise, exactly as in the parent game of whist; namely: Players must follow suit if they can; otherwise, they may trump or discard from a side suit. The highest card of the suit led wins the trick unless trumped, when the highest trump wins. The winner of each trick leads to the next until all thirteen have been taken.

In bridge, tricks are scored in ascending value, according to which suit is trump, or whether the declarer is playing no-trump. In clubs (♣) or diamonds (◊) each trick bid and won over six counts 20 points. Thus, with a bid of one diamond, the declarer would have to take seven or more tricks to score 20; with a bid of two clubs, eight or more tricks to score 40; and so on.

With hearts (♡) or spades (♠) each trick bid and won over six counts 30 points; thus with a bid of three hearts or three spades, the declarer would have to take nine or more tricks to score 90; and so on upward. With no-trump (NT) a bid of "one" scores 40 points, with 30 points for each additional trick bid and won, so that a bid of one NT (seven tricks) would count 40 if successful; two NT, 70 points; three NT, 100. All these count double if the bid is "doubled," four times if "redoubled."

The first team to score 100 trick points wins "game" and the teams start again at 0, until one team has won two games, which constitute a "rubber." It is possible to win game with a bid of "five" in a "minor suit" (♣ or ◇), since $20 \times 5 = 100$; or with a bid of "four" in a "major suit" (♡ or ♠), since $30 \times 4 = 120$; or with a bid of "three" in no-trump, as $40 + 30 + 30 = 100$. With lesser bids, a team must win at least two hands to make game. When a team has won one game, it becomes "vulnerable."

In bridge, a special scoring pad is used, with a separate column for each team and a horizontal line across the center. All trick points are entered "below the line" and all bonus points are entered "above the line," according to the scoring table shown. It will be noted that bonus scores increase when a team is "vulnerable," a factor that has an important bearing on the bidding, as the risk becomes proportionately greater.

After a team wins a game, a single line is drawn beneath the score; and after a team wins a rubber, a double line is drawn beneath. Each column is then added and the lower total is placed beneath the higher and subtracted, to ascertain the winning team's margin of victory. Here is an example of a rubber that required five hands for its completion:

	WE		THEY
(B)	50	(E)	700
(A)	30	(C)	30
(A)	90	(C)	130
		(D)	120
	170		980
			—170
			810

Bidding and play represented by the above score ran thus:

In hand "A" the first team, "We," bid three hearts and took 10 tricks, scoring 90 below the line for making contract; and 30 above for the "overtrick," or extra trick.

In "B," the other team, "They," bid three NT but took only 8 tricks, so "We" scored 50 above the line for one undertrick.

In "C," "They" bid four NT and took 11 tricks, scoring 130 below the line for making contract, and 30 above for the overtrick.

In "D," "They" bid four spades and made it by taking exactly 10 tricks, scoring 120 below the line.

Score "E" represents a 700-point bonus above the line, since "They" won the rubber by winning two games (in Hands "C" and "D"), while "We" won none.

A bid of "six," if successful, is termed a "small slam," and the bidding team scores a special bonus above the line for taking the required twelve tricks. A successful bid of "seven," in which all thirteen tricks are taken, is a "grand slam," with a still higher bonus.

The only score that has nothing to do with taking tricks is the "honor score," a carry-over from whist, in which either team, regardless of which declared trump, is credited with bonus points for holding four or five "trump honors" (A, K, Q, J, 10) in one hand; or all four aces in one hand, if the final bid is no-trump.

All these are listed in the scoring table below.

Evaluating and Bidding the Hand: In order for two partners to bid their hands effectively, they must follow a set system, and the most popular is the "point count," which was originally applied to no-trump hands and later developed to include suit bids. This consists of evaluating the high cards as follows: ace, 4; king, 3; queen, 2; jack, 1. These alone are used in no-trump bids. With trumps, each card over four in a trump suit counts 1 point; each over three in a side suit counts 1 point.

Instead of noting such "long suits," this can be calculated on a basis of "short suits." A suit with only two cards, termed a "doubleton," counts 1 point; a suit with only one card, known as a "singleton," counts 2 points; total lack of any suit, called a "void" or "blank suit," counts 3 points. It comes out the

SCORING TABLE FOR CONTRACT BRIDGE

After making contract, declarer's team scores below the line:

For each odd trick over six	Ordinary Contract	When Doubled	When Redoubled
Clubs ♣ or diamonds ◇	20	40	80
Hearts ♡ or spades ♠	30	60	120
No-trump: first trick	40	80	160
Additional tricks:	30	60	120

Declarer's team scores bonus points above the line:

	When Not Vulnerable		When Vulnerable		For Making Contract
	♣,◇	♡,♠,NT	♣,◇	♡,♠,NT	
For each overtrick	20	30	20	30	No bonus
If doubled	100	100	200	200	50
If redoubled	200	200	400	400	50
For small slam	500	500	750	750	
For grand slam	1000	1000	1500	1500	

When declarer's team fails to make contract, opponents score above the line:

	When Not Vulnerable ♣,◇,♡,♠,NT	When Vulnerable ♣,◇,♡,♠,NT
For each undertrick	50	100
Doubled: first undertrick	100	200
Each additional	200	300
Redoubled; first undertrick	200	400
Each additional	400	600

Game consists of 100 points or more.
Winner of two games wins rubber:

Bonus points above the line	Rubber in two games	Rubber in two out of three	One game in unfinished rubber	Part score in unfinished game
Team scores:	700	500	300	50

For honors held by one player, either team scores above the line:

	Trump honors (A, K, Q, J, 10)		No-trump honors (A, A, A, A)
	Four in one hand	Five in one hand	All in one hand
Bonus points	100	150	150

same either way, and these are termed "distributional points" to distinguish them from "high-card points."

To open with a suit bid, one of the following potential trump suits is needed: A four-card suit with 3 or preferably 4 high-card points; a five-card suit with at least 1 high-card point; or any six-card suit or longer. Such a hand, however, must contain a total of 12 or 13 points to warrant a bid of "one"; with 14 points a bid of "one" is a must in order for a player to alert his partner to the hand's potential strength. With two "biddable suits" it is usually preferable to bid the longer one; while with two of equal length, the one with the higher scoring value is preferable. Either way, there may be a chance to bid the other suit later.

To open with a trump bid of "two," a player should have 22 points with a seven-card suit, or two good five-card suits; 23 points with a good six-card suit; and 25 points with only one good five-card suit. This is a "demand bid," requiring the partner to keep the bidding open until game level is reached.

A trump opening bid of "three" or "four" denotes a "freak" hand containing a long, fairly strong suit of at least seven cards, but with a low point count, especially in high cards. This is termed a "shutout" bid, as it prevents the opposing team from bidding and is therefore worth the risk. For example:

♠ K J 10 9 8 5 3 2   ♡ 5   ◇ K 10 9   ♣ 9

Although this hand has only 7 high-card points (K-J-K) and a total point count of 11 (due to extra spades as trump), it should take six or seven tricks in spades and one in diamonds. Hence it is worth a bid of three spades or four spades, as normal support from the partner will clinch the contract; and at worst the declarer can go down only one or two tricks.

In opening with a suit bid of "one," which is the most frequent procedure, a player should check his hand for "quick tricks," which include the following combinations in individual suits ("X" standing for any small card): A-K-Q=2½; A-K= 2; A-Q=1½; A-J-10=1½; K-Q-J=1½; A=1; K-Q=1;

K–J–10=1; **K–X**=½; **Q–J–X**=½. A 12-point hand usually needs two and one half quick tricks to open; while a 13-point hand and even a 14-point hand should show two quick tricks, no longer rating as a "must" bid if it bogs down in that department. For example:

    ♠ K   ♡ K 8 7 3 2   ◇ Q 8 6 4 3   ♣ Q J

Even with 14 points (11 high-card, 3 distributional) this is inadequate for an opening bid, as it has only one half quick tricks in hearts.

For an opening bid in no-trump, a hand should contain suits distributed in one of the following ratios, which are known as "balanced" hands: 4–3–3–3, 4–4–3–2, 5–3–3–2. A point count of 16, 17, or 18, all in high cards, is needed for "one no-trump," and the bidder should have a stopper in each of three suits. A "stopper" is a card that sooner or later can take an opposing lead in its particular suit, thus enabling the bidder to gain the lead. Aces are stoppers in their own right, but kings, queens, and jacks require one, two, and three cards respectively to qualify. Example:

    ♠ K J 8   ♡ J 9 8 4   ◇ A K Q   ♣ Q 10 2

The above hand, with 4–3–3–3 distribution, has a point count of 16, with a stopper in every suit, automatically calling for an opening bid of "one no-trump." As already specified, stoppers in three suits would be enough, but with 4–4–3–2 or 5–3–3–2 distribution, the two-card suit must have a stopper, or the hand would be too risky. As examples:

(a) ♠ A K 9   ♡ K 8   ◇ A Q 7 2   ♣ 8 5 4 2
(b) ♠ 8 6   ♡ A K 7   ◇ K J 9 5 3   ♣ A Q 9

In (a) the count of 16 is good for "one no-trump" because the short suit (♡) has a stopper in a guarded king and three suits (♠, ♡, ◇) are protected. But in (b) the higher count of 17 is offset by the lack of stoppers in the short suit (♠). The correct bid for this hand would be "one diamond."

Balanced hands with 19, 20, or 21 high-card points call for an opening suit bid of "one" rather than a "no-trump" bid, even though three or four suits have stoppers. This enables a bidder to size up the situation from his partner's response or opposing overcalls, so he can continue the bidding accordingly. With a balanced hand containing 22, 23, or 24 high-card points, the proper bid is "two no-trump," provided all suits have stoppers. With 25, 26, or 27 points in that same type of hand, the bid should be "three no-trump."

Responses to Opening Bids: Since a suit bid of "one" is the commonest of all openers, a partner's response to such a bid deserves prime consideration. Such responses are of three types:

(a) Raising the bid in the same suit.

(b) Making a higher bid in a new suit.

(c) Making a bid in no-trump.

Each of these depends upon the type of hand held by the partner, whose response should adhere to the following patterns:

(a) If the responder has three cards of the original bidder's trump suit, headed by a jack or better, he can bid "two" in the same suit, if his hand contains 7 to 10 points. He can also raise to "two" on the strength of four small trumps (all below jack) if he has the required count. For a singleton, he can add 1 extra point; for a void, 2 extra points, toward his over-all count.

Example: ♠ 9 8 7 5 ♡ K 10 9 8 7 5 4 ◊ 6 ♣ 9

With an original bid of "one spade," this hand would normally add to 7 points, 3 for the ♡ K and four extra cards in hearts. But as a responding bid, the singleton ◊ would be worth 1 point more and a ♣ singleton 1 point, making a total of 9 points for a bid of two spades. Good judgment must be used, however, for if the hand just shown contained the ◊ K instead of the ♡ K as a singleton, it might be worthless in play, although the count added up to the same total.

With a hand that contains four of the original bidder's trump and adds up to 11 or 12 points, it is usually wise to switch to another suit, then come back to the original trump (if possible or advisable) on a later bid. However, such a hand that totals 13 to 16 points by the stepped-up count is worth a "jump raise" to "three" in the original bidder's trump, namely spades:

Example: ♠ K 8 7 5   ♡ 9   ◇ Q 7 3 2   ♣ K Q 8 6

High-card points total 10, plus 3 distributional points—1 for an extra ◇; 1 for an extra ♣; and 1 extra for the singleton (♡ 9). That makes 13, good for a response of three spades. Again, judgment is a factor; with a strong hand, a responder can always add an extra point to reach the needed bracket. Simply be cautious with doubtful hands, particularly those of the "balanced" type, as their lack of singletons or voids is a handicap when raising a trump bid.

When a responder has a hand containing five or more of the original bidder's trumps, with a singleton or void, and less than 10 high-card points, he should make a "shutout" raise to "four" of the original trump. The logic of this is simple: Since the original bidder has at least four trumps and the responder five, they must have nine or more trumps between them, with the responder's singleton offering the original bidder good trumping opportunities from the dummy hand. In bridge, as in whist, "trumping" is commonly termed "ruffing."

With "four" in a major suit (♠ or ♡) there is a chance for game; while with a minor suit (◇ or ♣) the original bidder can go "five" with a strong hand, hoping for the same result. Either way, the partners can't go down too badly, so it is worth the risk to shut out the opponents from a possible strong bid of their own.

(b) With an opening bid of "one," a partner who lacks support in the suit named can switch to a new suit in which he holds four or more cards and a total of 6 to 10 points, provided he can keep it at the "one" level. This type of bid, known as the "one over one" is always possible following an opener of one club; while an opening bid of "one" in either minor suit (♣

or ◇) can always be overcalled by "one" in a major suit (♡ or
♠).

With a count of 11 to 17, a responder can still bid "one" under such circumstances, but when that is impossible, he can
go to "two" in his own suit: Thus, an opening bid of one heart
would require a response of two clubs or two diamonds; while
a one spade opening would mean a bid of "two" in any other
suit. This is known as a "two over one." Either type—the "one
over one" or "two over one"—is a "forcing bid," which calls
upon the original bidder to keep the bidding open.

With a count of 18 or more, a responder can "jump" an
opening bid of "one" to "three" in another suit, thus "forcing"
the bidding to game level. Therefore, he should either be very
strong in his new suit or have good support for the original
bidder's trump, in order to switch back to it if need be. Often,
such bidding leads to a potential slam.

(c) With a "balanced hand" containing 6 to 10 high-card
points, the usual response to an opening suit bid of "one" is one
NT. This is not a "forcing bid," as it is often easy to wangle the
one trick needed over "book," so it does not matter if the original bidder and both opponents pass. However, with a balanced hand having 13 to 15 high-card points, a response of
two NT is in order; while a balanced hand with 16 to 18 high-
card points, three NT is proper. In *each case,* however, the
responder must have a "stopper" in every suit except the suit
named by his partner, the opening bidder. A two NT response
is "forcing" to game; but three NT is good for game, so the
original bidder can let it ride unless he sees prospects for a
slam.

An opening suit bid of "two" is a demand to keep the bidding open until game is reached. Hence with less than 7 high-
card points, a partner should respond with two NT as the
cheapest way to show that he has a negative hand, which may
prove worthless. With 7 or more high-card points and one quick
trick, a positive response is in order. That would mean "three"
in the opening bidder's suit or a lower-ranking suit; or "two"

in a higher-ranking suit. With a balanced hand of 8 or 9 points and anything more than one quick trick, the response should be three NT, which represents a positive bid.

An opening bid of "one no-trump" specifies a balanced hand with 16 to 18 high-card points, as already stated. A partner who also has a balanced hand should respond as follows: With 8 or 9 high-card points, two NT. With 10 to 14 such points, three NT. With 15 or 16 points, four NT. With 17 or 18, a jump to six NT is justified. With 21 high-card points, the response can be seven NT.

With an unbalanced hand containing less than 8 points, the responder may pass or bid "two" in a five-card suit, to show where his strength lies. With 10 or more points, the response should be "three" in a biddable suit—particularly a major—forcing to game. This is termed a "takeout bid," telling the opener that the responder has the points needed for three NT but wants to show strength in a specific suit.

With an opening bid of "two no-trump," a responder holding a balanced hand can raise the bid to three NT with only 4 high-card points; or jump to four NT with 9 such points. With 11 points, the bid can jump to six NT; with 13 points, to seven NT. If the responder holds an unbalanced hand, he can go to "three" in a five-card suit if the hand has more than 5 points. With a six-card suit, particularly a major suit ($\heartsuit$ or $\spadesuit$), a response of "three" should be sure-fire.

An opening bid of "three no-trump" is a game contract, so the responder should bid higher only if he sees chances for a slam. He knows that his partner, the opening bidder, has at least 25 points, which leaves only 15 for the rest. So if the responder holds 5 or 6 of those high-card points, he may as well let the "three" ride. But with 7 points, he can raise to four NT; with 8 points to six NT; with 12 points, to seven NT. Any long suit of five or more cards, with 5 points in high cards, is worth a takeout bid of "four" in that suit.

With a shutout bid of "three" (*or* "four") *in a suit,* the best response is to pass, as the bidder is depending upon the responder to have some strength to aid his freakish hand. However, if the responder's hand is good for three and one half quick tricks, or has four or more cards in the bidder's trump suit, a raise may be in order in the suit named.

Rebidding the Hand: After an opening bidder gains some clue to his partner's hand from the latter's response, he can rebid if their combined point count promises 26 or more, which normally should produce game during play. Hence, with an opening bid of "one" in a suit, the procedure is:

With opening bid of "one." Response "two" in same suit: If opening bidder has *12 to 15 points,* he should generally pass, since responder has only 6 to 10 points. However, if the opener has six or more cards in that suit, he can raise the bid to "three."

If opening bidder holds *16 to 18 points,* he can rebid "three" in the original suit; or, with a balanced hand with 16 high-card points, he can change to two NT. Or, he can make a bid in a new suit if it has the required count. With *19 to 21 points,* he can jump to game in his original suit, or bid a new suit.

Opening bid of "one." Response "three" in same suit: If opening bidder holds *12 to 15 points,* he can count on his partner's 13 to 16 to produce the total of 26 for game. Hence he can raise that suit to "four" or switch to three NT with a balanced hand of the 4–3–3–3 or 4–4–3–2 type. If the original bid is in a minor suit, one club or one diamond, the original bidder can "show" a strong major suit by bidding three hearts or three spades, and letting the responder take it from there. If opening bidder holds *16 to 21 points,* he should try for a slam.

Opening bid of "one" in a suit. Response "one" in no-trump: If the opening bidder has *12 to 15 points,* he can rebid "two" in that suit or another, unless he holds a balanced hand. In that case, it is better to let the response of one NT stand. With *16 to 18 points,* the same rule holds, but a response of two NT is allowable if the count is in high cards. With *19 to 21 points,* a bid of "three" or "four" can be made in a strong suit. A bid of three NT should also be considered.

Opening bid of "one" in a suit. Response "two" in no-trump: Here, the original bidder knows that his partner must have a balanced hand with 13 to 15 high-card points and that all suits are stopped, which definitely forces the bidding to game. Hence:

If the opening bidder holds *12 to 15 points,* he can rebid three NT with a balanced hand, unless it is a 5-3-3-2 distribution with a five-card major suit, which should be bid instead. With an unbalanced hand, the rebid should be in a suit. With *16 to 18 points,* the original bidder should consider slam prospects; with *19 to 21 points,* he should definitely go for a slam.

Opening bid of "one" in a suit. Response "one" in another suit: This is the familiar "one over one," indicating that the responder has a point count of 6 to 18 in the new suit; hence the original bidder has a variety of choices. If his own count is *12 to 15,* he can rebid his original suit if it has six or more cards. Or, he can treat the new suit as an original bid and respond by raising it if he has the proper support. Otherwise, he can show a new suit by bidding "one," or "two" if necessary. Finally, he can bid one NT to keep the bidding going for that round, though one NT is good in its own right with a balanced hand.

With *16 to 18 points,* the original bidder can jump to "three" in his own suit or jump the responder's suit to "four" if he holds four cards in that suit; otherwise, the regular procedure holds. With *19 to 21 points,* he can jump either his own suit or his partner's suit to game; or rebid two NT with a balanced hand, or even three NT if he is very strong in the suits that neither he nor his partner bid.

Opening bid of "one" in a suit. Response "two" in another suit: This applies to "two over one" in a lesser suit than the original bid, as two diamonds over one spade. Since it indicates that the responder has more than 10 points in the new suit, hence the original bidder can rebid more strenuously than with the "one over one." If his own count is *12 to 15 points,* he should at least rebid his original suit. But instead, he can show a new biddable suit at the two level; or, with balanced distribution and blockers in one or both of the unbid suits, he can rebid two NT. Or he can raise his partner's bid, with proper trump support.

With *16 to 18 points,* he could rebid the same as with the "one over one," and the same applies with *19 to 21 points.*

Opening bid: One no-trump. Response "two" in no-trump: This shows that the original bidder has 16, 17, or 18 high-card points, while his partner, as responder, has 8 or 9, so the combined total runs from 24 to 27 points. The original bidder should pass with only 16, raise to three NT with 17 or 18, provided he has all suits stopped.

Opening bid: One no-trump. Response "two" in a suit: The original bidder should pass with only 16 or 17 points, but with 18 points and strength in the responder's suit, he can bid "three" in that suit.

Rebidding by the Responder: After the original bidder has made a rebid that is forcing to game, his partner must comply with whatever rebid he can, to keep the bidding open. Otherwise, he should estimate the original bidder's count, add his own according to a potential bid, and figure how close they can go toward game, at 26 points, or slam at 33 points. A good working rule is to make one rebid on the strength of a 6-point hand; two on 11 or 12 points; and go for game with 13+ and slam with 18+.

Defensive Bidding: The Overcall: Since any opening bid, other than the "shutout" type, shows a hand with a higher-than-average point count, an opposing bidder is often on the defensive and must act accordingly. To overcall the initial bid, he usually needs a strong trump holding rather than a high point count; in fact, his very lack of points may mean that his partner has a high count, making it all the more important that he should furnish some key to his own holding.

Opinions vary in regard to overcalls, but generally speaking, it is safe to overcall at the "one" level with a count of 8 points or more, provided the hand has at least five trumps including two of the four top cards and is good for four tricks in play (or five, if vulnerable). For example:

♠ 8 7   ♡ Q J 10 8 7   ◇ 8 3   ♣ A 10 9 6

Assuming that the opening bid was 1 ◇, this hand, with a count of 9 points in hearts, would warrant an overcall of one heart, since it has five trumps headed by the Q–J and its "playing tricks" can be calculated thus: If the opponents win two heart tricks with the A and K, the ♡ Q, J, 10 become sure tricks, along with the ♣ A. Since clubs are a four-card suit, the ♣ 10 is high enough to be a likely winner, bringing the total of playing tricks to the required five.

Had the opening bid been one spade, an overcall of two hearts would have been needed; and for that, a count of 12 points is usual, with five or six playing tricks. The hand just cited would fall short of that, but if strengthened at spots, it would qualify, as follows:

♠ 8   ♡ K Q 10 8 7 2   ◇ 8 3   ♣ A 10 9 8

This just makes a point count of 12. In trumps, the opponents will win the ♡ A and possibly the ♡ J, but this hand will take four, along with the ♣ A and probably the ♣ 10, for six in all. The possibility of capturing the ♣ J, and the trumping prospects afforded by the singleton in the opener's suit (♠) are both helpful factors that should be taken into account when making an overcall.

For a three-level overcall, a point count of 15 is in order, with a six-card trump suit—or longer!—and six or seven playing tricks. In all cases, this factor is important: Since overcalls are primarily defensive, the opposing team is always apt to bid higher. Hence a great purpose of an overcall is to inform your partner what suit to lead in case an opponent becomes the declarer. That is why an overcaller needs at least two high cards in the suit he bids, as a lead to anything less could prove futile.

A no-trump overcall following a suit bid is practically the same as an opening bid in no-trump, with one NT requiring a balanced hand with 16, 17, or 18 high-card points and stoppers in three suits. In this case, however, one of those must be the suit named by the opening bidder. Higher no-trump overcalls follow the opening pattern.

A takeout double, or *informatory double,* is used as an overcall with a hand that has a normal opening point count (13 points or better) but with strength in all three suits except the one named by the opening bidder. Thus a 4–4–4–1 distribution is often an ideal setup, as:

♠ 10   ♡ A 10 9 7   ◇ K Q 9 3   ♣ Q J 8 4

Assuming that the opening bid was one spade, this hand, with 14 points, counting 2 for the singleton spade, meets requirements for an opening bid in hearts, diamonds, or clubs, but is not worth an overcall in any. So the overcaller doubles the one spade bid, thereby enabling his partner to bid his best or longest suit, no matter how weak it may be. A distribution of 5–4–4–0 is good for a "takeout double" (the void being in the opening bidder's suit) provided the usual requirements are met. So is a 5–4–3–1 or a 5–3–3–2; but opinions vary with a 4–4–3–2 hand.

To be recognized as a takeout, a double must be made before the doubler's partner has already made a bid. It should also represent the doubler's own first bid. Only a bid of "one" or a "two" in a suit should be doubled; and a no-trump bid, never. Otherwise it becomes a "business double," with no takeout needed, as the doubler's intent is to "set" the opponents for a substantial loss.

A cross between a takeout and a business double is allowable in overcalling an opening shutout bid of three or four in a suit. The overcaller needs a strong hand of about 18 points, which in itself is an indication that the opening bidder holds a low-point freak. The partner of the overcaller can make a takeout bid or let the double stand, usually preferring the latter if the opening bid was "four."

An overcall in the suit named in an opponent's opening "one" bid shows that the overcaller has a really strong hand, with either the ace of that suit or a blank in the suit. This is definitely a "forcing bid" for the coming round. This is known as a "cue bid."

Responses to Overcalls: An overcall is similar to an opening bid, in as much as the player making it is the initial bidder for his team. But since the overcall is figured chiefly on playing tricks, the responder must check his own prospects in that department before raising the overcaller's trump bid. Knowing that the overcaller has five or more trumps, the responder can add real help with two trumps headed by a queen or better, or with three small trumps. Generally, the hand also needs sufficient side strength to produce a count of 8 points or better.

It is better to pass than to bid another suit unless the responder has a suit holding that is worth an overcall in its own right, or his hand comes close to the requirement of an opening bid. If the responder has two stoppers in the opponent's suit, he can switch to no-trump with a high-card count of 11 points or more, though some cautious bidders are apt to hesitate at anything much short of a standard no-trump opening.

Following a takeout double, unless there is an intervening bid, the doubler's partner must respond at the lowest available level, even with a poor hand. In that case, the doubler can pass when his turn comes, unless: having 16 high-card points, he should raise the responder's "one" bid to the "two" level; with 18, to "three"; with 20, to "four." However, if the responder holds a good five-card trump suit and a point count of more than 10, he should make his bid at the next higher level, to let the doubler know the situation. After such a jump response, the doubler should raise the bid and aim for game.

Opposing Bidding Following an Overcall: If an opening bid is overcalled by the next player, the opener's partner may pass or make a "free bid" in the opener's suit or one of his own, provided he has a somewhat stronger hand with 2 or 3 more points than required for the usual response to an opening bid. However, if the opening bid is doubled, the opener's partner may make a free bid on the usual holding, while with a stronger hand, he can redouble, giving the opener a chance to rebid.

Either way, this puts the doubler's partner in what amounts to a free bid situation of his own, enabling him to pass or bid accordingly, knowing that his partner will be able to rebid.

Note: The "takeout double" and "redouble" fall in the category of accepted bidding conventions that are used by experienced partners to acquaint each other with special holdings or situations not recognizable through ordinary bidding. Conventions are allowable if confined to those that are generally recognized as standard, or if they are announced and described beforehand, with due acceptance by all concerned. Some are used only by experts and are therefore beyond the range of bridge as ordinarily played.

THREE-HANDED BRIDGE: Known also as "cutthroat bridge," this is a game for three players, but a fourth hand is dealt and placed aside face down, while the players bid, each on his own. The successful bidder, or declarer, then turns up the odd hand, placing it between the two other players, who act as his opponents during the play that follows, with the odd hand serving as dummy for the declarer exactly as in *Contract Bridge,* though scoring can be the same as in *Auction Bridge,* page 18, if preferred.

The declarer scores in the usual manner when he makes his contract, just as though he represented a team. If he is defeated, however, each of his opponents scores the full amount for setting him. Similarly, if the opponents hold honors, each scores for them in full. In contract scoring, each player can be individually vulnerable or not vulnerable, as the case may demand. The first player to win two games scores 500 points for rubber; this is increased to 700 points if neither of the other players has scored. In auction, the premium is 250.

CONTRACT PINOCHLE: A form of *Partnership Pinochle*, page 210.

CONTRACT RUMMY: A popular form of rummy, with three or four players using a double pack of 104 cards, usually with two or preferably four jokers added as wild cards. With five to eight players, a triple pack of 156 cards is used, usually with three or preferably six wild jokers added. In both versions, each player is on his own. Cards rank in descending order, as in standard rummy, except that the ace is both high and low, terminating each end of the sequence: **A, K, Q, J, 10, 9, 8, 7, 6, 5, 4, 3, 2, A.** Each ace is valued at 15 points; face cards **(K, Q, J),** 10 each; others according to their spots. Jokers, when included, are valued at 15 each.

The game consists of seven separate deals, each with its own "contract" involving special melding rules. Each player is dealt ten cards during the first four deals; twelve cards during the last three. After each player has been served, the next card is turned up to start a discard pile. Here, as in standard rummy, the first player on the dealer's left has the choice of taking the face-up card or a card from the top of the pack, *but:*

If the player does not want the card from the discard pile, he must wait and give the next player a chance to take it. The next player, if he does so, must also take the top card of the pack, adding both to his hand as extras, retaining them for later play in proper turn. If he does not want the card from the discard pile, the privilege of taking it—plus a card from the top of the pack—is given to the next player; and so on.

After a player has exerted this privilege, or all have refused it, the original player continues his turn by drawing the top card from the pack. He adds it to his hand and proceeds as in regular rummy, melding if he can and wants to do so, then discarding an odd card face up on the discard pile. Melds, as in the standard game, are of two types: "sets," composed of at least three cards of the same value, as **9–9–9;** and "sequences," formed by three or more cards of the same suit, in descending order, as ♠ **8 7 6.** He may also "lay off" cards from his hand by adding to a set or continuing a sequence from either end.

However, as already mentioned, in this game, a player's melds must meet the "contract" requirements of a given deal, as follows:

First Deal: A player must meld two separate sets of only three cards each (as **K–K–K, 5–5–5**).

Second Deal: A player must meld one set of only three cards, and one sequence of only three cards (as **9–9–9** and **♠ 5 4 3**).

Third Deal: A player must meld two separate sequences of only three cards each (as **♡ J 10 9** and **♢ 4 3 2. ♡ J 10 9 8 7 6** is not allowable, as it forms a six-card sequence; but **♡ J 10 9 ♡ 7 6 5** qualifies because of the gap).

Fourth Deal: A player must meld three separate sets of three cards each (as **Q–Q–Q, 10–10–10, 2–2–2**).

All the above are ten-card deals, with Deals 1 to 3 requiring the layoff of four cards for a player to clear his hand and "go rummy." In Deal 4, it is only necessary to lay off one card. Those that follow are twelve-card deals, with further contract provisions:

Fifth Deal: A player must meld two sets and one sequence, all of three cards each (as **Q–Q–Q, 8–8–8**, and **♡ 7 6 5**).

Sixth Deal: A player must meld one set and two separate sequences, each of three cards (as **4–4–4** and **♠ A K Q, ♢ J 10 9**).

Seventh Deal: A player must meld three separate sequences, each of four cards, as **♡ A K Q J; ♠ 8 7 6 5; ♢ 6 5 4 3**.

Three cards must therefore be laid off in Deals 5 and 6, while in Deal 7, the entire hand must be melded, with no layoffs, in order to go rummy. But it should be specially noted that in cases where a player picks up two extra cards, as described earlier, he will be forced to lay off two extras during one of his turns because he overloaded his hand.

In each deal, after a player goes rummy, each player must show whatever cards he still has in his hand, add up the values, and mark the total toward his score. At the finish of the seventh deal, all totals are added and the player with the lowest score wins. If chips are used, he collects from each of the other players according to the difference between his score and theirs.

A joker, being wild, can be used as part of a meld. Thus **joker–8–8** would represent **8–8–8;** while in the sequence ♡ **7 joker** ♡ **5** the joker would stand for the six of hearts. A player can also lay off a joker on any meld, naming it as a card that would ordinarily be placed there. Finally, after a player has completed his contract meld for a given deal, he has this privilege: If he holds an actual card represented by a melded joker, he can exchange it for the joker, which can then be laid off elsewhere. As a special rule, now in general use, such an exchange can be made only when the joker is part of a melded sequence (as ♠ **6 joker** ♠ **4 3 2**) and not when it has been melded with a set of the same value (as **joker–10–10).**

The joker can also be moved from one end of a melded sequence to the other, in order to aid a layoff. As an example, suppose that ◊ **9 8 7 joker** has been melded. A player holds ◊ **Q J** and ◊ **6.** In the meld, the joker represents ◊ **6,** so he moves it to the other end, forming **joker** ◊ **9 8 7,** with the **joker** representing ◊ **10.** This enables him to lay off the ◊ **Q J** at the upper end and the ◊ **6** at the lower end, for a final meld of ◊ **Q J joker** ◊ **9 8 7 6.**

In early forms of contract rummy, the deuces served as the wild cards and are still often used as such, in addition to the wild jokers. Other values may be designated as "wild" either instead of deuces or in addition to them. As a usual rule, only jokers are exchangeable; other wild cards, not. But all wild cards are movable, from the top of a sequence to the bottom, or vice versa. These points should be decided by agreement prior to play.

As a general rule, a player must complete his contract meld before he is allowed to lay off any odd cards from his hand. Also, it is often specified that he make his entire meld all at once, reserving any layoffs for a later turn. Even in games where single melds are allowed, the "all at once" rule is usually applied in the seventh deal, giving losing players a last chance to turn the tide.

In contrast to these restrictive measures, a special rule may be introduced allowing players to make additional melds— either as new sets or new sequences—beyond those required in the contract for any deal. That rule, when used, adds action to the game by encouraging players to draw from the discard pile out of turn, as the two extra cards thus acquired are doubly disposable through melds as well as layoffs.

The reason for so many options is that several games of earlier origin are actually included under the general head of "contract rummy"; namely: Hollywood rummy, joker rummy, king rummy, Liverpool rummy, progressive rummy, seven-deal rummy, Shanghai rummy, and Zioncheck. All have their own variations, mostly interchangeable, so that in the course of evolution the names have become practically synonymous, with earlier differences now being disregarded.

One truly "progressive" rule that has been gaining in popularity concerns the number of cards required for each contract, with the total being increased card by card in each successive deal, so the contracts run: first deal, six cards; second deal, seven; third deal, eight; fourth deal, nine; fifth deal, ten; sixth deal, eleven; seventh deal, twelve. This is managed by simply increasing the requirement for a contract sequence from three cards to four. Check this against the contract requirements listed earlier and it will be apparent how neatly they conform.

CONTRACT WHIST: *Contract Bridge* without a dummy. See page 72.

COON CAN: The Americanized form of *Conquian,* page 71, played with a forty-card pack ranking **10, 9, 8, 7, 6, 5, 4, 3, 2, A.** Also known as Double Rum.

COQUETTE: Another name for *Betrothal Solitaire,* page 325.

CRAPETTE: Another name for *Russian Bank,* page 296.

CRAZY ACES: The same as *Crazy Eights,* but using aces instead. See *Eights,* page 106.

CRAZY EIGHTS: A game of the "stops" type, with eights wild. See *Eights,* page 106.

CRAZY JACKS: Like *Crazy Eights,* but with jacks as wild cards.

CRIBBAGE: One of the most popular of two-handed card games, played with a fifty-two-card pack, ranking in descending value: **K, Q, J, 10, 9, 8, 7, 6, 5, 4, 3, 2, A.** Each card counts according to its spots, with **K, Q,** and **J** counting 10 each. These cards, like the 10 itself, are termed "tenth cards," but each retains its individual status.

Six cards are dealt to each player; and after looking at his hand, each discards two cards face down, reducing his hand to four. The discards are put together, forming an extra hand known as the "crib," which is laid aside for later reference. The pack is then cut by the opponent and the dealer turns up the top card of the lower half, which is termed the "starter." This card does not figure in the actual play, but it is used toward scoring certain points. Such scoring, in cribbage, is termed "pegging" because players customarily use a special board with four rows of thirty holes, two rows for each player, with "game holes" at the ends. Pegs are inserted in these holes as play proceeds.

If the starter is a jack, termed "His Heels," the dealer pegs 2 points; otherwise, there is no score. The opponent opens play by laying a card face up on his side of the board and announcing its count, as "Three" for the ♡ **3.** The dealer does the same on his side, adding the count of his card, making "Eleven" for the ♣ **8.** This continues alternately until the account approaches 31. A player is not allowed to exceed that total, so if his remaining cards are too high to play, he says, "Go!" giving his adversary the opportunity of playing whatever cards he can toward reaching 31. Whether or not the adversary is able

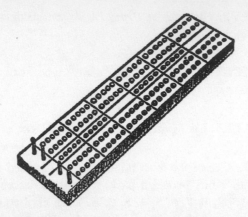

The cribbage board. One player uses the two rows at the left; the other, the two rows at the right. Each player pegs along his entire outside row away from him, and back along the inside row toward himself. After going out and back twice, he places the peg in the hole at the near end of the inner row to mark the final point of 121. For a 61-point game, a player goes out and back once.

The extra holes in the center section of the board are for keeping count of games won, each player using a row of ten holes. If one player is "lurched" (that is, his opponent has attained game before he, the player mentioned, has passed the halfway mark), the winner moves a peg two holes ahead in his game row.

to play, he pegs 1 point for "Go," and if he can play a card or cards that bring the total to exactly 31, he pegs 1 point more.

The cards so far played are turned face down and play reverts to the other player, who starts a new series beginning with 0 and aiming for 31. If one player uses all his cards, the other simply plays his out, pegging 1 point for playing the last card, with 1 point more if it brings the total to exactly 31. In all cases where a player hits exactly 31, he pegs 2 points regardless of whether "Go" or "Last Card" is involved.

Such are the simple mechanics of the play; now for the complexities that make cribbage such an intriguing game. During the play, either player pegs points by completing certain combinations that are scored as follows:

A Pair of the same value (as ♡ **Q** ♠ **Q**)   2 points
Pairs Royal or *Threes* (as ♠ **9** ♡ **9** ♣ **9**)   6 points

(Actually three pairs: ♠ 9 ♡ 9; ♠ 9 ♣ 9; ♡ 9 ♣ 9.)
Double Pairs Royal or *Fours* (as ♠ 5 ♡ 5 ♣ 5 ◇ 5) 12 points
(Actually ♠ 5 ♡ 5; ♠ 5 ♣ 5; ♠ 5 ◇ 5; ♡ 5 ♣ 5; ♡ 5 ◇ 5; ♣ 5 ◇ 5.)
Sequence of three cards (as **8 7 9** or **3 2 A**) 3 points
Any additional sequence card (as **5 2 4+3**) 1 point
(The addition of the three forms a sequence worth 4 points.)
Fifteen: Bringing the count to 15 (as **3 2 K**) 2 points

Note that suits have no significance where sequences and fifteens are concerned. Nor do sequences have to be in exact order, providing that no other card intervenes.

As a sample hand, consider the following:

Opponent: ◇ **Q** ♣ **5** ♣ **4** ♠ **A**   *Dealer:* ◇ **7** ♣ **6** ◇ **5** ♠ **5**

Opponent plays ◇ **Q**, announcing "Ten." Dealer plays ♠ **5**, declaring, "Fifteen and two." The "Fifteen" refers to the count; the "two" to the points the dealer pegs. Opponent plays ♣ **5**, declaring, "Twenty and a pair," pegging 2 for the pair. Dealer plays ◇ **5**, declaring, "Twenty-five and three," pegging 6 for three fives. Opponent plays ♣ **4**, saying, "Twenty-nine." Dealer, with ◇ **7** and ♣ **6**, cannot play without going over 31, so he says, "Go." Opponent plays ♠ **A**, saying, "Thirty," and pegs 1 for the Go.

The board then stands:

Opponent: ◇ **Q**   ♣ **5**   ♣ **4** ♠ **A**
Dealer: ♠ **5**   ◇ **5**

Cards are turned down and play reverts to the dealer, who plays both ◇ **7** and ♣ **6** (in either order) as the opponent is out of cards. This makes a new count of 13 and the dealer pegs 1 point for playing the last card.

Up to here, the opponent has pegged 3 (2+1) and the dealer has pegged 9 (2+6+1), but there is more to score. The hands, which were kept separate, are turned face up and each is scored individually for its combinations: the opponent's first, then the dealer's. In addition, the "starter" serves as an extra card in each player's hand. Following that, the "crib" is turned up and its combinations are pegged as a bonus for the dealer, the starter again serving as a fifth card.

In addition to the scoring combinations so far listed, there are these:

His Nobs, the jack of same suit as starter	1 point.
Flush, formed by four cards of one suit in hand	4 points.
Flush, with starter of same suit, either in hand or crib, 1 point extra, namely	5 points.

Assuming that the ♡ **3** was turned up as follows, the hands would stand as follows:

Opponent: (♡ **3**) ◊ **Q** ♣ **5** ♣ **4** ♠ **A**

Two fifteens **(Q–5; Q–4–A)** for 4 points. Three-card sequence **(5 4 3)** for 3 points. Total of hand: 7 points.

Dealer: (♡ **3**) ◊ **7** ♣ **6** ◊ **5** ♠ **5**

Two fifteens: **(3–7–5; 3–7–5)** for 4 points. Double sequence **(7–6–5–5)** consisting of two runs **(7–6–5; 7–6–5)** and a pair **(5–5)** for 8 points. Total of hand: 12 points.

Now suppose that the opponent had unfortunately discarded the ♡ **K** and the ♡ **8,** while the dealer discarded or "laid away" the ♡ **A** and ♡ **2.** When turned up, these would show:

Crib: (♡ **3**) ♡ **K** ♡ **8** ♡ **2** ♡ **A**

One fifteen **(3–10–2)** for 2 points. Three-card sequence **(3–2–A)** for 3 points. Flush with starter (all ♡) for 5 points. Total of crib: 10 points.

Totals: Opponent: In play, 3. In hand 7. 3+7=10.
Dealer: In play, 9. In hand. 12. In Crib, 9. 9+12+10=31.

Cribbage is a game with many intricacies and fine points that can be learned only through experience, and then usually through encountering and observing skilled players. However, rudimentary factors of play should be noted from the outset. Pairs, pairs royal (threes), and double pairs royal (fours) must appear in immediate succession, as ♣ 6, ♡ 6, ◇ 6, which would be pegged first as a pair (6–6) and then as a pair royal (6–6–6). If another card should intervene, as ♣ 6, ♡ 6, ♠ 3, ◇ 6, only the pair could be pegged. If the ♠ 6 should be played next, making ♣ 6, ♡ 6, ♠ 3, ◇ 6, ♠ 6, the cards would merely represent two pairs, pegged at 2 points each; but if they appeared in the order ♣ 6, ♡ 6, ◇ 6, ♠ 6, ♠ 3, it would be pegged as a pair (6–6), then as a pair royal (6–6–6), and finally as a double pair royal (6–6–6–6).

While sequences can follow a similarly progressive pattern, they can be gathered climactically, with startling results. For example, take cards played in the following order:

♠ 8, ♡ 7, ♣ 6, ♣ 5, ◇ 4

That would be pegged as 8–7–6 for 3 points; as 8–7–6–5 for 4 points; as 8–7–6–5–4 for 5 points. But suppose it ran:

♣ 5, ◇ 4, ♡ 7, ♠ 8, ♣ 6

There would be no pegging anywhere along the line until the fifth card laid a sequence (5–4–7–8–6=8–7–6–5–4) squarely in the pegger's lap. He would peg 5 from what had been a 0 until then.

To win a game in cribbage, a player must peg either 61 points, which is once around the board, or 121 points, which is twice around, according to previous agreement. In modern six-card cribbage, the form that has been described, 121 points is the customary game and is therefore understood unless otherwise stipulated. If the opponent goes out after showing his hand, he wins, regardless of what the dealer may have in his own hand or the crib. If the winner goes out before the loser reaches the halfway mark, the loser is "lurched" and the winner is paid double, or credited for two games.

As with most two-handed games, each deal alternates between the opponent and the original dealer until the game is completed.

Partnership Cribbage is a four-handed game between teams of two players (seated opposite) for 121 points. Each is dealt five cards and each puts one in the crib. When one player is told to "Go!" the privilege is passed along until completed. Scores made by each team are pegged as 1.

Three-handed Cribbage follows the two-handed pattern, but each player is dealt five cards instead of six and contributes one to the crib, which is dealt an extra card to bring its quota up to four. Each is on his own and both "Go" and the deal moves to the left.

Five-Card Cribbage is the early form from which the modern version was derived, and it is seldom played today. Each of the two players lays away two cards, playing with a hand of three. When shown, the hands have four, counting the starter, but the crib contains the usual five. Game is customarily 61 points.

Certain penalties are essential in cribbage:

A player who falsely announces "Go" must correct the mistake before the next card is played; otherwise the opposing player, once aware of it, may demand that any cards involved be rejected from play and peg 2 points for himself. Similarly, a player's failure to play available cards after his adversary declares "Go" is subject to the same penalty under the same conditions.

If a player overpegs his hand, he must correct the mistake before he plays his next card, or if at the end of the deal, before the starter is turned up for the next deal. Otherwise, the opposing player may demand the correction and peg two points for himself.

CRISSCROSS: An extension of *Cincinnati*. See page 247.

CROSS OVER: Another name for *Crisscross*. See above.

CROSS WIDOW: A variant of *Crisscross*. See above.

CUBAN CANASTA: Wild-card *Canasta* with special bonus melds. See *Wild Card Canasta,* page 378.

CUCKOO: Another name for *Ranter-Go-Round*. See page 288.

CUTTHROAT BRIDGE: See *Three-handed Bridge,* page 90.

CUTTHROAT EUCHRE: A three-handed game described under *Euchre,* page 110.

DARDA: Similar to *Klaberjass,* page 151, using the same thirty-two-card pack but with either two or three players and with these differences: Trumps rank Q, 9, A, 10, K, J, 8, 7, with queen counting 20 and jack 2 (like plain jacks). Trump is turned up and may be changed, but there is no "schmeiss." Plain suits rank A, 10, K, Q, J, 9, 8, 7 as in klaberjass. After each player is dealt three extra cards, the entire pack is turned bottom up and a player holding the seven of trump may exchange it for the card that shows; or he can use the eight if the seven was turned up and kept as trump. If the next card that shows is a trump, the same player may exchange any card for it; and that applies with succeeding cards that show.

Players meld as in klaberjass, with this addition: If a player holds four of a kind, he scores 4 points toward game for queens; 3 for nines; 2 for aces, tens, kings, or jacks. This is automatic; no play follows, and with two such sets the higher wins. If no one melds fours, the hand is played by the usual rules, except that whoever "made" trump leads to the first trick. To score, the trump maker must have a higher total in meld and counters than his opponent, or either opponent with three players. If his own total is under 100, he scores 1 point toward game; under 150, 2; under 200, 3; 200 and up, 4. Game is 10 points.

DEALER'S CHOICE: A *Poker* game in which the dealer can decide what type of game is to be played in the coming hand or round. See page 241.

DEMON: A variation of *Fascination Solitaire*, page 329.

DEUCES WILD: A form of *Poker* with variants covering other wild cards. See page 239.

DEUCES WILDER: See page 247.

DISCARD HEARTS: A name for *Hearts* when passing cards to the player on the left is included. *See Hearts*. page 140.

DIVISION LOO: Another term for *Lanterloo* or *Loo*, page 156.

DOCTOR PEPPER: See page 248.

DOMINO HEARTS: A variant of *Hearts* in which only six cards are dealt to each player. When a player cannot follow suit, he must draw cards from the top of the pack until he can. When the pack is gone, play continues as in standard *Hearts*, but with each player dropping when out of cards, play being continued by the next player on his left. The one remaining player must add his own cards to his tricks along with any still in the pack. Each heart counts 1 point against the player taking it. See *Hearts*, page 140.

DOMINO WHIST: Another name for *Fan-Tan*. See page 115.

DOM PEDRO: Described under *Pedro*, page 172.

DONKEY: A juvenile game practically identical with *Pig*, page 173.

DOUBLE-BARRELED SHOTGUN: A name for *Texas Tech*, page 271.

DOUBLE DUMMY BRIDGE: A two-player game in which each is dealt two hands, but looks at only one and bids on it, as in *Bridge.* The other two hands, or "dummies," are turned face up and set so that the declarer is *South;* opponent's dummy, *West;* declarer's dummy, *North;* opponent, *East.* Opponent leads from his dummy (*West*) and play is the same as in bridge, with each player scoring as a team. See page 72.

DOUBLE-HANDED HIGH-LOW: *Poker;* see page 248.

DOUBLE HASENPFEFFER: A form of partnership *Euchre,* page 107, played with a forty-eight-card pinochle pack. Cards in plain suits rank **A, A, K, K, Q, Q, J, J, 10, 10, 9, 9,** but the trump suit is headed by the two jacks, as right bowers, followed by the two jacks of the same color as left bowers; then **A, A, K, K, Q, Q, 10, 10, 9, 9.** With four players, twelve cards are dealt to each and single bids are made, starting at the dealer's left. Each bidder must guarantee that he and his partner—seated opposite—will take six tricks or more if he names the trump suit. If all pass, the bidder must take the bid at six.

With six players, there are three pairs of partners and each player is dealt eight cards, the minimum bid in this case being four tricks. Play proceeds exactly as in euchre, with bidder making the first lead and high card of suit led taking trick, unless the trick is trumped, which is optional whenever a player is out of the suit. If two cards of identical value (as ♣ J and ♣ J) appear as high cards in the same trick, the first one played wins the trick, as in pinochle.

As in single hasenpfeffer, the bidding team scores 1 point for every trick it takes, unless it falls short of its bid, when it is set back the number bid; but if the dealer is forced to bid and loses, his team is set back only half the number. Game is 62 points. A bidder may decide to play alone, discarding any two cards and being given the best two cards from his partner's hand, which is then entirely discarded. The bidder scores double if he makes more than his bid. The game may also be played three-handed, with sixteen cards dealt to each player, the minimum bid being six tricks, with the high bidder playing against the other two.

DOUBLE HEARTS: Another term for *Cancellation Hearts*. See page 55.

DOUBLE-PACK PINOCHLE: See *Army and Navy Pinochle*, page 204.

DOUBLE PEDRO: Another name for *Cinch*. See page 65.

DOUBLE RUM: A popular term for *Coon Can*. See page 94.

DOUBLE SOLITAIRE: A name applied to various types of *Solitaire*, most notably *Canfield*, page 55, or *Klondike*, page 338, in which two players, seated opposite, play with individual packs but are allowed to add to the opposing player's build. The first player to dispose of all his cards is winner; if neither manages to do so, the player who disposed of most cards wins the game. See also *Spite and Malice*, page 357.

DOWN THE RIVER: A popular name for *Seven-Card Stud*. See *Poker*, page 229.

DRAW CASSINO: Standard *Cassino*, page 57, but with only the opening deal. After playing a card, each player draws one from the top of the pack until all are drawn and the hand is played out.

DRAW HEARTS: *Hearts* for two players. Each is dealt thirteen cards and play proceeds, with the winner of each trick drawing the top card from the pack and the loser drawing the next, until the hand is ended. See *Hearts,* page 140.

DRAW POKER: The modern and most popular form of the basic game of *Poker,* described under that head. See page 226.

DUTCH BANK: See *Banker and Broker,* page 22.

DYNAMITE: *Two-Card Poker.* See page 248.

EARL OF COVENTRY: A form of *Stops,* page 364, in which three to eight players are dealt cards singly until the pack runs out. The first player lays a card—as the ◊ 6—face up, saying, "There's as good as six can be." The next player who holds a card of that value plays it, saying, "There's a six as good as he." Continuing in rotation, another player does the same, asserting, "There's the best of all the three," and the fourth is played to conclude the rhyme with, "And there's the Earl of Coventry!" That player then leads a card of a new value, which is named in the rhyming process; and so on. As soon as a player is out of cards, he wins. The others pay him 1 chip per card for whatever each still holds.

ÉCARTÉ: A once highly popular French game for two players utilizing a thirty-two-card pack with suits ranking **K, Q, J, A, 10, 9, 8, 7.** Each is dealt five cards and the next is turned up and laid aside to establish trump; if a king, the dealer automatically scores 1 point. The opponent looks at his hand, and if he thinks he can win three tricks, he says he will "play" with what he has. Otherwise, he "proposes" that they draw fresh cards. If the dealer "accepts" the proposal, the opponent discards any number up to five and is dealt cards to replace them. The dealer then discards any number and deals himself replacements. If either player holds the king of trump, he announces it and scores 1 point.

The opponent leads any card to the first trick. The dealer must follow suit and play higher if possible. If out of suit, he must play a trump if he has one; otherwise, he plays from another side suit. The winner of each trick leads to the next, and whichever takes three or four tricks scores 1 point; or taking all five tricks counts 2 points, which is called *vole.* If the opponent plays without "proposing," or the dealer "refuses" a proposal, the opponent scores 2 points for taking three or more tricks, but gets no extra point for *vole.* The next deal is made by the opponent and the game continues until one player reaches a total of 5 points and wins.

At gambling clubs, écarté includes a "gallery" of bettors, who back one player or the other; hence the play has been reduced to a series of mathematical probabilities called *jeux de règle;* and the game is overloaded with stringent rules on misdeals, discarding, etc., with penalties that would hardly apply in social play.

EIGHT-CARD STUD: See page 230.

EIGHTS: A form of *Stops,* page 364, with two to four players who are dealt seven cards each; or five or six players, who are dealt five cards each, from a fifty-two-card pack. Normally, each is on his own; but with four players, those seated opposite can serve as partners. The top card of the pack is turned up as a starter, and the player at the dealer's left must cover it with a card of either the same value or the same suit. If unable or unwilling to do so, the player must draw cards from the pack until he matches the turned-up card, as described. The turned-up cards are formed into a special pile.

All eights are "wild," so far as suits are concerned. Hence, if a card like the ◊ J is played, a player would normally cover it with a jack or a diamond; but if he holds the ♠ 8, he can place it on the ◊ J and declare it to be any suit he chooses. The next player must then cover it with a card of the suit named or another wild eight. When a player disposes of all his cards, he receives chips or points from each of the other players, according to the cards they hold: Each eight, 50; each face card (K, Q, J), 10; each spot card, its value from 10 down to ace, 1. If play is blocked, the player with lowest score collects the difference from the others. With points, 500 are needed for game. With partners, both must "go out" to win.

EIGHTY-EIGHT: *Poker.* See page 248.

ENFLÉ: Pronounced *Enflay* and also called *Rolling Stone* or *Schwellen.* A game for four players using a thirty-two-card pack with cards ranking in descending order, **A, K, Q, J, 10, 9, 8, 7.**

With five players, add each **6** and **5**; with six players, each **4** and **3**. Each player is dealt a hand of eight cards, and the player on dealer's left leads to the first trick. All the rest must follow suit, as there is no discarding and no trump in this odd game. Nor do tricks have any value; if everybody manages to follow suit, the trick is turned down and tossed aside; then whoever played the highest card leads to the next trick.

However, if a player cannot follow suit, he must pick up the cards already played to that trick and add them to his hand. He then leads to a new trick, using whatever suit he wants, and play continues on the same basis. Each player's object is to get rid of all his cards; when one does, play stops instantly, even in the middle of a trick, and the winner collects 1 chip per card for those still held by the other players. The deal then moves to the left.

ENGLISH POKER: A term for *Blind Opening*. See page 245.

ENGLISH STUD: A cross between *Draw Poker* and *Stud Poker*. See page 248.

ENGLISH WHIST: Whist as originally scored in England. See page 376.

EUCHRE: Once the most popular "trump game" in America, euchre still has its followers and is worthy of them. As a fast-moving "short game," it is hard to beat; and you will find it equally hard to beat a good euchre player!

The pack: Usually thirty-two cards, running in value from aces down to sevens, with the exception of the trump suit, in which the jack, termed the *right bower,* is highest, followed by the other jack of the same color, known as the *left bower,* then the ace, followed in order by the remaining trumps.

As an example, with hearts as trumps, the suits would run:

Trumps: ♡ J, ◇ J, ♡ A, K, Q, 10, 9, 8, 7
Other suits: ◇ A, K, Q, 10, 9, 8, 7
            ♠ A, K, Q, J, 10, 9, 8, 7
            ♣ A, K, Q, J, 10, 9, 8, 7

Number of players: Usually two, three, or four, more in some special games. Since the rules vary, the two-handed game, being the simplest, will be explained first.

TWO-HANDED EUCHRE : *The Deal:* After the pack is shuffled and cut, five cards are dealt to each player; either first three cards, then two, or vice versa. The dealer turns the next card face up on the pack, its suit becoming the first choice as trump.

The players look at their hands, and if the opponent feels that his hand is strong enough to take three tricks with the turned-up suit as trump, he states, "I order it up." This means that the dealer must place an unwanted card from his hand face down beneath the pack and add the turned up card to his hand instead, the trump standing as shown.

Example: Opponent holds ♠ J, ♣ J, ♠ K, ♡ A, ◇ 9.
The ♠ 10 is turned up as potential trump.

Since the hand contains both bowers and the fourth highest spade (♠ K) it is sure of three tricks if properly played, so the opponent "orders up" the turned-up ♠ 10, making spades trump.

With a hand too weak to go along with the turned-up suit, the opponent would say, "I pass." That puts the choice up to the dealer. If he decides that his hand, with the turned-up card added, is strong enough to take three tricks, he says, "I take it up." He then discards an unwanted card and takes the turned-up trump instead. But if the dealer's hand is too weak to risk that particular trump, he also says, "I pass" and either turns down the turned-up card or places it face up beneath the pack, leaving it crosswise so one end can be seen as a reminder that its suit has been eliminated as a possible trump.

The opponent is now free to make any other suit trump, or he can again pass if his hand seems too weak. If the opponent passes, the dealer may make the new trump, or he too can pass. If both pass, the hands are thrown in and the deal goes to the opponent.

Here is an example of two hands and what occurred with them:

Opponent: ♣ J, ♠ 9, ◇ A, ◇ 9, ♡ Q   Turned up:
Dealer: ♣ K, ◇ J, ◇ K, ◇ 10, ♡ A   ♣ A

The opponent, with only the right bower (♣ J), cannot risk "ordering up" the ♣ A as a trump for the dealer. *Opponent passes.*

The dealer, with neither bower, cannot risk "taking up" the ♣ A, thus accepting clubs as trump. *Dealer passes,* turning down the ♣ A. The opponent's hand is too weak generally to make any other suit. Again, *opponent passes.*

The dealer, with three diamonds headed by the right bower (◇ J) and high card in two other suits (♣ K and ♡ A), has a strong chance of taking three tricks in diamonds. *He makes diamonds trump.*

Playing the Hand: The opponent leads any card to the first trick. The dealer must follow suit if possible; if not, he may discard from another suit or trump a lead from an ordinary suit. The highest card of the suit led takes the trick unless trumped. The winner of each trick leads to the next until all five tricks have been taken. The left bower, if in play, is treated as a trump card.

Purpose of Play: Each player tries to win as many tricks as possible, but whichever decided upon the trump suit must take three or four tricks to score 1 point. If he takes five tricks, he scores 2 points for a "march." If he takes less than three tricks, he is "euchred," and 2 points are credited to the other player's score.

Scoring the Game: Each new deal is made by the other player and the score is added after each hand, with the first person who wins 5 points being declared the winner. This may be extended to 7 or 10 points by agreement beforehand. When 5 points constitutes "game," it is customary to play a "rubber," which is won by the player who wins two out of three games.

Special Note: In two-handed euchre, many players reduce the pack to twenty-four cards by removing the sevens and eights. This improves the hands by increasing the high cards, with more chance of holding bowers. It is a good thing to remember when only a pinochle pack is available, as the twenty-four cards represent just half of a pinochle pack.

THREE-HANDED EUCHRE (CUTTHROAT EUCHRE): Similar to two-handed euchre, this game involves three players, using the regular thirty-two-card pack, with rank as already stated. The deal goes in the usual clockwise rotation, with players receiving the customary five cards each and following the same general procedure, but with these factors to be noted:

Either of the first two players can "order up" the turned-up trump card; and if one does, he takes upon himself the burden of winning three out of five tricks against two other players, who for that hand only are teamed to stop him. Similarly, the dealer, if he "takes up" the trump card, must battle the two others. If all pass the first round, whoever "makes trump" on the next round is faced by the same double opposition. Hence a very strong hand is often needed to assume such a risk.

Scoring the Hand: Since three players must be scored individually, this differs from the two-handed game as follows: For taking three or four tricks, 1 point. For a "march" of five tricks, 3 points. When a player is "euchred" by failing to take three required tricks, each of the other players receives 2 points.

This method has one great disadvantage. Assume that two players, *A* and *B,* are tied at 3 (or 4) points each in a 5-point game. If the third player, *C,* is euchred, both *A* and *B* receive

2 points each and the game ends in a tie, requiring another hand that in turn could result in more hands being needed to break the tie.

To eliminate this fault, a more realistic mode of scoring was introduced and is now generally used, namely: For taking three or four tricks, 1 point. For a march, 2 points. When a player is euchred, 2 points are deducted from his score, none going to the other players. This may put a player in the minus column; for example, if euchred in the first hand, his score would become —2, so he would need 7 points to win a 5-point game.

In this mode of scoring, a march can be counted as 3 points instead of only 2, as it is worth it; but that should be specified in advance. Game can be for 7 or 10 points instead of only 5.

Notes on Play: Normally, the two teamed players are eager to defeat the player who made trump. But with the old mode of scoring, that changes as the game progresses. Example: In a 5-point game, scores stand: *A,* 2; *B,* 1; *C,* 3. If *B* makes trump and is euchred, *A* and *C* would each gain 2 points, making the score *A,* 4; *B,* 1; *C,* 5, with *C* becoming the winner.

Hence it behooves *A,* in such a situation, to throw tricks to *B,* letting him take the three needed for a 1-point score, which would then stand: *A,* 2; *B,* 2; *C,* 3. It was from this practice of turning against a temporary partner (as *A* favoring *B* and deserting *C*) that the game derived its name of "cutthroat euchre." Persons who prefer that feature should use the old-style scoring method, as it is eliminated by the new mode.

FOUR-HANDED EUCHRE: This is regarded as euchre at its best. The players, seated opposite each other, play as partners; thus *A* and *C* form a team opposed to *B* and *D.* Hence the basic rules and scoring are the same as in two-handed euchre, but with additional features that will be detailed in due order.

Five cards are dealt to each player in the usual fashion by the dealer (*D*), who turns up the next card as prospective trump. The first player, *A,* may "order it up" into the hand of the dealer, *D,* or he may pass. In the latter case, the choice moves to *B;* and if *B* likes that trump, instead of ordering it up, he says, "I assist," signifying that the card is to be taken up by his own partner, *D,* on the same basis as if ordered up. If *B* passes, *C* can order it up into *D*'s hand; while if *C* also passes, *D,* the dealer, can either "take it up" or "pass."

If all four players pass, the turned-up card is turned down as in the two-handed game, and each player, beginning at the dealer's left, may name another suit as trump or pass that privilege along to the next player. If all pass, the hand is dead and the deal moves to the player at the dealer's left, in this case Player *A.*

Playing and Scoring: Once trump has been made, as so far described, the player at the dealer's left leads to the first trick and others follow as in the two-handed or three-handed game. Each trick taken by a player counts for himself and his partner; and scoring is exactly as in the two-handed game, but as teams, not individuals. However, the four-handed game includes a special option termed:

Playing Alone: A player making trump in either round may also say, "I'll play it alone." His partner thereupon tosses in his hand, face down, and the lone player takes on both members of the other team, as in the three-handed game. As usual, the player at the dealer's left (Player *A*) leads to the first trick, unless his partner (*C*) happens to be the lone player. In that case, the dealer's partner (*B*) leads to the first trick.

The object of playing alone is to win all five tricks for a "march" that scores 4 points for the lone player's team, instead of the customary 2. Other scores remain the same: For taking three or four tricks, 1 point; for being euchred, 2 points for the other team. In some circles, when a lone player is euchred, the other team scores 4 points; and this is highly recommended, for unless a player's hand is good for at least three tricks, he has no real right to "play it alone." As with other optional rules, this one should be specified beforehand.

Of the many variants of euchre that have come and gone with the years, the following are the most popular and most practical. They are described here in simplified form:

Auction Euchre: A four-handed game without a turned-up trump. Instead, players in turn may bid three, four, or five for the privilege of making trump. Play is as usual and the bidding team, if successful, scores the amount bid, but no more. If they are euchred, the opposing team scores the amount bid. Game is 15 or 20 points as agreed.

Blind Euchre: Played by two, three, or four players, each on his own. Hands are dealt as usual, but two extra cards are dealt face down as a "blind," which goes to the player who orders up, takes up, or makes trump; he then discards and plays alone against all opponents. If all refuse to take the blind, the deal moves on.

Call-Ace Euchre: Basically a four-handed game in which a player orders up, takes up, or makes trump on his own, then picks a partner for that deal by calling for the holder of the ace in any suit, except in trump, to act in that capacity. If no one has the ace, the call goes to the player holding the best card in the suit named, though he is not identified until play is completed. For winning three tricks, caller and partner score 1 point each; for 5 tricks, 2 points, but if euchred, opponents score 2 points each. If a player elects to play alone, he scores 1 point for taking 3 tricks; 4 points for taking all 5 tricks. Opponents score 2 points each if he is euchred. A twenty-four-card pack (aces down to nines) is generally used in this game.

Joker Euchre: A game with the joker added to the pack as the "best bower," or highest trump. If it is turned up as trump, the card below it is noted to establish the potential trump suit.

Railroad Euchre: A fast-moving four-player game that includes the joker as "best bower," along with other special features; namely: If a player decides to "play alone," he may discard any unwanted card and be given his partner's best card, face down, to replace it. But to even matters, an opponent may decide to play alone against him, discarding his "worst" card and being given his partner's "best" in return. Scoring follows the usual rule if the lone player wins; but if he is euchred, by taking less than 3 tricks, the other team scores 4 points.

Two subsidiary games are features of railroad euchre; they are known respectively as "jambone" and "jamboree," meaning that a lone player has two privileges, the first being to announce:

Jambone: Here, his hand is so good that he can afford to lay it face up and let the opponents decide what he is to lead or play, according to the strength of their own hands. If he wins all five tricks under such circumstances, he scores 8 points instead of only 4. However, he can go even further by declaring:

Jamboree: In this case, he lays down a hand composed of the top five trumps: joker, right and left bowers, ace, and king. It seldom happens, but when it does, there can be no argument. A "jamboree" collects double of a "jambone"—16 points instead of 8—without having to play it out.

Game, in railroad euchre, is usually established as 10 points. That is still not enough to allow for a jambone following an earlier score, or a jamboree in its own right. So a scoring rule is included, known as:

Laps: Any time a winning score runs over the required total, any extra points are credited toward the next game. Thus, with 10 set as the total, a player declaring jamboree in the opening deal would win that game with 10 of his 16 points and would mark up the other 6 as a lead toward the next game. Another feature is:

Slam: This consists of winning a game before anyone else has managed to score. A player making a "slam" is credited with winning two games instead of one. Hence in the case of a jamboree in an opening hand—as cited—the winner would have two games to his credit with 6 points toward a third.

Note: Both *five-handed* and *six-handed euchre* can be played with a thirty-two-card pack (or thirty-three with joker) on a "call-ace" basis. The six-handed game can be played as "auction" with alternating players as partners, forming two teams of three players each. A seven-handed game can be played with a larger pack, but such games are cumbersome and require special rules.

EVERLASTING: See *War,* page 373.

FAN-TAN: One of the best of all "stops" games, with three to eight players, using a fifty-two-card pack with **K** high and **A** low. Cards are dealt singly, clockwise, until the pack runs out. Player at dealer's left then lays a seven face up on the table if he has one. If not, he puts a chip in a mutual pool or pot. The next player lays down a seven or adds to the first player's starter (if any) either upward with an eight or downward with a six. (Example: First player sets ♣ 7; the next puts ♣ 6 to the left or ♣ 8 to the right.) If unable to do so, he chips into the pot. Others continue, ♣ 5 down to ♣ A, and ♣ 9 up to ♣ K; the same with other suits. The first player to "go out" by thus disposing of his entire hand wins the pot, plus one chip per card for any cards left in opposing hands, paid by the individual players holding them.

FARM or FARMER: Similar to *Blackjack,* page 32, using a pack from which eights and sixes are removed, except for the ♡ 6. Ace counts 1 and other cards according to their spots (up to 10) with face cards (**J, Q, K**) as 10 each. Players put one chip each into a pool called the "farm," and the dealer, or "farmer," serving as the banker, gives each a card face down. Each player then calls for a face-down card, which he notes, and calls for more if he wants them, his aim being to hit a count of 16, though he can stop short of that total. Hands are finally shown, and whoever hits 16 with the ♡ 6 wins the pot and the deal as well. Without the ♡ 6, whoever hits 16 with the least cards wins, beginning at the dealer's left. If nobody hits 16, the deal stays with the farmer, but the farm or pot remains intact. The player nearest 16, but under, receives a chip from each of the others. Any player going over 16 must pay the farmer a chip per point.

FARO: An old-time gambling-casino game, using a fifty-two-card pack that is dealt by drawing cards face up from a special open-framed box. Only values count in faro, and these are represented on a painted layout, as follows:

	6	5	4	3	2	A
7						
	8	9	10	J	Q	K

Players put chips on the layout, designating cards which they think will win or lose; in the latter case, the chip is "coppered" by placing a penny or special disk on it. Dealer discards the card showing on the pack (called the *soda*), then draws the next card and lays it beside the box as a "loser," while the next card showing is a "winner." This is termed a "turn," and the dealer collects or pays off the bets accordingly. New bets are made, the two cards are discarded, and the dealer proceeds with another turn.

A player may bet on two or more cards by placing chips between them, or setting chips on a corner of a card to designate a group of three. Bets are paid off proportionately, but if two of the cards appear in the same turn, it is a standoff. However, if two cards of identical value show up in the same turn (as ◇ 8 and ♣ 8), it is known as a "split," and the dealer collects half of a bet on that value.

When the box holds only four cards, players bet on the next pair and also try to "call the turn" by betting on the order in which the final three cards will appear. The final card, termed the "hock," is discarded, like the soda, after being shown.

For a simplified form of faro, see *Stuss*, page 364.

FASCINATION: A form of *Solitaire*, page 329.

FELSOS: Similar to *Alsos,* but with Queen highest instead of Jack. See *Klaberjass,* page 151.

FIERY CROSS: *Poker.* See page 249.

FIFTEEN: An Americanized—or Anglicized—term for *Quinze.* See page 286.

FIND THE LADY: A term for *Three-Card Monte* (page 366).

FIREHOUSE PINOCHLE: A form of Partnership Pinochle. See *Pinochle,* page 197.

FISH: Short for *Go Fish,* page 135.

FIVE AND DIME: A form of seven-card stud. See page 249.

FIVE AND TEN: Another name for *Forty-five.* See page 123.

FIVE CARDS or FIVE FINGERS: An old form of *Spoil Five,* with jack of trump ranking below ace. See page 360.

FIVE-CARD STUD and variants. *Poker.* See pages 228, 249.

FIVE HUNDRED: Early in the twentieth century, this game was specially designed and introduced to meet the needs of a playing public, and it gained a deserved popularity that it has retained ever since, although other games may have grown to greater proportions.

The Pack: The thirty-two-card euchre pack, plus a joker, making thirty-three cards in all, with additional cards according to the number of players, as will be specified.

Number of Players: Three to six, with odd numbers playing on their own; even numbers playing as partners. Hence the three-handed game will be described first, as it constitutes the basic form that the others follow with slight modifications.

THREE-HANDED FIVE HUNDRED: Here, the suits of the thirty-three-card pack range in value from aces down to sevens, with the exception of the trump suit, which is headed by the joker, or *best bower,* followed by the jack, or *right bower,* then the other jack of the same color, as *left bower,* and after that the remaining trumps from ace on down.

Thus, with spades as trumps, the suits would run:

Trumps: joker, ♠ J, ♣ J, ♠ A, K, Q, 10, 9, 8, 7
Other suits: ♣ A, K, Q, 10, 9, 8, 7
          ◊ A, K, Q, J, 10, 9, 8, 7
          ♡ A, K, Q, J, 10, 9, 8, 7

In no-trump, a player may lead the joker, declaring it the highest card in any suit he names; otherwise, it rates as a trump suit of its own and can be used to trump an opponent's lead, provided its holder is out of the suit led.

The Deal: Ten cards are dealt to each player, usually a round of three cards each, then three cards as a "widow," followed by a round of three each, then a round of four each, all cards face down. Other modes of dealing are allowable.

Bidding: Beginning at the dealer's left, players bid the number of tricks they will attempt to take, with a specified trump suit or no-trump. Any player may "pass" if he chooses; otherwise bids are raised or "jumped" according to the following schedule:

Trump Suit	6 Tricks	7 Tricks	8 Tricks	9 Tricks	10 Tricks
Spades (♠)	40	140	240	340	440
Clubs (♣)	60	160	260	360	460
Diamonds (◊)	80	180	280	380	480
Hearts (♡)	100	200	300	400	500
No-trump	120	220	320	420	520

Originally, each player was allowed only one bid, but later, auction bidding came into vogue and is preferable, as it encourages higher bidding, which is a main aim of the game. In auction, a player may pass, then bid or rebid, until those following him have passed in succession; then his bid stands.

The highest bidder takes up the widow without showing its

cards, which he adds to his hand. He then discards three unwanted or least desirable cards from his hand, also face down.

Note: If all players pass, the hand is void and the deal moves on to the player on the left.

The Play: The successful bidder leads to the first trick, and the others follow suit if possible. If out of suit, a player can discard from another suit, or he may trump a lead from an ordinary suit. The highest card of the suit led wins the trick unless trumped, in which case the trump wins unless overtrumped. In no-trump, the joker (as mentioned earlier) can be used as a trump when its holder is out of suit, or he can lead it as the highest card of any suit he declares.

Scoring the Hand: At the conclusion of the hand, the bidder counts his tricks, and if he took the required number or more, he is credited with the amount of his bid. Thus, if he should bid seven spades and make it, he would gain 140 points, regardless of whether he took eight or nine tricks, instead of only seven. So there is no credit for taking extra tricks, with this exception: If the bidder takes all ten tricks, he scores 250, provided his bid was lower than that amount.

If the bidder fails to take the required number of tricks, the amount of his bid is deducted from his score, sometimes putting him in the minus column (below zero). In any case, an opponent scores 10 points for each trick that he takes. Usually, they act as temporary partners to prevent the bidder from making his bid; but, with that accomplished, each opponent naturally takes whatever tricks he can for himself.

Making Game: As the name "five hundred" implies, 500 points constitutes game, and the first player to reach or exceed that total is the winner, scores being added or subtracted after each deal. If the bidder and another player reach 500 in the same hand, the bidder wins the game; with two nonbidders, the one who reached 500 first becomes the winner.

By previous agreement, if a losing bid puts the bidder's score more than 500 "in the hole," that is, below —500, the game ends and the player with the highest score is declared the winner. Though optional, this rule is really a must in some circles, where opponents continually make wild, impossible bids to prevent a sound bidder from reaching 500. The losing limit may be set at —1000 if preferred.

Bidding Nullo: Also optional but generally accepted is the "nullo" rule, whereby a bidder undertakes to lose every trick. Nullo counts 250, hence such a bid outranks eight spades (240) but falls just below eight clubs (260). If a nullo bidder holds the joker or draws it in the widow, he must naturally discard it; otherwise it would be a sure trick against him. If a bidder loses at nullo, 250 points are deducted from his score and the opponents are credited with 10 points apiece for each trick taken by the bidder. Whether the nullo bidder wins or loses, tricks taken by his opponents do not count.

Various Options: Ordinarily, if all players pass, the hand is dead, the cards are gathered, then shuffled and dealt by the next player to the left. If preferred, an unbid hand can automatically be played as no-trump, with each player scoring 10 points for each trick he takes. The widow is simply laid aside, face up or face down, as preferred. In some circles, it is customary to turn the widow face up, letting everyone see it before the successful bidder takes it into his hand, though he does not have to show his discard.

FOUR-HANDED FIVE HUNDRED: Very similar to the three-handed game but with a forty-three-card pack that includes the sixes, fives, and red fours in descending value. Thus with hearts as trumps, the suits would run:

Trumps: joker, ♡ J, ◇ J, ♡ A, K, Q, 10, 9, 8, 7, 6, 5, 4
◇ A, K, Q, 10, 9, 8, 7, 6, 5, 4
♣ A, K, Q, J, 10, 9, 8, 7, 6, 5
♠ A, K, Q, J, 10, 9, 8, 7, 6, 5

(Black fours can be used instead of red fours if preferred.)

Considering the players as *A, B, C, D* in that order, *A* and *C* are teamed against *B* and *D*. Cards are dealt as usual (ten to each player with three for a widow), and bidding follows the regular pattern, each player having one bid, or more if auction bidding is agreed upon. A player may raise his partner in the same suit, and in any event, whoever makes the highest bid gets the widow and leads to the first trick.

All tricks taken by either partner count toward the team's score, in which the same rules apply as in three-handed, except that there are only two columns, *A* and *B* vs. *C* and *D*.

Note: Often a player can switch his partner's bid to the suit of the same color (as ◇ to ♡ or vice versa), indicating that he has a long run that will benefit from any bowers held by his partner. This intriguing feature is augmented when unrestricted auction is allowed, as it enables the original bidder to raise either suit to a still higher level.

FIVE-HANDED FIVE HUNDRED: This game utilizes the full pack of fifty-three cards (joker included) with ten cards dealt to each player, along with the usual three-card widow. The hands rank as in the other versions, with the trump suit headed by the joker and the right and left bowers. Each player is on his own, but bids are made with the understanding that the highest bidder can call upon another player to serve as his partner during the play of that particular hand.

By one system, the bidder can choose any partner he pleases; and he usually does this on a basis of the bids. Example: A player winning the bid at seven hearts is apt to choose a partner who bid seven diamonds, as they may have bowers in common.

To encourage high bidding, a player bidding eight or more may be allowed to choose two partners instead of only one. This is an optional rule, based on the fact that play will prove more difficult.

Another system is for the successful bidder to call upon the player holding a specific card to act as his partner pro tem. (The "call" is invariably for the joker unless the bidder holds it himself.) The player holding the "called card" shows it and play proceeds.

Here, another option may be introduced, that of playing "blind" without the temporary partner declaring his identity until he plays the card the bidder called for. This, however, is apt to overstress the element of luck.

Scoring the hand: Each temporary partner scores the amount of the bid if successful, or is set back that amount. Opponents score 10 points for tricks taken individually. As an option: Winning or losing hands may be scored as half the amount of the standard bid.

SIX-HANDED FIVE HUNDRED: This may be played in two ways: (a) With three teams, each formed by two partners seated opposite, in which case it follows the rules of three-handed five hundred, each team scoring as an independent player; or (b) With two teams of three partners seated alternately, which is played like four-handed five hundred. In either case, a sixty-three-card pack is used, containing specially manufactured cards of the following denominations: ♡ **13, 12, 11;** ◊ **13, 12, 11;** ♣ **12, 11;** ♠ **12, 11.** These rank just below the face cards but above the ten.

FIVE HUNDRED RUMMY: See *Rummy,* page 295.

FIVE IN ONE: As the name implies, this consists of five games in one. Dealer starts with a round of *Plus or Minus,* page 217, and at the finish, the hands are left face up. Hands are then rated as in *Cold-Hand Poker,* page 246, and the winner collects a chip from each of the other players. Hands are left face up, but discards are shuffled back into the pack and a deal of *Bango,* page 22, follows. Extra cards are shuffled into the pack for a deal of *Put and Take,* page 285. Entire pack is shuffled and dealer plays a final hand called a "consolation," counting from one to ten and turning a card face up on each count. If he hits a number as he names it, he collects a chip from each player. Also known as *Garbage* or *Variety.*

FIVE OR NINE: A form of *Fan-Tan,* page 115, in which the starting player lays down a five or a nine (instead of a seven) to start a two-way sequence. Whichever he plays (five or nine) must be used to start the three other suits during that deal.

FLIP: Another name for *Mexican Stud.* See page 255.

FLIP STUD: *Poker.* See page 250.

FLOWER GARDEN: A form of *Solitaire.* See page 334.

FOOTBALL: A specially wild form of *Poker* (similar to *Baseball*). See page 250.

FORTY-FIVE: The modern form of *Spoil Five,* page 360, played without the "spoil," scoring points for tricks instead. While it can be played by three to five players, each on his own, it is preferable with four, those opposite being partners; or six, with two teams of three each. Individually, each trick counts 5 points, and the first player to reach 45 wins the game; but in the standard partnership play other modes are used: (a) Each trick counts 5 points, but the lower total is subtracted from the higher; so for taking three tricks, a team scores 15—10=5; for taking four tricks, 20—5=15; for taking five tricks, 25—0=25. (b) A team taking the odd trick scores 5 points; for taking all tricks, 10 points. Either way (a) or (b), game is still 45.

In "auction forty-five," each trick counts 5 points, and the team holding the highest trump scores 5 more, making a total of 30. Players bid by fives for the privilege of naming trump, but the dealer, who bids last, can "hold" the bid and take it at the level named by the previous player, though others can rebid higher, with the dealer again holding if he wants. Both teams score what they take in tricks, but a bid of 30 counts 60 if made. A team failing to make a bid has the amount of the bid subtracted from its score. Game is 120, and a team with 100 points or more must bid 20 or higher. This game is very popular in the Canadian Maritime Provinces.

FORTY THIEVES: Another name for *Lucas.* See *Solitaire,* page 339.

FOUR-CARD POKER: Played with hands of four cards, combinations ranking four of a kind, four-card straight flush, four flush, four straight, three of a kind, two pair, pair, high card. See page 250.

FOUR-DEAL BRIDGE: Known also as *Chicago,* this is played like *Contract Bridge* but with special scoring rules that speed the action. Four deals constitute a "rubber," and if all players pass during a deal, the cards are dealt again by the same dealer until a hand is finally bid. Teams bid, play, and score as in contract, but vulnerability follows a set procedure; namely:

First Deal: Neither team vulnerable.
Second Deal: Only the dealer's team vulnerable.
Third Deal: Only the dealer's team vulnerable.
Fourth Deal: Both teams vulnerable.

As special premiums, a team that completes a game of 100 trick points or over is credited with 300 points if not vulnerable; and with 500 points if vulnerable. A part score made during one deal carries into the next, as in the usual form of rubber bridge; but once a team makes game, any part scores are eliminated. A team making a part score on the fourth and final deal receives a bonus of 100 points if its score falls short of game. Any part score already made by the opposing team is thereby disregarded.

FOUR-FLUSH POKER: Two forms of *Dealer's Choice: Four-Flush Opener* and *Four-Flush Stud.* See page 250.

FOUR FORTY-FOUR and FOUR FORTY-TWO: Similar types of wild *Poker,* page 250.

FOUR JACKS: Americanized term for *Polignac,* page 283.

FRAGE: See *Frog,* page 125.

FREAK HANDS: *Poker.* See page 251.

FREE WHEELING: *Poker.* See page 251.

FREEZEOUT: A game from which a player must drop when he has lost his original quota of chips. Chiefly *Poker,* page 251.

FRENCH BOSTON: An obsolete variant of *Boston,* with the ◇ J the top trump in any suit but its own, when the ♡ J becomes top trump and the ◊ **J** ranks below the ◊ **Q**. See *Whist,* page 375.

FRENCH EUCHRE: A name sometimes applied to *Euchre* with an auction. See *Auction Euchre,* page 113.

FRENCH RUFF: An old term for *Triomphe,* or *Triumph,* an early trump game. See page 369.

FRENCH WHIST: A variant of *Scotch Whist* with the ◊ **10** counting 10 points when taken, even though another suit is trump. See *Scotch Whist,* page 302.

FROG: A variant of *Solo,* page 352, with only three bids. In the lowest bid, "frog" (from German *"Frage,"* question), the bidder turns up the widow, takes its cards into his hand, and discards three face down. Play follows the pattern of solo, with hearts trump, bidder winning a chip for each point over 60. "Chico" is a higher bid played without the widow, with bidder naming any trump except hearts and gaining two chips per point (as in a bid of solo). In the highest bid, "grand," played without the widow, hearts are trump (as in a bid of "heart solo") at 3 points per chip. If opponents score over 60, bidder must pay each one, two, or three chips per point, according to his bid.

GAIGEL: A four-handed development of *Bezique,* with players seated opposite as partners. It can be played with a regular forty-eight-card pinochle pack, each suit ranking **A, A, 10, 10, K, K, Q, Q, J, J, 9, 9.** (Originally sevens were used instead of nines, but the latter are preferable today, as pinochle packs are common.)

Five cards are dealt to each player, and the next is turned up as trump, the pack being laid across it. Player at the dealer's left leads any card to the first trick, and the others, in turn, play whatever they want, with no need to follow suit or trump. Highest card of suit led wins unless trumped, when highest trump wins. The winner draws the top card from the pack, adding it to his hand, and the other players do the same in turn. The winner then leads to the next trick.

When all cards have been drawn, the hands are played out, but now each player must follow suit and play higher if he can. If out of suit, he must trump if he can and also trump higher whenever possible. Partners pool their tricks, and cards taken by each team are counted according to the original schedule used in bezique and pinochle: Each ace, 11; ten, 10; king, 4; queen, 3; jack, 2. Last trick counts 10, so that 250 points are possible in play; but the first team to reach 101 must declare "out," thereby winning the game. This is done by either partner knocking on the table before a new trick is played. Tricks already taken are then turned up and their points are counted, to make sure the claim is correct.

Other points may be gained during play by the following melds:

Royal Marriage (**K, Q** of trump)	40 points
Double Royal (**K, K, Q, Q** of trump)	80
Ordinary Marriage (**K, Q** of plain suit)	20
Double Marriage (**K, K, Q, Q** of suit)	40

Such a meld can be made only by a player who has just won a trick, or by his partner if he failed to meld, and before the next card is drawn from the pack. Also, once a marriage is melded, another is not allowable in the same suit; hence to meld a double marriage, a player must lay down all four cards at once. When all cards have been drawn from the pack, no further melds are allowed, with this exception:

Five nines may be melded *at any time* for 101 points.

Thus, a player holding or drawing such a combination has only to show it and his team wins automatically.

Having won a trick, a player may exchange a dix for the turned-up trump. Usually, there is no score for this; but an optional rule allows 10 points for the exchange. In that case, the holder of the second dix can score 10 by simply showing it.

As already mentioned, a team *must* declare "out" as soon as it hits 101 or higher. This means that both partners must keep an exact count of the points their team takes, which is one of the intriguing features of the game. In most instances, the team that goes out is credited with winning a single game, but there are special cases where a team scores a "gaigel," which counts as two games, in accordance with the following rules:

> When a team scores 101 before the opposing team wins a trick.
> If an opposing player knocks before his team has attained a total of 101; or:
> If neither opponent knocks when their team has reached the required 101.

Before knocking, a player can ask to see the trick just taken, to check his mental calculation; but if he looks further back through either trick pile, his team forfeits the game and the opposing team scores a gaigel.

Special Note: Gaigel can be played by two, three, five, or eight players, each on his own, with the cards coming out evenly in both the deal and the draw. The more players, the more likely that the game will go into extra hands requiring fresh deals, before reaching the needed 101.

GARBAGE: An inelegant term for *Five in One,* page 121.

GENTLEMEN'S AGREEMENT: A sophisticated form of *Contract Bridge,* page 72, in which hands are abandoned unless the declarer has been doubled or has made a bid that will ensure game if successful.

GERMAN SKAT: This is *Skat,* page 314, as originally played, including the bid of *"Frage"* (see *Frog,* page 125) and other features no longer generally used.

GERMAN SOLO: A modern development of *Ombre,* page 166, with four players, each on his own, using a thirty-two-card pack, ranking **A, K, Q, J, 10, 9, 8, 7** in descending order, with these exceptions: The ♣ **Q,** known as "spadilla," is always the highest trump; the seven of the trump suit, called "manila," is next; and the ♠ Q, or "basta," is always the third highest trump, the ace of trump being fourth; and so on, down to the eight. One suit, usually clubs, is known as "color" and takes precedence over the other suits when naming a trump.

Hence, each suit, when trump, would be ranked as follows:

Clubs (Color):
   ♣ Q 7   ♠ Q   ♣ A K J 10 9 8
Spades:
   ♣ Q   ♠ 7 Q A K J 10 9
Hearts:
   ♣ Q   ♡ 7   ♠ Q   ♡ A K Q J 10 9 8
Diamonds:
   ♣ Q   ♢ 7   ♠ Q   ♢ A K Q J 10 9 8

Eight cards are dealt to each player, and, beginning at the dealer's left, players bid for the privilege of naming trump and playing the hand on the following ascending scale:

Simple Game: Player names a trump suit after gaining the bid and calls for the holder of a nontrump ace to serve as his partner; or if the bidder holds all such aces, he calls for a king in a nontrump suit. Either way, the specified card is revealed by its holder only in the course of play. Bidder and temporary partner must take five of the eight tricks. Each then collects one chip from an opponent; or each pays one chip if they fail to make the bid. The trump named is any suit except "color."

Simple in Color: The same game, but the bidder states that he will name color as the trump suit if he gains the bid. Bidder and partner each collect two chips from another player, or each pays two chips if they lose.

Solo: In this game, the bidder plays alone against the three other players, naming any trump suit except color. For taking five or more tricks, he collects two chips from each opponent; if he fails, he pays two chips to each.

Solo in Color: Played like regular solo, but in bidding the player states that he will name color as trump. If he wins his five tricks, he collects four chips instead of only two, or pays four if he loses.

Solo Tout: After gaining the bid, the player names any trump except color and must take all eight tricks to win, collecting eight chips from each of the other players if he does, or paying eight to each if he loses.

Solo Tout in Color: Played like solo tout, but with color named as trump during the bidding. Bidder collects sixteen chips if he wins, and pays sixteen chips if he loses.

Optional Nullo: By previous agreement a bidder may offer to play his hand face up—which is termed "ouvert"—without winning a trick. There is no trump suit, and if the bidder succeeds, he collects seven chips from each of the others, or pays each seven chips if he fails.

In any case, once the trump is known, play begins at dealer's left, with highest card of suit led taking the trick unless trumped, then highest trump wins. Players must follow suit if possible and when out of suit can either play trump or discard from another suit. Winner of each trick leads to the next. In case all players pass, whoever holds the highest trump—the ♣ Q—must show it and take the bid at a simple game or at simple solo. Once a player passes, he is out of the bidding from then on; but when a player gains the final bid, he can decide to play the hand at a higher level, assuming the additional risk involved.

GERMAN WHIST: A two-player form of *Whist*, page 375, with the usual fifty-two-card pack. Each is dealt thirteen cards and the next is turned up as trump. The opponent leads and the dealer follows suit if able; otherwise discarding or trumping as in whist. Winner of trick draws the face-up card from the pack; loser draws the card beneath. The next card is turned up and the winner of the trick leads to the next trick. This continues until the entire pack is drawn, the remaining cards being played out. The player taking the most tricks collects the difference between his total and the loser's.

Note: The card originally turned up continues to represent trump throughout the play of the entire hand.

GILE or GILET: A game too antiquated to deserve consideration beyond the fact that it was the ancestor of *Brelan, Brag,* and *Poker.*

GIN RUMMY: Originally known as "poker gin," this has developed into perhaps the most popular of all two-handed games and is therefore worthy of consideration in its own right. Gin, as it is familiarly known, follows the pattern of *Knock Rummy,* page 154, with cards ranking from king down to ace and with ten cards being dealt to each player, the purpose being to form matched sets of three or four cards of the same value (as **J–J–J** or **9–9–9–9**) and sequences of three or more cards of the same suit (as ♡ **J–10–9** or ♠ **5–4–3–2–A**). As in rummy, face cards **(K, Q, J)** count 10 points each; all others according to their spots.

After dealing ten cards each to the opponent and himself, the dealer places the pack between them and turns up the top card beside it, as an upcard representing a discard pile. Opponent either takes the upcard to open play, discarding another card instead, or extends that privilege to the dealer, who in turn must either take the upcard or let the opponent open play by taking the top card of the pack. He may discard it, or keep it and discard some other card; in any case, a new upcard is now on display, and from then on each player in turn may take either the top card of the pack or the upcard, discarding as he chooses.

No melds are made until a player, after drawing, finds that he can reduce his "deadwood" or extra cards to 10 points or less. He can then knock on the table to end the play; after that, he melds his sets and sequences, makes a discard, and displays his unmatched deadwood.

As a simple illustration:

After a draw, Player *X* decides to knock on the strength of the following holding:

♣ J ♢ J ♠ J   ♡ 8 7 6 5   ♢ 8 ♠ 2 A ♡ A

He melds his set **(J–J–J)** and his sequence (♡ **8 7 6 5**) and discards the ◊ **8**, leaving him with ♠ **2 A and** ♡ **A** as deadwood for a count of 4 points (2+1+1=4).

Player *Y* then melds whatever he can, with the added privilege of laying off extra cards on *X*'s melds, by extending sets or sequences. Assume that *Y* holds these ten cards:

♡ **J 10**   ♠ **10**   ♣ **10 9**   ♠ **6**   ◊ **6 5 4**   ♡ **4**

He melds his set **(10–10–10)** and his sequence (◊ **6 5 4**). *Y* then lays off his ♡ **J** on *X*'s set (making **J–J–J–J**). *Y* also lays off his ♡ **4** on *X*'s sequence (making it ♡ **8 7 6 5 4**). That leaves *Y* with two cards as deadwood: ♣ **9** and ♠ **6** for a count of 15 (9+6=15).

In scoring, the player who knocked subtracts his points from the other player's and credits himself with the difference, which goes into his column on a score sheet. In the above example, *X* would subtract his 4 points from *Y*'s 15, scoring 11 for *X* (15−4=11). The winner of the hand always deals the next hand, and the new score is entered in the proper column, continuing hand by hand until one player reaches 100 points or more, thereby winning game and receiving a bonus of 100 points. Both the box score and the bonus are doubled if a player wins every hand in the game, shutting out the other player. Each player receives a bonus of 25 points for each hand he won; and at the finish, one score is subtracted from the other to determine the margin of the victory.

That, however, is not all.

Any time a knocker melds his entire hand, so his count is 0, he "goes gin," and the other player is not allowed to lay off on his hand. For going gin, he gains an additional 25-point bonus, even if the other player should meld all his cards as well, though that seldom happens, for by then the opposing player should have already knocked.

Frequently, however, a knocker may be tied or "undercut"

by the other player. Here is an example of how that may happen:

Player *X* knocks and melds:
♣ **9 8 7** ♠ **7 6 5 4** Deadwood: ♣ **3** ◇ **3 2** (3+3+2=8)
Player *Y* happens to hold the following:
♠ **9 8 3 A** ♡ **9 3** ◇ **9 A** ♣ **2 A**
So *Y* melds two sets: ♠ **9** ♡ **9** ◇ **9** and ♠ **A** ◇ **A** ♣ **A**

Then, instead of being stuck with a count of 16 points (8+3+3+2=16), *Y* lays off ♠ **8** and ♠ **3** at the ends of *X*'s sequence (making it ♠ **8 7 6 5 4 3**), which leaves *Y* with only ♡ **3** and ♣ **2** (3+2=5). So *Y* receives 25 points, which is customary for equaling the knocker's count, plus 3 points representing the margin of difference (8−5=3) for a total of 28 points for the hand.

In short, the opposing player scores as if he had knocked and picks up 25 points above that. He also becomes winner of the hand and therefore deals the next hand.

Hollywood Gin is a term applied to the popular practice of playing three (or more) games simultaneously, in overlapping style. A player scores his first winning hand in Game 1; his second winning hand in both Games 1 and 2; his third winning hand in Games 1, 2, and 3. From then on, all winning hands are scored in all three games until a player reaches 100 in any game, ending that game; but the others are played to their conclusions.

The following example will illustrate the precedure:

In the initial hand, Player *X* has 13 points, which is entered as his first hand in Game 1. In the next hand, *X* scores 25 points, so it is entered in both Game 1 and Game 2, thus:

Game 1		*Game 2*		*Game 3*	
X	*Y*	*X*	*Y*	*X*	*Y*
13	—	25	—		
38	—				

Now, Player *Y* comes up with a winning hand of 22 points, which is his first win and therefore is entered only in Game 1:

Game 1		Game 2		Game 3	
X	*Y*	*X*	*Y*	*X*	*Y*
13	22	25			
38					

In the next hand, Player *X* scores 8 points, which apply to all three games, 1, 2 and 3, as follows:

Game 1		Game 2		Game 3	
X	*Y*	*X*	*Y*	*X*	*Y*
13	22	25		8	
38		33			
46					

Player *Y* gets busy and wins four hands in a row, scoring 30, 28, 5, and 18, respectively, resulting in the following *successive* entries:

	Game 1		Game 2		Game 3	
	X	*Y*	*X*	*Y*	*X*	*Y*
	13	22	25	30	8	28
	38	52	33	58		33
(Total)	46	80		63		51
		85		81		
		103	(Total)			

3 Hands		+100	Bonus for game
Won	+ 75	+125	For five hands won
	121	328	
		−121	*X*'s score
		207	*Y*'s margin of win

Now, *X,* who gained a nice head start, is at a disadvantage, since he can't score in three games anymore, as *Y* did for two hands. Assuming that *X* wins three consecutive hands with scores of 4, 16, and 29, but that Y then undercuts X's knock and comes through for 27. Games 2 and 3 would then stand:

	Game 2			Game 3		
	X	Y		X	Y	
	25	30		8	28	
	33	58		12	33	(Game 3 still
	37	63		28	51	to be
	53	81		57	78	finished.)
(Total)	82	108	(Total)			
5 Hands		+100	Bonus for game			
Won	+125	+125	For five hands won			
	207	333				
		−207	X's score			
		126	Y's margin of win			

Oklahoma Gin introduces one seemingly slight rule that utterly changes the pattern of play from that of standard gin. The rule is that the value of the upcard sets the number of points required for a knock during the ensuing deal. A face card or a ten makes no change in the 10-point minimum; while a nine, eight, or seven does not matter much. Lower values, however, greatly affect the play, and with an ace (1 point) the knocker practically has to go gin; in some circles, that is required. Due to the stepped-up play, game is usually set at 150, 200, or 250 (as preferred) with a bonus for winning the game set at the corresponding levels. Another rule often included is "spades double," meaning that if the upcard is a spade all scores resulting from that hand are doubled.

Variants of Gin Rummy include the "round the corner" feature of standard rummy, in which an ace is both high and low, with a value of 15 points. In some circles, the opposing player is allowed to "lay off" on the knocker's hand when he has "gone gin"; and a further rule may be introduced, eliminating any score for that hand if the opposing player reduces his count to zero, thus matching the knocker's gin. Several forms of partnership gin rummy have been devised, along with versions of three-handed play, but gin is essentially a two-handed game, and other types of rummy are preferable when the accommodation of additional players becomes a matter of moment.

GLEEK: An old English three-handed game with a forty-four-card pack, lacking threes and twos, in which players were paid off for "gleek" or three of a kind, and "mournival," or four of a kind, with only **A, K, Q, J** counting. Those four paid off as honors in a turned-up trump suit (as ♡ **A, K, Q, J),** and the hand was finally played out as in *Whist,* page 375, with a further score for tricks.

GO BOOM: A juvenile game with two to six players utilizing a fifty-two-card pack ranking A, K, Q, J, 10, 9, 8, 7, 6, 5, 4, 3, 2. Each player is dealt seven cards, and, beginning at the dealer's left, a player leads any card, which the others must match in suit or value. (Example: ♠ 9 is led; it could be followed by ♠ J, ♡ 9, ♠ 3, ♣ 9.) Anyone unable to play must draw up to three cards from top of pack until he can. After that, he can pass.

Tricks are tossed aside as worthless, but whoever plays the highest card of the suit led has the privilege of leading to the next. The player who first disposes of all his cards wins the game.

GO FISH: This game is similar to *Authors,* page 20, but simpler. With two or three players, each is dealt seven cards; with three to five players, each is dealt five cards. First player demands of any other, "Give me your nines," or any other value he may name, provided that his own hand contains a card of that denomination. The player given the demand must hand them over if he has any, and the first player can make a new demand from anyone he chooses. But if a player cannot meet the demand, he says, "Go fish!" and the demander must draw the top card of the pack.

If it proves to be the value wanted, or fills a "book" by matching three cards of a value he already holds, he can continue. Otherwise, the call moves to the player on his left. This goes on until one player has laid down his entire hand in matched sets of books of four cards each, thereby winning the game.

GRAND: An intriguing composite game in which a fifty-two-card pack is dealt equally among four players, those seated opposite being partners. Beginning at dealer's left, each player in turn may pass or make a bid in a multiple of five, going as high as 100. The high bidder then has several choices. He may decide to play a hand of *Whist,* page 375, where he names the trump suit and leads to the first trick. For each trick that his team takes over the "book" of six, it scores 5 points. As an example: with a bid of "15" a team would have to take nine tricks but would score 5 points more for each extra trick. Taking all thirteen tricks would score 35 points, but also gives the team a bonus of 30, so a bid of "65" is possible. After the opening lead by the bidder, play proceeds exactly as in whist. If a team falls short, it is "set back" the amount of its bid and opponents score 5 points per trick for any they take over the book of six.

A bidder may decide to play a hand of no-trump, which in this game is termed "grand," and is played just like whist but without a trump. In grand, each trick counts 9 points, with a bonus of 40 for "big slam," so taking all thirteen tricks would score 103 points $(7 \times 9 + 40 = 103)$. Bids are still made in multiples of 5, hence a player bidding "20" could decide to go for ten tricks in whist $(4 \times 5 = 20)$ or only eight in grand $(2 \times 9 = 18)$. Thus a choice of grand is not revealed until the bidder announces it, which adds to the zest of the game. A team scores what it makes in grand; if it falls short, it is set back the amount of the bid and opponents score 9 points for each trick they take over book of six.

As a further twist, a bidder can switch to *Euchre,* page 107, with the suits ranking as in that game. Here, each player discards all but five cards from his hand, but no one can keep a trump lower than the eight. With a bid of "5," a team must take three tricks; with a bid of "10," four tricks; with a bid of "20," all five tricks. Bidder leads to the first trick, and his team scores for all it takes; if short, it is set back the amount bid plus 20 points, but the opponents do not score. Possible losses would therefore be: 5+20=25; 10+20=30; 20+20=40.

A player bidding "20" can decide to "play alone," with the privilege of asking for his partner's best card in exchange for one of his own, giving the opponents the same privilege. In this case, he scores 25 for taking all tricks, but is only set back the usual 40 if he fails. However, if he finds himself forced to bid "25," he can do so, with the understanding that he must play a lone hand, with the exchange privilege if he chooses euchre. If he makes his bid, he scores 25; if he fails, he is set back 25+25=50.

To illustrate this interesting situation: The trump suit consists of the jack (right bower), jack of the same color (left bower), followed by A, K, Q, 10, 9, 8 in that order. Assume that the bidder holds ♠ J, ♣ J, ♠ A, ♠ Q, ◊ K as his best possible hand, and names spades as trump. He decides to play a "lone hand," discarding the ◊ K, in the hope that his partner's best card is a spade, because a fifth trump will mean a sure win for the bidder.

However, his partner has no spade. His best card, though, is the ♡ A, and upon gaining that, the bidder still has this chance: If the four remaining trumps, ♠ K, 10, 9, 8, are evenly divided between his opponents, the opponent gaining the other's best card still will only have three trumps. So the bidder plays his bowers and ace, clearing the trumps, and takes the next two tricks with the remaining trump and the odd ace. But if one opponent holds ♠ K, 9, 8 and the other holds the ♠ 10, he can take the ♠ 10 as his partner's best card, giving him an odd card in return. Holding ♠ K, 10, 9, 8, he is sure to win the fourth trick with the ♠ K and probably the fifth trick as well, thus setting the bidder back 40, if his bid was 20, or 50 if he was forced to bid 25.

As if all this were not enough, anyone bidding up to 50 has still another option; namely, to declare *Hearts*, page 140, as the game for that hand. The bidder leads, and if his team avoids taking any hearts, they score 50 points and the opponents are set back 1 point for each heart, or 13 in all. If the bidder's team takes any hearts, it is set back the amount of its bid (which may be anything from 5 to 50) and 1 point for each heart. Opponents are also set back 1 point per heart.

Game is 100 points. If a team scores a big slam in grand, it wins the game, even though it may have a minus score at the time. If the dealer's team reaches a score of 70, the player at dealer's left can simply declare hearts as the game, with no other bids allowed. In any case, a "pass" by the first player indicates that he would like to play at hearts but is leaving the choice to his partner. If nobody bids, the dealer must take it at a minimum of "5," choosing whatever game he regards as the least deadly.

Scoring involves other angles in grand. Often, when the bidding is spirited, opposing teams are set back so often that they frequently go in the hole and never climb out sufficiently to reach the goal of 100. So it is frequently decided to terminate play after a specified number of additional hands or at a certain time. Then the team with the highest score is credited with a final total of 100, just as if it had actually reached that figure. The losing team's score is subtracted from 100 to establish the winner's margin of victory. Examples: Team A goes out with 108 when Team B has only 45 points. Team A is credited with $100-45=55$ points. But if Team A had only 48 points against B's 45, Team A would still be credited with $100-45=55$.

However, that still is not final. Setbacks also figure in the score. Each time a team is set back, an "X" is marked beside the deduction. At the finish, each team's setbacks are counted and the lesser deducted from the greater. The difference is multiplied by 10 and credited to the team with less setbacks. That margin is either added or deducted to playing score, as the case may be. Examples: In the case given above, if A had 5 setbacks and B had 7, the difference would be in A's favor—$2\times 10=20$—and that would be added to A's score, giving A a winning margin of 75.

But if A had 12 setbacks—some very small—against B's

7, the difference would be in *B*'s favor—5×10=50—which would be deducted from *A*'s playing score of 55, reducing *A*'s margin of victory to a mere 5 points. This is both a unique and important feature of grand, when settlements are made in chips or otherwise.

Note: Detailed rules for *Whist, Euchre,* and *Hearts* will be found under those heads, and are followed in the play of grand, with the important exception that in grand the bidder always leads to the first trick.

GRAND DEMON: A variant of *Fascination—Solitaire,* page 329.

GRUESOME TWOSOME: *Poker.* See page 251.

GUTS: *Poker.* See page 251.

HALF-POT LIMIT: *Poker.* See page 251.

HASENPFEFFER: A cross between *Euchre,* page 107, and *Five Hundred,* page 117, played with a twenty-five-card pack, aces down to nines, with joker included as highest trump or "best bower"; followed by jack of trump as right bower, jack of same color as left bower, then A, K, Q, 10, 9 as in euchre. Plain suits rank A, K, Q, (J), 10, 9.

There are four players, those seated opposite being partners. Each is dealt six cards, the odd card also being dealt face down as a "widow." Each player has a single bid as to the number of tricks (from one to six) that he thinks his team can take if he names the trump. Highest bidder takes up the widow without showing it and discards any card he does not want.

The high bidder then names trump and opens play, with others following suit as in euchre; if out of suit, they may trump or discard from another suit. If a partnership makes its bid, it scores 1 point for each trick won. If it fails, it is set back the amount bid, its score being marked with a minus sign if need be. Game is 10 points, and if both teams go out during the same hand, the one making the bid is the winner.

During the bidding, if all players pass, whoever holds the

joker must show it and bid 3 points. If all pass and the joker is in the widow, a new hand is dealt.

See: *Double Hasenpfeffer,* page 103.

HEARTS: Though basically very simple, this popular game has been stepped up with some intriguing elaborations that will be described in due course, making it among the most exciting of round games, with each participant playing for himself.

The Pack. The standard fifty-two cards, running in descending values **A, K, Q, J, 10, 9, 8, 7, 6, 5, 4, 3, 2.** In the basic game, one to four cards of lower values are removed, as the **♣ 2, ◊ 2, ♣ 3, ◊ 3** (for six players), in the order given, so the deal will come out even, according to:

Number of Players: From three to eight. The full pack is used with four players; with three, one card (**♣ 2**) is removed; with more players, additional cards are removed as specified.

BASIC HEARTS: *The Deal:* The cards are dealt singly, face down, in clockwise order. Each player looks at his hand and the player at the dealer's left leads to the first trick. Others must follow suit if possible, otherwise they discard from another suit. The highest card of the suit led takes the trick, which the player lays face down in front of him and leads to the next trick. This continues until all cards are played.

There is no trump suit in hearts, nor do tricks have any value in themselves. The whole purpose of the game is to avoid taking any hearts, as they score 1 point each for the player taking them, and in this game the player with the highest score is the loser. After each hand, the deal moves to the left, and game itself is usually 50 points. When one player goes over that, the player with the lowest score at the finish of the hand is the winner, unless some other form of settlement is used, as will be specified later.

Hearts, in modern form, can best be described under the head of "omnibus hearts," a term that includes any or all of the elaborations that have added to the popularity of the game.

OMNIBUS HEARTS: Foremost among the features that enliven the play of modern hearts is the designation of a penalty card:

Black Lady: This refers to the ♠ Q, which in itself counts as 13 points toward the score of the player who is unfortunate enough to take it, as that lone card is as bad as all the hearts together. This adds greatly to the strategy of the game, as the ♠ A and ♠ K though adding no count of their own, are dangerous to hold, as they may force the player to take the black lady, with its 13 points.

To offset the penalty card, at least partially, the general rule is to include a:

Bonus Card: This is usually the ◊ J, though many groups prefer the ◊ 10, so the choice should be specified beforehand. Either way, the player who takes a trick containing the bonus card deducts 10 points from his score, sometimes putting himself in the minus column (below zero), which is all for the better in this game. Use of the bonus card also adds to the strategy, as players holding high diamonds (◊ A, ◊ K, or ◊ Q) have more chance of capturing the bonus card and can govern their play accordingly.

Passing the Cards: As a further aid to good strategy, immediately after the deal each player is allowed to lay three of his cards face down and pass them to the player on his right, thus improving his own hand until he picks up the three cards from the player on his left, which may prove worse. Hence he must pass his three cards before looking at those passed to him.

Good policy here is to pass high hearts and also the ♠ A and/or ♠ K, unless the player is holding ♠ Q as well. Sometimes it is smart to pass clubs or diamonds, to go short in those suits and make it easy to unload high hearts or the ♠ Q on unfortunate opponents during play. With five or more players, the number of cards passed may be reduced from three to two, by agreement.

The Third Trick: By this excellent rule, no player can lead a heart until the third trick; otherwise, a player could pass along high hearts and lead low hearts, gaining an undue initial advantage.

The Widow: Instead of reducing the pack so that all hands

come out even, the full fifty-two-pack is used, and any card or cards left over can then be laid aside, face down, as a "widow." Whoever takes the first trick gets the widow with it and can look at its contents without showing it to anyone else. Generally, it is wise to dodge the first trick, as there is more chance of getting a heart or the ♠ Q in the widow than there is of catching the desired ◊ J.

Scoring in Hearts: Scoring includes the following variations:

Instead of game being set at 50 or 100 points with lowest score denoting the winner, it can be limited to a specified number of hands. All scores are then added and divided by the number of players to strike an average. Players above average contribute chips or counters to a pool according to their scores; and those below average collect on the same basis.

Example: At the end of five hands, four players stand:

$A, +5.$ $B, +11.$ $C, +20.$ $D, +44.$ Total, $+80.$

Dividing 80 (the total) by 4 (the players) brings an average of 20. D therefore puts 24 chips in the pool. A collects 15, B, 9, and C, 0.

Hearts may also be scored on a "hand-to-hand" basis. After every hand, each player contributes a chip for each heart that he took in play. The pool is won by the player with the lowest score.

Examples: $A, +5.$ $B, +3.$ $C, +2.$ $D, +6.$

C wins 14 chips, as he contributed 2 of the 16.

A player with a minus score would gain additional chips proportionately, as:

$A, -6.$ $B, +2.$ $C, +2.$ $D, +18.$

Being less than zero, A naturally contributes nothing but takes the chips put in the pool by the other players, for a win of 22.

PINK LADY: Though comparatively little known, this unusual

option adds much zest to the game of hearts and is therefore highly recommended. It consists simply of counting the ♡ Q (or pink lady) as 13 points, so that it becomes a companion penalty card along with the ♠ Q (or black lady). This raises the point level from 26 (with 13 hearts at 1 each, plus ♠ Q as 13) to 38 (with 12 hearts at 1 each, plus ♠ Q and ♡ Q at 13 each). In both cases the bonus card (as ◊ J) reduces the count by 10.

The advantage of counting the ♡ Q as 13 is that a player who takes the ♠ Q (with its 13 points) can frequently retaliate in the same deal by foisting the ♡ Q on someone else. Occasionally, too, a player with a very low score may be saddled with both queens, thus putting him on close terms with the others. When the "pink lady" option is included, game can be raised from 50 to 100 points to allow for the heavier scoring.

Also included under "omnibus hearts" but worthy of individual discussion is:

TAKE-ALL HEARTS: This feature, which may be included with any type of hearts, provides that if a player takes all of the hearts, as well as any penalty or bonus cards, he may subtract all points that ordinarily would have been added to his score. Thus a high-card hand that would ordinarily be classed as a sure loser can sometimes be adroitly transformed into a big winner.

This varies, however, with the type of game, as follows:

Originally "take-all" was incorporated with a form of hearts termed "black lady," in which the ♠ Q figures as a penalty card, but there is no bonus card (as ◊ J). In "black lady," a player holding the ♠ Q was forced to unload it at the first opportunity; namely, when someone else played the ♠ A or ♠ K; or when the ♠ Q could be discarded. Thus a player taking the ♠ Q in an early round could go after all the hearts in order to get clear, but if he managed that, the score was merely nullified, giving everyone zero for the hand.

Such heroic effort deserved a greater reward, so the rules were amended. Today a player may hold the ♠ Q until he wants to play it; and a player who takes all hearts and the ♠ Q subtracts 26 points from his score, as already stated. However, when the ◇ J is rated as a bonus card (as is customary in modern hearts) it must also be taken by the player who is endeavoring to "take all," though taking it does not affect his score one way or the other.

Should a player fail to take all the hearts and the ♠ Q and ◇ J as well, the hand is scored in the usual manner. Hence, when playing with a widow it is advisable for a player to take the first trick in order to go after "take-all," as a lone heart in the widow could ruin his chances, if taken by another player.

Note: When counting both the ♠ Q (black lady) and ♡ Q (pink lady) as 13 points each, a player taking all hearts (and the ◇ J) deducts 38 points from his score. This increases the incentive but adds to the risk as well.

Other forms of the game will be found under: *Auction Hearts,* page 20, *Cancellation Hearts,* page 55, *Discard Hearts,* page 102, *Domino Hearts,* page 102, *Draw Hearts,* page 104, *Joker Hearts,* page 149, and *Spot Hearts,* page 362.

HEARTSETTE: *Hearts* played with the widow. See page 141.

HEART SOLO: Another name for *Frog,* page 125. Also a type of bid in *Six-Bid Solo,* page 309.

HEINZ: A wild form of *Seven-Card Stud.* See page 251.

HIGH FIVE: Another term for *Cinch,* page 65.

HIGH-LOW DRAW: *Poker.* See page 232.

HIGH-LOW JACK: A once common name for *Pitch,* page 214, and similar games in which high, low, and jack of trumps represent three of the points. Also called *High, Low, Jack and Game,* to include the fourth point.

HIGH-LOW POKER: A popular, modern form of *Poker,* in which "high" and "low" hands split the pot. See page 232.

HIGH-LOW RUMMY: See page 293.

HIGH-LOW STUD: *Poker,* played with five, six, or seven cards. See pages 233–34.

HIGH POKER: See page 251.

HIGH SPADE SPLIT: See page 251.

HILO: In *Poker,* a term for *Automatic Lowball,* page 243.

HILO PICOLO: *Take It or Leave It,* page 270.

HIT THE MOON: An English term for *Omnibus Hearts.* See page 140.

HOC or HOCK: An obsolete game resembling *Ambigu,* page 15.

HOGGENHEIMER: An English card game resembling roulette, with any number of players using a thirty-three-card pack (joker included) and a special layout, as follows:

♠ A K Q J 10 9 8 7
♡ A K Q J 10 9 8 7
◊ A K Q J 10 9 8 7
♣ A K Q J 10 9 8 7

Players place bets on individual cards (at equal odds); on two adjacent cards (2 to 1); on an entire column of four (4 to 1); or a row of eight (8 to 1). Cards are then dealt face up from the shuffled pack, each on its proper place in the layout, with any wagers on those cards being paid off by the dealer. But if the joker turns up, payoffs end and the dealer collects outstanding bets.

Instead of a special layout, cards can simply be dealt face down to form the rows indicated, with the last card placed to one side. After bets are laid, the odd card is turned up (as the ♡ **4**) and is put in its proper position in the layout, the card already there being removed and turned up next (say the ◊ **J**), which is put where it belongs; and so on, with appropriate payoffs for turned-up cards, columns, and rows until the joker appears and wins for the dealer.

HOKUM: Similar to *Hole-Card Stud.* See *Hokum,* page 252.

HOLD 'EM: A form of *Dealer's Choice.* See page 252.

HOLE-CARD STUD: A form of *Five-Card Stud Poker* with a first round of betting on the hole card alone. See page 252.

HOLLYWOOD: *Poker.* See page 253.

HOLLYWOOD CANASTA: A cross between *Samba,* page 300, and *Bolivia,* page 37, played according to the general rules of samba, as described under that head, but with these additions or modifications:

A *sequence canasta* can contain one wild card, thus becoming a *mixed sequence,* which reduces its value to 1000 instead of the 1500 for a *natural sequence.* Each meld must contain at least three natural cards unless a player goes for a *wild-card canasta,* which is allowable, and scores 2000 points. Every canasta is limited to seven cards.

A natural matching pair can always take the discard pile; and this applies to a pair of deuces or a pair of jokers. Unless the pack is frozen, the top card can be taken to lay off on any meld except a wild-card meld.

HOLLYWOOD GIN: See *Gin Rummy,* page 132.

HONEST JOHN: Another name for *Banker and Broker,* page 22.

HONEYMOON BRIDGE: A two-handed game with a standard fifty-two-card bridge pack, in which thirteen cards are dealt to each. Opponent leads first and dealer follows suit if he can, exactly as in no-trump. Winner of each trick draws a card from top of pack and the loser takes the next card. The winner leads to the next trick, and this continues until the whole pack has been drawn. No count is kept of those tricks, each player's purpose being to get rid of unwanted cards. But now, with each player holding his final 13 cards, bidding begins with the dealer as in *Contract Bridge,* page 72. Highest bidder becomes declarer; the other player leads and the hand is played and scored as in contract, each player representing a team. Deal then moves to the opponent.

HOUSE IN THE WOODS: Another name for *La Belle Lucie.* See *House in the Woods,* page 334, and *Trefoil,* page 348.

HOUSE ON THE HILL: A variant of *House in the Woods*. See page 335 and *Trefoil*, page 348.

HURRICANE: A form of *Two-Card Poker*. *See* page 273.

IDIOT'S DELIGHT: Another name for *Aces Up Solitaire*, page 323. See entry below.

IDIOT'S DELIGHT: A name appropriately applied to a game of tossing, skimming, or scaling cards one at a time into a wastebasket or some similar receptacle from a predetermined distance of five feet or more. Each player may toss an entire pack; or with two players one may toss reds, the other blacks; with four, each may toss a separate suit. Whichever lands the most cards wins. See entry above.

IDLE YEAR: A variant of *Accordion Solitaire*, page 323.

I DOUBT IT: A fifty-two-card pack is dealt singly to three or four players until all cards have been dealt. Player at dealer's left takes one to four cards from his hand, lays them face down and declares, "Aces." Next player does the same, declaring "Twos"; the next, "Threes," continuing around to "Kings," after which it begins again with "Aces."

Each player's aim is to discard his entire hand; and he can bluff by miscalling cards when he lacks the value named, or deems it expedient to retain some. However, immediately after any discard, the next player—or another following— may assert, "I doubt it." The cards are then shown, and if they prove to be miscalled, the player who discarded them must take them into his hand along with all other cards so far discarded.

Should the call be correct, the burden is on the player who said, "I doubt it," and he must take all the discards into his own hand. When one player successfully disposes of his entire hand, play ends, and he collects a chip or point for each card held by another player.

With four to eight players, a double pack is used, allowing discards of one to eight of each value. With eight to twelve players, use of a triple pack allows discards up to twelve.

IMPERIAL: A game similar to *Piquet,* page 211, but played with trump suit and with cards ranking **K, Q, J, A, 10, 9, 8, 7.**

IRISH LOO: See page 158.

ITALIAN CANASTA: A variety of *Samba.* See *Three-Pack Canasta,* page 52.

JACKPOTS: A highly popular form of *Draw Poker,* requiring jacks or better to open the betting. See page 253.

JACKS BACK or JACKSON: *Poker.* See page 253.

JACKS HIGH: *Poker.* See page 253.

JAMBONE and JAMBOREE: Special rulings optionally applied to the game of *Railroad Euchre,* described under *Euchre,* page 113.

JASS: A game similar to two-handed *Pinochle,* page 175, but with a single pack of thirty-six cards, ranking as in *Klaberjass,* page 151; Trump: **J, 9, A, 10, K, Q, 8, 7, 6** (dix). Other suits: **A, 10, K, Q, J, 8, 7, 6.** Jack of trump is "Jass"; **9,** "Nell."

Each player is dealt nine cards; the next, turned up and laid aside as trump, may be exchanged by player holding the dix, but with no score involved. Opponent leads to the first trick, but dealer does not have to follow suit or trump. High card of suit led wins unless trumped; and winner of trick draws the top card of the pack; loser draws the next. When all have been drawn, the hands are played out; but now a player must follow suit or trump the trick if out of suit if he can. If trump is led, he must play a higher trump if he has one. However, such rules do not apply to the Jass. A player may hold it (the jack of trump) as long as he wants.

Points are scored for the following cards taken during play: Jass, 20; Nell, 14; aces, 11 each; tens, 10; kings, 4; queens, 3; ordinary jacks, 2; last trick, 10. A player winning a trick and making his draw may meld one of the following scoring combinations: four jacks, 200; four aces, tens, kings, or queens, 100; five cards of a suit in sequence, 100; four in sequence, 50; three in sequence, 20; king and queen of trump, 20. The deal alternates and game is 1000, with a player "calling out" when he reaches it.

In three-handed Jass, each is dealt nine cards, and the next is turned up as trump. Dealer may exchange his hand for the nine left in the pack; otherwise, succeeding players have that privilege. All melds are made before play begins at dealer's left, and a trick must be taken for a player's meld to count. Four can play, each on his own, the dealer showing his final card as trump.

JIG: A variation of *Earl of Coventry,* page 105, or *Snip Snap Snorem,* page 320, with this difference: When a card is led (as ♡ 3), instead of adding others of that value (as ♣ 3 or ◇ 3), players must add the next higher value of the same suit (as ♡ 4, ♡ 5, ♡ 6). But when *four such cards* have been played, the sequence ends; and a new one must be started.

Note: A sequence beginning with ♡ Q, ♡ K, ♡ A can be continued into ♡ 2.

JOKER EUCHRE: See page 113.

JOKER HEARTS: Regular *Hearts,* page 140, but with a joker added to the pack, ranking below ♡ J and above ♡ 10, but also representing the highest card in any other suit, and counting 5 points against a player's score if he takes it during play. To unload it, he must play it on a trick headed by a higher heart, as ♡ A, ♡ K, ♡ Q, ♡ J.

JOKER POKER: Any form of *Poker* with a joker added to the pack as a wild card. See page 253.

JOKER RUMMY: Any form of *Rummy* utilizing a joker. See page 291.

KALOOCHI or KALUKI: An elaborated form of *Rummy,* page 291, played with two fifty-four-card packs, containing four jokers as wild cards. Either two, three, or four players are dealt fifteen cards each; a card is turned up for the discard pile, and play proceeds as in rummy, with an ace ranking either high or low and a joker representing any card a player chooses. Cards are valued: ace, 11; face cards (K, Q, J), 10 each; others according to their spots, with joker whatever value named in meld, but counting 25 points against a player if he is caught with it unmelded. Players may meld "sets" of three or four of the same value, provided all suits are different, as ♡ J, ♠ J, ◊ J, ♣ J; or "sequences" of three or more cards in the same suit (♡ 8, 7, 6).

However, special rules apply as follows: A player cannot take the upcard of the discard pile unless he can use it in an opening meld of more than 50 points (as ♡ Q, ◊ Q, ♣ Q, ♠ Q and ♠ 9 8 7), or until after he has made such a meld. Nor can he "lay off" cards on an opposing meld until after he has made his own opening meld. But any time a joker appears in a meld, a player holding the card it represents may, during his turn, exchange his card for the joker. (Example: Player X melds ♡ 10, ♡ 9, joker, ♡ 7 as a sequence. Player Y, holding a ♡ 8, inserts it in X's meld and takes the joker into his own hand.)

A player "goes out" by melding all his cards and making a final discard if necessary. He then collects a chip per point from each opponent for unmelded cards in the opponent's hand; and the deal moves to the left. Kaloochi can be played by five players, each being dealt thirteen cards; or by six, with eleven cards dealt to each.

KANKAKEE: A form of "dealer's choice." See *Poker*, page 253.

KING ALBERT: A form of *Solitaire*. See page 335.

KING RUMMY: Another name for *Contract Rummy*. See page 91.

KINGS BACK or KINGSTON: *Poker*. See page 253.

KINGS IN THE CORNERS: A game for two to six players. Each is dealt a face-down hand of five cards; then, a layout of four cards is dealt face up with corner spaces reserved for kings; and the pack is placed face down in the center. For example:

(K)	♡ 9	**(K)**
♣ 8	(Pack)	◊ 8
(K)	◊ 2	**(K)**

Beginning at the dealer's left, each player may build on the layout cards in descending order, and in alternating colors, as ♣ 8 on ♡ 9; ◊ 7 (or ♡ 7) on ♣ 8; and so on, down to ♡ A or ◊ A. Builds may be made from the board or from the player's hand; and whenever a space becomes vacant on the board (as when ♣ 8 is placed on ♡ 9), the space can be filled by a card from the hand. Whenever a king appears, either in the original layout, or in the player's hand, it is placed in one of the corners **(K)** to start a new layout pile that is then built downward in the same manner (as red queen on black king, then black jack on red queen) as far as possible.

When a player is unable to play further from the board or from his hand, he draws a card from the top of the pack and may use it to continue his turn, including another draw from the pack; but when a drawn card cannot be played, the turn moves to the next player. The first player to dispose of his entire hand wins the game.

KLABERJASS or KLOB: Highly popular along Broadway during the "guys and dolls" era, this two-player game utilizes a thirty-two-card pack, ranking as follows during play: Trump: **J, 9, A, 10, K, Q, 8, 7.** Other suits: **A, 10, K, Q, J, 9, 8, 7.**

Six cards are dealt to each player and the next is turned up under the pack. The opponent may either accept it as trump or pass, in which case the dealer may accept it or pass. If trump is accepted, a player holding the seven, or dix, may exchange it for the turned-up trump card. As another option, either player may announce, *"Schmeiss,"* pronounced "shmice," signifying that he is willing either to accept the turned-up trump or abandon the hand, as the other player chooses. If both pass, the opponent may "make" another trump by simply naming a suit; if he passes again, the dealer may make trump, or pass, which calls for a new deal.

If a trump is accepted or made, three more cards are dealt to each player for a total of nine. Each player then considers *melding* certain cards, in sequences of three or four in individual suits, ranking A, K, Q, J, 10, 9, 8, 7. A four-card meld, as ◊ 10, 9, 8, 7, is worth 50 points; a three-card meld, as ♣ A, K, Q, is worth 20 points. However, only the player with the highest sequence is allowed to meld, the opponent first announcing "50" or "20" or saying that he has no meld. If the dealer cannot equal it, he says, "Good" and the opponent melds and scores whatever sequences he holds. If the dealer can beat "20" with a "50," or has 20 when the opponent has no meld, the dealer says, "No good" and proceeds to meld.

If the dealer merely matches the opponent's figure, he asks how high the sequence is. The opponent names his top-ranking card, as "ten" with ◊ 10, 9, 8, 7, and if the dealer's sequence is higher, as ♡ Q, J, 10, 9, he gains the melding privilege. With a tie, a trump sequence has priority: if both sequences are in plain suits, neither player melds. However, during the play that follows, another meld—known as "bella"—may be made by either player. This consists of the king and queen of trump and scores 20 points, provided the player who holds it announces, "Bella" after he has played both of the cards.

In the play, the opponent leads any card to the first trick; and the winner leads to the next. A player must follow suit if he can; if not, he must trump if possible; otherwise, he discards from any suit. The high card of a suit led wins unless trumped. Whenever a trump is led, the other player must trump higher if he can. The object is to take cards with point values as follows:

Jack of trump, or *Jass,* 20. Nine of trump, or *Menel,* 14. Any ace, 11; ten, 10; king, 4; queen, 3; ordinary jack, 2. Another 10 is scored for taking the last trick. These are added to whatever meld a player has already made, which is generally an advantage. However:

The player who "accepted" or "made" trump must score more than his adversary in order for each score to stand. But if the adversary scores more, he gets the total of both scores, while the player who accepted or made trump gets nothing and is said to "go bate." If the score is tied, the usual rule is for the adversary to score his own points, against none for the trump maker. This is called "half bate." Game is either 300 or 500 points; preferably 500.

KLONDIKE: A form of *Solitaire*. See page 338.

KNOCK POKER: This game, played with a fifty-two-card pack by three to five players, is practically *Knock Rummy*, page 154, but with hands ranked as in poker. Each is dealt five face-down cards as in draw poker; and the top card of the pack is turned up alongside. Beginning at the dealer's left, each player draws either the top card of the pack or the turned-up card, which represents a pile on which he must make a discard. Players continue this in rotation, each trying to improve his hand with every draw, in conformity with poker combinations, which run in ascending order: pair, two pair, three of a kind, straight, flush, full house, four of a kind, straight flush. (See *Poker*, page 219.)

When a player thinks he has a winning hand, he knocks on the table after discarding, and all other players may make one more draw and discard before the hands are shown, as in poker, with the highest hand winning. The deal then moves to the left. In this game, each player contributes an equal number of chips at the start and the pool goes to the winner; hence there is no betting, as in poker, or any scoring or laying off, as in rummy. So it belongs in its own category and should not rightfully be used in "dealer's choice," though that is allowable if the dealer makes a usual ante of his own and all players agree. See *Dealer's Choice* (page 241).

The game has slight variations, which may be specified, as requiring a player to have a minimum holding, as a pair of jacks, two pair, or even something higher, before knocking. It can also be played with deuces or other cards wild, bringing it more into the poker realm. Some groups play that hands are shown immediately after a knock, without further draws or discards.

KNOCK RUMMY: A fast form of Rummy, page 291, that rates as a game in its own right. Cards rank in the customary descending order: **K, Q, J, 10, 9, 8, 7, 6, 5, 4, 3, 2, A.** With two players, each is dealt ten cards, but it is usually played by three, four, or five, with seven cards each. Players draw from the pack or discard pile as in rummy and arrange their hands in sets (three or four of one value) or sequences of three or more cards of the same suit, but there are no melds whatever until one player, after making a draw, knocks on the table to signify that play is over. The knocker then discards, and all players meld whatever they can but are not allowed to lay off extra cards on other melds.

Each then adds the points on his unmelded cards, or "deadwood," each face card counting 10 and others according to their numerical value, with each ace counting 1. The knocker collects the difference between his count and that of each opponent, plus 25 points from each if he "goes rummy" by melding his entire hand. A player who ties the knocker collects instead, according to a long-accepted rule; but in modern play, the knocker is generally specified as the winner.

Should the knocker be beaten for low, he pays the difference in count, plus 10 points. No knock is allowed if the pack is reduced to the same number of cards as players. Draws continue until all cards are gone, when hands are melded and the one with the smallest count in deadwood wins. As an optional ruling, when the pack is reduced as described, a player cannot take an up-card unless he can use it in a meld and shows cards to prove the fact.

Poker Rum is an early form of knock rummy which carries the proviso that a player cannot knock until his deadwood is reduced to a total of 15 points or less. Poker rum is also a progenitor of *Gin Rummy,* which is described under that head. See page 130.

KONTRASPIEL: An old-time trump game.

KREUTZ-MARIAGE: A form of four-handed *Sixty-six.* See page 313.

LA BELLE LUCIE: A variant of *Trefoil Solitaire,* page 348.

LALAPALOOZA: *Poker.* See page 254.

LAMEBRAIN PETE: Another name for *Cincinnati Liz,* in *Poker.* See page 246.

LAMEBRAINS: The same as *Cincinnati,* in *Poker.* See page 246.

LANSQUENET: A famous old dealing game. Two cards of different value are turned up, one for the players, on which they place bets, the other for the dealer. More cards are turned up one by one, and if they represent new values, players can wager on them as well. As soon as a card appears matching a player's card, the dealer pays off all bets on it; and cards of that value are rejected from then on. But if the dealer matches his own card in value, he collects all outstanding bets, and the deal ends. The game is frequently played with two or more packs shuffled together. Sometimes it is played in reverse, with the dealer winning when he matches a player's card and paying all remaining bets when he matches his own.

LANTERLOO: See page 156, under *Loo.*

LAPS: A form of *Euchre,* page 107, in which the winner of a game applies his excess score as a start to the next. This mode of scoring is sometimes used with other games. See page 114 for *Laps.*

LAST IN: A typical trump game with a fifty-two-card pack ranking A, K, Q, J, 10, 9, 8, 7, 6, 5, 4, 3, 2. With six players, each is dealt four cards; five players, five cards; four players, six cards. The last card is dealt face up to establish trump, then is taken into the dealer's hand. Player at dealer's left leads any card; others follow suit if possible; otherwise they trump or play another suit. Highest card of suit led wins the trick unless trumped; then highest trump wins. Now comes the important feature:

The player who wins the trick draws a card from the top of

the pack before leading to the next trick; but nobody else draws. This applies to every trick that follows. So the game narrows down to the point where only one player is left, automatically becoming the winner. If down to two players on the last trick, whoever takes the trick wins. Hence the game is usually played with all players contributing to a pool to start.

LAZY EDNA or LAZY LUCY: Popular terms for *One-Card Poker*. See page 258.

LEFTY LOUIE: *Poker*. See page 254.

LEG IN POT: See page 254 for *Leg in Pot*.

LIFT SMOKE: An old and somewhat debatable title for the game of *Last In,* which is described under that head. See page 155.

LIVERPOOL RUMMY: Another name for *Contract Rummy,* page 91.

LONG WHIST: See *English Whist,* page 376.

LOO or LANTERLOO: Highly popular around the year 1800, this is still an intriguing, fast-moving trump game, involving any number of players from four or five, up to a dozen, or even more, using a fifty-two-card pack with each suit ranking A, K, Q, J, 10, 9, 8, 7, 6, 5, 4, 3, 2 in descending order. The dealer places three chips or counters in a pool, which is termed a "simple" or "single" pool, and deals three cards face down to each player. The first player on the dealer's left leads any card, and the rest follow suit in rotation, with the proviso that each must play a higher card if he has one; otherwise, he plays from an odd suit. High card of the suit led wins the trick, and the winner of each trick leads to the next, making three in all. However, each player must keep his tricks face up in front of him because:

Any time a player is unable to follow suit, the top card of the pack is turned up to designate a trump suit. If a player happened to discard from that suit, he wins the trick, unless another player discarded higher in the same suit. That suit stands as trump for the next trick, or tricks, if two are still to be played; and the winner of a trick must lead a trump to the next trick, if he has one; and others must overtrump if they can. If a player is out of the suit led, he must trump if able.

For each trick won, a player takes one third of the pool. Any player who failed to take a trick is "looed" and must contribute three chips to the next pool, along with the customary three put up by the new dealer. The deal moves to the left and is termed a "double" pool, although it may contain far more than twice the usual three. Example: In a seven-player "simple" pool, four players are sure to be looed, which means that twelve additional chips must be put into the double pool that follows.

Play with a Double Pool follows a special pattern. An extra hand is dealt, termed the "miss," which serves as a "widow"; and following the deal, the top card of the pack is turned up as trump. Each player, in turn, may then "pass," putting his hand face down; or he may "stand" and play out the hand. If he stands, he can exchange his hand for the widow, if he wants; but only one player has that privilege.

If all players pass until the dealer, he simply stands and wins the pool automatically. If only one player stands and takes the widow, he wins the pool; but if he does not take the widow, the dealer must do one of two things: (a) Stand and play his own hand, also ignoring the widow; (b) Exchange his hand for the widow and play against his lone opponent merely to defend the pool, by preserving as much of it as possible for the next deal. In this case, the dealer neither wins nor loses, but simply acts in behalf of the players who passed.

Rules vary regarding play with a "double pool," the simplest being that a player must always lead a trump if he has one; and that if he holds the ace of trump, he must lead it, or the king, if the ace happened to be turned up as trump. Otherwise, the play is the same as with a simple pool, including the rule that each succeeding player must try to take each trick by "heading" it, even when the next player is apt to go higher.

The winner of each trick takes one third of the double pool, and if no one is looed (as may happen if only three players or less decided to stand), the next deal reverts to the simple or single pool. If any players are looed, they must each put up the usual three chips for the next deal, so that the double pool still holds.

If a player is dealt a "flush," consisting of three trumps, or if he takes the widow and finds a flush therein, he waits until everyone has decided to pass or stand, and then shows his hand. The flush gives him the entire double pool automatically, and each player who decided to stand is automatically looed and forced to put three chips into a new double pool. In the case of two or more flushes during the same deal, the player nearest the dealer's left is the winner.

Popular developments of loo include the following:

Irish Loo: This is "double pool" without a widow. The dealer puts up three chips and deals three cards to each player, finally turning up trump. Players pass or stand, and whoever stands can discard any cards he does not want, drawing replacements from the top of the pack, the turned-up trump being laid aside to facilitate that action. Play then proceeds as with a double pool, the flush rule being optional.

Five-Card Loo: Played like Irish loo, but with the dealer putting up five chips and dealing five cards to each player. Players pass, stand, draw, and play as usual, with the winner of each trick taking one fifth of the pool. In this game, the ♣ J, known as "Pam," may be rated as the highest trump by preliminary agreement. As another option, a flush in any suit wins the pool, with Pam counting as a card of that suit; and in some circles, a blaze, consisting of any five cards, has equal rating with a flush. For further ratings see *Pam-Loo,* page 168.

Unlimited Loo is any form of the game in which any player who is looed must put up an amount equal to the existing pool.

Irregularities in Loo, if serious, carry the simple penalty of having the offender put three chips into the pool, or five in five-card loo. This applies to both deal and play.

LOUIS NAPOLEON: A *Solitaire* game, variant of *Napoleon's Favorite.* See page 344.

LOWBALL: A highly developed form of *Low Poker,* with special rules of its own. Very popular in California. See *Lowball,* page 237.

LOW POKER: Any form of *Poker* in which the low hand wins instead of the high hand. See pages 254, 255.

LUCAS: A form of *Solitaire,* page 339.

MACAO: Similar to *Blackjack,* page 32, with cards valued by their spots, from ace, 1, up to nine, 9. Tens and face cards (J, Q, K), 0. Players bet and each is dealt one card; if a seven, he collects the amount he bet from the dealer; if an eight, he collects double; if a nine, triple, unless the dealer's card is higher, when he collects on the same terms from every player with a lower card. If the dealer's card is under seven, any players under seven may call for more cards, hoping to approach nine without going over. Any that does go over is "bust" and pays the dealer, who then can draw cards for himself in an effort to beat any others who drew extra cards. In case of ties, bets are off. All cards are dealt face up.

MA FERGUSON: *Poker.* See pages 255, 266.

MARRIAGE: A game played like *Sixty-six,* page 311, but with an added bonus of 60 points for holding the ace and ten of trumps; and 30 for the same in another suit; also 20 extra points for taking the last six tricks. Each deal constitutes a complete game.

MATCH 'EM: *Poker.* See page 255.

MATRIMONY: An old English game played by any number of players—up to two dozen!—and a fifty-two-card pack. A simple layout is also required, marked with these divisions: matrimony (any **K** and **Q**); intrigue (any **Q** and **J**); confederacy (any **K** and **J**); pair (any pair); and best ($\lozenge$ **A**). Each player puts up a specified number of chips, distributing them among the sections as he wishes. Each is then dealt two cards; one face down, the other face up. Any player receiving the $\lozenge$ **A** face up immediately takes all the chips, not only from "best" but from every other section. If the $\lozenge$ **A** does not appear, each player, beginning at the dealer's left, turns up his downcard; and if his two cards form any combination named, he collects the chips from that section. The $\lozenge$ **A** has no value as a downcard. Any chips not won remain for the next deal, which moves to the left, with players putting up the same number that they did before, so that some very sizable pots are often built before the $\lozenge$ **A** appears as an upcard, to take all.

MAW: The earliest form of *Five Cards,* which later developed into *Spoil Five.* See *Spoil Five,* page 360.

MEDIATOR: A variation of *Tresette,* page 368, without melds or regular partners, in which a player may play alone for added stakes.

MEMORY: Another name for *Concentration,* page 70.

MENAGERIE: A juvenile game, best with a dozen or more players. Each takes the name of a wild animal—from antelope to zebra!—and cards are dealt around until they run out. Each player holds his packet face down, and, starting at dealer's left, each turns a card face up in front of him. When two match in value (as $\heartsuit$ **Q** and $\spadesuit$ **Q**), each player calls the "animal name" of the other. First to call wins the other's face-up cards and places them face down beneath his own packet. Play resumes where it left off, and whenever a player has dealt all his cards face up, he turns the packet over and begins again. Winner is the player who eventually garners all the cards.

MEXICANA or MEXICAN CANASTA: A three-pack form of *Canasta,* page 43, with six jokers (152 cards), with thirteen dealt to each player. After his opening meld, a player can draw thirteen cards from the pack, adding them to his hand; but in team play, only one member can do so. In one accepted mode of scoring, a canasta of seven counts 1000, but a player cannot match a seven when it is an upcard. To go out, a team must have two or more canastas, with a red three to go with each.

MEXICAN STUD: Five- or seven-card stud, involving a special mode of play. See page 255.

MEXICAN WILD: A wild version of Mexican stud with five cards. See page 256.

MICHIGAN: A modern game of the "stops" type, played with a standard fifty-two-card pack, with cards running in ascending value, 2, 3, 4, 5, 6, 7, 8, 9, 10, J, Q, K, A. A special requirement is a "layout" consisting of four cards from another pack, usually the ♠ J, ◇ Q, ♡ K, ♣ A, which are laid face up as "pool" or "boodle" cards. Each player puts four chips on these in whatever way he wants, as four on one, two on two, etc.

The pack is dealt singly to from three to seven players, with an extra hand at dealer's left, until cards run out, as an added card in a hand does not matter. The dealer may exchange his hand for the extra hand—or "widow"—laying his own hand face down; or he may auction the widow to the highest bidder, beginning at his left, if anyone wants it. The first player then places his lowest card in any suit face up in the center of the table and follows with others of that suit in ascending sequence (as ◇ 4, ◇ 5, ◇ 6) until he strikes a gap, when the turn moves to the next player and so on, until play reaches the ace or is stopped by a missing card. The player then begins a new sequence with his lowest card in another suit; if all are reduced to the suit just played, the player who was stopped can resume it when the turn comes around to him.

Whenever a duplicate of a boodle card is played, either in proper sequence or as the player's lowest card in that suit, the player collects all the chips that were placed on the corresponding card in the layout. When a player "goes out" by being the first to get rid of his final card, he collects one chip from each player for each card that player holds. If any chips remain on a boodle card, they stay there as a bonus for the next deal, which moves to the left, unless it is previously agreed that they are to be taken by the player who goes out.

Additional Boodle Cards and *Combinations* may be used on the layout, as the ♡ **J** and the ◊ **10**, which function like the regular boodle cards; or two cards in sequence, as ♠ **10 J**, which one player must hold and play in order to collect. A layout combination of **7–8–9** means that by playing a card of each value during one deal, a player collects, regardless of the suits or the order in which the three cards are played. Other combinations are optional, such as winning on a layout of ♣ **10 J Q**, by playing two of those three cards. At the finish of a game, any chips still left on boodle cards are divided among the players.

MICHIGAN RUMMY: A transitional form of *Rummy,* page 294.

MIKE: Stud poker with all cards dealt face down. See page 256.

MISS MILLIGAN: A form of *Solitaire.* See page 342.

MISTIGRIS: An old name for *Joker Poker.* See page 253.

MONTE: Another name for *Three-Card Poker.* See page 271.

MONTE BANK: A money game in which the dealer draws two cards from the bottom of the pack and turns them face up; then two from the top, which are turned face up. Players bet on either pair and the banker-dealer turns the entire pack face up, revealing the bottom card, which is termed the "gate." If a pair shows a card of the same suit as the gate, the dealer pays off that pair; if not, he collects. Cards are gathered, pack is shuffled, and the deal repeated.

MONTE CARLO: A form of *Solitaire.* See page 343.

MORTGAGE: *Poker.* See page 256.

MUGGINS: A name applied occasionally to *Cribbage,* page 95, when played with a penalty for an oversight; also to various simple games.

MULTIPLE KLONDIKE: *Klondike* played by three or more persons; procedure as in *Double Solitaire,* page 104.

MUSTACHED JACKS or KINGS WILD: *Poker.* See page 256.

MY BIRD SINGS: A simple game with up to a dozen players. Each is dealt a hand of four cards; and if the first player finds that his are all one suit, he announces, "My bird sings," shows his cards, and wins the deal. Otherwise, he passes an odd card face down to the player on his left; if he can show four of one suit, he makes the announcement and wins; otherwise he passes a card along; and so on and on, until one player gains a "flush" of four. Deal moves to the left, and the game continues until one player gains a specified total of wins. Variants are played under similar titles with different numbers of cards, one popular name being *My Ship Sails.*

NAPOLEON: A popular English game for the past two centuries and still good. A fifty-two-card pack, with values running **A, K, Q, J, 10, 9, 8, 7, 6, 5, 4, 3, 2,** is used by two to six players, each being dealt a hand of five cards. Each player bids from one to five—unless he prefers to pass—and the highest has the privilege of naming trump by leading a card of the suit he prefers. Others follow suit if possible and the highest trump wins the trick. From then on, the winner of each trick leads to the next, using any suit; all must follow suit if they can; otherwise, they may discard from another suit or trump the trick. Highest card of suit led wins the trick unless trumped; then the highest trump wins.

If the bidder takes the specified number of tricks, he collects that many chips from each opponent. If he fails, he must pay each that number. A bid of "five" is a "napoleon," and the bidder collects double—ten chips from each—if he wins; but he only pays singly—five to each—if he loses.

By agreement, a special bid of "wellington" may outbid a "nap," the bidder agreeing to go for "double"—twenty chips from each opponent if he takes all five tricks, but paying ten to each if he fails. A still higher bid of "blucher" can be added for triple stakes: thirty chips from each opponent for a win, or a payment of fifteen to each for a loss. This is at least historically correct, since Wellington defeated Napoleon at Waterloo, but only because Blücher arrived in time to save the day.

A "nullo" bid may also be included in "Nap," rating above three, but below four; but paying only three chips, win or lose. Such a bid, also called "misere," is played as no-trump, and the bidder must lose all tricks to win.

NAPOLEON AT ST. HELENA: Another name for *Lucas Solitaire,* page 339.

NAPOLEON'S FAVORITE: A form of *Solitaire*. See page 344.

NAPOLEON'S SQUARE: A variant of *Napoleon's Favorite*. See page 344.

NESTOR: A form of *Solitaire*. See page 346.

NEW GUINEA STUD: *Poker*. See page 256.

NEW MARKET: The English counterpart of *Michigan,* page 161, the only difference being that the extra hand, or "widow," is never taken up for play but is "dead" from start to finish. This helps pile chips on the boodle cards (traditionally ◊ J, ♣ Q, ♡ K, ♠ A), so if any are unclaimed at the finish, the pack is shuffled and cards simply dealt around face up, the boodle going to the players who receive the proper cards. This device is applicable to *Michigan* as well.

NEW YORK STUD: A variant of *Five-Card Stud Poker*. See page 257.

NINE-CARD STUD: See page 257.

NINETY-NINE: *Poker*. See page 257.

NODDY: An earlier and simpler form of *Cribbage*. See page 95.

NO DRAW: A *Poker* game, page 257.

NO LIMIT: *Poker*. See page 257.

NO LOW CARDS: *Poker*. See page 257.

NORWEGIAN WHIST: A form of no-trump *Whist,* page 375. Players, starting at dealer's left, may "pass" until one decides his team will play at "grand," which means taking odd tricks at 4 points each, or "nullo," losing odd tricks at 4 points each. If a team fails, the opponents score 8 points for each odd trick they take. Game is 50 points.

OH, HELL!: A unique game for four players, each on his own, using a fifty-two-card pack in thirteen successive deals. On the first, each player is dealt one card; the next is turned up as trump. After the hand is played, the deal moves to the left, and each player is dealt two cards, the next being turned up as trump. Again, the deal moves to the left, and three cards are dealt to each; and so on, one more card being dealt with each deal and the next card being turned up as trump.

Play is the same as in whist or bridge. Player to dealer's left leads to the first trick. Highest card in suit led wins the trick unless it is trumped, when highest trump wins. The winner of each trick leads to the next, and play continues in that wise. However: Immediately after a deal, each player in turn must state the number of tricks he expects to take. Thus, on the first deal, which consists of a single trick, it would be either 0 or 1. On the second deal, it would be 0, 1, or 2; on the third deal, 0, 1, 2, 3; and so on.

If the player's statement is correct, he scores 10 points, plus the number stated. Example: On first deal, he might score 10+0=10 or 10+1=11; on the second deal, 10+0=10, 10+1=11, 10+2=12. This increases with every deal, so that the game becomes more intriguing as the hands become more complex. On the final deal, all fifty-two cards are dealt (thirteen to a player), so instead of turning up a trump, the hand is played at no-trump. The player with the highest score wins.

OKLAHOMA: Another name for *Arlington*. See apge 16.

OKLAHOMA GIN: An advanced form of *Gin Rummy* in which the minimum points for a "knock" are determined by the spots of the upcard. See page 134.

OLD MAID: A popular children's game using a fifty-two-card pack from which the ♣ Q is removed, so that the ♠ Q becomes the "old maid." Cards are distributed about equally among two to five players and each lays aside any pair of cards that are the same in value and color (as ♡ 6 and ◇ 6 or ♠ 9 and ♣ 9). Then each in turn spreads his hand face down so that the next player can take a card for his own hand, pairing it if possible, so as to lay two more cards aside. This continues until one player is left with the unpaired "old maid" and becomes the loser.

Note: If desired, a fifty-three-card pack may be used, including the joker, which becomes the equivalent of the "old maid."

OLD SLEDGE: A name for *Seven Up*. See *All Fours,* page 13.

OMAHA: A compact version of *Seven-Card Stud* crossed with *Cincinnati,* enabling as many as twenty-three players to participate in each hand. See page 257.

OMBRE: A famous old Spanish game for three players, using a forty-card pack with cards ranking as follows:

Red plain suits (♡ or ◇): **K, Q, J, A, 2, 3, 4, 5, 6, 7**
Black plain suits (♠ or ♣): **K, Q, J, 7, 6, 5, 4, 3, 2**

Note the absence of aces in the black plain suits. That is because both those cards (♠ A and ♣ A) always belong to the trump suit, which runs in the following order:

♡ as trump: ♠ A; ♡ 7; ♣ A; ♡ A, K, Q, J, 2, 3, 4, 5, 6
◇ as trump: ♠ A; ◇ 7; ♣ A; ◇ A, K, Q, J, 2, 3, 4, 5, 6
♠ as trump: ♠ A, 2; ♣ A; ♠ K, Q, J, 7, 6, 5, 4, 3
♣ as trump: ♠ A; ♣ 2, A, K, Q, J, 7, 6, 5, 4, 3

Nine cards are dealt to each of the three players, to the right, or counterclockwise, as customary in Spanish games. The first player may pass or announce himself as Ombre, allowing him to name the trump suit and to discard any cards he does not want and draw replacements from the pack. If he passes, the second player can announce himself as Ombre; if he passes, the third can. If all pass, the deal moves along to the next player.

Assuming that one player's announcement is made and stands, the others have the privilege of drawing from the pack as he did; and the last of the three can look at any leftover cards to see what the others missed. Play starts with the player on Ombre's right, who leads any card he wants, and the others must follow suit if they can; otherwise, they can discard or trump the trick. Highest card of suit led wins the trick unless trumped; in that case the highest trump wins. Play proceeds to the right, or counterclockwise. There is, however, an exception to the rule just given. The top three cards of trump are called *matadores* or "mats"; and a player holding one may renege— that is, refuse to play it—unless a higher mat is led and he has no other trump.

The matadores are known respectively as *spadille, manille,* and *basto;* when a red suit is trump, its ace (♡ A or ◇ A) is called *ponto* but is not classed as a "mat."

The game's purpose is this: Before cards are dealt, each player puts three counters or chips into a pool. If there is no Ombre on that deal, it moves along, with each player adding a chip. Whoever becomes Ombre must take more tricks than *either* foe; it is *sacardo* and he wins the pool. If Ombre is tied by either foe in tricks taken, he must double the pool for the next deal; this is called *puesta.* If either foe takes more tricks than Ombre, it is termed *codille;* and Ombre pays the player instead of the pool, which remains intact. If Ombre takes the first five tricks, he naturally scores *sacardo;* and play ends, unless he decides to go for *vole,* by taking all nine tricks. If he wins it, he collects half the amount of the pool from each foe; if he fails, he pays them instead. However, his *sacardo* still stands.

There is one important proviso in announcing oneself as Ombre, by stating, "I will play." Another player may override it by declaring in turn, "I will play *sans prendre,*" meaning that he will play as Ombre *without discarding.* However, the original announcer can override that by saying that he too is willing to be Ombre, with no discard. The game then proceeds on that basis. Other minor rulings may be introduced in Ombre.

OMNIBUS HEARTS: The modern form of *Hearts,* which includes any or all popular innovations. See *Hearts,* page 140.

ONE-CARD POKER: Known as *Lazy Lucy.* See page 258.

ONE-EYED JACKS or KING: A form of wild-card *Poker,* usually in conjunction with other wild games. See page 258.

OPEN GIN: A term covering the doubling feature in *Gin Rummy,* page 130.

OPEN POKER: See page 258.

OPTION: *Poker.* See page 258.

PA FERGUSON: Wild-card *Poker.* See page 258.

PAM-LOO: The modern development of *Five-Card Loo,* page 158, with Pam (♣ J) as highest trump. These holdings automatically win without any play, in the following order: Pam flush (♣ J with four of one suit) or Pam blaze (♣ J with four other face cards); trump flush (five trump cards); plain flush (five of one ordinary suit); blaze (five face cards). If two players tie, first on dealer's left wins.

PANGUINGUE Popularly Known as PAN: An elaboration of *Conquian,* page 71, played with half-a-dozen to a dozen packs of cards from which the tens, nines, and eights have been removed, so that the cards are ranked **K, Q, J, 7, 6, 5, 4, 3, 2, A.** The packs are shuffled together by as many as fifteen players, who keep trading clumps until they are thoroughly mixed and gathered into one huge pack, from which the dealer takes a batch and deals each player ten cards (usually two groups of five), utilizing further batches if required and replacing any leftovers on the pack. Originally, cards were dealt to the right, not the left; but that is optional today.

The purpose of the game is to meld sets and sequences, some of special value. Each player puts two chips into a pool, and if anyone is not satisfied with his hand, he can turn it down and drop from play. The dealer turns up the top card of the pack and lays it alongside to begin a discard pile. Each player in turn, with the exception of any who dropped out, draws either the top card of the pack or takes up the card showing on the discard pile. He may then make any melds he can, keeping such cards in front of him. After that, he discards an odd card from his hand, placing it on the discard pile as a new upcard.

This continues, with players melding and adding extra cards to their melds, until one player "goes out" with a total meld of eleven cards, which includes the one he just drew. If he can meld only ten cards, he still must discard the eleventh and continue to draw whenever his turn comes, in hope of adding a final card to his meld. The player just ahead of him is not allowed to make a discard that will enable the man with the ten-card meld to go out, unless that preceding player has no other discard.

Melds are of the following types:

Any sequence of three or more cards in the same suit, as ♠ J 7 6 or ♡ 7 6 5 4 3.

Three or more identical cards of the same value and suit, as ♡ 4 4 4 or ♣ 6 6 6 6 6 6.

Three or four cards of the same value, but each of a different suit, as ♠ 7, ♡ 7, ♣ 7 or ♡ 2, ♣ 2, ♠ 2, ◇ 2.

Three or more kings of any suits, as ♡ K, ♡ K, ◇ K; or

Three or more aces of any suits, as ◇ A, ◇ A, ♡ A, ♡ A.

Among the above are certain combinations known as "conditions," which, when melded by a player, entitle him to collect chips from each player except those who dropped out, as follows:

A "high" sequence, as ♡ K Q J, or a "low" sequence, as ♣ 3 2 A, one chip from each. If in spades, as ♠ K Q J, two chips. For each card added to such a sequence, one chip in ordinary suits, two chips in spades.

Any set of three identical cards, as ♡ Q Q Q, one chip. If in spades, as ♠ J J J, two chips. For each ordinary extra, one chip; spades, two chips.

If these sets are composed of threes, fives, or sevens, they are known as "valle cards," and the holder collects double for the original set of three, with one chip for each ordinary extra, two for each extra spade.

A set of three valle cards, with all different suits, one chip; for the fourth card of a different suit, one chip.

All conditions are paid off as they occur; hence a player making strong melds in spades may pile up a nice profit during the course of play. As for nonpaying melds, a player may "borrow" from those to make up other sequences or sets, which may be made into conditions. For example: A player melds ♡ Q, ♣ Q, ◇ Q, ♠ Q, a nonpaying meld. He holds the ♠ J and later draws the ♠ K. He promptly borrows the ♠ Q, leaving a legitimate meld of three queens (♡ Q, ♣ Q, ◇ Q) on the board, and adds the ♠ Q to the ♠ K and ♠ J, making a high sequence in spades, which brings him two chips from each opposing player. If he also held the ♠ 7, he could include that in the meld, as ♠ K Q J 7, and collect two more from each.

When a player goes out, he collects one chip from each of

the participating players, plus the pool contributed by the players who dropped out. He also collects again from each participating player for the conditions that he melded. The deal then moves on to the next player in rotation.

Special rulings are often used in pan. One is that a player can take the upcard from the discard pile only if he is able and willing to meld it. To prove that, he does not take the upcard into his hand, but lays the other meldable cards with it. Another such rule is that a card drawn from the pack must be melded in the same manner or discarded, never being taken into the hand, and that only such a discard may be taken by the next player, and then only toward a meld.

A player who can use the upcard as an addition to a meld is forced to do so if another player insists.

PAPILLON: A French forerunner of *Cassino*, very similar in play. See *Cassino,* page 57.

PARLIAMENT: The English form of *Fan-Tan,* following exactly the same rules with the exception that the ◊ **7** must be used for the opening play. See page 115.

PARTNERSHIP GAMES as *Canasta,* page 43, *Cassino,* page 57, *Euchre,* page 107, *Gin,* page 130, *Pinochle,* page 174, and various others will be found under general headings for such games.

PASS ALONG: *Poker.* See page 259.

PASS AND BACK IN: *Poker.* See page 259.

PASS ON HEARTS: Standard *Hearts,* page 140, incorporating the feature of passing cards along to the next player. Often used interchangeably with *Omnibus Hearts.*

PASS OUT: A form of *Draw Poker* in which a player must bet or drop. See *Bet or Drop,* page 244.

PASS THE GARBAGE or PASS THE TRASH: A wild-card

form of *Poker* in which players pass cards along. See page 259.

PATIENCE: An English term for games of *Solitaire*, page 320.

PEDRO: This covers developments of *Auction Pitch* (see *Pitch*, page 213), which include two interrelated features: Simplification of play, and additional points for various trump cards taken in play, as follows:

High, low, and jack count 1 point each, but low must be taken in play. The single point of game is represented by the ten of trump, thus eliminating any "counters." The five of trump, known as "pedro," scores 5 points when taken in play. Thus there are nine possible points in each deal, and a total of 21 is needed to win the game.

Pedro Sancho is the same game, but with the nine of trump, called "sancho," also scoring 9 points when taken in play, making a possible 14 points in each deal, with a total of 50 needed to win the game.

Dom Pedro includes the three of trump, called "dom" as a scoring card, for an additional 3 points, making a possible 17 in each deal. Usually the joker is added as an extra trump known as "snoozer," which ranks below the two but is not regarded as "low," and scores 15 points when taken in play. Since that makes a possible 32 points in each deal, a total of 100 is usually required to win the game.

Bidding is unrestricted in all forms of pedro, continuing until all players but the bidder have passed in succession. In "going out," points are counted in the order: high, low, jack, game (ten), dom, pedro, sancho, snoozer. Sometimes, by agreement, the single point for "game" is scored last. These depend on the type of pedro being played, and any that do not appear in the course of play are naturally not counted.

PEDRO: A *Poker* game. See page 259.

PEEK POKER: The original form of *Seven-Card Stud*. See page 229.

PEEP AND TURN: A name for *Mexican Seven-Card Stud*. See *Seven-Card Flip*, page 263.

PEEP NAP: *Napoleon*, page 163, with an odd card dealt face down as a "widow." Any player can peep at the card before passing or bidding if he contributes one chip to the pool. The widow goes to the highest bidder, who can then discard any card from his hand.

PENCHANT: A game similar to *Cinq Cent*, page 68.

PENNIES FROM HEAVEN: A name given to *Mexicana*, page 161, and other variants of *Canasta*.

PENNY ANTE: A form of *Poker*. See page 259.

PERSIAN PASHA: Another name for *Pisha Pasha*, page 214.

PERSIAN RUMMY: The partnership form of *Five Hundred Rummy*, page 295.

PIG: A juvenile game involving up to thirteen players, with sets of four cards of the same value, according to the number of players. Example: A pack for a five-player game could include four kings, four jacks, four tens, four sevens, four fives, making twenty cards in all. These are shuffled and four cards are dealt to each player, who pass cards to the left in unison, each picking up the card from the right and adding it to his hand. The first to match a set of four lays down his hand and makes an established signal, such as tapping his nose with his finger. Others must immediately lay down their hands and make the same signal; the last to do so is "pig" and loses the hand.

PIG IN POKE: Another name for *Wild Widow* in *Poker*.

PINK LADY: An extension of *Hearts,* with the ♡ **Q** or "pink lady" counting 13 points against the player taking it, like the ♠ **Q** or "black lady." See *Hearts,* page 143.

PINOCHLE: In its early form, pinochle was a two-handed trump game in which half the pack was dealt out and the remaining cards drawn progressively during the play. Later, other elements were incorporated into it, so it became practically a new game, which in turn produced striking offshoots. Auction pinochle is the most popular of these; but all forms of pinochle have two features in common, the special pack and a preliminary procedure termed a "meld." So those take priority, as follows:

The Pack: This contains forty-eight cards, with two of each value in each suit from aces down to nines, but with the ten ranking next to the ace. Hence their values run: **A, A, 10, 10, K, K, Q, Q, J, J, 9, 9.** Duplication of values creates no problem during play, as whichever is played first is regarded as higher than the one that follows.

The Meld: Before playing certain cards from his hand, a player is allowed to lay them face up on the table, thus "melding" them to form special combinations, which score as follows:

Trump Sequence **(A, 10, K, Q, J** of trump)	150
Royal Marriage **(K, Q** of trump)	40
Ordinary Marriage **(K, Q** of any suit)	20
Four Aces, all of different suits	100
Four Kings, all of different suits	80
Four Queens, all of different suits	60
Four Jacks, all of different suits	40
Pinochle, consisting of ♠ **Q** and ◊ **J**	40
Dix, pronounced *deece,* the 9 of trump	10

A card from one meld may be used with a meld of another type. Example: A player could meld ♡ **Q,** ◊ **Q,** ♠ **Q,** ♣ **Q** for 60 points; then add ♡ **K** to the ♡ **Q** and call it a marriage for 20 points, or 40 for a royal marriage if hearts happened to be trump. He could then add the ◊ J to the ♠ Q, scoring 40 for a pinochle; and he could even tack ♡ J, ♠ J, ♣ J onto the ◊ J and score 40 points for four jacks.

But he cannot meld the ♣ K and ♣ Q for a marriage and then add the other ♣ K to the same ♣ Q for another marriage, as bigamy is not legal even in pinochle. Nor, after melding a combination like ♠ A, ♣ A, ◊ A, ♡ A for 100 points, would it be allowable to add three other aces (as ♠ A, ♣ A, ◊ A) to an ace already melded and score another 100 points. For such a score, he would have to meld another complete set of aces; and the same applies to four kings, four queens, and four jacks.

A few special rules apply to melds according to the particular type of pinochle being played; these will be mentioned under their proper heads. In addition to points scored by melding, there are points that can be scored during play by taking tricks containing cards of certain value. There are three types of "count" used with such cards, as follows:

Original Count

Each ace,	11 points.	Each ten,	10 points.
Each king,	4 points.	Each queen,	3 points.
Each jack,	2 points.	Each nine,	0 points.

For taking last trick   10 points.

Simplified Count

Each ace, ten, or king, 10 points. No others count.

For taking last trick   10 points.

Modified Count

Each ace or ten, 10 points. Each king or queen, 5 points. No others count. For last trick, 10 points.

Note: In all types of "count," the total of the counters, including "last trick," comes to 250 points.

TWO-HANDED PINOCHLE: In this original form, utilizing the forty-eight-card pinochle pack, twelve cards are dealt to each player by threes or fours. The next card is turned face up to represent trump and the pack is laid face down across it, with the dealer giving himself 10 points on a score sheet, if the card is the dix, or nine of trump. The opponent leads whatever card he wants and the dealer places any card upon it, as at this stage of the game it is not necessary to follow suit or trump.

However, the highest card of the suit led wins the trick, unless trumped, which is important because the player winning the trick is allowed to make a single meld by laying the proper cards face up in front of him and its total is immediately entered in his column of the score sheet. If he holds a dix, he may meld it also, by placing it face up beneath the pack and taking the trump already there as a replacement in his hand. Whether or not he melds, the winner draws the top card from the pack, adding it to his hand; and the loser draws the next card, to maintain his quota of twelve.

The winner of the trick leads to the next trick; either from his hand or his meld, and play continues in this fashion. A new meld may be made by the winner of a trick, and it may include cards that he already melded, but only if he adds a fresh card from his hand. For example, if he should meld four queens for 60 and later meld four jacks for 40, he could not simply point to the ♠ Q and ◊ J and call the combination a "pinochle" for 40. The proper way would be to first place the ◊ J with the ♠ Q, scoring 40; then later add the three remaining jacks to the ◊ J for the other 40. However, if a player melds a royal marriage— as ◊ K Q, with diamonds as trump—he can later meld the ◊ A 10 J as additional cards for a trump sequence of 150, over and above the 40 gained for the royal marriage.

This goes on until all cards have been drawn from the pack, with the face-up dix being the last taken into the hand of the player who lost the twelfth trick. From then on, the hands are simply played out, with the winner of each trick leading to the next, but during this phase, a player must follow suit if he can; if not, he must trump, if he can; and if a trump is led, he must play a higher trump if he can. Originally, a player was required to play a higher card to a plain suit led, if possible; but this rule, though still optional, is seldom used by modern players.

A running score of melds is kept during play and at the finish of the hand, each player adds his counter, using the "original count" (A=11, 10=10, K=4, Q=3, J=2) with 10 for last trick. This is added to his total; and the deal moves to the other player. The game continues, with 1000 points as the objective; and during play, a player may announce that he has reached 1000. Play then stops, and if he has actually taken sufficient counters, he wins; but if he overestimated his take and is short, he loses.

If both players go over 1000, play is continued with 1250 as the goal, or 1500 if both pass that mark; and so on. In some circles, a player is not allowed to "call out," in which case the hand is played to the finish and the player with the higher final score is winner.

Special Melds in *Two-Handed Pinochle:*

Originally, a player who melded a *pinochle* (◇ J ♠ Q) for 40 points could later add another pinochle to it and call the combined meld a *double pinochle* (◇ J J ♠ Q Q) for 80 points, making 120 in all. This rule is seldom used today, but in many circles a player holding a *double pinochle* (◇ J J ♠ Q Q) is allowed to meld it as a unit for 80 points instead of being forced to make two melds of single pinochles.

Similarly, in many circles, a player may combine a *spade marriage* (♠ K Q) with a pinochle (♠ Q ◇ J) as an individual meld (♠ K Q ◇ J) for 60 points, or 80 if spades happen to be trump. This combination was once termed *grand pinochle* and counted for 80, whether or not spades were trump. Both combinations, *double pinochle* for 80 and *grand pinochle* for 60 or 80, are recommended, as they enable a player to meld more rapidly, which is an important adjunct in this game. However, they should be specified beforehand.

AUCTION PINOCHLE: *The Pack:* The standard forty-eight-card pinochle pack.

Number of Players: Three, four, or five, but only three are active in each deal. With four, the dealer stays out; with five, the dealer and the player to his left stay out. Since the deal moves to the left, each "extra" player becomes active in rotation.

The Deal: Fifteen cards to each active player; three rounds of four cards each, with an odd round of three; or simply by threes. At the end of the first round, three cards are dealt aside as a "widow."

Bidding: After looking at their hands, the active players, beginning from the dealer's left, begin bidding the number of points that each thinks or hopes his hand can take. This is termed an "auction," as each player may increase his bid if an opponent bids higher. If a player wishes he can "pass" and drop out of the bidding; when only one bidder remains, his bid stands. If all pass to start, the hand is abandoned and the deal goes to the next player.

Usually, 250 is decided upon as the minimum opening bid, though a player can go higher if he wants. Some groups prefer 300 as their minimum. Bids are increased by 10 points or more; here, again, a bid may be jumped to any height. The highest bidder has the privilege of naming the trump suit; hence bids are based on the hand's potential meld and the probable number of counters that it can take during the play that follows.

Note this hand as a bidding sample:

♣ A A 10 K Q   ♡ A K Q   ◇ K Q J   ♠ A 10 10 Q

Figuring on clubs as trump, this hand can meld 40 for a royal marriage (♣ K Q), 40 for two ordinary marriages (♡ K Q and ◇ K Q), 60 for four queens (each of a different suit), and 40 for a pinochle (◇ J and ♠ Q), which adds up to 40+40+60+40=180. In play, it should be good for 80 points or better, so it is definitely worth a 250 opening bid; and if someone else should open at 250, this hand could go to 260 or even 270. Many players would regard this as an almost sure 300 opener, as the bidder has the privilege of:

Turning up the Widow: Before melding, the highest bidder turns the three widow cards face up, then adds them to his hand in order to improve its meld or playing strength. He then discards any three cards face down and proceeds to meld. When play begins, he adds the discard to whatever tricks he takes. Usually, a bidder can depend on a few points from the widow.

For example, with the hand given above: Assume the bidder turns up ♣ 9, ♡ A, ◊ K. The ♣ 9 (dix) adds 10 points to his meld; the ♡ A is a sure trick and is a "counter" in itself; he can discard ♠ 10, ♠ 10, and the unneeded ◊ K that he drew, all three being counters that will help his score during play.

However, with many hands, the widow represents much greater possibilities on which keen bidders often bank. Our sample hand is a fine example, because it offers three chances for a "fill," which would enable the player to jump the bid to as high as 400.

(1) If the widow contains the ♣ J, it will give the hand a sequence or run in trump (♣ A, 10, K, Q, J) for 150 points. He will lose the 40 points for royal marriage (♣ K Q) as in auction pinochle; it is considered simply as part of the sequence; but he gains 110 points in all.

(2) If the widow contains ◊ A, it will give the hand four aces (of different suits) for 100 points and help its playing strength.

(3) If the widow contains ♠ K, it will give the hand four kings (of different suits) for 80 points and a spade marriage (♠ K Q) for 20 points, a total of 100 points.

Note: In that case the hand would have four kings and four queens, which is termed a "roundhouse" and rates as a special meld of 240 points in auction pinochle, reducing to 200 if the hand also has a trump sequence, which eliminates the royal marriage from the roundhouse.

The fact that a bidder does not have to name the trump suit until after he turns up the widow is also a great advantage, as shown by the following example:

♠ A 10 Q J   ♡ A 10 K J   ♣ A 10 Q J   ◊ A J 9

This hand has four aces for 100, four jacks for 40, and a pinochle (♠ Q ◊ J) for 40, a total of 100+40+40=180. With an estimated playing strength of about 80, it is a sure 250 opener. But it hasn't a single marriage, nor any chance for four kings or four queens. Still, any keen player would bid 400 with it.

Why? Because there are three possible fills for a trump sequence of 150; namely, the ♠ K, ♡ Q, ♣ K. If one of those should turn up in the widow, the bidder would simply declare its suit as trump and become a 400 winner.

In contrast, such glittering snares as the following should be avoided:

◇ 10 10 K K Q J 9 9 ♠ A A Q ♡ A A ♣ A J

This hand holds a royal marriage (◇ K Q) for 40, two "deeces" (◇ 9 9) for 20, and a pinochle (◇ J ♠ Q) for 40, making a total of 40+20+40=100. But look at what just *one* key card, the ◇ A, will do! It will give the bidder 150 for a diamond sequence and 100 for four aces. Add 10 for each dix, 40 for the pinochle, and the meld alone is 310, while in play, by forcing the opposing trump ace, 190 more points are assured for a grand total of 500.

A fine hand, if there is a ◇ A in the widow, but with only that one possible fill, the chances are about five to one that it won't be there. At least two possible fills are needed to bid beyond what the hand already shows; and three possibilities are needed for a must bid.

Only the highest bidder makes a meld in auction pinochle. No matter what the other players hold, it does not count. They are not allowed to show any of their cards; while the bidder shows only the turned-up widow and the cards that he melds.

Playing the Hand: The bidder, after discarding, takes his melded cards into his hand and leads to the first trick with any card he wants. The two other players follow suit in clockwise order. If a player is out of suit, he must play a trump card if he has one; if not, he discards from another suit. If a trump is led, the next player must play a higher trump if he has one; and the third player must go still higher if he can.

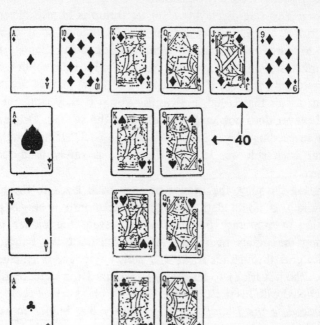

AUCTION PINOCHLE

This hand has the highest possible meld in auction pinochle, consisting of sequence with dix (160), four aces (100), four kings (80), four queens (60), three marriages (60), and a pinochle (40), for a total of 500.

In play, however, the hand is weak. Even if the player can discard three top spades, **A, 10, 10**, as shown, for 30 points (simplified count), he will be lucky to pick up more than 100 points in play, making this about a 600 hand—or perhaps 650 at best.

Otherwise, a lower trump is played; and if out of trump, the player discards from any other suit.

Note: This rule of playing a higher trump is termed "heading the trick," and it is very helpful to the bidder, as it enables him to force high trumps from the opposing hands, thus making his lower trumps sure winners. The rule applies only when trumps are led; if the second and third players are both out of a suit that is led, both must trump if they can, but the third player does not have to overtrump the second. Originally, each succeeding player had to "head the trick" if he could, no matter what suit was led, but that rule is rarely used today, if ever.

During the play, the winner of each trick leads to the next; and the two nonbidders pool their tricks into a single pile, forming a temporary partnership to prevent the bidder from making the points he needs. At the finish of the hand, the bidder goes through his tricks and adds any counters (including 10 for the last trick) to his meld. His discard (as stated earlier) is included with his trick pile.

Conceding the Hand: Often, a conservative bidder turns up enough favorable cards in the widow to increase his meld to the amount of his bid, or to come so close that he is sure to make the few additional points needed in play. In that case, the opposing players, by mutual agreement, can concede the hand to the bidder without going through the formality of playing it out.

Conversely, if the bidder fails to turn up cards that he needs to make his bid, or if he feels that his hand lacks enough playing strength to take the counters that he requires over and above his meld, he may concede the hand to his opponents before starting play. This option on the bidder's part has a special bearing on:

Scoring the Hand: In auction pinochle, each hand or deal is a game in itself, and the simplest way to settle it is with tokens or chips. In the basic scoring method, the bidder wins one chip from each of the other players if he bids 250 and makes it; two chips each, if he bids 300 and makes it; three chips each for 350; and upward in the same ratio. These scoring brackets are shown in Column A below; other systems, mostly involving "steeper" jumps, appear in the other lettered columns:

		Scoring Systems					
Brackets	A	B	C	D	E	F	G
250–90	1	2	1	–	–	1*	–
300–40	2	3	2	1	1	3	3
350–90	3	4	4	2	3	5	5
400–40	4	5	6	4	7	10	10
450–90	5	6	8	6	10	15	20
500–40	6	7	10	8	13	20	40
550–90	7	8	12	10	16	25	80
600 and Up	8	9	14	12	19	30	160

* When playing with 250 as a minimum bid.

However, if the bidder sees that play is useless and concedes the hand as being lost, each of the other players collects from him on the same terms. If he decides to play the hand out and loses, he must pay double to the others. Thus, if scoring by the basic method, a player bidding 370 and making it would collect three tokens from each opponent; if he should concede the hand, he would pay them three each; and if he should play and lose, six tokens each.

When there are four or five players in the game, those who are inactive during the hand still participate in the settlement, paying the bidder if he wins and collecting from him if he concedes or loses.

Pinochle can be scored with paper and pencil by giving each player a column and marking him plus (+) or minus (−) for each hand. Here is an example, using System C, with three players (*X, Y,* and *Z*) in the game:

	X	Y	Z	
First Hand	−4	+8	−4	*Y* bids 360. Makes it.
Second Hand	−8	+10	−2	*X* bids 320. Concedes.
Third Hand	−10	+8	+2	*Z* bids 330. Makes it.
Fourth Hand	+2	−16	+14	*Y* bids 400. Plays and loses.

AUCTION PINOCHLE

Here is what many auction pinochle players would regard as the "perfect hand." Its meld of two sequences, each with a dix (160+160), with four aces (100), comes to only 420 points, but no matter how it is played, it will bring in all the counters for 250 points, making a total of 670.

When score is kept in this manner, settlement can be made after playing a specified number of hands or at the end of a designated time.

Spades Double: When a bidder declares spades as his trump suit, he collects double if he wins the hand; hence if he plays and loses, he must pay each player four times the usual number of tokens. However, if he concedes the hand, he only pays the single amount to each opponent, since his declaration of trump is abandoned along with the hand itself.

This is now an established rule of auction pinochle and is a very important feature because of the impetus it gives to the bidding. A player who holds a spade sequence or has a good chance of filling one, will naturally take greater risks in bidding, since he stands to win twice as much if he can make his points or if the widow holds a key card; while if he fails, he can concede the hand with only a single loss.

Hearts Triple: To stimulate the bidding still further, the players, by agreement beforehand, can count hearts (or some other chosen suit) as paying triple, but still with the privilege of conceding the hand and taking a loss of the amount bid. If the bidder plays out such a hand and loses, he has to pay six times the ordinary amount. In many circles, "hearts triple" is classed as too "wild" or freakish, hence it is not an established rule of pinochle.

Playing with a Kitty: When playing with chips or tokens, the game can be stepped up by forming a pool called the "kitty," to which all players contribute equally at the outset. The player at the dealer's left is required to bid 300 no matter how poor his hand may be; and if the other two players pass, he is allowed to drop without turning up the widow. In that case, he must pay the kitty the amount of a 300 bid (according to the schedule used), but he does not pay anything to the other players.

On all other bids, where the bidder naturally turns up the widow, the kitty functions as an extra player where settlements are concerned, collecting the regular amount if the bidder loses and paying him if he wins. Any time the kitty runs short, the players must "feed" it an equal amount to make up the deficit and provide it with further funds.

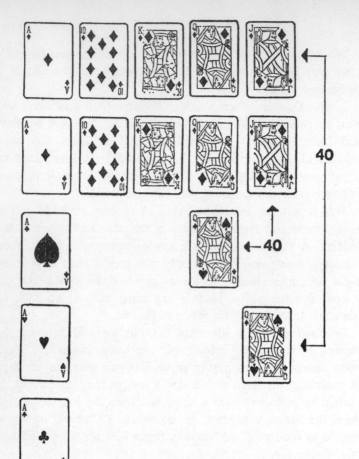

AUCTION PINOCHLE

This auction pinochle hand tops those previously shown. Its two sequences (150+150), four aces (100), and a double pinochle (80), come to 480. If the player can discard three top spades (A, 10, 10) for 30 points, he has simply to lead with trumps and he can be sure of 210 points in play, for a total of 690. If one opponent holds ♠ K, ♠ K, with no other spades, the hand will take 230 for 710; and if the opponent discards both kings during play (preferring to hold cards in other suits), the hand will take 250 in play, hitting a high of 730.

If any player leaves the game, the kitty pool is divided equally among those who remain, and a new pool is immediately provided by those players and any newcomers. At the end of the game, a final division is made on the same equal basis. Various optional rules may apply to the kitty, one of the best being to have the kitty collect from all losing bidders, but never pay off a winner unless the bid is higher than 350. This helps to feed the kitty and at the same time spurs the bidders to greater risks.

THREE-HANDED PINOCHLE: This is the game from which *Auction Pinochle*, page 177, is derived, and is still popular in modernized form, as follows:

The entire pack is dealt by fours, giving sixteen cards to each of the three players, there being no widow in this game. The final card is turned face up to represent trump. Beginning with the first player on the dealer's left, whoever holds a dix (the nine of trump) is temporarily credited with 10 points by exchanging the dix for the turned-up trump, which then goes into his hand, while the dealer's hand retains the dix. All players then meld and each is credited according to the established trump. For example:

Suppose that the ♢ K is turned up as trump and that the three players, *X*, *Y*, and *Z* (the dealer), hold these cards:

X: ♢ A A K Q Q J   ♣ 10   ♡ A 10 K Q J 9   ♠ 10 Q Q
Y: ♢ 10 J 9   ♣ K Q J 9   ♡ 10 K Q J   ♠ 10 J J 9 9
Z: ♢ 10 K 9   ♣ A A 10 K Q J 9   ♡ A 9   ♠ A A K K

Since Player *Y* has the first dix (♢ 9), he gives it to Player *Z* and takes the turned-up ♢ K in return, scoring a tentative 10 points. The ♢ K does not help *Y*'s meld, however, as he has nothing to go with it. The melds are as follows:

X: ♢ K Q, 40 (royal marriage). ♡ K, Q, 20 (marriage).
    ♢ J, ♠ Q, 40 (pinochle). Total, 100.

   Y: ◊ J, ♣ J, ♡ J, ♠ J, 40 (four jacks). ♣ K, Q, 20
      (marriage).
      ♡ K Q, 20 (marriage). Dix (exchanged for ♣ K) 10.
      Total, 90.
   Z: ♣ K Q, 20 (marriage). Dix (◊ 9) from deal, 10. Total, 30.

Note that *X* holds a sequence **(A, 10, K, Q, J)** in hearts
and that *Z* holds the same in clubs, but that neither of those
runs can be counted because a diamond was turned up as
trump.

Play begins at the dealer's left and proceeds exactly as in
auction pinochle. Highest card of suit led wins the trick unless
trumped; if out of suit, a player must trump; when trump is
led, each succeeding player must play a higher trump if he
can. Counters are added to each player's score (according to
the type of count used), with 10 points going to the player
taking last trick. Here, an important rule should be noted,
namely:

If a player fails to take any tricks, he scores zero for that
hand, his meld being wiped out along with it. In the hand
shown above, *Y*'s holding is so weak that he would be in
danger of going trickless if *X* and *Z* should guess his plight
and combine their play to "blank" him. But two players seldom
gang up on a third in three-handed pinochle unless he is so
far ahead that drastic measures must be taken to keep him
from reaching 1000 points, which wins the game in three-
handed pinochle.

Scoring the Game: In each hand, the counters won in play
are added to each player's meld as his score for the hand. The
deal moves to the left, a new hand is played and scored. This
continues until one player reaches or passes 1000, thus becoming the winner.

There are two options here: Originally a player was allowed
to declare "out" after taking sufficient points in play to reach
1000. A more modern rule is that the hand must be completed,
and if more than one player goes over 1000, the game continues with 1250 as the goal. If two players pass that mark in
the same hand, it goes on to 1500, then to 1750, and so on

if required. This should be specified before play begins, as with all options.

Four-handed Pinochle can be played in the same way, with each player on his own, but receiving only twelve cards in the deal. This reduces the melds proportionately and at the same time increases the chance of a player being blanked with a weak hand, as he is faced by three opponents instead of two and there are four less tricks in the deal. As a result, this game promises plenty of competition before the chief contenders approach the 1000 mark. However, when four players are in the game, they usually prefer the more modern form of "partnership pinochle," which will be described under its own head.

PARTNERSHIP PINOCHLE : Basically, this game is almost the same as three-handed or four-handed pinochle, the main difference being that the players seated opposite are partners. Thus, if we term them *A, B, C, D* in clockwise rotation, with *D* representing the dealer, players *A* and *C* would be teamed against players *B* and *D*.

Cards are dealt by fours, giving each player twelve cards, and the final card is turned up for trump, with the first player who holds a dix claiming the turned-up trump and scoring 10 points for the exchange, as in the three-handed game. Players then meld individually, but in this case their melds go to a team score. For example, with spades as trump:

A melds: ◇ J, ♠ Q, 40 (pinochle). Total 40.
B melds: ♠ K Q, 40 (royal marriage). Dix (exchanged) 10. Total 50.
C melds: ♠ K, ♡ K, ♣ K, ◇ K, 80 (four kings) with ♡ Q, ♣ Q, ◇ Q, 60 (three marriages at 20 each) Dix, 10. Total 150.
D melds: ♠ J, ♡ J, ♣ J, ◇ J, 40 (four jacks). Total 40.

Note that *A* cannot put his meld with that of his partner, *C,* to add 40 more points for a royal marriage (♠ K Q) and 60 more for four queens, or, in other words, a roundhouse.

THREE-HAND PINOCHLE

Many pinochle experts overlook the high-scoring possibilities in the old three-handed game, due to the sixteenth card that a player receives. Here is a hand so nearly perfect that it is practically sure of 750. Its meld consists of two sequences (150+150) and eight aces (100+100) for a total of 500. By leading any two trumps, the player can then take all 250 points in play for his 750.

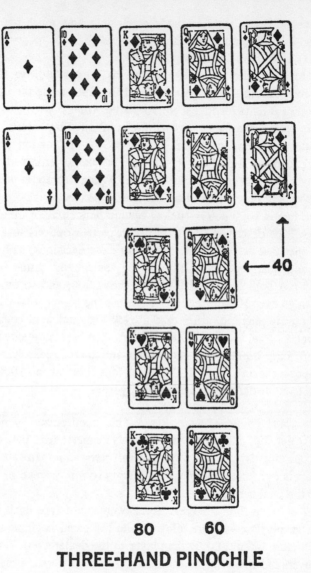

THREE-HAND PINOCHLE

Here is a sixteen-card hand that is high in meld but disappointing in play. With two sequences (150+150), four kings (80), four queens (60), three marriages (60), and a pinochle (40) it hits a total meld of 540. But it can leaves only 100 for the player holding the hand, which is therefore worth a 640 and no more.

Each partner's meld is made separately and must remain so. Similarly, *B* cannot use the ◊ **J** melded by *D* to go with the ♠ **Q** as 40 points for pinochle.

However, the melds are added as they stand, so that the team of *A* and *C* would score 40+150=190; while the opposing team of *B* and *D* would score 50+40=90.

In play, the same procedure applies. Play starts at the dealer's left and continues clockwise. As in auction pinochle, high card of suit led wins the trick, unless trumped; and a player must trump if out of suit. When trump is led, each succeeding player must head the trick if he can.

Game is 1000 points (unless certain *bonus melds* are allowed, as will be described later), but with certain options that should be specified beforehand to settle any close decisions; namely: (a) If both teams go over 1000 in the same hand, game becomes 1250; if both go over that, 1500; then 2000; and so on. (b) If both go over 1000, whichever team has the higher total wins. (c) If, during play, one team take a trick with sufficient counters to bring its total score to 1000, the two members may agree to declare out, winning the game then and there, regardless of the opposing team's score. If the count falls short of the 1000 mark, the team declaring out automatically loses.

Partnership Pinochle with Bids: This modernized version of "partnership pinochle" has largely superseded the original game and is played with several variations. In all forms, players bid for the privilege of naming trump, instead of turning up the final card dealt.

The "One Bid" Version: Here, twelve cards are dealt to each of the players, who are allowed one bid each, beginning with a minimum bid of 100 by the player at the dealer's left. Naturally, players bid according to the strength of their possible melds and the number of counters they expect to take. Melds and score follow the partnership procedure, but with this proviso:

If the bidder's team fails to make its bid, it loses its meld and the amount of bid is deducted from the team's score, putting the team in the minus column if need be.

If the bidder's team makes its bid, it is credited with the full amount that it scores in melds and counters. The bidding team's score is always listed first; hence if both teams go over the 1000 mark in the same deal, the team that made the bid is the winner.

"Auction" bidding is a more popular procedure in which players can continue to raise the bid, usually by amounts of ten or more, but once a player passes, he cannot re-enter the bidding, though his partner is free to continue unless he has also passed. In both versions, the lead ordinarily is made by the player at the dealer's left, but the modern trend is to have the bidder lead, as this encourages higher bidding because of the advantage thus gained. This rule, if used, should be specified before the start of the game.

Auction with Widow: Only eleven cards are dealt to each player, the best procedure being to deal them singly, laying aside a fifth card for a "widow" of four cards; from then on, the deal continues singly with each player.

Bidding proceeds as usual and the highest bidder turns up the widow and adds it to his hand before naming trump, unless he prefers to start melding then and there. Trump must be named, however, before other players meld. After the dealer has melded, he discards four cards face down, these being included with his team's tricks so that any "buried" counters are added to the team's score.

As with three-handed auction pinochle, page 177, the generally accepted procedure is for the bidder to lead to the first trick, although the old rule of opening on the dealer's left is allowable by agreement. (See "Playing the Hand," page 180.)

Variation with Widow: Here, the highest bidder is the only person who looks at the widow. He keeps one card for himself and hands each of the other players a single card face down. He then names the trump, melds are made, and play follows, each player having twelve cards.

This does not deter high bidding, as a sound bidder never needs more than one key card from the widow to "fill" his hand; hence others, though helpful, are really superfluous.

Often, he can give his partner a card that may increase the latter's meld, while handing worthless cards (as nines) to the opponents.

Bonus Melds: Special bonus melds are frequently used in partnership pinochle. These must appear in an individual hand and score as follows:

Double sequence (A, A, 10, 10, K, K, Q, Q, J, J of trump)　1500

Eight aces	1000	Eight queens	600
Eight kings	800	Eight jacks	400
Double pinochle (◊ J, ◊ J, ♠ Q, ♠ Q)		300	

When these are used, game should be at least 3000, but preferably 5000 or even more, by agreement. It would be ridiculous to play for only 1000 when one player's hand might meld more than that amount at the very start, though this seldom happens.

Informative Bidding in Partnership Pinochle: Special bids can be introduced in partnership pinochle, to inform a partner how to bid. In a game where each player is limited to a single bid, the simplest procedure is for A, the first player, to evaluate his hand and bid an *even figure,* as 200, 240, 280, unless he holds a sequence (A, 10, K, Q, J) in one suit. In that case, he bids an *odd figure* of 270 or higher, telling his partner, C, to pass, so that A can take the bid and name the trump. However, if C also has a sequence and thinks his hand is stronger than A's he naturally can bid higher.

The opposing team can bid on the same basis, with B naming an *even figure* to overbid A, or bidding an *odd figure* (270 or higher) so that his partner, D, will know that B has a sequence enabling D to pass or bid accordingly.

With a Continuous Auction: Here, the first bidder, A, can make a minimum bid of 100 to indicate that he has no meld. If he has a meld, he adds it to the minimum, bidding 120 if he holds a simple marriage (20); 140 if he holds a pinochle (40); 160 if he holds both (20+40); and so on. This tells C the exact amount of A's meld, so that C can raise by the amount of his

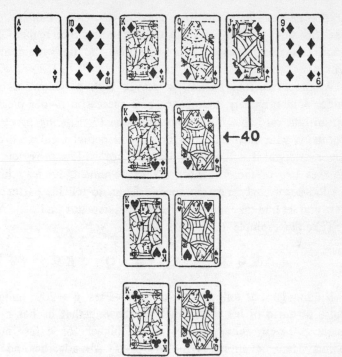

FOUR-HAND PINOCHLE

Here is a twelve-card hand in partnership pinochle that melds sequence and dix (160), four kings (80), four queens (60), three marriages (60), and a pinochle (40) for a total of 400. Give the player's partner an identical hand and they will meld 800 together. However, the hands are sure of only 100 points in play, for a total of 900.

own meld, plus any special playing strength. *A* can then pass or bid higher if he sees fit.

The *even* and *odd* form of bidding applies in this case also, but a special exception may be included, particularly where the opposing bidders are concerned. Suppose that *A* opens with a bid of 180, telling *C* that he has 80 points in meld. *B*, the first opposing bidder, either has a meld of 160 with a strong playing hand, or a 180 meld that equals *A*'s. Rather than pass, as if he had a "nothing" hand, *B* could bid 190, telling his partner,

D, that he has a hand almost as good as A's. Other bidders may use this same device, with the understanding that a mere 10-point raise from even to odd has nothing to do with naming trump.

When partnership auction is played with a widow, a new factor enters; namely, the chance of a successful bidder picking up an odd card that fills an important meld. Bidding proceeds normally, with each bidder signifying his actual meld until one becomes stymied and studies his hand for widow prospects. If he sees two or more chances for improvement, he may jump his bid accordingly, naming an *odd* figure to tell his partner to pass and let him take the widow as his bid depends on it.

Take this example. Player A holds:

♣ A K Q Q J ♡ A K ♠ A Q ◇ K 9

Bidding goes as follows: A—140. B—Pass. C—200, indicating a 60 meld of his own, D—310, showing that he has a sequence, thereby telling B not to bid higher for a few more points. Here, A appraises his prospects. Already, he and his partner have a combined meld of 100. With clubs trump, A is strong enough to take the majority of the counters, which means 130 more, a sure total of 250.

Now for his prospects of a fill. If he finds the ♠ K in the widow, he will gain 100 points for four kings (80) and a plain marriage (20). If the ◇ A is there, he will pick up 100 for four aces. If he gets the ♣ 10, it will mean 150 for a trump sequence less 40 for the royal marriage that will be absorbed, or a gain of 110. Counting on one of these three chances, A jumps his bid to 350. So his partner, C, passes, unless he should have still better widow prospects of his own, then he could bid 370, or a higher odd figure. Too, there is a chance that the opponent, D, may jump his solid bid of 310 to speculative heights.

Other conventional bids have been injected into partnership pinochle. One of the simplest is to set a specific figure—say 250—to represent a hand that has four aces, but little or nothing else in way of a meld. If this is used as an opener, particularly in the single-bid game, it is an invitation for the bidder's partner to go higher and name the trump, as four aces are worth 100 as a meld and should easily help a team score 160 or more in play, in connection with a long trump suit.

In some circles, bidding values are allotted to sequences in specific suits, as spades, 260; hearts, 270; clubs, 280; diamonds, 290. Such a tip-off enables the partner to go the limit with a bid of his own, as he can name the original bidder's trump and can often lead into it. Of course, the original bidder can still go higher, after sounding out his partner's reaction. All such informatory bidding should be agreed upon by both teams, beforehand.

FIREHOUSE PINOCHLE: This form of partnership pinochle follows the "one bid" version, but with informative bids established for every level from 200 to 300 inclusive. These apply only to the first two players, A and B, as their respective partners, C and D, are naturally free to go to the limit on the strength of the information given.

A typical bidding schedule runs:

A hand of little or no value: Pass or bid	200
A strong trump suit, but less than 60 meld:	210
A meld from 60 to 120 (without four aces):	220
A similar hand but with a strong trump suit:	230
A meld from 140 to 220 (without four aces):	240
A meld of four aces (100) and maybe 20 more:	250
A meld of four aces (100) with strong trump:	260
A meld of four aces (100) with 40 or 60 more:	270
A meld of four aces (100) with 80 more:	280
A roundhouse or another meld of 240 or more:	290
Any hand containing a trump sequence:	300+

(Here, a sequence with little else would be worth only the 300 minimum, with higher bids according to additional melds and extra playing strength, based on the premise that the bidder

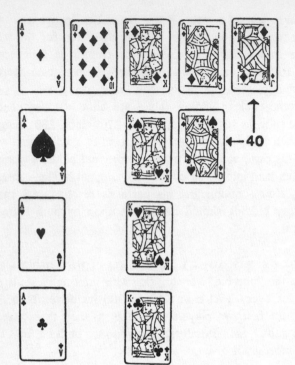

FOUR-HAND PINOCHLE

This partnership hand melds a sequence (150), four aces (100), four kings (80), a marriage (20), and a pinochle (40) for a total of 390. Give the partner the same holding and they will have 780 between them. In play, however, they can take every trick but one, losing only 20 counters when each plays his ♠ Q. So the hands are worth a phenomenal 1010!

(*A* or *B*) must make the final bid in order to name the trump suit and thus cash in his 150-point sequence.)

In this game, if the first three players pass, the dealer, *D*, is forced to bid 200. So the first player, *A*, will normally pass on a poor hand, hoping the dealer will have to take it. In contrast, *B*, the second player, will usually bid 200 on anything, thus informing his partner, *D*, that he has little to offer and at the same time giving *D* a chance to bow out if he feels that his own hand may be worse. This is like giving information in reverse. Otherwise, the game follows the accepted rules of partnership pinochle.

CHECK PINOCHLE: A development of firehouse pinochle which includes auction bidding and special rules peculiar to itself. Each team is provided with "checks" in the form of chips or counters, and after each melds, one side collects from the other according to the following melds:

Trump sequence, four checks; four aces, two checks; four kings, queens, or jacks, one check; roundhouse (four kings and four queens), five checks; double pinochle (♠ Q Q ◊ J J), two checks. If a team fails to make its bid, it must pay these back.

The high bidder leads, and if the bidding team wins, it collects from the losers as follows: For a bid of 200 and up, two checks; 250, four checks; 300, seven checks; 350, ten checks; 400, fifteen checks; 450, twenty checks; 500, twenty-five checks; and so on, five more checks for each 50 points. However, if a team loses its bid, the opponents collect twice the number of checks specified at the bidding level.

A team collects additional checks, as follows: Five checks for winning all twelve tricks in the hand; four checks for winning less than twelve tricks but taking all 250 counters; ten checks for winning game of 1000 points; plus one check for each 100-point margin over the losing team; and five checks if losers have a minus score. At the end of a hand, each team scores its meld plus points taken in play and applies them toward game, except that if the bidding team fails to make its bid, it loses its meld and playing count and is set back the exact amount that it bid.

A special bidding rule applies in check pinochle, namely, that a player cannot bid unless he holds a marriage, but if the first three players pass, the dealer must bid the usual 200 minimum. Originally, he could bid no higher without a marriage, but that rule has been modified, allowing the dealer to go as high as he wants when forced to bid 200. Thus if A, B, and C pass, and the dealer, D, finds himself with four aces

(100) and a strong trump but no marriage, he could easily bid 250, in order to collect four checks at the 250 level, instead of only two checks for a bid of 200.

An important penalty rule should be noted here: After the meld, if any player who participated in the bidding fails to show a marriage, the opposing team can demand redress because of the illegal bid, which naturally could have affected the entire bidding procedure. The simplest action is for the opposing team to call for another deal, particularly if they have poor hands. Instead, they can take the bid themselves, at either the highest or the lowest level that they bid, or they can demand that the offending opponents take the bid at the highest level that it named.

Bidding conventions vary because of the marriage requirement and the unlimited auction. If two partners each have a marriage but little else, they can bid upward by degrees, but naturally won't go very high. If the first bidder has a strong hand, he may do well to go the limit, as in the single-bid game, rather than restrict himself to a low, unprofitable level, if the rest pass, including his partner, who may lack a marriage and therefore have to pass.

Bids of 250 to signify four aces, 290 for a roundhouse, 300 or higher for a trump sequence are accepted openers; but some groups have more exacting conventions and any group is free to adopt its own. The simplest response to any opening bid is to raise it a mere 10 points; this shows that the responder has the required marriage but generally not much else. It also gives the original bidder a chance to keep the bidding open with another 10-point raise, or go as much higher as he judges his hand is worth.

A jump response to show a strong meld is also a popular procedure, such as a raise of 100 to show four kings (80) and the marriage (20); or 120 to show four aces (100) and the marriage (20). Here, the *odd-figure* bid, as described under *Informative Bidding in Partnership Pinochle,* page 194, can be used, beginning with the 310 level, to inform a partner that the bidder has a sequence or so strong a suit that he must take the bid to name the trump.

Note: A sequence fulfills the marriage requirement of this game, as a meld of 150 for a trump sequence includes the king and queen that would otherwise be melded as a plain marriage.

SIX-HANDED PARTNERSHIP PINOCHLE: An exciting modern form of partnership pinochle with six players forming three teams of two each, those seated opposite acting as partners. A double pack of ninety-six cards is used, so in the simple game, in which the final card is turned up as trump, each player is dealt sixteen cards. That not only gives a player more cards that may prove meldable; it increases the frequency of "double" melds and allows multiple melds in the form of "triples" and in some instances "quadruples." These are scored according to the schedule given below.

The pack is dealt by fours and the last card is turned up as trump and given to the first player on the dealer's left who holds a dix, or nine of trump. That player scores 10 and gives the dix to the dealer instead. However, if the dealer turns up a dix, he automatically scores the 10 points himself. All players meld separately, but the members of each team add their melds, as in the usual partnership game. However:

Since there are three teams, play follows the procedure of three-handed pinochle, page 187, with each team playing as an individual. Since there are twice as many counters in the double pack, 480 points can be taken in play, with 10 for the last trick, making a total of 490. Modern players frequently count the last trick as 20, making a total of 500, so that should be settled by agreement beforehand.

Game should be set at 3000 or higher (as 4500 or 6000) to allow for both the heavier melding and the frequent bonus melds, as well as the extra points scored in each deal.

SIX-HANDED PARTNERSHIP WITH BIDS: This more popular version follows the pattern just described, but instead of turning up trump, players bid for the privilege of naming it,

MELDS IN SIX- & EIGHT-HANDED PINOCHLE
(WITH NINETY-SIX-CARD PACK)

Trump Sequence (**A, 10, K, Q, J** of trump)		150
Double Sequence 1500	*Triple Sequence*	3000
Royal Marriage (**K, Q** of trump)		40
Double 300	*Triple* 600	*Quadruple* 1200
Ordinary Marriage (**K, Q** of any suit)		20
Double 300	*Triple* 600	*Quadruple* 1200
Four Aces (one each in ♠ ♡ ◊ ♣)		100
Eight Aces 1000	*Twelve* 2000	*Sixteen* 3000
Four Kings (one each in ♠ ♡ ◊ ♣)		80
Eight Kings 800	*Twelve* 1600	*Sixteen* 2400
Four Queens (one each in ♠ ♡ ◊ ♣)		60
Eight Queens 600	*Twelve* 1200	*Sixteen* 1800
Four Jacks (one each in ♠ ♡ ◊ ♣)		40
Eight Jacks 400	*Twelve* 800	*Sixteen* 1200

(All eights, twelves, and sixteens must
have an equal number in each suit.)

Pinochle (♠ **Q** and ◊ **J**) 40	*Double Pinochle*	300
Triple Pinochle 600	*Quadruple Pinochle*	1200
Dix (9 of trump) 10	*Each extra Dix*	10

Note: *Six-handed Pinochle* is often played by two teams of three players each, instead of three teams of two players each. Similarly, *Eight-handed Pinochle* can be played by four teams of two players each, rather than the customary form of two teams of four players each.

beginning at the dealer's left. As with four-handed partnership pinochle, this can follow the *"one bid" version,* with each player bidding at full strength; or *"auction bidding"* can be agreed upon. (See page 193.) Either way, a bidding team is "set back" if it fails to make its bid, so play follows the general rules of auction pinochle, the three-handed game described on page 187, each team acting as an individual player.

The same applies to six-handed partnership *auction with a widow,* which is close indeed to the popular three-hand auction with a widow, but here two highly important factors should be considered:

First, in order that the cards should come out evenly, only fifteen are dealt to each player, leaving six cards for the widow. This gives the dealer a remarkable opportunity for "fills" if the rule is used that he can pick up all six, which is customary.

Second, since each player's hand is limited to fifteen cards (including the dealer's after he has discarded six), it is impossible for anyone to make a quadruple meld of sixteen aces, kings, queens, or jacks. So in this version, a player holding fifteen cards in any of those denominations is credited with a quadruple meld.

If preferred, the alternate rule may be used, wherein the bidder keeps only one card from the widow and hands one face down to each of the other players. In this case, nobody discards, so the hands are brought to the usual sixteen-card quota in which a quadruple meld must be complete to be allowed.

As with three-handed auction (page 187) play customarily starts with the bidder, and since teams frequently go deep into the minus column, game of 3000 points is usually satisfactory, as a big bonus meld may do no more than merely pull a team out of the hole.

EIGHT-HANDED PINOCHLE: Played with the double pack of ninety-six cards, eight-handed partnership pinochle involves two teams of four players each, with the "odd" players forming one team, the "even" players the other. Since each is dealt only twelve cards, no quadruple melds are possible. When played with a widow of eight cards, with the bidder picking up eight, each player is dealt only eleven cards, so a hand of eleven aces, kings, queens, or jacks counts as a triple meld. It is better, however, to follow the rule that the bidder keeps one card for himself and hands one each to the other players, so that each has twelve cards, with no discard. Here, all procedures are the same as in four-handed partnership pinochle (page 189), since only two teams are involved; but the scoring is the same as in six-handed pinochle.

EIGHT-HANDED PINOCHLE WITH THREE PACKS: In this elaboration of the eight-handed partnership game, a triple pack of 144 cards is used, so that each player is dealt eighteen cards when no widow is involved. With a widow, each gets seventeen cards, while an eight-card widow goes to the bidder, who selects and discards as usual; or, if so agreed, he keeps one and gives one each to the other players so that all have eighteen cards. Rules are the same as with the double-pack version, but due to the additional pack, certain quintuple and sextuple combinations are possible; and the following bonus scores are applicable, if so agreed:

Quintuple Marriage (five kings and queens of same suit)	1800
Sextuple Marriage (six kings and queens of same suit)	2400

Quintuple Pinochle   1800   Sextuple Pinochle   2400

Higher values, as 2400 for quintuples and
3600 or 4800 for sextuples, may be used if preferred.

Since there are seventy-two counters in the triple pack, 730 points can be taken in play, with the last trick counting 10 points; or 750 points, if the last trick is rated at 30 points, which is preferable. With the added scoring opportunities, 5000 is a logical minimum for game, with 7500 or 10,000 acceptable alternates.

ARMY AND NAVY PINOCHLE: A highly popular development of modern pinochle, played by three or four players with an eighty-card pack consisting of two pinochle packs without the nines; or played by six players with a 120-card pack consisting of three pinochle packs without the nines. The terms "double-pack pinochle" and "triple-pack pinochle" are sometimes used to designate these games, but this is apt to confuse them with regular partnership pinochle played by six or eight players (as previously described), hence the title "army and navy" is preferable.

With the eighty-card pack, the standard melds are used—with the exception of the dix, which is absent—and certain multiple melds may be made, as in the table on page 206. It will be noted that there are no special scores for multiple trump sequences or marriages; only for multiple aces, kings, queens, jacks, or pinochles. In the course of its evolution, the game was at one time played on a single-bid basis, but unlimited auction has become the generally accepted rule, with, of course, the proviso that once a player passes he can bid no longer.

FOUR-HANDED ARMY AND NAVY PINOCHLE: This is the most popular version of the game, hence will be treated first. Each player is dealt twenty cards and the auction begins with the player at the dealer's left, 500 being the required minimum, which is low indeed, considering the large potential melds (due in part to the absence of the useless nines), and the fact that the eighty-card pack holds forty-eight counters, worth 480 points, plus 20 for the last trick, making a total of 500 points.

Bids can be "cued" to tell a partner that the bidder holds a sequence and therefore wants the final bid. The simplest way is to use an "odd" bid to indicate the presence of a sequence; an "even" bid for a nonsequence hand. After the high bidder announces trump, all players meld individually and each team scores its total, but the bidding team loses its meld if it fails to make its bid, being set back the amount of its bid, as in other forms of partnership pinochle. Always, the bidding team scores first and therefore wins whenever both sides score enough to reach game.

Game can be fixed as low as 3500 points, but 5000 was

MELDS IN ARMY AND NAVY PINOCHLE WITH
EIGHTY-CARD PACK

Trump Sequence (**A, 10, K, Q, J**)			150
Royal Marriage	40	*Ordinary Marriage*	20

(No multiple melds with the above.)

Four Aces	100	*Eight Aces*	1000
Twelve Aces	1500	*Sixteen Aces*	2000
Four Kings	80	*Eight Kings*	800
Twelve Kings	1200	*Sixteen Kings*	1600
Four Queens	60	*Eight Queens*	600
Twelve Queens	900	*Sixteen Queens*	1200
Four Jacks	40	*Eight Jacks*	400
Twelve Jacks	600	*Sixteen Jacks*	800
Pinochle (♠ **Q,** ◇ **J**)	40	*Double Pinochle*	300
Triple Pinochle	600	*Quadruple Pinochle*	3000

Note: *Six-handed Army and Navy Pinochle* can be played by two teams of three players each, instead of three teams of two players each.

the original "army and navy" figure and is still the best, unless players prefer an extended game and therefore agree upon 7500 or 10,000. If desired, a four-card widow can be used in this game, with each player being dealt nineteen cards instead of twenty. The usual rules of partnership pinochle apply where a widow is involved.

Informative Announcements: If so agreed, rules may be introduced allowing players to make specific announcements regarding their hands, these serving as bidding cues. As preliminary to the actual bidding, each player, starting at the dealer's left, may name a figure representing part or all of his forthcoming meld, thus giving his partner an idea of what he can depend upon. Some groups allow a player to name any figure he wants, even in excess of his actual meld, as a means of confusing the opposition. But this is not recommended, as it is apt to confuse the partner as well and if overdone can become nonsensical.

In the actual bidding, each player may announce a potential trump sequence if he holds one, or he can state that he is bidding on the playing strength of a long nonsequence suit. Either way, this cues his partner to let him have the final bid, unless his partner responds with a similar cue or thinks he can do better. In such an announcement, the bidder cannot name the suit involved, either as a sequence or otherwise. He can, however, announce a meld, over and above the potential sequence, which naturally does not count unless its suit becomes trump. This figure can cover part or all of a player's actual meld, but not more, though he is free to bid as high as he wants.

Any infraction of these rules—such as naming a suit, or specifying a type of meld by name—gives the opponents the privilege of calling for a new deal if they are so inclined. However, no player is compelled to bid after making a preliminary announcement, as one of its functions is to determine if a hand is biddable at all. If all players pass, the hands are thrown in and the deal moves to the left. This applies whether or not announcements are allowable; in short, no one is ever forced to take the bid at the 500 minimum.

Note: Originally, the multiple melds used in six-handed pinochle with the ninety-six-card pack were also used with the eighty-card pack. In that schedule (given on page 202), additional sequences and marriages increase proportionately, as do other multiple melds, with the exception of pinochles. The original schedule can still be used with the eighty-card pack, if so agreed, but the one given here is better geared to the added scoring opportunities in the eighty-card game.

SIX-HANDED ARMY AND NAVY PINOCHLE: This elaboration of the four-handed eighty-card game is very similar in rules and procedure but involves six players, using a 120-card "triple" pack, from which the nines have been removed. Hence there are three teams of two players each, the players seated opposite acting as partners; and each player is dealt the usual twenty cards. However, due to the fact that there are six cards of each denomination, instead of only four, additional multiple melds are possible and score as follows:

Twenty Aces	2500	*Twenty Queens*	1500
Twenty Kings	2000	*Twenty Jacks*	1200
(All the above must have an equal number of each suit.)			
Quintuple Pinochle	4000	*Sextuple Pinochle*	5000

Bidding is the same as in the four-handed game, and announcements can be made if agreed beforehand, but the minimum bid in six-handed is 750, as the 120-card pack contains 72 counters, making 720 points that can be taken in play, with the last trick as 30, for a total of 750 points. Each team is on its own, but occasionally two gang up on the third if they see an opportunity to defeat a bid and put the bidder in the hole. Melding and play are exactly as in four-handed.

Game may be as low as 4500, but 5000 is a better figure and 7500 is more realistic. It can be extended to 10,000 or 12,500 if so agreed. If a widow is used, only nineteen cards are dealt to each player, with six for the widow. Players can decide beforehand whether the entire widow goes to the high bidder, who discards accordingly, or whether he keeps just one card and gives one to each of the five other players, so the hands will have their full quota of twenty cards each.

If each player is dealt only nineteen cards, a player will need only nineteen aces, kings, queens, or jacks to score as "twenty."

THREE-HANDED ARMY AND NAVY PINOCHLE: A high-powered version of *Army and Navy Pinochle,* utilizing the eighty-card double pack and the multiple melds that go with it (page 206). Each player is dealt twenty-five cards, with five extra for a face-down widow. Players bid beginning at the dealer's left, with 500 as the lowest bid; and the dealer must take it at that figure if the two others pass. As multiple bids are common with twenty-five-card hands, continuous auction is preferable to single bids, though either type may be agreed upon.

The high bidder must name trump before taking up the widow. All three meld, the high bidder discards five cards and leads to the first trick, adding his discard to any tricks he takes in play. If he fails to make his bid, he loses his meld and is set back the amount of the bid. There is a total count of 500 points in play, including 20 for the last trick; and any player who fails to take a trick containing a counter loses his meld for that hand.

Game is 4500 or 5000, preferably the latter. The bidder's score is always counted first at the end of the hand, but sometimes he may wind up short of game while the other players both drift out. The best procedure in that case is to extend the game another 1000 points, with all three players staying in it.

Certain variants may be introduced if desired. One is to deal each player twenty-six cards, leaving only two for the widow instead of five. In this case, the high bidder may pick up the widow before naming trump. The other is to allow the high bidder to throw in his hand if he has overbid it, without wasting time in play. He loses his meld and is set back, as usual, while each of the other players is credited with 100 points in addition to his meld.

CONTRACT PINOCHLE: A unique form of partnership pinochle with a bidding system borrowed from contract bridge. Four players, *A, B, C, D,* in that order, form two partnerships, *A–C* and *B–D.* Each player is dealt twelve cards from the standard forty-eight-card pack. Beginning with the dealer, *D,* each player may pass or bid, the minimum being 100 points; but in bidding, he must also name a trump suit. Thus, a spirited bidding might run:

D, the dealer: "100 clubs." *A,* the next bidder: "Pass." *B,* next: "120 hearts." *C,* next: "150 diamonds." *D,* back again: "160 spades." *A,* finally: "300 diamonds." And that settles it, with everybody passing from there on. So *A*'s bid stands.

By the rules, only the high bidder's team melds; and each can add to whatever the other lays down. So, in this instance, suppose that Player *A,* the high bidder, melds ♠ Q ◊ J ♡ K Q, which amounts to 40+20=60 points. Player *C,* his partner, merely melds ♣ K Q for 20 points, which is rather dismal. But Player *A* responds by adding the ◊ Q for four queens, worth 60 points; and Player *C* adds the ♠ K to score 20 more for an ordinary marriage: 60+60+20=140.

Fairly good for a mutual meld. But at this point, *A,* the bidder, can ask his partner, *C,* for a single card that will complete a meld. So *A,* holding ◊ A K, asks *C* for the ◊ 10; and *C* delivers it. That enables *A* to lay down the ◊ A 10 K on the Q J for a meld of 150, which clinches the bid, since 140+150= 290 is only 10 points short of the 300 that the two partners must take.

The bidder can keep asking for meldable cards—one at a time—as long as his partner can deliver them. But once that stops, the partner is allowed to ask the bidder for a meldable card; and then another, as long as the bidder can deliver. During all this, either member of the team can add to the mutual meld whenever the opportunity arises.

Suppose that Player *C* happened to be holding the ♠ A, ♡ A, ♣ A, when the bidder, Player *A,* completed the trump sequence in diamonds. Without even asking, Player *D* could have laid his three aces on the ◊ A and announced "100 aces," even though by that time they were totally unneeded. But they could have been if the bidding had been forced higher. Therefore:

Once the team's meld has been counted, each player picks up his own cards and the hand is played out. The bidder leads to the first trick, with play proceeding as in partnership pinochle. Often, play is unnecessary—as in the example just cited—because the meld approaches or exceeds the amount required by the bid. But conversely, there are times when a team overbids and its mutual meld falls so far short of expectations that it may as well concede without playing out the hand.

A team scores the amount that it bid; nothing more. In the example just given, the partners *A* and *C* might easily have taken 160 points in play, which, added to their 190 meld, would have given them 350. But they would have had to be content with 300 for that hand, since 300 was their final bid. If a team fails to make its bid, the opposing team adds that total to its score. If a bid is doubled, so is the score for that hand—whichever team gets it. If redoubled, the score is quadrupled.

The first team to reach 3000 wins the game.

PINOCHLE POKER: See page 259.

PINOCHLE RUMMY: See page 295.

PIQUET: An outmoded French game for two players, using a thirty-two-card pack, ranking **A, K, Q, J, 10, 9, 8, 7.** Each is dealt twelve cards (by twos or threes), leaving a "stock" of eight. If the opponent's hand contains no face cards (**K, Q, J**), he announces "carte blanche" and scores 10 points. Regardless of that, he discards from one to five cards and draws replacements from the top of the stock, looking at any that he does not draw. The dealer may then announce and score for "carte blanche"—if he has it!—and then discard and draw.

Other scoring combinations are then "called" as follows:

Point: Opponent names the number of cards in his longest suit, scoring 1 point for each card if dealer cannot equal it. If dealer has more, he scores 1 point for each card. If equal, opponent and dealer tally up the value of the cards in their respective long suits: Ace, 11; face cards, 10 each; others according to their spots. Whichever is higher scores the usual 1 point for each card of his long suit.

Sequence: Opponent names the number of cards in his longest suit sequence of three or more, counting 1 for each card, plus 10 for any sequence of five or more cards, unless the dealer has a longer sequence, enabling his to score instead. If equal in length, the top card determines the winner, ♡ **Q J 10 9 8** overpowering ♠ **J 10 9 8 7.** If absolutely equal, neither wins. But where there is a winner, he may also score for lesser sequences in other suits. Example: Player scoring 5+10=15 for ♡ **Q J 10 9 8,** would add 3 for ♣ **10 9 8** and 3 more for ◊ **A K Q.**

Fours and Threes: Opponent names his longest and highest set of the same value, provided they consist of tens or higher, with four of a kind, termed a *quatorze,* counting 1 for each card, plus 10 (4+10=14) and taking precedence over three of a kind, termed a *trio,* which counts 1 for each card, or 3. A pair does not count. Player declaring the highest of such combinations can score them all. Example: Player holding **10– 10–10–10** and **J–J–J** would score 14+3=17, while the other player, holding **A–A–A** and **K–K–K,** would score 0. As with "point" and "sequence," the dealer responds to opponent's declaration by naming a higher holding if he has it.

These two hands will illustrate the procedure:

Opponent: ♠ **A K Q J** ♡ **K Q J 7** ◊ **Q J 10** ♣ **Q**
Dealer: ♣ **J 10 9 8 7** ♡ **10 9 8** ♠ **10 9 8 7**

Opponent calls, "Four" as his longest suit (in ♠) for point.
Dealer, having five (in ♣), responds, "No good."
Opponent calls, "Four in sequence" (♠ **A K Q J**) (see note below).
Dealer, who has five (♣ **J 10 9 8 7**), responds, "No good."
Opponent calls, "Quatorze" or "Four queens."
Dealer, who has only a trio of three tens, says, "Good."

Opponent announces that he has a trio (J–J–J), and scores are made as follows: Opponent 10+4=14 for quatorze; plus 3 for trio, a total of 17. Dealer 5 for point; plus 10+5=15 for five in sequence; plus 4 for four in sequence; plus 3 for three in sequence, a total of 27.

Note: In piquet parlance, a sequence of three is termed a *tierce;* of four, a *quatrieme* or *"quart";* of five, a *quinte;* of six, a *sixieme;* of seven, a *septieme;* of eight, a *huitieme.*

Opponent opens play by leading any card he chooses; the dealer must follow suit if he can. Highest card of suit led always wins the trick, as there is no trump suit in piquet. Winner of each trick leads to the next, and points are scored during play as follows: For leading an honor (A, K, Q, J, 10) a player scores 1 point. If the nonleader takes a trick with an honor, he scores 1 point. For winning the last trick, 1 extra point. For winning more than six tricks, 10 points for "cards." For winning all twelve tricks, 40 points for *capot,* which includes the last trick and cards, making it actually 29+1+10=40.

If a player can score 30 or more points prior to play and before the other player makes any score whatever, he can claim *repique,* adding 60 points to his score. As an example:

♠ Q J 10 9 8   ♡ J 9   ◊ J 8 7   ♣ K J

Assuming that all the player's calls are "good," he would score as follows: 5 for point; 15 for quinze sequence; 14 for quatorze, a total of 34. Add 60 for repique, making 94.

If short of the needed 30, the opponent can sometimes make up the difference by scoring points in play before the dealer registers any score. In that case, the opponent claims *pique,* which adds 30 points to his score.

Game consists of 100 points, with the deal alternating until a player reaches that total. If the other player fails to reach 50, he is "lurched," and the winner is credited with a double game. A player can "call out" as he approaches 100, scores being registered in the following order: carte blanche, point, sequence, four or three, repique. Leading or winning tricks; pique; cards, capot.

PIRATE BRIDGE: A briefly popular form of *Auction Bridge,* page 18, in which an individual bid by one player could be accepted by another, who thereby became the bidder's partner for that hand.

PISHA PASHA: A fast but simple two-player game with a fifty-two-card pack, suits ranking in descending order: **A, K, Q, J, 10, 9, 8, 7, 6, 5, 4, 3, 2.** The pack is equally divided in two face-down heaps, and the players simultaneously turn up cards to form individual piles until two cards of the same suit appear (as ◊ **J** and ◊ **7**). Player with the higher card takes or captures the other player's pile and lays it aside with his own. Play continues until the pack runs out, when player with greater number of cards wins. As an option, cards thus taken can be placed beneath the winner's original packet, as in *War,* page 373, and when a packet runs out, it can be turned face down to continue play as in that game.

PISTOL PETE: Also known as *Pistol* or *Pistol Stud,* all being terms for *Hole-Card Stud,* page 252.

PITCH: This modern game developed from those of the *High-Low Jack* type, which date back to *All Fours.* Its most popular form is *Auction Pitch* (also called *Setback*), which is described herewith, with notes on *Standard Pitch* to follow.

The Pack: The standard fifty-two cards, running in descending values, **A, K, Q, J, 10, 9, 8, 7, 6, 5, 4, 3, 2.**

Number of Players: Two to eight, each for himself.

The Deal: Six cards to each player, usually by threes, in clockwise order.

The Bidding: Beginning at the dealer's left, each player either "passes" or bids from one to four, according to the number of points he thinks he can gain during play. Each new bid must top the one before; but the dealer, as final bidder, may take it for the amount of the previous bid, provided it is less than four.

Examples, with four players, *A, B, C,* and *D* (dealer):

(1) *A*, "One." *B*, "Three." *C*, "Pass." *D*, "Three."

(2) *A*, "Pass." *B*, "Two." *C*, "Four." *D* must "pass."

If all players pass, the cards are gathered and shuffled by the dealer, who then deals another round of hands.

Playing and Scoring: The highest bidder names trump by playing or "pitching" a card of that suit face up on the table. The other players must follow suit to the trump lead if they can; otherwise, they may discard from any side suit. Highest trump played takes the trick, and the winner leads to the next trick.

If a trump is led, the original rule applies; if another suit is led, players may either follow suit or trump the trick, as they prefer. If out of the suit led, they may discard from another side suit or trump the trick. The highest card of suit led wins the trick unless it is trumped; in that case, the highest trump played wins it.

Each player's purpose is to score as many points as he can, the possible points being four in number; namely:

High: Gained by the player who holds (and plays) the highest trump in that particular hand.

Low: Gained by the player who simply holds the lowest trump in that hand.

Jack: Gained by the player who wins a trick that includes the jack of trump, regardless of who held it.

Game: Gained by the player who takes the highest count in "honor cards," which are valued as follows, regardless of suit: ace, 4; king, 3; queen, 2; jack, 1; ten, 10.

Important toward the bidding is the fact that if nobody holds the jack of trump it cannot be taken, and therefore the jack point is lost in that hand. Also, if the highest game count results in a tie between two or more players, there is no game point in that hand.

Points are scored at the end of the play; and if the bidder fails to gain the number that he specified, he is "set back" (hence the name "setback") that many points, which will put him in the minus column—or "in the hole"—if this occurs in the opening hand, or whenever his total score happens to be less than the amount of his losing bid.

The Game itself is won by the first player who gains a total of 7 points, unless a higher total (as 9, 10, 11, 21) is specified beforehand. All hands are played to completion, so if the bidder "goes out" along with any other players, he is declared to be the winner. If only nonbidders go out, their points are reckoned in the order, high, low, jack, game; and the first to reach the required total is the winner.

Smudge: A name applied to a widely accepted rule whereby a player who bids "four" and makes it gains a "smudge" or "slam" and is given enough points to win the game immediately, unless he is already in the hole. In that case, he gains only the four points that he bid. This rule should be specified beforehand.

Low-Card Variant: Another option often used is that the point for "low" goes to the player *taking* the lowest trump instead of the player merely *holding* it. This rule (if specified) greatly encourages higher bidding, hence often is included with "smudge."

Joker as Fifth Point: Some modern players include the joker in auction pitch, ranking it either above the highest trump in play or, preferably, below the lowest. Either way, the player taking the joker gains one point; hence the bidding can be increased from four to five, with "smudge" (if used) requiring a "five" bid, so that it becomes harder to make.

Some go by the rule that, if the bidder "pitches" the joker, it establishes spades as trump; but unless that is agreed upon, the bidder should be allowed to name his own trump when leading the joker.

Settling the Score: When players are using tokens or chips, the most popular method is for each loser to pay a chip to the winner, plus one chip for each time the loser was set back, with an extra chip from any loser whose final score is zero or below, making it a minus score.

Standard Pitch: In the earlier or standard form of pitch, there is no auction and therefore no setback. The player on the dealer's left establishes trump by pitching whatever card he wants. The play follows the rules as already described, and each player is credited for whatever points he scores, high, low, and possibly jack or game. The first player to reach a total of 7 points (or any other specified total) becomes the winner.

This is still an intriguing game, even though it represents a transitional stage. With two players, it gives the opponent an opportunity to balk a stronger hand held by the dealer; while with seven or eight players, it produces action at times when mediocre holdings might lead to a succession of "passed" deals in the auction version.

Most interesting is the fact that the player making the "pitch" can occasionally win all four points with a single card; namely, the jack of trump, if neither he nor any other player holds another trump or counter card. In that case, the lead becomes high, low, jack, and game. With only two players, this becomes a well-calculated risk on the part of the opponent.

PIVOT BRIDGE: A form of party bridge in which players change seats after each rubber so that partnerships are equalized. See *Contract Bridge,* page 72.

PLACE POKER and PLACE AND SHOW: See page 260.

PLAFOND: A French game similar to *Auction Bridge,* page 18, but with special features that were utilized in the transition to *Contract Bridge,* page 72, which later supplanted it.

PLAY OR PAY: A name applied to an early and simple form of *Fan-Tan,* page 115, with which it is often identified. From three to seven players contribute equally to a pool and are dealt cards singly from a fifty-two-card pack until all are dealt. Player at dealer's left plays any card face up, and he or others add cards of the same suit in ascending order, as ◇ **6, 7, 8, 9, 10, J, Q, K, A, 2, 3, 4, 5;** and whoever plays the final card begins another suit, with any card he wants, on the same ascending scale. Any player unable to play in turn must add one chip to the pool, which goes to the first player who gets rid of all his cards, exactly as in fan-tan.

PLUS OR MINUS: A game played like *Draw Poker* but with hands valued according to the spots on the cards, ace=1;

two=2, etc., with face cards (J, Q, K) at 10 each. Red cards count plus and black cards minus. Each player is dealt five cards and can discard any number, drawing others instead. The hand with the highest plus total wins, unless the game is played with high and low splitting the pot, which is usually preferred. Either form can be called for in "dealer's choice." See *Draw Poker,* page 226.

POCHEN: An old-time game with a thirty-two-card pack (aces down to sevens) and a layout with eight sections marked **A, K, Q, J, 10,** marriage, sequence, and pochen, which is a central section termed "poche" or "pool." Each player puts a chip in each section and is dealt a face-down hand, consisting of nine cards with three players; seven cards with four players; six cards with five players; five cards with six players. The next card is turned up to signify the trump suit.

Players then collect from the layout automatically as follows: Any high trump, as ace, king, queen, jack, ten, wins from **A, K, Q, J, 10,** respectively; and a player holding both king and queen of trump collects from the "marriage" section. Sequences of three or more cards of a single suit are next shown, and the player with the longest collects from the "sequence" section. (Thus **J, 10, 9, 8, 7** would win over **A, K, Q, J.**) With sequences of the same length, the highest wins. (Thus **K, Q, J** would beat **Q, J, 10,** which in turn would beat **J, 10, 9.**)

Next, high hands are shown as in poker, four of a kind outranking threes, which in turn outrank a pair. Here again the highest breaks a tie (as **J–J–J** beating **10–10–10,** or **9–9** beating **8–8),** and the winner takes the pool. The hands are played out, with the player at the dealer's left leading any card (as ♡ **9)** and the rest following suit in ascending order (as ♡ **10, J, Q, K, A)** until play in that suit is stopped, when the player can lead any other card. During that procedure, anyone unable to play simply lets his turn go by. The first player to dispose of his entire hand collects a chip for each card remaining in an opponent's hand.

When a high card is turned up as trump, or if a high trump happens to remain undealt, no one collects from that section, so the chips remain there for the next deal, which is made by the player on the original dealer's left. The same applies when there is no "marriage" or a winning "sequence," though with tied sequences (as ♠ **J, 10, 9, 8** and ◊ **J, 10, 9, 8**), the players divide that section, the one nearest the dealer's left taking an odd chip.

By agreement, the deal may be limited to a specified number of cards, usually five to each player, regardless of how many are in the game. Also, the hands may be played out as tricks, each player following suit to the first player's lead but passing his turn if out of suit. High card wins the trick and leads to the next; and the player who first clears his hand collects a chip per card from the rest.

For a more modern version of this game, played with a fifty-two-card pack, see *Tripoli*, page 369.

POKER: Primarily a simple game, poker through the years has developed more elaborate versions, all suited to serious play; while from these have stemmed innumerable offshoots, some with rules as fanciful as their names. These can be readily understood and appreciated if taken in due order, from standard types to those that have gained wide acceptance and finally listing a grand array that comes under the head of "dealer's choice," in which almost anything goes.

Generally, poker is played with a fifty-two-card pack, ranking **A, K, Q, J, 10, 9, 8, 7, 6, 5, 4, 3, 2, A,** the ace sometimes being low instead of high. Suits are important but none takes precedence over the others. Players, usually from three to seven but in some games more, are dealt hands that are customarily reduced to five cards each. Betting and sometimes bluffing are followed by a "showdown" in which all hands are fully revealed; and the one with the best combination becomes the winner, according to the following table of standard poker hands, given in order from highest down to lowest:

FIVE OF A KIND

With deuces wild,
five aces is the
highest possible hand.

STRAIGHT FLUSH

As a natural hand
—no wild card—a royal
flush is highest.

Next to a straight flush comes four of a kind.

The highest is either four aces or four kings
with an odd ace.

Others rank in descending order.

POKER

Examples of poker hands

With a full house, the highest trio wins.

With a flush,
the one with the highest card wins.

Here the king high beats the queen high.
If the highest cards are identical in value,
the next highest decides it——or the next highest.

With the four top cards identical in value,
the fifth card is the decider: here the four of diamonds
versus the three of hearts.

POKER

Examples of poker hands

**With a straight, the one with the highest
top card wins.**

Here, the queen high beats the ten high.

With three of a kind, the highest trio wins.
Here, the three kings beat the three queens.

With deuces wild, the "side cards" sometimes mean
the difference. Three jacks with a ten and a seven beat three jacks
with a ten and a five.

POKER

Examples of poker hands

Two pair. Two pair with aces up beat two pair with kings over tens—

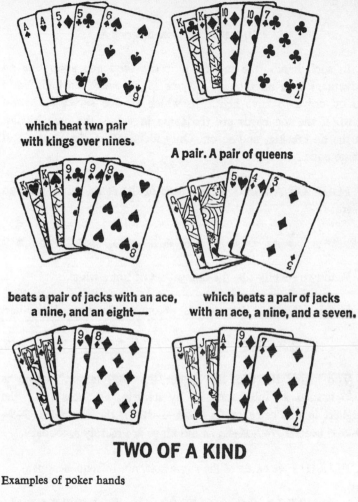

**which beat two pair
with kings over nines.**

A pair. A pair of queens

**beats a pair of jacks with an ace,
a nine, and an eight—**

**which beats a pair of jacks
with an ace, a nine, and a seven.**

TWO OF A KIND

Examples of poker hands

ROYAL FLUSH: The five highest cards in one suit, as:

◇ **A**   ◇ **K**   ◇ **Q**   ◇ **J**   ◇ **10**

This can be tied by a similar hand in another suit. It is sometimes termed a "royal straight flush" to identify it as the highest hand in the next group, namely:

STRAIGHT FLUSH: A sequence of any five cards in one suit, as:

$$\heartsuit\ J\ 10\ 9\ 8\ 7 \quad \text{or} \quad \spadesuit\ 5\ 4\ 3\ 2\ A$$

In such hands, the top card of the sequence gives one an advantage over another, as a "jack high" over "ten high," and so on down to "five high," in which an ace serves as lowest card. If the top cards are the same in value, the next highest is the tie breaker, and so on. Only identical hands are ties and share equally.

FOUR OF A KIND: Four cards of the same value, with an extra:

$$\spadesuit\ A \quad \heartsuit\ A \quad \clubsuit\ A \quad \diamondsuit\ A \quad \heartsuit\ 5 \text{ or } \clubsuit\ 3 \quad \diamondsuit\ 3 \quad \spadesuit\ 3 \quad \heartsuit\ 3 \quad \spadesuit\ 9$$

With two such hands, the highest set of fours wins.

FULL HOUSE: Three cards of one value; two of another:

$$\clubsuit\ 9 \quad \diamondsuit\ 9 \quad \heartsuit\ 9 \quad \clubsuit\ 6 \quad \heartsuit\ 6 \text{ or } \spadesuit\ 7 \quad \diamondsuit\ 7 \quad \clubsuit\ 7 \quad \heartsuit\ K \quad \spadesuit\ K$$

The higher the trio, the higher the "full house," which is also termed a "full hand" or by its trio, as "aces full," the highest in this category (A–A–A–J–J). In the examples, 9–9–9–6–6 beats 7–7–7–K–K, as the kings are merely secondary.

FLUSH: Five cards of the same suit, not in sequence, as:

$$\diamondsuit\ A\ 8\ 5\ 3\ 2 \quad \text{or} \quad \clubsuit\ Q\ J\ 9\ 8\ 6 \quad \text{or} \quad \heartsuit\ Q\ 10\ 9\ 8\ 6$$
$$\text{or} \quad \spadesuit\ Q\ 10\ 9\ 8\ 5$$

The hand with highest card takes precedence, with a tie for high, the second highest; then third, fourth, or fifth. Ace is always high.

STRAIGHT: Five cards in sequence, of different suits, as:

♡ A ♠ K Q ◇ J ♠ 10 or ♣ 5 ♡ 4 3 ♣ 2 ♠ A

Highest is an "ace high straight," popularly termed a "Broadway," going down the scale to a "five high," in which an ace is lowest card.

THREE OF A KIND: Three cards of the same value with two extras:

♡ J ♠ J ♣ J ♡ 8 ♣ 3 or ♠ 6 ◇ 6 ♣ 6 ♡ K ♠ 10

As with "four of a kind," the highest set wins.

TWO PAIR: Two sets of two alike in value with an extra card:

♣ A ♠ A ♣ 5 ♡ 5 ◇ 10 or ◇ K ♠ K ◇ J ♡ J ♣ 8

The hand with the higher pair wins, "aces up" beating "kings up."

♣ Q ♠ Q ♣ 4 ◇ 4 ♡ 6 or ♡ Q ◇ Q ♠ 3 ◇ 3 ♣ J

However, with top pairs equal (Q–Q), the lower pair denotes the winning hand, in this case 4–4 taking precedence over 3–3.

◇ 9 ♣ 9 ◇ 7 ♡ 7 ♠ 10 or ♡ 9 ♠ 9 ♣ 7 ♠ 7 ◇ 5

With two pairs equal (9–9, 7–7), the extra card decides, the hand with the ♠ 10 beating the one with the ◇ 5.

ONE PAIR: A single pair alike in value; other cards different:

♠ J ◇ J ♠ K ♡ 4 3 or ♣ J ♡ J ◇ Q 10 ♣ 6

With each pair alike (J–J), the highest odd card wins (K beats Q).

♠ A ◇ A ♡ 8 7 4 or ♣ A ♡ A ♠ 8 6 ♣ 5

With each pair alike (A–A) and also the highest odd card (8 and 8), the next-highest odd decides (♡ 7 vs. ♠ 6). If those tie, the lowest odd card may sometimes decide as 9–9–5–4–3 beating 9–9–5–4–2.

HIGH CARD: A hand of mixed suits and values; no combinations.

♠ A K ◇ Q ♡ J 9 or ♣ J ♠ 9 6 ◇ 5 3 or ♠ 7 5 ♡ 4 ♣ 3 2

These range from highest (A–K–Q–J–9) to lowest (7–5–4–3–2) of such hands. Ties are decided by highest, second high, third high, and so on down.

Other types of combinations are possible in special forms of poker that will be discussed under their respective heads.

STANDARD FORMS OF POKER: Starting from "straight poker," in which each player was simply dealt a hand of five cards and forced to bluff his way from then on, various improvements were introduced to enliven the game. First and foremost of these innovations was "draw poker," which became so dominant that most persons have come to regard it as the original game, although it too has undergone some definite changes. It is described here in modern form:

Draw Poker: Preferably played by three to seven persons, "draw" utilizes the fifty-two-card pack as already described and valued. Each player puts up an "ante," or a specified number of chips, to form a pool or "pot," or each dealer, in turn, puts up an ante for the entire group, which is essential when playing "dealer's choice." Five cards are dealt singly to each player, and the first on the dealer's left, after looking at his hand, has the privilege of "opening" the pot by adding one or more chips. Instead, he may "pass," letting the next player open if he wants; and so on. If all pass, the hands are gathered and the deal moves to the dealer's left, a new ante being added to the one already in the pot.

After one player opens a pot, each in turn may pass, or, in poker parlance, "drop" by throwing in his hand face down; or he may "call," also termed "stay," by putting up the same number of chips; or he may "raise," popularly styled "bump," by calling and adding some extra chips of his own. Other players, successively, must meet the rise in order to stay, or else drop; and any that stays can make a further raise. This continues until all surviving players have finally called any raise or raises.

Now comes the distinctive feature of draw poker. Again starting at the dealer's left, each player may discard whatever cards he does not want, by laying them face down and drawing others to replace them. The term "draw" is slightly a misnomer; actually, the fresh cards are dealt by the dealer instead of being drawn by the player, but it amounts to the same thing where improving the hands is concerned. Another round of betting follows, exactly like the first but usually with the added proviso that a player can "check" instead of betting, meaning that he puts the decision up to the next player, who may do the same. When everybody has checked, bet and called, or dropped, the active players show their hands and the best wins the pot. If only one player remains, nobody being willing to call his bet, he wins automatically and does not have to show his hand.

Note: The player who opens is first to bet after the draw. If he drops, the next player bets, and so on.

Some groups do not allow a player to check; still more go by the rule that a player cannot draw more than three cards. Most include a so-called "jackpot" ruling, meaning that a player must hold a pair of jacks or something better to open the pot originally, though others may stay on anything. A player does not have to open if he wants; but sometimes when he does, he may decide to "split his openers"; for example, holding ◊ **K** ♣ **K** ◊ **Q** ♠ **J** ♣ **10,** he might open on his pair of kings, then decide to discard one and draw a single card, hoping that an **A** or a **9** will give him a straight **(A–K–Q–J–10** or **K–Q–J–10–9)**. In that case, he should keep his discard separate from others, so that he can later show it and prove that he opened on "jacks or better."

Five-Card Stud: In contrast to "draw," in which no cards are seen until the "showdown," the form of poker known as "five-card stud" seems virtually a giveaway, though such is not the case. Originally this game was played without an ante, but one is now customary, particularly in "dealer's choice."

A round of face-down cards is dealt, then a round of cards face up, so that each player has a "downcard" and an "upcard." Each player looks at his "hole card," as the "downcard" is termed; and the player with the highest upcard either bets or drops, by turning down his upcard, which is termed "folding" in stud. Others call, raise, or fold, in turn, until all survivors have called.

Another upcard is then dealt to each active player, and another round of betting follows, beginning with the player who shows the best upcards, with a pair being better than just a high card. This player may check, bet, or drop.

A third upcard is dealt to each player and bet in the same manner, this time beginning with the player who shows the three best. Finally, a fourth upcard is dealt and bet on the same terms; and after the final call, the hole cards are turned up and the best hand wins.

Expert poker players really go for this game, because of the intriguing situations it may produce, such as two hands, X and Y, shown below. The asterisks are hole cards dealt face down.

X:	*	♣ J	◇ K	♡ J	♣ 3
Y:	*	◇ Q	◇ 9	◇ 7	◇ 3

Here, Player *X* has a pair of jacks showing, that Player *Y* can outmatch only by a pair of queens, which he may have had to start. As it now stands, *X* could have three jacks, or two pair—as kings over jacks, or jacks over threes. But meanwhile, *Y* may have been sitting back with ◇ **A** in the hole, hoping for a pair of aces, or a pair of queens, only to find himself the proud possessor of a flush, running ◊ **A Q 9 7 3,** which beats all of *X*'s chances.

Unfortunately, such hands are too few and far between; hence five-card stud became too slow for modern play. As a result, the game underwent expansions, the best of which was:

Six-Card Stud: This is simply *Five-Card Stud* with an added deal of a face-down card and another betting round. The result is two hole cards—first and last—with four upcards in between. But the important factor is that the player is given choice of his five best cards, with the privilege of discarding the extra. As a result, the hidden possibility of the sixth card is tremendous. In the example given under five-card stud, such an extra hole card could almost clinch a diamond flush for Player *Y,* yet at the same time enable Player *X* to win with a full house (as **K–K–K J–J** or **J–J–J K–K**). But six-card stud, much though it has been extolled by veteran poker addicts, still fell short of the action that most players demanded. That has been met by:

Seven-Card Stud: This spells action from the start, as indicated by its nickname, "down the river." Each player is dealt three cards to start; two hole cards, face down, and an upcard. That livens the betting so that most players are apt to stay, as two hidden cards may do much toward future prospects. The player who has the highest upcard starts the betting; then three more upcards are dealt to each player, making four in all, with a betting round on each; and finally, another hole card, with its own betting round.

In contrast to the extremely limited prospects at the conclusion of a five-card hand, almost anything is possible after the final card has been dealt in seven-card stud. As an example:

    *   *   ♠ K   ♡ 6   ♣ J   ◊ 3   *

Here, the only impossible holding is a flush—or a straight flush—because the four upcards are each of a different suit. But this hand, in itself, could represent anything else from a pair to four of a kind; and if the ♣ J happened to be the ♠ J, it could stand for a flush—or even a royal flush!—as well. Sometimes, in contrast, a hand that already looks sure has limitations, as:

*   *   ♣ 7   ◇ Q   ♠ Q   ♡ 7   *

With two pair on display (Q–Q–7–7) this looks fine for a full house (Q–Q–Q–7–7 or 7–7–7–Q–Q), or four of a kind (Q–Q–Q–Q or 7–7–7–7). But anything else is out. No straight is possible, as the Q and 7 are too far apart; nor can the player hold a flush with four different suits showing. Usually, a hand like this winds up no better than it looks; merely two pair (Q–Q–7–7).

In both examples given above, the real clue to a player's holdings may be gained by studying the upcards of other hands. In particular, where a Q or 7 is needed, only four such are available (♣ Q, ♡ Q, ♠ 7, ◇ 7), and if all those were visible elsewhere, the player's chances would be nil. Since many players are more apt to "stay" than "drop" during a hand of seven-card stud, such surveys are often highly productive.

Eight-Card Stud: This may be played with the seventh card as an upcard and an eighth card as a hole card with an added betting round; or both the seventh and eighth cards may be hole cards, either bet separately or together, as agreed upon beforehand. Other variants are also allowable. This game is generally regarded as too liberal for serious play, but it still has well-defined limitations and therefore comes within the fringe of standard games. Anything beyond it, however, can be classed as a "wild" game.

Important Note on Standard Poker: In games involving an unusual number of players, the dealer may run out of cards if too many stay in. The remedy is simple: The dealer gathers any hands that have been dropped or folded, shuffles them, and uses them as the remainder of the pack. Examples: *Draw Poker* with eight players, who are dealt forty cards. Two drop and four demand three cards each, making a total of fifty-two, with two more players to be heard from. Dealer uses the ten cards belonging to the first two players to serve the last two.

Seven-Card Stud with nine players. One folds after the third card; another after the fifth. The rest stay through the sixth, so the dealer has dealt $3+5+42=50$ cards. The seven players remaining each want a seventh card, so the dealer shuffles the two remaining cards with the early discards and has $2+3+5=10$ cards for the final round.

Betting Limits: In the vast majority of poker games, specific limits are agreed upon, ranging from "penny ante" to "dollar limit" or higher. In "draw," there are three factors: The ante, the minimum bet, and the limit; all these can be established as desired. Thus in the highly popular form of "five-ten poker," with each chip worth five units, the ante could be set at a single chip, with a bet of one chip and a raise of two. Sometimes the lower figure is used to represent the limit before the draw; while the higher figure applies after the draw. Often, three figures may be named, as "Five-ten-twenty-five," to mean that a player must bet at least five units, but can only go as high as ten before the draw; while after the draw, his minimum bet would be ten units, but he could go fifteen, twenty, or as high as twenty-five.

Summarized, players may decide among themselves what the betting procedures and limits should be. The same applies to stud poker; but since it has more betting rounds, the tendency is to keep them all the same, though many groups like to double the bets on the final card. Sometimes, a high ante is advisable, since it encourages a player to "stay" because he already has something at stake; but that applies only when all players put up an ante, rather than the dealer alone.

Betting limits also figure strongly in:

SPECIAL FORMS OF POKER: Many efforts have been made to speed the action in poker by offering more players inducements to "stay" with hands that would ordinarily be regarded as worthless. By far the most popular of such devices and perhaps the soundest is:

High-Low Poker: This differs from standard poker in one very important respect, which does not change the comparative values of the game; namely: Instead of the highest hand winning the entire pot, it splits it with the lowest hand. This may stem from the universal rule that when two hands are tied—as can occasionally happen with flushes, straights, and pairs—the pot is divided; but whatever its origin, once the notion of splitting high and low was introduced, it took over to stay.

In all forms of "high-low," hands are rated exactly as in standard poker, from a royal flush—as ♡ A K Q J 10—down to a seven-five high, or "seventy-five," as ♡ 7 ◇ 5 ♡ 4 ♣ 3 ◇ 2. For clarity, the game will be described on this basis; but it should be noted that in fairly recent years certain important options have been introduced in regard to low hands and should be given due consideration as they occur.

Otherwise, the game follows these general patterns:

High-Low Draw: The procedure is almost identical with *Draw Poker* except that more players stay because of extra objectives. As an example, suppose that two players hold these hands:

X:	♠ J	♣ J	♡ 7	♠ 7	♡ 9
Y:	♣ Q	♠ 7	♣ 6 4	◇ 2	

Player X makes the usual one-card draw, discarding the ♡ 9 in hope of making a full house with a jack or seven, for "high." Player Y discards the ♣ Q and makes a one-card draw, hoping for something lower, which would give him a good hand for "low." Even a 9 or an 8 might do, but of course a 5 or a 3 would almost be a clincher. Y's real worry is that he may "pair" a card already in his hand, by drawing a 7, 6, 4, or 2.

Better still are hands like the following:

X: ◇ 8   ♠ 8   ♡ 7   ♠ 6   ♣ 5
Y: ◇ 9 6 5 3   ♣ K

By discarding an eight and making a one-card draw, *X* may make a straight (9–8–7–6–5 or 8–7–6–5–4) for "high," or by drawing a 3 or 2, come up with a fairly good bid for "low." In *Y*'s turn, a discard of the ♣ K might result in drawing a fifth diamond to produce a flush for "high" or an 8, 7, 4, or 2 for a possible "low." Even a doubtful hand is often worth betting, because sometimes two or more players may all be going for "high" without the others knowing it, so the worst hand automatically wins "low" when the showdown comes. Conversely, all could be going for "low," only to have one win "high."

By the original rules of "high-low draw," the hands "speak for themselves" at the showdown, which is an old poker custom. Their values are noted and the pot is divided between the players with the high and low hands; if there is an odd chip, it goes to the player with the high hand. This is still a good way to play the game, but in a more modern form, players must declare whether they are going for "high" or "low." This can be a progressive declaration, beginning with the last player who raised or bet; but a preferable mode is a *simultaneous declaration,* with a player secretly taking a red chip in his hand for "high" or a white chip for "low." Fists are raised and opened all together, to establish the choices.

Betting follows the usual procedure, but with an added proviso: Often, a player with an almost certain "high" and another with an equally strong "low" will keep raising each other indefinitely. A third player may thereby be "caught between" with only a fair hand, being forced to stay, because both his opponents might be going for the same thing—"high" or "low." So in fairness to such "in-betweeners," players are allowed only three successive raises during a betting round.

High-Low Five-Card Stud: The regular game, but with players betting on either "high" or "low" prospects on each round, with hands decided by "cards speak" or "declarations," as preferred. It is productive of some sharply competitive results, but some players are often obvious losers. Hence the game often includes a feature termed *Option,* whereby each player, beginning with the highest hand showing, can discard one card and draw another instead; a hole card for a hole card, or an upcard for an upcard, as the case may be, immediately after the final betting round. Additional options or "twists" may be included if so agreed; but always a player can "stand pat," keeping his hand intact, if preferred. With a single option, this game is much like:

High-Low Six-Card Stud: This is coming into popularity and wisely so. After five cards have been dealt, a sixth is dealt, face down, with a final betting round, as in the standard game. But that leads into:

High-Low Seven-Card Stud, most popular of all. Exactly like *Seven-Card Stud,* but giving the player a choice of five out of seven when he declares his hand as either high or low. Take this hand as an example:

Player *X:* (♢ 6) (♢ 3) ♢ Q ♣ Q ♢ 7 ♠ 8 (♢ 4)

Here, a player can choose between a diamond flush for "high" and an eight-high hand for low, as follows:

♢ Q 7 6 4 3 or ♠ 8 ♢ 7 6 4 3

Possible straights also figure heavily in such hands, as with the following:

Player Y: (♣ 6) (♠ 4) ♡ 7 ♣ 8 ♢ 10 ♠ 2 (♡ 9)

From these, a player could make up either a ten-high straight for high, or an eight-seven hand for low, as:

♢ 10 ♡ 9 ♣ 8 ♡ 7 ♣ 6 or ♣ 8 ♡ 7 ♣ 6 ♠ 4 2

If playing "cards speak," each player could make up his best high hand and his best low hand, with the prospect of winning with one or the other. Example: Since X's flush beats Y's straight for high, Y forms an **8–7–6–4–2** for low and wins in that department. Neither would suffer from the presence of an in-betweener, such as:

Player Z: (◇ 8) (♡ 2) ♡ 5 ♣ 5 ◇ 5 ♡ 6 (♠ 9)

This hand would simply lose either way, when arranged thus:

♡ 5 ♣ 5 ◇ 5 ♠ 9 ◇ 8 or ♠ 9 ◇ 8 ♡ 6 5 2

However, with "declarations," a new situation arises. If X should panic at sight of Z's three fives—which could mean a full house or four of a kind—X might declare low, like Y, while Z, knowing his hand looks strong, might declare high. In that case, Z would win "high, while X, who has the best high hand, would be beaten by Y for "low" (X 8–7–6–4–3 vs. Y 8–7–6–4–2).

Conversely, if both X and Y should decide on high—each thinking that Z had only three of a kind—and Z, feeling they both had him beaten, should go for low, X's flush would beat Y's straight for high, and Z's **9–8–6–5–2** would win low, even though X and Y both held lower hands.

If two hands are tied for either high or low, they simply split that portion of the pot between them. Only five cards can figure in a hand; any extras do not count. In brief, all decisions conform closely to the rules of standard poker. However, complexities can develop when a new and highly popular feature is included; namely:

Declaring Both High and Low: Here, any player who so chooses can go for both high and low either in his proper turn, if declarations are progressive, or by holding a blue chip in his fist if they are simultaneous. Such a player may use any five of his seven cards to form his high, then use any five for his low. He must win both to take the entire pot; if tied for either high or low, he divides that portion with the player who tied him. But if he misses either high or low, he is automatically eliminated; and the contest is restricted to the other players. If only one player remains, he takes the entire pot.

In checking back to the sample hands listed on pages 234–235, the following results would apply:

X declares "high and low." Y declares high. X wins both as his flush beats Y's straight. Z's declaration does not matter, as X beats him both ways.

X declares high and low, Y declares low. X loses both as Y's 8–7–6–4–2 beats X's 8–7–6–4–3 for low. If Z declared high, he would win it with three fives, since X is eliminated. But if Z declared low, his 9–8–6–5–2 would be beaten by Y's 8–7–6–4–3. Since Y is still in the game, Z would be eliminated and Y would take the high half of the pot as the only remaining player.

X and Y each declare high and low, thereby literally canceling each other out. So if Z declared either high or low—but not both!—he would win whichever he declared and take the other half as the only remaining player, gaining the whole pot. But if Z also declared high and low, there would be a triple elimination. In that case, the hand would be settled on a "cards speak" basis, with the declarations being disregarded.

Similar situations may be decided in much the same manner. Some groups agree upon special rules for specific circumstances; but generally it boils down to simple terms, with logic the final factor. However, another element has come to the fore in modern "seven-card high-low," namely: *The Swinging Option:* In its most widely accepted form, this allows aces, which are classed as high in a high hand, to be classed as low in a low hand. The rule is fair, indeed, because aces have long been treated as high or low, in straights (as A–K–Q–J–10 or 5–4–3–2–A). Thus the "swinging ace" was introduced to high-low poker and is now practically a fixture of the game. It means simply this:

With the swinging ace, the lowest hand, instead of simply being

7–5–4–3–2, includes the following lower hands: **7–5–4–3–A, 7–5–4–2–A, 7–5–3–2–A, 7–4–3–2–A, 6–5–4–3–A, 6–5–4–2– A, 6–5–3–2–A,** and, lowest of all, **6–4–3–2–A.** But it also influences high hands, because an ace takes on new stature where they are involved. In the old days, these two holdings, ♡ **A 7 6 3** or ♡ **K 7 6 3**, were almost equal when going for a flush, because each needed a fifth heart to "fill." But today, if the card should be another suit, the difference would be great:

♡ **A 7 6 3** ♠ **5** would be a beautiful **7–6–5–3–A** for low whereas ♡ **K 7 6 3** ♠ **5** would be an utter bust for either high or low. So an ace is a vital card in the game as played today. Hence the rule of the swinging ace should be definitely established before play begins. The same applies to other "swinging options" that have been introduced and should be specified as follows:

A "swinging straight"—the same five cards high or low:

♠ **7**   ◇ **6**   ♠ **5**   ♣ **4**   ♠ **3**   or   **7–6–5–4–3**

A "swinging flush," shown here with a swinging ace, as:

◇ **A 7 5 3 2**   or   **7–5–3–2–A**

And best of all, the "swinging straight flush":

♡ **5 4 3 2 A**   or   **5–4–3–2–A**

Obviously, when one type is allowable, all should be. This is particularly applicable to the modern and popular game of:

Lowball: When *High-Low Poker* was introduced, it was played at intervals between standard forms where the "high hand" alone was winner. As a novelty, that procedure was reversed, resulting in occasional games of "low-hand poker" where only low counted, with **7–5–4–3–2** as the best hand in the game, which is still playable for those who want it. But from it developed a newer game, "lowball," based on this premise:

In poker, only pairs, triplets, and four of a kind were recognized originally. Straights and flushes were injected later to increase the possibilities of high hands. In going for low, nobody could afford to stay on a straight or flush in a game of high-low draw, so those combinations were relegated to the limbo from which they had emerged; and the ultimate result was "lowball," in which an ace is always low; and since straights and flushes are ignored, the lowest possible hand is any 5–4–3–2–A, which is termed a "wheel" or "bicycle."

Lowball is essentially a form of *Draw Poker*, played exactly like the standard version of that game, except for the rating of the hands. It can, however, be adapted to any other form of the game, particularly *Five-Card Stud*, in which low hands are ordinarily all too frequent, and therefore can pep up the play. Many legalized "poker parlors" feature lowball, with house rules forming a part of the game.

Poker with the Stripped Deck: A popular way of stepping up the action in standard "high-hand" poker is to strip the low cards from the pack, as the twos, threes, and even the fours, in games where only three or four players are involved. With *Draw* or *Five-Card Stud,* this improves the chances for high hands, although it greatly alters the usual probabilities toward certain hands. In "straights" an ace still rates as high or low; thus in a forty-card pack, the lowest straight would be 8–7–6–5–A.

Poker with the Bug: This game utilizes the standard fifty-two-card pack plus a joker, termed the "bug," which serves as an extra ace in a "high-hand" game, so that the joker and two aces would rank as A–A–A; while a hand containing the joker and and all four aces would be counted as five aces and as such is higher than a royal flush. The bug can also be used to fill a straight, such as:

♠ Q joker ◇ 10 ♠ 9 ♣ 8 counts as Q–J–10–9–8

The bug can also fill a flush, as:

joker ♡ K J 7 5 counts as ♡ A K J 7 5

Lowball with the Bug: Here, the joker also counts as an ace toward low, but if the player already has an ace, he can give the bug any value he wants, as:

> ♢ **7**   ♡ **6**   **joker**   ♠ **2**   ♢ **A** counts as **7–6–3–2–A**

Joker Poker: Originally termed "mistigris," this game includes the joker as representing *any card* that its holder wants. Hence it is the forerunner of *Wild-Card Poker*, which today has spread like wildfire. Since most modern packs contain two jokers, both may be used. Any five of a kind (as **joker 6–6–6–6**) beats a royal flush.

WILD-CARD POKER: In this ever-expanding category are all forms of poker in which certain "wild cards" can be used to represent other cards, both real and imaginary. Thus such a card can belong to a "fifth suit," giving a player "five of a kind," a hand that outranks a royal flush. This has already been mentioned under *Joker Poker,* but the game that really sets the pace for all to follow is:

Deuces Wild: This may be played as *Draw,* any form of *Stud,* or even *High-Low.* Each deuce is wild, making the highest hand five aces, as:

> ♡ **2**   ♡ **A**   ♣ **A**   ♠ **A**   ♢ **A** or ♡ **2**   ♢ **2**   ♣ **2**   ♠ **2**
> ♠ **A**

Any variation of deuces and aces counts as **A–A–A–A–A;** and so on down, from **K–K–K–K–K** to **3–3–3–3–3**, which is the lowest "five of a kind." Deuces can also be used to complete a "straight flush," so that:

> ♠ **A**   ♣ **2**   ♡ **2**   ♠ **J**   ♠ **2** represents ♠ **A K Q J 10**

The same applies to a "full house" but with a "Flush," an odd situation may develop. Assume that Players *X* and *Y* hold these hands:

X: ♡ A   ♠ 2   ♡ 8 7 4   Y: ♣ A K 8 7 4

This could be a tie: heart flush vs. club flush (each **A–K–8–7–4**).

But according to another school of thought, X's hand would be the winner by this interpretation:

X: ♡ A   ♠ 2   ♡ 8 7 4 represents ♡ A A 8 7 4
Y: ♣ A K 8 7 4 represents ♣ A K 8 7 4

By the rule that a wild card can represent any card, X holds a "double-ace flush," which takes precedence over Y's "ace-king flush."

This should be agreed upon in advance, as otherwise another rule would take precedence; namely, that a "natural" hand wins over a "wild" hand. Here is an example, involving straights:

X: ♠ J   ♣ 10   ♢ 9   ♣ 8   ♠ 7=J–10–9–8–7
Y: ♣ 2   ♠ 10   ♡ 9   ♠ 2   ♢ 7=J–10–9–8–7

Each is a "jack-high straight," but Player X, with the "natural," wins over Y's "wild-card straight." However, a moot question arises with lesser hands, as "three of a kind." Take these samples:

X: ♡ K   ♣ K   ♢ K   ♠ 9   ♣ 4=K–K–K
Y: ♢ 2   ♡ 2   ♠ K   ♣ 9   ♢ 5=K–K–K

Here, X and Y each have three kings, but X's "naturals" are supported by a nine and a four, whereas Y's wild holding is backed by a nine and a five, making Y the winner. If X's ♣ 4 had been the ♣ 5, X would have won on the strength of naturals over wild cards. Here, again, is a rule that should be understood beforehand.

All this adds up to the fact that "deuces wild" is a good game in its own right. Far from being unpredictable, it can be played quite scientifically. A player holding all four deuces is a sure winner; a player holding three deuces is nearly so. Holding just a pair of deuces gives a player an excellent edge, since he automatically has three of a kind, which is generally good enough to win. But with only one deuce—or none—a player's chances may be shaky unless he holds a high straight or a flush.

From "deuces wild" have developed many wilder games along with other variants that come under the head of:

Dealer's Choice: This represents poker in its ultramodern and most sociable form, in which the dealer decides what type of game is to be played in the next deal or round, subject to any restrictions agreed upon beforehand. As a result, "dealer's choice" can be limited to standard games, where serious poker addicts are concerned, but the general practice is to let the dealer call for any game he wants and even invent a few variations. Usually, however, it is customary for each dealer to put up the same amount as an ante; and in some cases, a specified game should be played for an entire round, rather than a single deal, if the majority of the players want it that way.

These games run the gamut from mere variants of standard games to those that are wild beyond belief. Since many readers may recognize many of them by name, rather than by type, they have been listed alphabetically, rather than in groups, with reference to the parent games on which they are based:

ACE POTS: Regular *Draw Poker*, page 226, with aces or better as openers.

ANACONDA: Each player is dealt a hand of seven cards from which he discards two without showing them. Each then lays a card face down; these are turned up and bet as in *Five-Card Stud,* page 228. This is repeated with the remaining cards, one by one, with players dropping if they think they are beaten. Similar to *Seven-Card Reverse,* page 264.

ANACONDA WITH PASS ALONG: In this addition to *Anaconda,* above, each player first lays three of his cards face down; and when all are ready, each passes his trio to the player on his left, as in the game of *Hearts,* page 140. This may cause a player to break up a "pat hand" or otherwise upset his plans. The game then proceeds like simple *Anaconda,* though as a general rule, a player is required to arrange his final five cards in the exact order in which he intends to turn them up. *Screwy Louie,* page 263, is a similar game; and both come under the head of *Pass the Garbage* or *Pass the Trash,* page 259.

ANY CARD WILD: Usual *Draw,* page 226, or *Stud Poker,* pages 228–231, until the showdown, when each player may use any card in his hand as a wild card. Example:

♡ K ♠ Q ♣ 10 ♠ 9 ♡ 6 Make ♡ **6** wild to form K–Q–J–10–9

ANY SUIT WILD: All the cards of a specified suit are declared wild, making it a wild game indeed. Also termed *Wild Suit,* page 274.

ANYTHING OPENS: *Draw Poker,* page 226, with no opening requirement and usually with the privilege of entering the betting after a preliminary pass.

ANY VALUE WILD: An extension of *Any Card Wild,* above, with any extra cards of the same value in the player's hand also being classed as wild.

Example: ◇ K ◇ J ◇ 9 ♡ 7 ♣ 7 Make sevens wild to form ◇ K Q J 10 9

AROUND THE WORLD: Each player is dealt a hand of four cards and a round of betting follows. A single card is dealt face up and regarded as part of each player's hand. Betting follows and three more cards are dealt face up on the same basis, each with its betting round. Active hands are then shown and player with the best five cards wins. Similar to *Seven-Card Mutual,* page 264, *Omaha,* page 257, and *Hold 'Em,* page 252.

AUSTRALIAN POKER: Another term for *Blind Opening,* page 245. Also called *English Poker.*

AUTOMATIC LOWBALL: Played with *Jackpots* (or *Acepots*), page 253, in *Draw Poker,* page 226. If no one opens, the players retain their hands and play them as in *Lowball,* page 237.

BANK NIGHT: *High-Low Five-Card Stud,* page 233, with two replacements or twists, as described under *Option,* page 258, and *Five-Card Stud with Replacement,* page 249.

BASEBALL: A form of *Seven-Card Stud,* page 229, with threes and nines wild; but a player who is dealt a three face up must either put chips in the pot equaling the amount already there or fold his hand. A player who is dealt a four face up is immediately dealt an extra downcard as a bonus. Sometimes played *High-Low,* page 232.

BEAT YOUR NEIGHBOR: Each player is dealt five cards in a face-down packet and cannot look at them. First player turns his top card face up and betting follows. Second player turns up cards one by one until he tops first player with a higher card or pair. Third player turns up cards until he shows something better than the second; and so on, with betting following each player's turn. Any player running out of cards drops and the next player continues. When only one player remains, he wins.

BEDSPRINGS: Five cards are dealt to each player, but no draw follows. Instead, two rows of five cards are dealt face down. Cards of top row are turned up one by one, with betting after each turnup; those of bottom row are turned up on the same basis, so rows might stand:

♡ K ◇ 3 ◇ 9 ♡ 8 ◇ 2
♠ 4 ♣ 4 ♡ A ♡ Q ♠ 6

Each player may add one card of the top row and the card directly below to the five he already holds, giving him seven from which he chooses his final five, as in *High-Low Seven-Card Stud,* page 234, toward either "high" or "low." If he goes for both high and low (see page 235), he can use the same two from the layout, or another two, as he prefers.

Player *A:* ♣ K ◇ K ♠ 8 ♣ 5 ◇ 4

Choices from the layout would be ♡ K and ♠ 4 toward "high" **(K–K–K–4–4)** with ◇ 2 and ♠ 6 toward "low" **(8–6–5–4–2).**

Player *B:* ♡ J ♡ 10 ♠ 7 ♡ 5 ♣ 2

Choice would be ♡ 8 and ♡ Q toward "high" (♡ **Q J 10 8 5)** with ◇ 3 and ♣ 4 toward "low" (7–5–4–3–2).

BEST FLUSH: Any game in which only flushes or partial flushes count. Hands rank in following order: royal flush; regular flush; four-flush; three-flush; two cards of one suit. Ties are decided by highest card (or cards) of the flush; if still tied, highest card in any other suit decides.

BET OR DROP: *Draw Poker,* page 226, with the rule that a player cannot "check" after the draw, but must either bet or drop.

BETTY HUTTON: *Seven-Card Stud,* page 229, in which fives and nines are wild.

BIMBO: A popular name for *Double-handed High-Low,* page 248.

BLIND OPENING or BLIND AND STRADDLE: A form of *Draw Poker,* page 226, in which the player at dealer's left must open the pot without looking at his hand; and the next player must raise under the same condition. Also known as *Australian Poker* and *English Poker.*

BLIND STUD: Any form of *Five-Card Stud,* page 228, in which no one looks at a hole card until all upcards have been bet. Can also be played by dealing the hole card last.

BLIND TIGER: Another term for *Blind Opening,* above.

BOBTAIL OPENER: Standard *Jackpots,* page 253, but with a player allowed to open with a "bobtail straight," or four cards in sequence but not of the same suit; and also with the privilege of opening on a "four flush." See *Four-Flush Stud,* page 250.

BOBTAIL STUD: *Five-Card Stud,* page 228, with a bobtail straight ranking above an ace-high and a four flush ranking above the bobtail. See *Canadian Stud,* page 246 and *Four-Flush Stud,* page 250.

BUTCHER BOY: Cards are dealt face up, one to each player in turn, until one is duplicated in value. Example: First player, ◇ 8; second, ◇ J; third, ♣ 4; fourth, ♡ J. The last card is given to the player who has that value (in this case, the second player) and he starts a round of betting. The deal is then resumed, beginning with the player who still has a card due him (in this case the fourth player), and when a value is again duplicated, the same rule applies. This continues until one player acquires all four cards of one value and wins the pot. Betting rounds can be numerous, hence many players find it advisable to "check" or "drop" in the early stages.

CALIFORNIA LOWBALL: Another name for *Lowball.* See page 237.

CANADIAN STUD: *Five-Card Stud,* page 228, with the special rule that a bobtail or open-end straight (as **K–Q–J–10**) beats a pair; and that a four flush (as ♡ **J 7 6 3**) beats a four-straight. Similar to *New York Stud,* page 257.

CHICAGO: *Seven-Card Stud,* page 229, with the player holding the highest spade splitting the pot with the player who has the highest hand. Absence of high spades among the upcards may encourage players to stay with weak hands.

CINCINNATI: Five cards are dealt to each player, as in *Draw Poker,* page 226, along with an extra hand that remains face down, like a "widow." After a round of betting, instead of a draw, the cards of the extra hand are turned up one by one, with a betting round on each, as those cards are shared mutually by all players who stay. In the showdown, each player makes up a five-card hand from his own cards and those on the table; and the highest hand wins. This game, with slight variants, is also known as *Lamebrains, Tennessee,* and *Utah.* It also forms the basis for several other games.

CINCINNATI LIZ: Also known as *Lamebrain Pete,* this is simply *Cincinnati,* above (or *Lamebrains*) with the added feature that the lowest card in the face-up center group is wild, as are all others of its value, including those held by individual players.

CLOSED POKER: Any game like *Draw Poker,* page 226, in which each player alone sees his own cards prior to the showdown. The opposite of *Open Poker,* page 258.

COLD HANDS: Each player is dealt five face-up cards and the best poker hand wins the pot. A purely automatic game dependent only on luck.

COLD HANDS WITH DRAW: After cold hands are dealt, each player openly discards unwanted cards and calls for others to be dealt face up. Here, judgment can be used in deciding on the type of draw. Example: A player holding ♠ 9 ♡ 9 ♠ 8 ♣ 6 ♡ 5 would normally keep his pair (9–9) and draw three cards, hoping to make three nines (9–9–9). But if he sees that another player already has three jacks (J–J–J), he would discard the ♠ 9 (or ♡ 9) and draw one card, hoping for a seven, which would fill his "inside straight," enabling him to win with 9–8–7–6–5.

CRISSCROSS: Exactly the same as *Cross Over*, below, but the center card and any others of the same value are wild, whether showing on the board or in a player's hand.

CROSS OVER: This is *Cincinnati*, page 246, with the extra hand forming a cross:

Betting follows the turning up of each card, the center card being turned up last. A player can only add one cross-row to his five cards in forming his final hand, thus limiting him to a total of eight cards, instead of ten, as in *Cincinnati*. See *Crisscross*, above.

CROSS WIDOW: A name applied to *Crisscross* or *Cross Over*, above, since each involves a "widow" of five cards dealt in cross formation.

DEUCES WILD: Any game in which all four deuces are wild cards. See page 239.

DEUCES WILDER: Games in which deuces and other specific cards are wild, such as: *Deuces and Joker Wild*, or *Deuces and Jokers* if two of the latter are used; *Deuces and One-eyed Jacks Wild*, those being the ♡ J and ♠ J; also *One-eyed King Wild*, namely the ◇ K; *Deuces and Treys Wild*, making eight wild cards in all; or any other cards as chosen by the dealer, one favorite being *Deuces and Pothooks Wild* (nines).

DOCTOR PEPPER: Deuces, fours, and tens all wild in *Seven-Card Stud,* page 229.

DOUBLE-BARRELED SHOTGUN: Another name for *Texas Tech,* page 271.

DOUBLE-HANDED HIGH-LOW: A form of *High-Low Five-Card Stud,* page 233, with two hands being dealt to each player, who bets them separately, with privilege of folding one and continuing to play the other.

DOWN THE RIVER: Another name for *Seven-Card Stud,* page 229.

DRAW POKER: See special description, page 226.

DYNAMITE: An appropriate name for *Two-Card Poker,* especially when played with deuces (or other cards) wild. See page 273.

EIGHT-CARD STUD: *Seven-Card Stud* with an extra card, as described on page 230. In "dealer's choice," the last two are usually hole cards, and wild cards are frequently specified.

EIGHTY-EIGHT: *Eight-Card Stud,* above, with eights wild.

ENGLISH POKER: Another name for *Blind Opening,* page 245. Also called *Australian Poker.*

ENGLISH STUD: This is *Seven-Card Stud,* page 229, as widely played in England. Each player is dealt two hole cards and an upcard, followed by two upcards singly, with a betting round after each deal, making three rounds as in the American game.

Then comes the difference: To receive a sixth and later a seventh card, a player must discard one he already has. If he discards a hole card, he is dealt a face-down card; for an upcard, he receives another face up. A betting round follows each deal, and in the showdown each player has exactly five cards, as in *Draw Poker,* page 226.

FIERY CROSS: This is dealt like *Crisscross,* page 247, but played as *High-Low,* page 232, with no wild cards. A player can go for both high and low, using a different cross-row for each.

FIVE AND DIME: *Seven-Card Stud,* page 229, with fives and tens wild. Usually played in the stepped-up form of *Woolworth,* page 274. Also refers to a freak hand with a ten high and a five low.

FIVE-CARD FINAL: *Five-Card Stud,* page 228, with the last card dealt face down, giving a player two hole cards. May be played with wild cards, as agreed; or as *High-Low,* page 232.

FIVE-CARD STUD: See description on page 228. When played as "deuces wild" or any similar game, a wild card is the first to bet, taking precedence over the highest card showing. A pair of wild cards takes precedence over any other pair; and a pair with one wild card takes precedence over a natural pair of the same value (as 2–K over K–K).

FIVE-CARD STUD, LAST UP OR DOWN: Here, each player can call for his last card down, turning up his hole card instead; or he may have it dealt face up as usual. See page 228.

FIVE-CARD STUD WITH REPLACEMENT: The usual game, page 228, but with the added privilege of discarding any card and drawing another in its place; face down if the hole card is involved, otherwise face up. This is termed a "twist" and is followed by another betting round. When played *High-Low*, page 232, this game is commonly termed *Option*. Also see *English Stud*, page 248.

FLIP: See *Mexican Stud*, page 255, and *Seven-Card Flip*, page 263.

FLIP STUD: Another name for *Mexican Wild*, page 256.

FOOTBALL: A form of *Seven-Card Stud*, page 229, with fours and sixes wild; with the rule that a player dealt a four face up must either put chips in the pot, equaling the amount already there, or fold his hand. A player who is dealt a two face up is immediately dealt an extra downcard as a bonus. Similar to *Baseball*, page 243, and can be played *High-Low*, page 232, like that game.

FOUR-CARD POKER: Either *Draw*, page 226, or *Stud*, page 229, with any variants, such as "wild cards" or "high-low," but with only four cards dealt to each player. Hands rank in the following order: four of a kind, straight flush, flush, straight, three of a kind, two pair, pair, high card. In *Draw*, a player may call for any number of cards up to four; in *Stud*, the first card is customarily a hole card; the rest, upcards.

FOUR-FLUSH OPENER: Standard *Jackpots*, but with the special privilege of opening with a "four flush" (as ♡ Q 9 7 6 ◊ K). See *Bobtail Opener*, page 245.

FOUR-FLUSH STUD: Any type of *Five-Card Stud*, page 228, with a "four flush" ranking above an ace-high hand, but below a pair. See *Canadian Stud*, page 246, *New York Stud*, page 257, and *Bobtail Stud*, page 245.

FOUR FORTY-FOUR: A form of *Eight-Card Stud*, page 230, with *four* hole cards, *four* upcards, and all *fours* wild, all easily remembered by the title.

FOUR FORTY-TWO: A variant of *Four Forty-four*, played the same way, but with deuces wild instead of fours. See above.

FREAK HANDS: Any form of poker with added action in the form of "freak" combinations not included in the standard game. A list of these with their comparative values is given on pages 278–283.

FREE WHEELING: Another name for *Poverty Poker* (page 260).

FREEZEOUT: Special poker games where any player must drop completely from play once he has exhausted his original supply of chips.

GRUESOME TWOSOME: *Two-Card Poker*, played like *Draw Poker*, page 226, but with each player having three chances to discard one card or stand pat, with a round of betting on each occasion. For rank of hands, see *Two-Card Poker*, page 273.

GUTS: Standard *Draw Poker*, page 226, with a player allowed to open on anything.

HALF-POT LIMIT: Any game in which a player may bet up to half the amount at present in the pot.

HEINZ: *Seven-Card Stud*, page 229, with fives and sevens wild; but if a player is dealt one as an upcard, he must contribute a specified amount to the pot or fold his hand. Similar to *Woolworth*, page 274.

HIGH-LOW POKER: See special description on page 232.

HIGH POKER: Any form of poker in which only the high hand wins.

HIGH SPADE SPLIT: Any game in which the player with the highest hand splits the pot with the player holding the highest spade. In *Draw*, it is usual to "open on anything"; in *Five-Card Stud*, the variant called *Mexican Stud* enables a player to keep his high spade hidden. In *Seven-Card Stud,* the game is called *Chicago,* page 246.

HILO: A term for *Automatic Lowball,* page 243, applied particularly to games in which a pair of kings or better is required to open on "high"; otherwise, the game becomes "lowball."

HILO PICOLO: *Take It or Leave It.* See page 270.

HOKUM: Each player is dealt a face-down card as a start toward a hand of *Five-Card Stud,* page 228, but is allowed to look at it before receiving the next card face up. If he wants, he can turn it face up and be dealt the next card as his hole card. Betting and further deals of single upcards follow, exactly as in *Five-Card Stud.* Can be played with first two cards dealt face down, letting the player turn up whichever he chooses, as in *Mexican Stud,* page 255. The rest are dealt face up already specified.

HOLD 'EM: A speeded-up version of *Omaha,* page 257. Each player is dealt two face-down cards and a round of betting follows; then three cards are dealt face up in the center for another betting round; next, two cards singly, each with a betting round; so that there are only four betting rounds in all.

The center group, termed the "flop," is common to every hand. So are the last two cards.

HOLE-CARD STUD: Each player is dealt a face-down hole card, which he looks at and bets, beginning at the dealer's left, with each player in turn having the right to call, raise, or drop. An upcard is then dealt to each, followed by another betting round, beginning with the highest showing, though that player may drop if he pleases. Three more upcards are dealt and bet singly, exactly as in *Five-Card Stud,* page 228, the only difference being that this game has an earlier or preliminary betting round.

HOLLYWOOD: An elaboration of *Cincinnati,* page 246, with ten cards being dealt on the table and turned up singly, with a betting round on each. All are mutual, giving each player fifteen cards (including his own) from which to form his hand.

HURRICANE: A popular name for *Two-Card Poker,* page 273. See also *Dynamite,* page 248.

JACKPOTS: Regular *Draw Poker,* page 226, with the rule that a player must have a pair of jacks or higher in order to open the betting. Otherwise, the deal moves along and the pot remains intact.

JACKS BACK or JACKSON: The same as *Automatic Lowball,* page 243.

JACKS HIGH: Regular *Draw,* page 226, or *Five-Card Stud,* page 228, played as *High Poker,* page 251, but with a pair of jacks the highest hand allowable, anything above that being disqualified, which produces some intriguing situations. A value other than jacks can be specified if preferred.

JOKER POKER: Any form of poker with the joker as a wild card. Can be played with modern two-joker packs with both wild. See page 239.

KANKAKEE: A game wherein a joker is dealt face up as a wild card for everybody's hand. From there on, cards are dealt as in *Seven-Card Stud,* page 229, with the usual betting rounds. The player with the best five cards (counting the wild joker) is the winner.

KINGS BACK or KINGSTON: The same as *Jacks Back* (or *Automatic Lowball*) above, except that a pair of kings (or better) is needed to open; otherwise the hand is played as *Lowball,* page 237.

KNOCK POKER: A form of *Rummy,* utilizing Poker combinations (see page 153). Not actually a form of *Poker,* but allowable as a form of *Dealer's Choice,* if all players agree.

LALAPALOOZA: A game in which an odd but fairly common hand is given top rating—above a royal flush—for the first player who is dealt one; but from then on, it reverts to its usual rank, during the remainder of that session.

LAMEBRAIN PETE: Another name for *Cincinnati Liz,* page 246.

LAMEBRAINS: A popular term for *Cincinnati,* page 246, often applied to any of its wild-card variants.

LAZY LUCY: Another name for *One-Card Poker,* page 258.

LEFTY LOUIE: All picture cards with faces looking toward the left are wild. An intriguing game, because the portraits vary with different makes of playing cards.

LEG IN POT: A round of *High Poker,* page 251, in which the winner of each pot must leave it until someone wins a second pot and thereby takes all.

LOWBALL: See special description, page 237.

LOW CARD WILD: Any type of game in which a player's lowest card is counted as wild, along with any others of that value that he happens to hold.

LOW ENGLISH STUD: Played exactly like *English Stud,* page 248, but with the low hand winning instead of the high, an ace being ranked as "low." Can also be played with cards ranking as in *Lowball,* page 237, thus eliminating straights, flushes, etc.

LOW HOLE CARD WILD: *Stud Poker,* page 228, with a player's lowest hole card wild, as are any other cards of that value in his hand. Especially popular as *Seven-Card Stud*, page 229.

LOW POKER: A game in which the lowest hand wins, but with hands ranked as usual, so that 7–5–4–3–2 was originally the lowest possible. Usually played with "ace low" so that 6–4–3–2–A is lowest. If straights are eliminated, making 5–4–3–2–A the lowest, the game takes on the character of *Lowball*, page 237.

MA FERGUSON: Nickname for *Seven-Card Stud, Low Upcard Wild*, page 266.

MATCH 'EM: *Five-Card Stud*, page 228, in which a player's hole card becomes wild if he matches it in value with an upcard, which also becomes wild, as do any more of the same value that he holds. Any pair thus matched automatically gives a player three of a kind. Example: (♣ 7) ♡ 9 ♣ K ◇ 7 ♡ J=K–K–K. Hence competition is often keen to the last card.

MEXICAN LOW CARD: *Mexican Stud with Low Card Wild*, below.

MEXICAN STUD: Basically a form of *Five-Card Stud*, page 228, in which each player is dealt two cards face down and after looking at them is allowed to turn up either card, keeping the other as his hole card. Each succeeding card is dealt face down with the same privilege of retaining it as hole card or turning it up, as preferred. All turnups are made simultaneously by the players, so that none can change his mind after another shows his card; hence the game is popularly and appropriately called *Flip*. With *Seven-Card Stud*, it is called *Seven-Card Flip* and is described under that head. See page 263.

MEXICAN STUD WITH LOW CARD WILD: The regular game until the hole card is finally shown. Then, each player's lowest card is wild for his hand, along with any more of the same value that he happens to hold. A game filled with surprises.

MEXICAN WILD: *Mexican Stud,* page 255, with each player counting his hole card wild, as well as any others of that value in his hand. This applies specifically to the five-card game but can also be used with *Seven-Card Flip,* page 263, the final hole card being the wild value.

MIKE: *Stud Poker,* page 228, without any upcards. Each player is dealt two cards face down, looks at them, and bets, beginning at the dealer's left. Single cards are then dealt, each followed by a betting round. Can be played with any specified number of cards, like various forms of *Stud,* with each player making up his best five card hand and showing it after betting ends. Can also be played as "high-low," page 232, with players making up separate hands for "high" and "low."

MISERE: The English version of *Lowball.* See page 237.

MISTIGRIS: The old name for *Joker Poker,* page 239.

MONTE: Another name for *Three-Card Poker,* page 271.

MORTGAGE: Another name for *Leg in Pot,* page 254, frequently used with *Seven-Card Stud,* page 229, when played on that basis.

MUSTACHED JACKS WILD: Same as *One-eyed Jacks Wild,* page 258, as it refers to the same two cards (♡ J and ♠ J). Usually designated as "mustached jacks and kings wild," making five wild cards (♡ J, ♠ J, ♠ K, ◇ K, ♣ K) in the game.

MUSTACHED KINGS WILD: Any game including the three mustached kings (♣ K, ◇ K, and ♠ K) as wild cards.

NEW GUINEA STUD: Each player is dealt four face-down cards, from which he chooses two and turns them face up. A round of betting follows and the game proceeds as in *Seven-Card Stud,* page 229, two more upcards and another hole card all dealt singly, with a betting round after each.

NEW YORK STUD: *Five-Card Stud,* page 228, with a four flush ranking higher than a pair but below two pair. See *Canadian Stud,* page 246, a similar game.

NINE-CARD STUD: *Eight-Card Stud,* page 230, with an added hole card, which may be dealt singly and bet accordingly, or the last two may be dealt together. Game should be limited to five players, and the exact mode of dealing and betting should be specified.

NINETY-NINE: *Nine-Card Stud,* above, with nines wild.

NO DRAW: Five cards dealt face down to each player, with a single round of betting and a prompt showdown, without a draw.

NO LIMIT: Any game in which betting is unlimited. The same as *Sky's the Limit,* page 267.

NO LOW CARDS: *Five-Card Stud,* page 228, in which a player may reject any hole card lower than a four and call for another instead, repeating the procedure if need be. If agreed, the rule may apply to upcards as well. It may also be used with variants of *Five Card Stud,* such as *Canadian Stud,* page 246, *Mexican Stud,* page 255, and others.

OMAHA: A highly popular cross between *Cincinnati,* page 246, and *Seven-Card Stud,* page 229. Two cards are dealt face down to each player, followed by a betting round, then five cards singly to the center, face up, each followed by a betting round. Where *Cincinnati* can accommodate nine players (five cards to each plus five center cards), this game can be played by as many as twenty-three (two cards to each plus five center cards), though it is seldom that so many participate. For closely related games, see *Hold 'Em,* page 252, and *Seven-Card Mutual,* page 264.

ONE-CARD POKER: Each player is dealt a single face-down card and bets that the highest will win. Can also be played with low to win; or high-low splits the pot. Ace is always high and deuce low. There is no draw (of a single card) unless so specified by the dealer.

ONE-EYED JACKS WILD: Any game in which the ♠ J and ♡ J, which appear in profile, are classed as wild cards. Sometimes specified as *All One-Eyes Wild,* to include the ◇ K.

ONE-EYED KING WILD: The ◇ K, the only king appearing in profile, as a wild card.

OPEN POKER: Any game in which some of the cards are dealt face up, as in various forms of *Stud,* page 228, as opposed to *Closed Poker,* page 246, in which all cards are dealt face down.

OPTION: *High-Low Five-Card Stud,* page 233, with a "twist" or replacement at the finish—either for a hole card or an upcard—followed by an added betting round. The twist is optional, hence the name, and sometimes the game is beefed up further by allowing two twists, each with a betting round. In that form the game closely resembles *English Stud,* page 248, with which it is frequently confused, the difference being that English stud has two hole cards to start and is generally played for "high," like regular stud, though *Low English Stud,* page 254, is also popular.

PA FERGUSON: Nickname for *Seven-Card Stud, Low Upcard Wild,* page 266, with high upcard wild.

PASS ALONG: *Seven-Card Stud, High and Low,* page 265, with the privilege of passing along an upcard on each round, as in *Push Poker;* but with no exchange of hole cards.

PASS AND BACK IN: Any game in which a player can enter a betting round after he has passed.

PASS OUT: The same as *Bet or Drop,* page 244.

PASS THE GARBAGE or TRASH: Any game in which face-down cards are passed to the next player, as *Anaconda* or *Screwy Louie.* See pages 241 and 263.

PEDRO: Another name for *Mexican Stud,* page 255.

PEEK POKER: The early form of *Seven-Card Stud,* page 229, in which only the first two cards were hole cards, a rule still followed in certain modern games, as *Omaha,* page 257.

PEEP AND TURN: Another name for *Mexican Seven-Card Stud,* page 255, or *Seven-Card Flip,* page 263.

PENNY ANTE: A game costing only a cent to open, with limits proportionately low.

PIG IN POKE or WILD WIDOW: *Draw Poker,* page 226, with an extra card turned up to establish all cards of that value as wild for that particular deal. The extra card does not figure in the play. Thus, if the ◊ 6 should be turned up as the "pig in poke," there would be three wild cards in the game: ♠ 6, ♡ 6, and ♣ 6. See *Wild Widow,* page 274, for a variation.

PINOCHLE POKER: Played with a *Pinochle* pack, page 174, ranking **A, K, Q, J, 10, 9** with all cards duplicated. Five of a kind is the highest hand, and a flush with two pair takes precedence over a one-pair flush, which rates above an ordinary flush.

PISTOL, PISTOL PETE, or PISTOL STUD: All names for *Hole-Card Stud,* page 252.

PLACE AND SHOW: Similar to *Place Poker,* below, but in this case the pot is split between the second-best and the third-best hands, all others being eliminated.

PLACE POKER: Any type of game with the special rule that the second-best hand wins the pot, instead of the best hand.

POKER SOLITAIRE: Five rows of five cards each are dealt at random; then rearranged so that each cross-row represents a poker hand ranking as a straight or higher. Example:

♠4 ◊J ♣3 ♡5 ♡7		♠J ◊J ♡J ♣J ♡A
♡K ♡J ◊3 ♣K ♣A	Can be	♡K ◊K ♣K ♠Q ♡Q
♣9 ◊K ♠J ♡A ♣10	formed	♣A ♣10 ♣9 ♣8 ♣3
♡Q ◊6 ◊9 ♣8 ◊5	into:	◊10 ◊9 ◊5 ◊4 ◊2
♠Q ◊4 ◊2 ◊10 ♣J		♡7 ◊6 ♡5 ♠4 ◊3

In competition, players can be dealt twenty-five cards each from different packs, and the first to complete a layout wins.

POTHOOKS WILD: A game with the nines as wild cards.

POT LIMIT: Any game in which the size of the pot or pool determines the limit of an immediate bet.

POVERTY POKER: A game in which a player is allowed to continue without paying after losing all his chips, until he wins a pot and is thus back in the game. Each player begins with the same number of chips, or the rule goes into effect after losing a specified number. Also called *Free Wheeling.*

PRIMERO: An almost forgotten Spanish antecedent of poker, from which both *Ambigu,* page 15, and *Ombre,* page 166, were partially derived.

PROCTER AND GAMBLE: A cross between *Cincinnati,* page 246, and *Option,* page 258, in which each player is dealt a hand of four cards, then three mutual cards are dealt face down. Each center card is "rolled," or turned up, and a round of betting follows, making three rounds in all, with the last card wild, along with all others of its value in a player's hand or on the board. Player forming the best five-card hand from his own and those turned up is winner.

PROGRESSIVE JACKPOTS: This begins as *Jackpots,* page 253, with a pair of jacks or better to open; but if a deal is passed, a pair of queens becomes the minimum. Another pass boosts it to a pair of kings; then to aces, as in *Acepots,* page 241, where it normally stays until a pot is opened, though by agreement, two pair may then be set as openers. After a pot is opened, the requirement reverts to a pair of jacks on the next deal.

PUSH POKER: A form of *Five-Card Stud,* page 228, but only the first player is dealt an upcard, which he can push along to the next player if he does not want to keep it. In that case he is dealt another upcard, which he keeps. The second player can do the same; and so on to the dealer, who can keep a card pushed to him, or put it under the pack and deal himself another. A second upcard is dealt to the first player, who again either keeps it or passes it along; and so on with successive players. This continues with the usual betting rounds, and after betting on the fifth card, each player may discard any card—even his hole card—and be dealt another instead, as in *Sixth Card Optional,* page 267. There is a final round of betting, then the showdown.

This game is also known as *Shove 'Em Along* and as *Take It or Leave It,* which is usually played as *High-Low,* page 232. Another name is *Rothschild.*

To pep up the game, a rule is generally included that allows a player to push along any upcard, not just the one dealt to him. As that is an advantage, it is often tempered by a further rule, requiring a player to add a chip to the pot every time he decides to "push" instead of "keep." Other variations may be introduced. See *Pass Along*, page 259.

PUSSY CAT: *Push Poker*, page 261, played *High-Low*, page 232, with the sly inclusion of an extra card dealt face down, instead of *Sixth Card Optional*, page 267. This "free ride" not only can improve a player's hand, but may enable him to go for "high and low" instead of only one, in which case he becomes the cat, while the other players are the mice. Since no player wants that extra sixth card unless he needs it, another rule may be added, requiring a payment in chips for such a card.

QUEEN CITY POKER: Another name for *Cincinnati*. See page 246.

RANGDOODLES: A round of *Roodles*, below, after a specified good hand.

RICKEY DE LAET: A form of *Mexican Stud* (page 255), but each player's hole card is wild in his hand.

ROODLES: Any game in which antes or limits are increased by agreement, sometimes for a single hand, but more often for a round of deals or more. Thus, a round of roodles may automatically follow any pot won by a full house; or two rounds after any pot won by four of a kind or better. Sometimes roodles are introduced spontaneously on any pretext that will step up a slow-moving game. Its more conservative forms are popularly known as *Rangdoodles*, above, or *Whangdoodles*, page 274.

ROTHSCHILD: Another name for *Push Poker*, particularly when extra payments are demanded for each push. See page 261.

ROUND OF JACKS: A game of *Draw Poker*, page 226, in which each player is required to deal a hand of *Jackpots*, page 253, until an entire round has been dealt. A form of *Whangdoodles*, page 274.

ROUND THE CORNER: A game in which an ace may be both high and low when forming a straight, as **4–3–2–A–K, 3–2–A–K–Q, 2–A–K–Q–J,** which should properly be rated in that order, all below **5–4–3–2–A.**

ROUND THE WORLD: See *Around the World*, page 242.

SCREWY LOUIE: Like *Anaconda*, page 241, with the "pass along" feature, but only two cards are passed to the player on the left. Thus each player is dealt five, passes two, and rolls five, betting after each turnup, those being made in a set order. The only difference is that a player can retain a "pat hand" (as **J–10–9–8–7**), which is not possible when three cards are passed as in anaconda.

SECOND HAND LOW: Any form of *Low Poker*, page 255, or *Lowball*, page 237, in which the second-lowest hand wins the pot instead of the lowest.

SEVEN-CARD FLIP: In basic form, this is exactly like *Mexican Stud*, page 255, but with seven cards instead of five. Each player is dealt three face down and keeps two as hole cards, turning up the third. Each succeeding card is dealt face down, again giving choice of any one out of three to turn up. Last card, however, stays face down, as in *Seven-Card Stud*, page 229. Betting is the same as in that game.

SEVEN-CARD FLIP, MODERN FORM: This popular version speeds and simplifies the action. Each player is dealt four cards face down, flips two, giving himself two upcards, so the first round of betting involves four cards. Procedure is then the same as *Seven-Card Stud*, page 229, two more cards being dealt face down with a round of betting after each. If so specified, the two cards can be flipped singly at the start, with a round of betting after each, making the same number as in seven-card stud. Either way, the game can be played high-low or with wild cards.

SEVEN-CARD HOKUM: A name occasionally applied to the modern form of *Seven-Card Flip*, see page 263, due to its similarity to *Hokum*, page 252.

SEVEN-CARD MUTUAL: A fast, practical form of *Seven-Card Stud*, page 229, that can accommodate as many as fifteen players. Each is dealt two face-down hole cards, then a single card is dealt face up in the center of the table, serving as a mutual upcard for every hand. A betting round follows, then three more mutual upcards are dealt, each followed by a betting round. Finally, each player is dealt a separate downcard, giving him a total of seven, counting the mutuals, for a final betting round. This game is a simplification of *Cincinnati*, page 246, but is actually more like *Seven-Card Stud*. Such games as *Hold 'Em*, page 252, and *Omaha*, page 257, are derived from it. The game is suited to high-low and wild-card variants.

SEVEN-CARD PETE: A term for *Seven-Card Stud*, page 229, when played with the sevens wild.

SEVEN-CARD REVERSE: Each player is dealt a hand of seven cards, which he holds as in *Draw Poker*, page 226. Each chooses one card and lays it face down. These are flipped face up and bets are made as in *Stud Poker*, page 229. This continues card by card until the fifth, which is bet while still face down, exactly like the finish of a hand of *Five-Card Stud*, page 228. The fifth card is then turned up to decide the winning hand, the two extra cards being discarded. An alternative procedure is to discard the two extras to start; then utilize the five cards as described. As a variant, players may be required to arrange their five cards in the order in which they plan to turn them up, thus preventing any changes after seeing another player's upcards.

SEVEN-CARD STUD: For the basic game, see page 229.

SEVEN-CARD STUD, DEUCES WILD: A highly popular game that has become a classic in its own right. Played exactly like *Seven-Card Stud,* page 229, but with each deuce representing anything, the game is replete with surprises, with comparatively low hands sometimes winning unexpected pots. It can be played high-low, as with the standard game.

SEVEN-CARD STUD, HIGH AND LOW: Form of *High-Low Seven-Card Stud,* page 234, in which a player can go for both, using five of his seven cards to form a high hand, then taking those back and using five of his original seven to form a low hand. Applicable to most variants of *Seven-Card Stud,* page 229.

SEVEN-CARD STUD, LOW CARD WILD: Each player counts his lowest card wild along with any others of that value in his hand. See page 229. Can be played with player's *High Card Wild,* if preferred.

SEVEN-CARD STUD, LOWEST CARD WILD: After the showdown, the lowest card in anybody's hand becomes wild in everybody's hand, along with all others of its value. Can be played with *Highest Card Wild,* if preferred.

SEVEN-CARD STUD, LOWEST HOLE CARD WILD: After the showdown, the lowest hole card in play is wild in everybody's hand, as are all others of its value. Can be played with *Highest Hole Card Wild* if preferred. See page 229.

SEVEN-CARD STUD, LOW HOLE CARD WILD: Each player counts his lowest hole card wild, along with any others of that value in his hand. Can be played with player's *High Hole Card Wild,* if preferred.

SEVEN-CARD STUD, LOWEST UPCARD WILD: Just before the showdown, the lowest upcard in any remaining hand becomes wild, along with others of that value in anybody's hand. Often, only one player has an upcard of the lowest value; if he should fold his hand, cards of that value would no longer be wild, as the rule would apply to the lowest upcard still on display. After the showdown, all cards of that value are "wild," whether "up" or "down," which means that this can be a grim game, indeed. This can also be played with *Highest Upcard Wild*.

SEVEN-CARD STUD, LOW UPCARD WILD: Each player counts his lowest upcard wild, along with any others of that value in his hand. This is also termed *Ma Ferguson*. It can be played with each player's *High Upcard Wild*, when it becomes *Pa Ferguson*.

SEVEN-CARD STUD, OPTIONAL WILD CARD: A player may declare any of his cards wild with others of its value. This can be restricted to an *Optional Hole Card*, though of course any upcard of that value will also be wild. Also it can be restricted to an *optional upcard*, though a hole card of that value will also be wild.

SEVEN-CARD STUD, WILD VARIANTS: If desired, this game can be played with some value other than the deuces representing wild cards. (as threes or sevens, etc.). Also, added values may be specified, as *One-eyed Jacks,* page 258, *Mustached Kings,* page 256, etc., or two values may be specified, as in *Five and Dime,* page 249. Other variants are given below.

SEVEN-TOED PETE: Another name for *Seven-Card Stud,* page 229, particularly applicable when played with *Deuces Wild,* page 265.

SHIFTING SANDS: Another name for *Mexican Wild,* page 256.

SHOTGUN: This is *Draw Poker,* page 226, but with a pause for a betting round after each player has been dealt only three cards, which he looks at. Two more are dealt, followed by a betting round. Then the usual draw with its betting round and showdown. As a variant, a betting round may be inserted after the fourth card, with another after the fifth. See *Texas Tech*, page 271.

SHOVE 'EM ALONG: *Push Poker*, page 261, also termed *Take It or Leave It*, page 270.

SHOWDOWN POKER: *Straight Poker*, page 269, without the draw. The same as *No Draw*, page 257, but the term is also applied to *Cold Hands*, page 246, dealt face up.

SIX-CARD STUD: *Five-Card Stud* with an extra card dealt as a second hole card, with the best five cards winning. Often played high-low. See special description on page 229.

SIX SIXTY-SIX: *Cincinnati*, page 246, with six cards dealt to each player, six cards in the center, and sixes wild.

SIXTH CARD OPTIONAL: *Five-Card Stud*, page 228, with the privilege of taking a sixth card in exchange for a hole card or an upcard from the pack, with another betting round. See *Option*, page 258; also *Push Poker*, page 261.

SIXTY-SIX: *Six-Card Stud*, page 229, with sixes wild.

SKY'S THE LIMIT: A game with unlimited betting. Same as *No Limit*, page 257.

SLIPPERY ELMER: *Five-Card Stud*, page 228, but before the showdown, an odd card is dealt face up, as in *Spit*, page 268, making all cards of that value wild, though the card itself does not figure in play. This is followed by another betting round.

SOUTHERN CROSS: A game of the *Cincinnati type*, page 246, played exactly like *Cross Over*, page 247, but with nine cards instead of only five, thus enabling a player to choose either of two five-card cross-rows:

May be played with center card wild, along with any others of its value, as in *Crisscross*, page 247. Also can be played *High-Low*, page 232, with players going for both. In all forms, the center card is turned up last.

SPADES AS SPOILERS: *Six-, Seven-,* or *Eight-Card Stud*, pages 229–230, with wild cards (as twos and threes; or fives and tens), but if a hand contains a spade, other than a wild card, none of its wild cards count. Example, in *Seven-Card Stud*, twos and threes wild: (♡ K) (♣ Q) ♠ 3 ♣ K ♣ 10 ◇ 2 (♠ 10). This would rate as a royal flush ♣ A K Q J 10 until the seventh card but the ♠ 10 kills the wild cards, reducing it to two Pair: K–K–10–10.

SPIT: The simplified term for *Spit in the Ocean*, which is described next.

SPIT IN THE OCEAN: A "wild game" that has become standard, with many wilder games developing from it. Basically, "spit" is a form of *Draw Poker*, page 226, in which only four cards are dealt to each player, after which an odd card is dealt face up on the table, to represent a fifth card in everybody's hand. That card and any others of its value automatically become wild. Thus, with ♠ 8 dealt as the center card, a player holding ♣ 8 ♡ A ♡ 10 ◇ 4 would have three aces, in the form of 8–8–A. He could (a) keep the ♠ 8 and discard the three other cards, hoping to catch another wild eight for a sure four of a kind or better; (b) he could keep the ♣ 8 and ♡ A, hoping for four aces or better, by drawing either an eight or an ace; or (c) he could discard only the ◇ 4, since a one-card draw of ◇ 8,

♡8, ♡ K, ♡ Q, ♡ J would give him a royal flush: ♡ A K Q J 10. Five of a kind is the highest hand in this game, and it usually takes something better than a flush to win a pot.

SPIT, NO CARD WILD: Truly a conservative development of *Spit in the Ocean,* page 268, or see above. The loner upcard, though belonging to each player's hand, is not wild, nor are any other cards wild. Much like standard *Draw Poker,* page 226, except that a player is unable to get rid of that one mutual card, much though he might like to do so.

SPIT, OTHER VARIANTS: These include the following: (1) The center card is counted as a wild card for each hand, but no other cards are wild. (2) The center card serves as a fifth card for each hand but is not wild, though all others of its value are. (3) Five cards are dealt to each player as in *Draw Poker,* page 226, while an extra card, dealt face up, establishes all cards of that value wild, though it does not form part of any hand. For other elaborations of *Spit in the Ocean,* see below.

STORMY WEATHER: This is *Spit in the Ocean,* page 268, with no wild cards; but three cards are dealt face up and each player can choose the one he wants as part of his hand. As a variant, the center cards can be turned up singly, with a betting round on each, instead of simply on all three. Either way, a draw follows after the cards are "rolled," or turned up; and there is a final betting round.

STRAIGHT POKER: Originally, the basic game of *Showdown,* page 267, or *No Draw,* page 257. Generally extended to include *Draw Poker,* page 226, in its basic form, later *Five-Card Stud,* page 228, and in many groups, *Seven-Card Stud,* page 229; but always limited to the standard type of game, without special rules or wild cards.

STRIPPED PACK: Any form of *Poker,* page 219, with a pack of less than the customary fifty-two cards.

STUD POKER: Various types of *Open Poker,* in which some of a player's cards are seen by others prior to the *Showdown.* See special descriptions beginning on page 228.

STUD WITH SPIT: Simply *Spit in the Ocean,* page 268, converted from *Draw Poker,* page 226, to *Five-Card Stud,* page 228. It begins like five-card stud and stays that way up to the fifth card, when a lone card is dealt face up in the center of the table as a mutual card for each player's hand. That card is wild, as are any others of its value already dealt, which encourages many players to stay to the end. Certain variants of five-card stud are also adaptable to *Spit in the Ocean,* and vice versa.

SUDDEN DEATH: An appropriate nickname for *Five-Card Stud,* page 228, when played *High-Low,* page 232.

TABLE STAKES: A game in which a player's bets are limited to the chips he has on the table at the beginning of a hand. He may increase his stake before the next except in *Freezeout,* page 251. For special betting procedure, see *Tap Out,* below.

TAKE IT OR LEAVE IT: *Push Poker,* page 261, played as *Five-Card Stud,* page 228, usually as *High-Low.*

TAP OUT: Any game like *Table Stakes,* above, in which a player running short of chips is allowed to raise or call with whatever he has left. If other players raise, they bet among themselves from that point on, with the player who "tapped out" participating in the original pot, with a chance of winning it in the showdown. If he wins, the next best hand takes the surplus.

TEN-CARD STUD: Like *Nine-Card Stud,* page 257, but with an extra card that may be dealt down or up, as decided beforehand. Dealer can announce any other variations.

TENNESSEE: The same as *Cincinnati,* page 246, but instead of dealing an extra hand, cards are dealt face up from the top of the pack, with a betting round following each. Often played with the last card wild, along with all others of its value, either in individual hands or showing on the board. This should be specified by the dealer.

TENNESSEE JED: *Tennessee,* page 270, with "last card wild" automatically specified or understood.

TENS HIGH: Any form of Poker in which any hand above a pair of tens is disqualified and the highest hand remaining in play becomes the winner. This produces keen competition where low Pairs are concerned, with players "standing pat" with holdings like **8–8–J–10–4** and **7–7–A–K–3.**

TEXAS TECH: Played like *Shotgun,* page 266, until after the betting round that follows the draw. Then, instead of a showdown, each player lays his hand face down and flips or turns one card face up. A betting round follows; then another flip and a betting round; and so on, until only one card remains face down, like a hole card in *Five-Card Stud,* page 228. After a final betting round, each player turns up his hole card to determine the winner, or the winners if the game is played high-low. This game is also appropriately known as *Double-Barreled Shotgun,* page 248.

THIRD HAND HIGH: Any form of *Poker* in which the third highest hand wins the pot, the two higher hands being eliminated. Good in games with seven or more players.

THREE-CARD MONTE: A popular misnomer for *Monte,* page 256, or *Three-Card Poker,* below.

THREE-CARD POKER: *Draw,* page 226, or *Stud,* page 228, with only three cards dealt to each player. Hands rank in the order: straight flush, three of a kind, flush, straight, pair, high card. In *Draw,* a player may call for any number of cards up to three; in *Stud,* the first card is dealt face down; the next two, face up. Often played as *High-Low Poker,* with other variants allowable, as specified.

THREE FORTY-FIVE: *Eight-Card Stud,* page 230, with three cards dealt face down, followed by a betting round; then four face up, each followed by a betting round; than a final hole card, with its betting round; and any five spot counting as a wild card.

THREE OUT OF FIVE: Played like *Five-Card Stud,* page 228, until the showdown. Then each player throws away two cards and those remaining in the hand are rated as in *Three-Card Poker,* page 271.

THREE PAIR HIGH: A game of *Six-, Seven-,* or *Eight-Card Stud,* pages 229–230, in which a player may keep a sixth card for the showdown in order to form three pair (as ♡ K ◇ K ♠ 9 ◇ 9 ♠ 7 ♣ 7). Such a hand wins the pot, even beating five of a kind. Can be played as a *Lalapalooza,* page 254, with only one such hand to a session.

THREE-TOED PETE: A name for either *Three-Card Poker,* page 271, or *Seven-Card Stud,* page 229, with threes wild.

THROW AWAY TWO: Here, cards are thrown away to start. Each player is dealt a closed hand of five cards, but instead of drawing, he throws away three cards and lays the other two face down and the game shifts from *Draw* to *Stud,* page 226–228. If *Five-* or *Six-Card Stud* is designated, each player keeps one card as a hole card and turns up the other, with a betting round to follow. If *Seven-* or *Eight-Card Stud,* both are kept as hole cards and each player is dealt an upcard to start the first betting round. See also pages 230–231.

TIGER: Another name for *Blind Opening,* page 245.

TNT: A combination of *Texas Tech,* page 271, and *Seven-Card Stud,* page 229. Each player is dealt a closed hand of three cards and a round of betting follows. Four single cards are then dealt face down, each followed by a betting round. Two cards are discarded and four of the remaining five are flipped or turned up singly, each with a betting round, ending with four upcards and a hole card, as in Texas tech.

TWIN BEDS: Dealt like *Bedsprings,* page 243, but cards are turned up alternately in top and bottom row, with a betting round after each. In forming hands for "high" or "low," a player may choose those from an entire cross-row to go with his own holdings, thus giving him ten cards from which to pick each hand. As a result, the hands run much stronger than in bedsprings.

TWIN BEDS WILD: In this version, the last card turned up in its row is wild; or the lowest card turned up; or the lowest card in a player's own hand. The preferred arrangement must be stated before the deal; and as usual, all cards of that value become wild. See above.

TWO-CARD POKER: Played as *Draw,* page 226, or *Stud,* page 228, with one hole card and one upcard, each dealt singly and followed by a bet. Highest pair wins; otherwise highest card. As *Hurricane,* it is often played high-low; and as *Dynamite,* with wild cards. See also *Gruesome Twosome,* page 251.

UP AND DOWN THE RIVER: Though not a form of *Poker,* this game is sometimes introduced as "dealer's choice." It is similar to *Put and Take.* See description on page 285.

UTAH: Practically the same as *Cincinnati,* with a row of five "mutual" cards being turned up singly, with a betting round on each. Sometimes played with the center card being turned up last, as a wild card, with all others of its value wild. This should be specified beforehand. See *Cincinnati,* page 246.

VICE PRESIDENT: *Draw Poker,* page 226, with the second highest hand winning the pot. A form of *Place Poker,* page 260.

WHANGDOODLES: The same as *Rangdoodles,* page 262, though occasionally limited to a single hand rather than a round.

WHISKEY POKER: See description on page 374. Though not actually a form of poker, hands are ranked in the same order; hence by agreement, whiskey poker may be introduced as a "dealer's choice."

WILD-CARD POKER: Any form of *Poker* in which certain cards are classed as wild, thereby representing any card the holder wants, even though it may duplicate a card held by someone else. See page 239.

WILD COURT CARDS: Any form of *Poker* with all kings, queens, and jacks wild, making twelve wild cards in all. Other cards are ranked A, 10, 9, 8, 7, 6, 5, 4, 3, 2, with ace also low in a straight. Highest possible hand is five aces, with ♡ A 10 9 8 7 the highest straight flush.

WILD FACE CARDS: Same as *Wild Court Cards,* above.

WILD SUIT: An entire suit is declared wild, and the game is accordingly played with thirteen wild cards. By making the wild suit either C, D, or H, this game can be played very effectively with *Spades as Spoilers,* page 268.

WILD WIDOW: *Draw Poker,* page 226, and a variation of *Pig in Poke,* page 259, with an odd card turned face up after the deal to establish all cards of that value as wild, though the turned-up card does not figure in play. Actually, the game is an extension of *Spit in the Ocean,* as described under variants of *Spit* on page 268. The term "wild widow" is somewhat of a misnomer, as the single card is unlike an ordinary widow.

WOOLWORTH: Like *Five and Dime,* page 249, this is *Seven-Card Stud* with fives and tens wild, but with the added feature that a player who receives one must either fold or put five chips in the pot for a five and ten chips for a ten.

X MARKS THE SPOT: This is like *Cross Over*, page 247, but also played in wild form like *Crisscross*, page 247. The only difference is that instead of forming a cross the cards are laid out as an X:

A player is dealt five cards of his own and can use any cards from one diagonal row to improve his final hand.

YOU ROLL TWO: The same as *New Guinea Stud*, page 256, the name signifying that a player "rolls," or turns up, two of four cards dealt to him as the start of a special form of *Seven-Card Stud*, page 229.

ZEBRA POKER: A game of *Draw*, page 226, in which the only hands that count are "zebras," consisting of five cards alternating in color (red, black, red, black, red; or black, red, black, red, black) in descending values, with ace either high or low (Example: ♣ A ♡ Q ♣ 6 ◇ 3 ♠ A). The zebra with the highest card or cards wins the pot. By agreement, a *Straight* of alternating colors can take precedence over any other hand (Example: ♠ 10 ◇ 9 ♠ 8 ♡ 7 ♣ 6).

ZOMBIE: *Draw Poker*, page 226, with an extra hand dealt as a zombie, or temporarily "dead hand." Anyone opens and game proceeds as usual until the showdown. Then, instead of the player with the highest hand winning the pot, he must wait while the second best player exchanges his hand for the zombie, which immediately comes to life. The second player can draw to improve the zombie; and if it beats the highest hand—with or without a draw—the second best player wins.

LIST OF POKER GAMES PREVIOUSLY DESCRIBED UNDER "DEALER'S CHOICE"

Acepots
Anaconda
Anaconda with
 Pass Along
Any Card Wild
Any Suit Wild
Anything Opens
Any Value Wild
Around the World
Australian Poker
Automatic Lowball
Bank Night
Baseball
Beat Your Neighbor
Bedsprings
Best Flush
Bet or Drop
Betty Hutton
Bimbo
Blind Opening or
 Blind and Straddle
Blind Stud
Blind Tiger
Bobtail Opener
Bobtail Stud
Butcher Boy
California Lowball
Canadian Stud
Chicago
Cincinnati
Cincinnati Liz
Closed Poker
Cold Hands
Cold Hands with
 Draw
Crisscross
Cross Over
Cross Widow
Deuces Wild
Deuces Wilder
Doctor Pepper

Double-Barreled
 Shotgun
Double-Handed
 High-Low
Down the River
Draw Poker
Dynamite
Eight-Card Stud
Eighty-Eight
English Poker
English Stud
Fiery Cross
Five and Dime
Five-Card Final
Five-Card Stud
Five-Card Stud,
 Last Up or Down
Five-Card Stud with
 Replacement
Flip
Flip Stud
Football
Four-Card Poker
Four-flush Opener
Four-flush Stud
Four Forty-four
Four Forty-two
Freak Hands
Free Wheeling
Freezeout
Gruesome Twosome
Guts
Half-Pot Limit
Heinz
High-Low Poker
High Poker
High Spade Split
Hilo
Hilo Picolo
Hokum
Hold 'Em

Hole-Card Stud
Hollywood
Hurricane
Jackpots
Jacks Back or
 Jackson
Jacks High
Joker Poker
Kankakee
Kings Back or
 Kingston
Knock Poker
Lalapalooza
Lamebrain Pete
Lamebrains
Lazy Lucy
Lefty Louie
Leg in Pot
Lowball
Low Card Wild
Low English Stud
Low Hole Card Wild
Low Poker
Ma Ferguson
Match 'Em
Mexican Low Card
Mexican Stud
Mexican Stud with
 Low Card Wild
Mexican Wild
Mike
Misere
Mistigris
Monte
Mortgage
Mustached Jacks Wild
Mustached Kings
 Wild
New Guinea Stud
New York Stud
Nine-Card Stud

Ninety-nine
No Draw
No Limit
No Low Cards
Omaha
One-Card Poker
One-Eyed Jacks Wild
One-Eyed King Wild
Open Poker
Option
Pa Ferguson
Pass Along
Pass and Back In
Pass Out
Pass the Garbage
Pedro
Peek Poker
Peep and Turn
Penny Ante
Pig in Poke
Pinochle Poker
Pistol, Pistol Pete, or
   Pistol Stud
Place and Show
Place Poker
Poker Solitaire
Pothooks Wild
Pot Limit
Poverty Poker
Primero
Procter and Gamble
Progressive Jackpots
Push Poker
Pussy Cat
Queen City Poker
Rangdoodles
Rickey de Laet
Roodles
Rothschild
Round of Jacks
Round the Corner
Round the World
Screwy Louie
Second Hand Low

Seven-Card Flip
Seven-Card Hokum
Seven-Card Mutual
Seven-Card Pete
Seven-Card Reverse
Seven-Card Stud
Seven-Card Stud,
   Deuces Wild
Seven-Card Stud,
   High and Low
Seven-Card Stud,
   Low Card Wild
Seven-Card Stud,
   Lowest Card Wild
Seven-Card Stud,
   Lowest Hole Card
   Wild
Seven-Card Stud, Low
   Hole Card Wild
Seven-Card Stud,
   Lowest Upcard Wild
Seven-Card Stud,
   Low Upcard Wild
Seven-Card Stud,
   Optional Wild Card
Seven Card Stud,
   Wild Variants
Seven-Toed Pete
Shifting Sands
Shotgun
Shove Them Along
Showdown Poker
Six-Card Stud
Six Sixty-six
Sixth Card Optional
Sixty-six
Sky's the Limit
Slippery Elmer
Southern Cross
Spades as Spoilers
Spit
Spit in the Ocean
Spit, No Card Wild

Spit, Other Variants
Stormy Weather
Straight Poker
Stripped Pack
Stud Poker
Stud with Spit
Sudden Death
Table Stakes
Take It or Leave It
Tap Out
Ten-Card Stud
Tennessee
Tennessee Jed
Tens High
Texas Tech
Third Hand High
Three-Card Monte
Three-Card Poker
Three Forty-five
Three Out of Five
Three Pair High
Three-Toed Pete
Throw Away Two
TNT
Twin Beds
Twin Beds Wild
Two-Card Poker
Up and Down the
   River
Utah
Vice President
Whangdoodles
Whiskey Poker
Wild-Card Poker
Wild Court Cards
Wild Face Cards
Wild Suit
Wild Widow
Woolworth
X Marks the Spot
You Roll Two
Zebra Poker
Zombie

RANKS OF HANDS IN POKER,
INCLUDING FREAK HANDS

(See pages 220–226 for descriptions of Standard hands)

This includes standard hands, wild card hands used in wild card games, special hands, used in specific games, and freak hands, which are either standard in certain limited circles or can be introduced as desired. They are given in descending order, and starred hands (*) are sometimes rated higher or lower than in the present listing, their exact evaluation being determined by agreement.

FIVE OF A KIND, with four wild deuces: ♠ A ◇ 2 ♣ 2 ♡ 2 ♠ 2. This represents five aces and, since a wild deuce can be any suit, the hand can be announced as ♠ A, ♠ A, ♠ A, ♠ A, ♠ A, giving it the added value of a flush, thus beating any hand with fewer than four wild cards, in games where other cards besides deuces are also wild.

FIVE OF A KIND, with deuces wild:

♠ Q ♡ Q ◇ Q ♠ 2 ♣ 2
or ♠ 9 ◇ 9 ♡ 9 ♡ 2 ◇ 2

Here, five queens, being higher than five nines, would win the hand.

ROYAL FLUSH (royal straight flush): See the standard hands.

STRAIGHT FLUSH: See the standard hands.

SKEET FLUSH:

◇ 9 7 5 4 2
or ♣ 9 5 4 3 2

A freak hand that *must* contain a 9, 5, and 2 of one suit, with two intervening cards of the same suit. In some circles, one must be between the 9 and 7, the other between the 5 and 2, as shown in the upper example. Such a hand is sometimes ranked above a royal flush.

SKIP FLUSH:

◇ J 8 6 4 2

An alternating sequence consisting of every other card in descending order, all of the same suit. With two such hands, the one with the higher sequence wins.

FOUR ACES (highest four of a kind):

♠ A ♡ A ◇ A ♣ A ◇ 7
♠ K ♡ K ◇ K ♣ K ♠ A

A standard hand, once the highest (before the straight flush was recognized). Four kings with an odd ace (as shown) is just as good, as it prevents any other player from holding four aces.

BLAZE FOURS:

◇ K ♣ K ♡ K ♠ K ◇ J
◇ Q ♣ Q ♡ Q ♠ Q ♠ K
◇ J ♣ J ♡ J ♠ J ♣ Q

A freak hand, regarded as special in some circles, consisting of all *face cards,* hence the term "blaze," but with four of a kind (kings, queens, or jacks), as shown. Properly, a blaze four should rank higher than four aces, as there are only twenty-four ways of forming a blaze four against forty-eight for four aces.

FOUR OF A KIND: See the standard hands.

BIG BOBTAIL with pair:

◇ Q J 10 9 ♠ J
♡ Q J 10 9 ♣ 9

Four cards toward a straight flush, with one pairing with the odd card. A higher sequence wins, but in case of a tie (as shown), the higher pair is the deciding factor.

BIG BOBTAIL:

♠ 10 9 8 7 ♣ 4
♡ 7 6 5 4 ♠ K
◇ 7 6 5 4 ♡ J

Four cards toward a straight flush, with top card deciding winner, as "ten high" over "seven high," as shown. With a tied sequence, the hand with the higher odd card wins, as ♠ K over ♡ J, when both sequences are "seven high."

BLAZE FULL:

♠ K ♡ K ◇ K ♣ Q ♠ Q
♣ J ♡ J ◇ J ♡ Q ◇ Q

A hand full of face cards, three of one kind, two of another. With two "blaze fulls," the higher trio wins.

FULL HOUSE or FULL HAND: See the standard hands.

FLUSH: See the standard hands.

BIG CAT or BIG TIGER: ◇ K ♠ J ◇ 10 ♣ 9 ◇ 8
A freak hand of mixed suits with king high, eight low, and three cards of intervening values; but all different, no pairs.

LITTLE CAT or LITTLE TIGER: ♣ 8 ♠ 7 ♣ 5 ◇ 4 ♡ 3
A junior edition of "big cat" with eight high and three low, with intermediate cards of different values.

BIG DOG: ◇ A ♣ K ♣ J ◇ 10 ♣ 9
A freak hand with ace high, nine low, mixed suits, and no pairs.

LITTLE DOG: ♡ 7 ♡ 5 ♠ 4 ◇ 3 ◇ 2
A freak hand with seven high, two low, mixed suits, and no pairs.
Note: In some circles, "big dog" and "little dog" are ranked above "big cat" and "little cat"; hence the comparative rating of such hands should be specified beforehand.

FIVE AND TEN or FIVE AND DIME: ♣ 10 ♠ 9 ♣ 8 ◇ 6 ◇ 5
A freak hand with ten high, five low, mixed suits, and no pairs. *Note:* This is sometimes ranked below a straight.

STRAIGHT: See the standard hands.

ROUND THE CORNER STRAIGHT: ◇ 4 ◇ 3 ♣ 2 ♡ A ♠ K
♣ 3 ♠ 2 ♠ A ◇ K ◇ Q
◇ 2 ◇ A ♣ K ♣ Q ♠ J

These are special hands, allowing the formation of "four high," "three high," and "two-high" straights, by classing the ace as both low *and* high in the same hand, thus serving as a link between deuce and king, which becomes lower than the ace. Inclusion of such straights should be agreed upon beforehand.

SKIP, SKIP STRAIGHT or DUTCH STRAIGHT:
♡ A ◇ Q ◇ 10 ♠ 8 ♣ 6
♠ 9 ♡ 7 ♣ 5 ♣ 3 ♠ A

A freak straight composed of alternating values, skipping those between. The lowest (9–7–5–3–A) is sometimes called a "kilter."

SKEET or PELTER: ♡ 9 ♠ 8 ♠ 5 ◇ 3 ♣ 2
                        or ♠ 9 ♣ 7 ♡ 6 ♣ 5 ♠ 2

A freak hand of mixed suits, containing a nine, five, two, with an intervening card in each bracket, as shown in the upper example. That rule is sometimes relaxed, allowing the two "in betweeners" to be in either bracket, as in the lower example. This should be decided upon beforehand.

KILTER or PELTER: ◇ 9 ♠ 7 ◇ 6 ◇ 5 ♠ 3
                        ♠ 8 ♡ 6 ◇ 4 ♣ 3 ♣ 2

These terms also denote a freak hand that consists of nothing higher than a nine or lower than a two, with mixed suits and no sequence or pairs. Truly a "nothing" hand, which is its great merit, as players stay in the game, hoping to catch one. With two such kilters in play, the winner is decided on a high-card basis.

STRIPED STRAIGHT or ZEBRA: ◇ J ♠ 8 ♡ 7 ♠ 5 ◇ 4

A hand without a pair or better, in which colors alternate, red and black, or black and red, in descending order.

BLAZE THREES: ◇ K ♣ K ♠ K ◇ Q ◇ J
                    ♣ Q ♠ Q ♡ Q ♡ K ♠ J

A freak hand full of picture cards, with three of one kind (as kings, queens, or jacks) and one each of the other. In case of a tie, the higher value wins, as three kings over three queens. This hand should properly rate just below blaze fours.

THREE OF A KIND or TRIPLETS: See the standard hands.

LITTLE BOBTAIL: ◇ K ◇ Q ◇ J ♣ 10 ◇ 4
                      or ♣ K ♣ Q ♣ J ♣ 9 ♡ 8
                         ◇ 9 ◇ 8 ◇ 7 ♣ 8 ◇ 3
                      or ♠ 9 ♠ 8 ♠ 7 ♣ A ♠ K

A freak hand containing three cards toward a straight flush, ranking from "ace high" downward. If tied, the hand with highest extra card wins, as shown in the upper example, unless one hand contains a pair, which takes precedence over a high card, as in the lower example.

FLASH: ♡ K ♣ 10 ♠ 7 ◇ 6 Joker
♣ Q ♡ J ◇ 8 ♠ 6 ♣ 2

A special hand that can be introduced when playing with the joker as a wild card. Here, the joker represents a "fifth suit," with the "flash" a hand of five different suits. By agreement, the same rule can be applied when playing "deuces wild," with each deuce classed as a fifth suit card when so desired.

SIMPLE BLAZE: ◇ K ♡ K ♠ J ♡ J ♡ Q
◇ Q ♠ Q ◇ J ♣ J ♠ K

A freak hand of picture cards, forming two pairs with an odd card. With two such hands, the one with the highest pair wins; or if both have the same, the next highest wins. Properly, a simple blaze should be ranked next in value to blaze threes.

TWO PAIR: See the standard hands.

FOUR FLUSH with pair: ◇ Q 6 4 3 ♠ 3
♣ 9 7 6 5 ♡ 9
♠ 9 7 6 5 ◇ 5

A special hand with four cards of one suit and an odd card to make up a pair. The hand with the highest card in the "four flush" wins; if two hands tie, the one with the higher pair is winner.

FOUR FLUSH: ♠ K 9 8 3 ◇ J
♣ K 9 7 5 ♠ 4
◇ K 9 7 5 ♡ 3

A special hand with four cards of one suit and an odd card of another. With two or more such hands, the one with highest card in its "four flush" wins; if those are the same, the next highest; and so on, down. If two "four flushes" are identical, the hand with the higher odd card wins.

FOUR STRAIGHT with pair: ♦ J ♠ 10 ♣ 9 ♦ 8 ♠ 9
            ♠ 8 ♠ 7 ♣ 6 ♣ 5 ♣ 7
            ♡ 8 ♦ 7 ♦ 6 ♡ 5 ♠ 5

A special hand with a sequence of four cards in mixed suits, with an odd card pairing up. Highest sequence, wins; if two are tied, the hand with higher pair wins.

FOUR STRAIGHT: ♠ K ♠ Q ♦ J ♣ 10 ♡ 6
           ♡ K ♣ Q ♣ J ♦ 10 ♡ 4

A special hand with four cards of mixed suits in sequence, with an odd, unpaired card. Highest sequence wins; if tied (as shown), the higher odd card marks the winning hand.

ONE PAIR: See the standard hands.

HIGH CARD: See the standard hands.

LOWEST STANDARD HAND: ♦ 7 ♡ 5 ♡ 4 ♦ 3 ♣ 2

Commonly termed a "seventy-five," this is the lowest possible hand in "high-low poker," since hands are ranked from the highest down; and the two is the lowest value.

LOWEST with swinging ace: ♣ 6 ♡ 4 ♣ 3 ♠ 2 ♦ A

This special hand is allowable by including the "swinging ace" rule, where the player can declare an ace "low" instead of "high," making this the lowest "high-low" hand.

WHEEL or BICYCLE: ♣ 5 ♦ 4 ♣ 3 ♡ 2 ♣ A
      or   ♠ 5 4 3 2 A

In the standard game of "lowball" the ace is always low, and combinations like straights and flushes are ignored; hence 5–4–3–2–A becomes the lowest possible hand and the sure winner!

POKER RUM: An early form of *Knock Rummy,* page 154.

POKER SOLITAIRE: See page 260.

POLIGNAC: An old French game very similar to *Hearts,* page 140, except that players avoid taking jacks instead of hearts. With four players, a thirty-two-card pack is used, each suit customarily ranking **K, Q, J, A, 10, 9, 8, 7.** The ♠ **J,** known as "Polignac," counts 2 points for the player taking it; other jacks, 1 point each. Play begins at dealer's left and players must follow suit if possible, with the winner of each trick leading to the next. The first to reach 10 points loses and must pay the difference to each of the others.

As a special rule, a player may announce, "Capot" before play starts, meaning that he intends to take every trick. If he does, 5 points are added to each of the other scores; if he fails, scoring is the same as in a regular hand. With three, five, or six players, the black sevens are removed from the pack so that the deal will come out evenly. By agreement, cards may be ranked **A, K, Q, J, 10, 9, 8, 7.** This game is also known as *Four Jacks* and *Quatre Valets.*

POLISH BEZIQUE: See *Bezique,* page 24.

POLISH RUMMY: See page 294.

POPE JOAN: A once popular but transitional elaboration of *Matrimony,* page 159, with a special division on the layout marked "Pope," representing the ◊ **9.** The ◊ **8** is first removed from the pack, forming a "stop," so that the ◊ **9** can be played only toward starting a new sequence. Other sections are included for "boodle cards" of a trump suit **(J, Q, K, A),** and an extra hand is dealt to provide more stops. From those added features, games like *New Market,* page 164, and eventually *Michigan,* page 161, were developed.

POTHOOKS WILD: See page 260.

POT LIMIT: A form of *Poker,* page 260, in which the size of the pot or pool determines the limit of an immediate bet.

POUNCE: A popular name for *Double Solitaire,* page 104.

POVERTY POKER: See page 260.

PREFERENCE: Simplified *Vint,* page 372, for three players using a thirty-two-card pack, ranking **A, K, Q, J, 10, 9, 8, 7** in descending order. Players contribute equally to a pool and each is dealt ten cards with two for a "widow." Each may bid for trump in ascending order of suits: ♠ ♣ ◇ ♡, guaranteeing to take at least six tricks in the suit named; no-trump not included. If no one bids, each has one turn to add chips to the pool; whoever puts in the most takes up the widow, discards two cards, and announces the trump. Play follows as in *Vint* or *Whist,* page 375, but for tricks only. Values are established beforehand for each trick over five taken by the bidder, these being scaled according to the trump. If successful, the bidder collects from the pool; if he falls short, he must pay a set penalty.

PROCTER AND GAMBLE: See page 261.

PROGRESSIVE BRIDGE: A series of bridge games in which players move from table to table in progressive order, according to established procedure. Applicable to other games, as *Euchre,* page 107, *Five Hundred,* page 117, *Hearts,* page 140, and *Whist,* page 375.

PROGRESSIVE JACKPOTS: *Poker.* See page 261.

PROGRESSIVE RUMMY: A name for *Contract Rummy,* page 91.

PUSH POKER: See page 261.

PUSSY CAT: *Poker.* See page 262.

PUT AND TAKE: A game for as large a group as nine players. Using a fifty-two-card pack, the dealer gives five cards face up to each of the other players. He then turns up a card for himself, say the ◇ 5. Every player holding a card of that rank must pay one chip to the dealer. He turns up another card, calling for two chips from anyone holding a card of that value; then another for three chips; for four chips; then five. Following that, the dealer turns up five more cards in succession. A player who matches the first in value takes one chip from the dealer; two for the second; three for the third; four for the fourth; five for the fifth.

The same game is sometimes played on a "doubling" schedule, "puts" and "takes" running 1, 2, 4, 8, 16. Either way, it is often used as a "dealer's choice" in *Poker.*

QUADRILLE: A once highly popular French game closely resembling *Ombre*, page 166, utilizing the same forty-card pack, but with four players instead of only three.

QUATRE VALETS: Another name for *Polignac*, page 283.

QUEEN CITY RUM: Played like *Rummy*, page 291, with seven cards dealt to each player. A player must "go rummy" to "go out," with or without a discard; but he is paid the point value of his cards from each opponent; not the other way about.

QUINELLA: A four-pack form of *Samba*, page 300, with four jokers (212 cards) or eight jokers (216 cards). Players are dealt eleven cards each (as in *Canasta*, page 43, or fifteen each (as in samba). A mixed canasta scores 300; a natural canasta, 500. Wild-card melds are allowed and can be built into an "all wild" canasta, scoring 2,000. Sequences can be melded as in samba, without wild cards, scoring 2,000 for a seven-card samba; but this can be extended to form a special eleven-card "escalera," scoring 3,000. A joker has the usual 50-point value, but can be cut to 30 by agreement, which may be desirable when eight jokers are used. Opening requirement is 50, going up to 90 at 3,000; and to 120 at 6,000. Game is 10,000 points. Various options may be introduced if desired.

QUINOLA: A variant of *Reversi*, page 289, in which the ♡ **J,** known as "quinola," is given a special value as a penalty card.

QUINZE: A two-player simplification of *Blackjack*, with 15 as the goal instead of 21, hence the game is also known as *Fifteen*. An ace counts only 1 point; other cards are valued according to their spots, with face cards (**J, Q, K**) 10 each, as in *Blackjack*, page 32, or *Twenty-one*, page 371. Dealer gives a face-down card to opponent and one to himself; opponent may stand or call for more face-down cards, one by one. Dealer does the same and hands are shown. Player nearest 15 wins a predetermined stake unless he alone goes over 15, in which case he loses. If count is tied, or both go over 15, the stake is simply doubled for the next hand. The deal alternates with each hand.

RACEHORSE: Another name for *Airplane* (page 13).

RAILROAD EUCHRE: *Partnership Euchre* with a variety of options. See *Railroad Euchre*, page 113.

RAMS: An old-time game for three to five players, using a thirty-two-card pack in which each suit once ranked **K, Q, J, A, 10, 9, 8, 7;** but in modern play **A, K, Q, J, 10, 9, 8, 7** is customary. The dealer puts five chips in a pool and deals five cards to each player usually dealing two, then three, or vice versa. He also deals an extra hand face down, to serve as a "widow," and turns up the top card of the pack to designate a trump suit. The player at dealer's left may "pass," by laying his hand face down; or he may "play," either with the hand dealt to him or by laying it face down and taking up the "widow" instead.

The remaining players may decide to pass or play in turn, but once the widow has been taken up, no further exchange is allowed. If all pass until the player just before the dealer, that player must play or pay the dealer five chips. If only one player decides to play, the dealer must play against him; but always the dealer can discard one card and take up the turned-up trump instead.

The first player who decides to play leads any card, and the rest must follow suit if they can; if not, they must trump if they can; in either case, always playing higher, if possible. Highest card of suit led wins unless trumped. Winner of each trick leads to the next, and for each trick won the winner takes one-fifth of the pool. Any active player who fails to win a trick must contribute five chips to the next pool; and the deal moves to the left, the new dealer putting up the usual five chips.

"General Rams" may be announced by a player who thinks

he can win all five tricks. Any who passed pick up their hands or exchange for the widow if available. All then play against the announcer, who collects five chips from each, plus the pool, if he wins. If he loses, he must pay five chips to each player and double the total chips in the pool. The player announcing "General Rams" leads to the first trick.

RANA: A form of *Frog* (page 125), played in Mexico.

RANGDOODLES: *Poker.* See page 262.

RANTER-GO-ROUND: A fast but simple game played by up to a few dozen players with a fifty-two-card pack, ranking **K, Q, J, 10, 9, 8, 7, 6, 5, 4, 3, 2, A.** Each is given three counters and is then dealt a single face-down card. The lowest card is a loser and each player, in turn, can say, "Stand," keeping a card that he thinks is high enough to be safe; or he can say, "Exchange" and pass a low card face down to the player on his left, receiving that player's face-down card in return. This continues around to the dealer; if he is dissatisfied with his card, he can replace it in the pack, drawing another instead.

Cards are then shown and player with the lowest puts a counter into a pool. The deal moves on and the game continues with a player dropping out after losing all his counters, until only one player remains in the game and wins the pool. In case two or more are tied for low, each loses a counter. Kings are immune; any player holding one turns it face up and is passed by in the play. The game may be played with minor variations and is also known as "chase the ace," because an ace is chased around the table.

RAP POKER: See *Knock Poker,* page 153.

RAZZLE DAZZLE: Another name for *Auction Cinch.* See *Cinch,* page 65.

RED AND BLACK: A name for *Trente et Quarante,* page 368.

RED AND BLACK: Each of several players announces a bet of "red" or "black." Each is dealt five face-up cards, and the dealer pays off if the majority are the color named. If not, the dealer collects. With all five of one color, the amount is doubled. This game may be played as "dealer's choice," in *Poker,* page 219.

RED DOG: A betting game played with a standard fifty-two-card pack, with each suit valued in descending order, **A, K, Q, J, 10, 9, 8, 7, 6, 5, 4, 3, 2.** All players contribute a specified number of chips to a common pool, or pot, and five cards are dealt face down to each player. Upon looking at his hand, each player in turn bets from one chip up to the entire pot that his hand contains a card higher in value than the top card of the pack, and of the same suit.

The dealer turns up the next card, and if the player beats it, he takes the amount of his bet from the pot. If he loses, his bet goes into the pot. For example, a player holding ♠ **K,** ♠ **5,** ♡ **10,** ♣ **9,** ♢ **4,** might bet five chips. If the ♡ **7** should turn up, the player would win; but if the ♣ **J** should turn up, he would lose. In winning, the player shows only the card that beats the one turned up by the dealer; if he loses, he throws in his hand without showing it.

Despite its simplicity, red dog can build up to high stakes if several players in succession "bet the pot" and lose. Whenever a player wins a pot, all must contribute to a new pot, so that play can resume. Obviously, a hand with four aces is a sure winner; but some hands with very high cards can lose, particularly those that are totally lacking in one suit; for any card of that suit can beat them. A variant of red dog is played with only four cards being dealt to each player, making it more difficult to hold a winning hand. It can also be played with only three cards per player, so that a "sure win" hand is impossible.

RED OR BLACK: Another name for *Plus or Minus,* page 217.

REVERSI: A forerunner of *Hearts,* page 140, in which players avoided taking any tricks, not just any hearts, or else tried to take all the tricks.

RICKEY DE LAET: A form of *Poker*. See page 262.

ROLLING STONE: Another name for *Enflé,* page 106. Also called *Schwellen.*

ROODLES: *Poker.* See page 262.

ROTHSCHILD: A form of *High-Low Five-Card Stud.* See Rothschild. page 262. Also called *Push Poker,* described on page 261.

ROUGE ET NOIR: A name for *Trente et Quarante,* page 368.

ROUNCE: A modernized version of *Rams,* page 287, with three to nine players using a fifty-two-card pack, ranking **A, K, Q, J, 10, 9, 8, 7, 6, 5, 4, 3, 2.** Players are dealt five cards each with six to the widow. After exchanging his hand for the widow, a player discards one card. Trump is turned up as in rams and the first player may lead any card; but others are not required to play higher or to trump if out of the suit led. However, whoever wins the first trick must lead a trump to the next trick if he has one. There is no "general call" as in *Rams.* In all other respects, play is the same.

ROUND THE CORNER GIN: See *Gin Rummy,* page 130.

ROUND THE CORNER RUMMY: See page 293.

ROUND THE WORLD: An abbreviated form of *Cincinnati,* page 246.

ROYAL CASSINO: Standard *Cassino,* page 57, but with face cards given numerical values: jack, 11; queen, 12; king, 13. This allows "building" to those totals, exactly as with spot cards. As an option, an ace can be valued at either 1 or 14, thus allowing further builds or combinations. Royal cassino is also played with special packs containing cards with eleven and twelve spots. In that case, face cards are valued: jack, 13; queen, 14; king, 15; with an option of ace, 1 or 16.

ROYAL DRAW CASSINO: *Royal Cassino* played with a draw instead of a repeated deal. See *Draw Cassino*, page 104.

ROYAL MARRIAGE: Another name for *Betrothal Solitaire* page 325.

ROYAL SPADE CASSINO: A combination of *Spade Cassino*, page 356, and *Royal Cassino*, page 290, played with the rules of both.

ROYALTON: A form of *Auction Bridge* with special scoring rules. See page 18.

RUBICON BEZIQUE: A modern form of *Bezique* played with a double pack (128 cards) and special scoring rules. See page 26.

RUBICON PIQUET: The most popular form of *Piquet*, played on a basis of deals, rather than score. See *Piquet*, page 211.

RUFFS AND HONORS: An early form of *Whist*, page 375.

RUMMY: One of the most popular of all card games, rummy forms the nucleus for many others, which will be described under various heads, but knowledge of the basic game will prove helpful in understanding all. The players number from two to six, each on his own, utilizing a standard pack of fifty-two cards, valued in descending order: **K, Q, J, 10, 9, 8, 7, 6, 5, 4, 3, 2, A.** With two players each is dealt ten cards singly, face down; with three or four players, seven cards in clockwise order; with more players, six cards. The pack is placed face down in the center of the table, and the top card is turned up beside it to start a discard pile.

The player at the dealer's left (or opposite him when only two are in the game) looks at his hand and draws a card from the top of the pack, or from the discard pile if he prefers. He adds this to his hand, which he arranges toward the formation of melds composed of three or four of the same value (as J–J–J–J) or sequences of three or more cards of the same suit (as ♠ 5 4 3 or ♣ Q J 10 9 8 7). He places any such groups face up in front of him, thus "laying down" a meld. Whether or not he melded, he then discards a single card face up on the discard pile, this being known as the "upcard."

The next player then draws from the pack or takes the up-card, and lays down whatever meld he can. He is also allowed to "lay off" one or more cards on any melds made by the previous player. For example, if the first player melded a "set" composed of ♡ 9, ♣ 9, ◇ 9, the next player could add the ♠ 9 for "four nines." Or, if the first player melded ♡ 7 6 5, the next could add ♡ 9 8 to one end and ♡ 4 3 to the other, none of these being sufficient for melds in their own right. The player then discards and the next takes his turn.

This continues player by player until one "goes out" by dis-posing of his last card by melding it, laying it off, or discarding it, thus becoming winner of that deal. He then collects chips or scores points for cards remaining in each opponent's hand: 10 for each face card; 1 for each ace; others according to their numerical value. If a player holds back on his melds, so that he can dispose of all his cards at once, by going out in a single turn, he "goes rummy" and collects double from each opponent. That, of course, is a calculated risk, because if someone else goes out in the meantime, the player hoping to go rummy must pay for all the cards he holds, even though some are ready to be melded.

Occasionally, the entire pack is drawn before anyone goes out. In that case, the next player may take the final upcard, then turn the whole pile face down as a new pack and discard alongside it. Or he can ignore the final upcard by turning the pack, drawing the top card, and making a discard as with the first play.

SIMPLE VARIANTS OF RUMMY: Special rules applicable to regulation rummy will be found in the forms listed below, some being used in combination with others.

Block Rummy: In going out, a player must finish with a discard. Hence he cannot meld if down to two cards, but can only lay off. Also, if the entire pack is drawn, players can draw only from the discard, until one declines; hands are then shown, and the player with the lowest count wins the difference from each of the others. In case of a tie, winners split the profits.

Boathouse Rummy: Whenever a player takes the upcard from the discard pile, he must draw from the pack as well; but he can only make a single discard. As an optional rule, the two top cards can be drawn from the discard pile. To win, a player must "go rummy" by laying down his entire hand; no earlier melds are allowed.

Call Rummy: If a player inadvertently discards a card that he could have "laid off" on an existing meld, another player can call, "Rummy!" and lay it off himself, then make a discard from his own hand. Play then resumes in proper order. If two players call, "Rummy" simultaneously, the one closer to the discarder's left takes precedence.

High-Low Rummy: Regular rummy but with an ace ranking high as well as low, so it can begin a sequence running A–K–Q as well as one ending 3–2–A. Each ace counts 11 points instead of only 1.

One-Meld Rummy: No one is allowed to meld until one player can announce, "Rummy" and lay down his entire hand in melds, discarding an odd card if necessary. He collects the total points represented by the cards in his own meld from each opponent.

Round the Corner Rummy: Here, an ace can be both low and high in the same meld, allowing a sequence of 2–A–K, with additions at either end. An ace counts 11 points as in *High-Low Rummy.*

Two-Meld Rummy: The standard game, but no one can "go rummy" by melding an entire hand. To prevent this, a player must make a preliminary meld, or lay off, holding back a final meld until his next turn, thus warning opponents that they had better meld or be caught.

Wild-Card Rummy: A player must "go rummy" by melding his entire hand, as in one-meld rummy, but deuces are "wild cards" representing any card the holder needs to fill a set or sequence. (Thus **9–9–2=9–9–9**; or **6–2–4=6–5–4.**) Each deuce counts 25 points and winner collects his total points from each opponent. One or two jokers can be added to the pack as additional wild cards, rating as extra deuces.

MICHIGAN RUMMY: An elaboration of rummy in which the discard pile is spread so that players can keep track of cards they want. A player may take up any card but must also take up all those above it; and he must use that card in an immediate meld, either with cards from his hand or from the pile, unless he can lay it off on a meld that somebody has already made. Cards rank in descending order: **A, K, Q, J, 10, 9, 8, 7, 6, 5, 4, 3, 2, A,** with the ace counting 15 points except in a low sequence as **3–2–A,** when it counts only 1. Face cards are worth 10 each, and all others are valued according to their spots.

A running score is kept of each player's meld, and whoever first disposes of his entire hand becomes the winner. As such, he scores additional points for all cards remaining in the hands of the other players. The game proceeds deal by deal until one player's total passes the 500 mark, when he wins the game and collects from each opponent according to the difference in their individual scores. If so agreed, settlement can be made at the end of each deal instead of playing to 500.

Polish Rummy is a name applied to a variant in which a player can pick up the entire discard pile whenever he wants to take it. In all forms, if the pack is exhausted before anyone goes rummy, the best plan is to turn it face down and continue. Otherwise, there is no winner and each player simply scores the total of his meld less whatever points are remaining in his hand.

FIVE HUNDRED RUMMY: Known also as *Pinochle Rummy*, this is an advanced form of Michigan rummy, involving special scoring features. Cards are valued according to the same schedule: **A, K, Q, J, 10, 9, 8, 7, 6, 5, 4, 3, 2, A,** with ace counting 15 points, except when lowest card of a sequence (as ♡ **3, 2, A**) when it counts only 1. Face cards are 10 each, with other cards according to their spots.

However, no score is kept during play; instead, a player keeps his melds in front of him, and although he can lay off on another's meld, he merely indicates that he has done so, still keeping all his cards intact. If a player "goes rummy," play ends before the pack is exhausted. Either way, each player then adds the total of his meld and from that deducts whatever points he still has in his hand. Thus a player melding 92 points might have 61 in hand, giving him a gain of 31 points; or another might meld 46 points and still have 80 in hand, giving him a loss of 34 points.

Such gains or losses are totaled deal by deal, with play continuing until one player reaches 500 and becomes the winner, collecting from each opponent individually according to the difference in the scores. The game can be played by four players, with those seated opposite operating as partners, keeping their melds separate but combining their scores at the end of each deal, until one team reaches 500 and wins.

PERSIAN RUMMY: Originally known as "five hundred joker rummy," this game gained a new name by getting away from the old scoring method. It incorporates these special features:

Four players participate as two teams of partners, each being dealt seven cards from a fifty-six-card pack that includes four jokers, each valued at 20 points, while the others rank: **A, K, Q, J, 10, 9, 8, 7, 6, 5, 4, 3, 2,** with aces valued at 15 each; face cards 10; the rest according to their spots. Note that an ace is high only, not high or low, as in earlier games of this type. The jokers are not wild cards, but simply form a value of their own, enabling them to be melded in sets of three or four.

The game proceeds as in partnership five hundred rummy, with each player melding individually, but with partners adding their scores at the end of each deal. However, if a set of four is melded intact (as **8–8–8–8**), it counts double, so players give preference to such melds. If a player goes rummy, ending the play for that deal, his team scores 25 points as a bonus.

The game ends after two or three deals, whichever is agreed upon, and the winning team counts the difference between its score and that of the losing team to determine the margin of victory. Otherwise, the rules of five hundred rummy prevail.

PINOCHLE RUMMY: See *Five Hundred Rummy,* page 295.

RUSSIAN BANK: A highly popular game resembling double solitaire, page 104, with two players each using a fifty-two-card pack, with each suit ranking **A, 2, 3, 4, 5, 6, 7, 8, 9, 10, J, Q, K,** in ascending order for building purposes only. From his shuffled pack, each player deals twelve face-down cards, placing them in a packet at his right to serve as his "stock." From there he deals a column of four face-up cards toward the other player. He places the remainder of his cards face down at his left as his "hand." The space between the columns is reserved for building, with aces as bases (see diagram page 297).

Whoever deals the lowest face-up card plays first, as Player *X*, the other being Player *Y*. If both are tied for low, the next lowest card is the decider, and so on. If all four cards are identical in value, whoever dealt the lowest first becomes Player *X*, and play proceeds as follows:

If an ace is showing in the layout, Player *X* must place it in the center space, and follow by building others of the same suit if available. In the example given in the diagram, Player *X* would put the ♡ **A** in the center and then build the ♡ **2** and the ♡ **3** upon it. The player can then move cards from one layout pile to another, in descending sequence, alternate in color, as red on black, or black on red. This is optional but it the usual procedure.

Thus, in the example given, Player *X* would put the ◇ **Q** on the ♣ **K** and the ♠ **J** on the ◇ **Q**. He could not put the ◇ **5** on the ◇ **6,** as they both are red and therefore do not alternate in color.

SAMPLE LAYOUT FOR RUSSIAN BANK

Player X

Stock			Hand
♣ **K**	*	*	◇ **6**
♡ **A**	*	*	♡ **2**
◇ **5**	*	*	◇ **Q**
♠ **J**	*	*	♡ **3**

Space for

Hand   Discard Pile   *Stock*

Player Y

Each star (*) represents a space
reserved for a building base.

Player *X* next turns up the top card of his stock. If it is an ace, he must start another base, or a card of another value must be built on an existing base if possible. In the example, if the ♡ **4** turned up, *X* would have to build it on the ♡ **3.** If unable to build, *X* can add a turned-up card to a layout sequence if suitable (as ◇ **10** on ♠ **J**), or he can fill a layout vacancy with any card that cannot be built, and can move a suitable layout card onto it, making another vacancy in the layout. He then turns up another card from the stock, treating it the same way.

In the example, there would be five gaps to fill, enabling *X* to turn up at least six cards on the stock, but due to builds and moves, he might continue to turn up cards on the stock almost indefinitely.

When this good thing comes to an end, Player *X* is still not fully frustrated. He now turns up the top card of his hand and uses it in builds or moves if possible. If this enables him to use the card that is showing on the stock, he does so, and continues turning up the stock, reverting to the hand later. When unable to use a card turned up on the hand, he lays it face up between the hand and the stock, to begin a discard pile, from which no card can be played. His turn ends there, with the top card of the stock face up, the top card of the hand face down, and a face-up card on the discard pile.

It is then Player Y's turn to go through the same procedure, but with an added privilege. He can "feed" or "load" cards from his stock, hand, or from the layout, if available, onto Player X's stock or discard pile, provided it is the same suit and in sequence, either up or down. As a simple example: X ends his play with the ◊ 8 showing on his stock and the ♠ Q on his discard pile. Y turns up the ◊ 7 on his stock and promptly feeds it on to X's ◊ 8, then feeds the ◊ 6 and ◊ 5 from the layout. This not only loads X with three cards he doesn't want; it gives Y two vacancies in the layout, which he can fill by turning up his stock. Assume that Y finishes his play by turning up the ♠ K on his hand. He could load it on the ♠ Q that X discarded and then turn up another card on his own hand.

In his turn, X can sometimes retaliate by feeding cards on to Y's stock or discard pile. So it goes, turn after turn, and as the game progresses, a player may have a chance to "unload" from his stock. If a base should be started with the ◊ A and followed by builds of ◊ 2, ◊ 3, ◊ 4, Player X would build ◊ 5, ◊ 6, ◊ 7, ◊ 8 from his stock, thus getting rid of those surplus cards.

When a player uses up his entire stock, he simply turns up the top card of the hand instead. When he uses up his entire hand, he turns his entire discard pile face down and uses it as a new hand. This gives him an opportunity to unload any cards that were fed to his discard pile. All this is in keeping with a player's main purpose; namely, to get rid of all his cards by building them onto bases, placing them on layout piles, or feeding them to his opponent. The player who does that becomes the winner.

Score for winning the game is 30 points, plus 2 points for each card that an opponent still is holding in his stock; and 1 point for each card still in the opponent's hand or discard. If neither player can get rid of all his cards, the game is a draw, regardless of how far ahead one player may be.

The following procedures govern the play in Russian bank:

A player must build on a base whenever possible; first from the stock instead of from the layout, if there is a choice—as is possible if the player has just built from his hand to a base. Also, a build must be made on a base before playing onto the layout, or moving cards there, or feeding cards to the opponent.

Spaces in the layout may be filled either from the stock or by moving the uppermost card of another layout pile into the vacancy. However, all such vacancies must be filled before a card is turned up on the hand, unless the stock is exhausted. In that case, the hand serves as the stock and all vacancies must be filled before discarding from the hand.

If a player violates any of those rules or starts one play and switches to another, his opponent can call, "Stop!" and begin his own turn from there. If a player turns up two cards on his stock at the same time or turns up a card on his hand too soon, the stop rule also applies. However, modern rules allow a player to turn up the top card of his stock before playing or moving from the layout, since the card on the stock might be playable on a base and therefore take precedence.

Dedicated devotees of Russian bank are sticklers on the stop rule, demanding its enforcement on the slightest provocation, which is quite justifiable, because oversights are common to the game and should be penalized accordingly. In contrast, minor infractions can be overlooked if so agreed, but that should be determined beforehand. However, the following rules are now generally accepted:

After playing from his stock, a player may turn up the next card before making layout moves or any plays from there. This is because that next card may have some bearing on the layout moves; and if playable to a base, it will take precedence over anything involving the layout.

Although layout moves are normally optional, the opponent may demand that the player add to sequences in order to provide a space that the player may then fill from his stock; for example, by putting a lone ♡ 8 in the layout onto a ♠ 9.

An opponent may also demand that a player shift layout cards in order to free a card that is playable on a base. Suppose a base has been built up to ◊ 8, leaving a space in the layout. There is a layout sequence running ◊ 9, ♣ 8, ♡ 7, and another, ♠ 10, ♡ 9. By moving the ♡ 7 to the space, then transferring the ♣ 8 to the ♡ 9, the ◊ 9 is freed and built on the ◊ 8.

The reason the opponent is allowed to "spell out" such procedures is that, when a player is far behind, he may try to block the play in order to produce a drawn game. That is contrary to the philosophy of Russian bank, and by letting the opponent "call the shots" it can be nullified. Also, there are times when the opponent is simply calling attention to a series of moves that the player has honestly overlooked.

A card built upon a base can never be withdrawn, and a player is not allowed to take a face-up card from his opponent's stock, though after calling, "Stop," he can demand that it be played to a base where it should have gone. By modern rules, no card can be drawn from either discard pile. If a player wants to look back through his discard pile, he may do so, but must show those cards to his opponent if the latter wants to see them.

SAMBA: Derived from three-pack *Canasta,* page 52, this is a game with its own distinctive features, from which still other games have been developed. It requires a pack of 162 cards, including six jokers, with four players, those seated opposite being teamed as partners. Each is dealt fifteen cards, and play begins at the dealer's left, following the rules of canasta, but with these additions:

In drawing, the player takes two cards from the top of the pack but discards only one as a new upcard. The pot, or discard pile, can be taken up only by matching the upcard with a natural pair from the hand, unless the pot is no longer frozen. Then, a player can take the pot if he can add the upcard to any meld already made by his team, short of a completed canasta.

In forming a mixed canasta, only two wild cards are allowed instead of the usual three, but the extra cards in the triple pack are a help toward that.

Most important, the game allows a special scoring combination in the form of sequences, consisting of three or more cards of the same suit, as ♡ 10 9 8 or ♠ K Q J 10 9. These are called *escaleras,* or "ladders"; and though wild cards cannot be included, a sequence of seven, as ◊ Q J 10 9 8 7 6, becomes a *samba* (or *canasta escalera*). No more cards can be added to a samba, but it carries a bonus of 1500, in addition to the point values of its cards; and a samba is turned face down to distinguish it from a canasta.

Going out requires two canastas, a sambra rating in that category, with a fixed bonus of 2000, regardless of whether a player goes out openly or with a concealed hand. Game is 10,000 points, and the opening meld requirement jumps to 150 points at the 7000 level. Red threes count 100 each up to five; the sixth, if held by the same team, counts an additional 500.

SARATOGA: A form of *Michigan,* page 161, in which each player puts exactly the same number of chips on each payoff card, so that all are equal.

SCHAFKOPF: The early form of *Sheepshead.* See page 304.

SCHWELLEN: Another name for *Enflé,* page 106. Also called *Rolling Stone.*

SCOOP: From the Italian *Scopa,* similar to *Cassino,* page 57, using a forty-card pack, valued K=10, Q=9, J=8, 7, 6, 5, 4, 3, 2 according to their spots; A=1. With two players, each is dealt three cards, with four face up on the table. Opponent can take up any card with one of the same value (as ♣ 8 takes up ♡ 8). If possible, he can take up cards with one of their total value (as ♣ 2, ◊ 2, ◊ 3 being taken up with the ♡ 7). But he cannot take two builds as one. If unable to take up any cards, he puts one of his own face up on the table, but if he can take up all the cards, it is a "scoop." The player making the final "take" can gather any extra cards with it, but those are not rated as a scoop.

Each player then scores: 1 point for most cards; 1 for most diamonds; 1 for taking the ◊ 7; 1 for each scoop; 1 for the highest count in all four suits, rated thus: Any 7=21; a 6=18; A=16; a 5=15; a 4=14; a 3=13; a 2=12; a K, Q, or J=10. Game is 11 points, a player declaring "out" when he reaches that total. Scoop can be played by four players, as teams of two each; or by six, as teams of three each.

SCOPONE: *Scoop* (see above), for four players, but with ten cards dealt to each player, so that the first must begin by discarding one to the table. The team first scoring 15 points wins the game.

SCOTCH WHIST: A fast-moving game played with a thirty-six-card pack, the trump suit ranking J, A, K, Q, 10, 9, 8, 7, 6 and plain suits A, K, Q, J, 10, 9, 8, 7, 6. With four players, those seated opposite are partners. Each is dealt the same number of cards, the dealer turns up the final card as trump, then takes it in his hand, play starts at the dealer's left and proceeds exactly as in whist, one player gathering the tricks taken by his team.

The difference is that tricks do not count in this game. The main purpose is to take trump honors during play, each counting as follows: jack, 11, ace, 4; king, 3; queen, 2; ten, 10. In addition, the team taking more than half the cards scores 1 point for each card over eighteen. Deals continue in rotation, as in whist, with game set at 41 points. If both teams go over, as they are apt to do on the third deal, they count out in the order: Ten of trump, extra cards, A, K, Q, J.

Since taking the ten is important, the game is also called "catch the ten," and it may be played by three, five, or seven players, each on his own. With five or seven, the odd card is turned up as trump, without being used in play. In counting cards, a player scores 1 point for any over the number dealt to him: In three-handed, 12; five-handed, 7; seven-handed, 5.

The game can also be played by six players, with two partnerships of three each or three partnerships of two each. In the variant known as *French Whist,* page 125, the ◊ **10** always counts 10 whether or not its suit is trump.

SCREWY LOOEY: See page 263.

SELLOUT: Known as *Commercial Pitch,* this is an early form of *Auction Pitch,* page 214, with the first player selling the bidding privilege to another, thus adding points toward his own score, or retaining the bid by going as high as anyone. See *Pitch,* page 214.

SETBACK: Another name for *Auction Pitch.* See *Pitch,* page 214.

SETBACK BID WHIST: A mode of scoring in *Bid Whist,* described under *Whist.* See page 375.

SETBACK EUCHRE: A mode of scoring used in *Euchre,* page 107. Each player starts with ten chips and disposes of one each time he makes a point. If "euchred" he must add two chips to his quota. First to dispose of all chips is the winner.

SEVEN AND A HALF: Similar to *Blackjack,* page 32, this game is played with a forty-card pack, with ace up to seven valued according to the number of their spots, with face cards (**J, Q, K**) counting one half each. One card is dealt face down to each player, who may "stand" or call for further cards, to be dealt face up, one by one. The aim is to approach or reach 7½ without going over that total. A seven and a face card form a "natural 7½," and the player not only wins the amount of his wager, but gains the deal as well, unless the dealer also gets a "natural." A natural (as **7+Q**) beats any other 7½ (as **2+A+K+4**). Any 7½ beats any lesser total on which a player may decide to stand (as a simple **7;** or **A+K+5=6½**). Dealer wins any ties, as in **Blackjack,** and can double the bets after looking at his face-down card. Seven and a half is also similar to **Quinze,** page 286, its count being just half the 15 used in that game.

SEVEN-CARD games of *Poker*. These are too numerous to include here but are indexed in the Glossary-Index.

SEVEN-CARD FLIP: *Mexican Stud* with seven cards. See page 263.

SEVEN-CARD REVERSE: A variant of *Seven-Card Stud*. See page 264.

SEVEN-CARD STUD: A highly popular form of *Poker* now recognized as a standard game. Page 229.

SEVENS: Another name for *Fan-Tan* or *Card Dominoes*. See pages 115 and 55.

SEVEN-TOED PETE: A nickname for *Seven-Card Stud*. See page 266.

SEVEN UP: The American version of *All fours*, page 13, a forerunner of *Pitch*, page 214.

SHAMROCKS: A variant of *Trefoil Solitaire*. See page 346.

SHANGHAI RUMMY: See *Contract Rummy*, page 91.

SHASTA SAM: *California Jack*, page 41, with draws made from a face-down pack. Trump is determined by cutting the pack before the shuffle.

SHEEPSHEAD: A game akin to *Skat*, page 314, using the same thirty-two-card pack, with the same value for counters: Each A, 11; 10, 10; K, 4; Q, 3; J, 2. In its most popular form, the game has a fixed trump suit, running in descending order: ♣ Q, ♠ Q, ♡ Q, ◇ Q, ♣ J, ♠ J, ♡ J, ◇ J, A, 10, K, 9, 8, 7. Plain suits run A, 10, K, 9, 8, 7. Three players are dealt ten cards each, with two for a "widow," or "blind." Each player, in turn, has the privilege of taking up the widow, discarding two cards which go with any tricks he takes, and playing against both opponents. Player at dealer's left leads to the first trick, and others must follow suit if possible; otherwise they may discard or play trump if an ordinary suit was led. Highest card of suit led wins unless trumped, when highest trump wins. Winner of each trick leads to the next.

If the lone player takes more than 60 points, he scores 2 points for "game." If he takes in more than 90 points, he scores 4 for a "schneider." If he takes every trick, he scores 6 for a "schwarz." If the lone player takes 60 points or less, he is set back 2 points, unless he scores 30 or less, when he is set back 4 points; while if he fails to take a trick, he is set back 6 points. If all the players refuse to take the widow, the hand is played without it, the widow cards going to the player taking the final trick. In this case, however, they play for "least," the player taking the fewest points scoring 2 toward game; or 4 if he takes no points at all.

The first player to reach a total score of 10 becomes the winner unless some higher total is agreed upon beforehand.

Two players may be tied for "least"; in that case, whichever took his final trick before the other becomes the winner. In case of a triple tie, at 40 points each, the dealer is the winner. Another rule provides that a player taking no tricks at all scores 4 points, while if a player takes all the tricks, he is set back 4 points, and the others do not score.

Another and popular mode of scoring is to play a specified number of deals, the player with the highest total becoming the winner.

FOUR-HANDED SHEEPSHEAD: With four players, each is dealt eight cards, with no widow or blind. The long-accepted rule is to treat each deal as a separate game, with the player holding the ♣ Q automatically becoming the partner of the holder of the ♠ Q, though neither may state that he holds his black queen until he actually plays it. Hence it often becomes good policy for a player to lead high trumps as soon as possible in order to determine who his partner is.

If a player holds both black queens, he must say so, and then name an ace other than the ◊ A, which is the third highest trump. Whoever holds the requested ace becomes the player's partner. In this case, although the holder of the ♣ Q and ♠ Q is known, his partner must remain silent until he plays the ace in question. Sometimes a player holds the two black queens and all three nontrump aces (♣ A, ♠ A, ♡ A). When that occurs, he must state the fact, and the first of the other players to win a trick automatically becomes his partner.

As in three-handed game, the player at the dealer's left leads to the first trick, enabling him to show a black queen if he has one. By leading a low trump next, he gives his partner an opportunity to reveal himself by taking the trick with the other black queen. Conversely, an opening lead of anything else usually marks the player as a member of the opposing team.

The simplest mode of scoring is treat each deal as a game in itself, since the partners may fluctuate with every deal. For scoring more than 60 points, each member of the winning team collects a specified number of chips from one opponent; for more than 90 points, twice that number for schneider; for taking all tricks, three times that number for schwarz. By agreement, a schwarz can be rated at four times the ordinary score.

AUCTION SHEEPSHEAD: In this modernized form, the partners are permanent and are seated opposite. Each is allowed to pass or bid, beginning at the dealer's left, usually with a single bid the limit. Each bidder names a number above 60 as the total points his team will guarantee to take. If the team makes good, it scores as in the standard three-hand game, being set back accordingly if it loses, game being 10 points. Or, if preferred, each deal can constitute a game, as in regular partnership.

However, there is no regular trump suit in this type of game. Instead, the highest bidder chooses his trump suit, which gives more leeway to the bidding. While queens and jacks can head the trump suit, in the order already given, a more popular procedure is to demote the queens to ordinary status, using only the jacks as tops. Thus, the trump suit would run ♣ J, ♠ J, ♡ J,

◊ **J,** followed by **A, 10, K, Q, 9, 8, 7** of the suit named, with plain suits **A, 10, K, Q, 9, 8, 7.**

As a compromise, the two black queens may be retained as top trumps, followed by the jacks in their usual order, while the red queens each rank just below the king in their respective suits. In any of these forms, instead of bidding, the player holding the highest trump—whether ♣ **Q** or ♣ **J**—must name the trump suit. In another variant, diamonds are always trump as in the parent game, and play simply begins at the dealer's left, with the team taking the majority of the 120 points scoring accordingly. In case of a tie, neither scores.

All these represent the evolution of the old German game of schafkopf into its modern equivalent of sheepshead. The process can be extended still further by playing the *four-handed partnership* game—with or without bidding—with a forty-eight-card pinochle pack, containing two cards of the same value in every suit, from aces down to nines. If identical cards are played in the same trick—as ♡ **10** and ♡ **10**—the first takes precedence.

Each player is dealt twelve cards, and since the pack contains 240 points, more than 120 are needed for game; and more than 180 for schneider. Conversely, a bidding team loses if it takes 120 or less, and is schneidered if it takes 60 or less. In a *six-handed* game, there are two teams of three players, those seated alternately being partners; and each player is dealt eight cards.

With a sixty-four-card bezique pack, containing duplicate cards from aces down to sevens, an *eight-handed* game can be played, with two teams of four alternating partners, each player being dealt eight cards.

FIVE-HANDED SHEEPSHEAD: An interesting cross between the three-handed and four-handed games, this is played with the regular thirty-two-card pack, with the four queens and four jacks heading the diamonds as the permanent trump suit. Each player is dealt six cards, with two for a "widow" or "blind," and each, beginning with the dealer's left, has the choice of picking up the widow or passing it up. Whoever takes it then calls for an ace in any suit but trump, and the player holding that ace becomes his partner for the deal, identifying himself during play.

If the caller has all three aces, he says so, and the first of the three other players to take a trick becomes his partner. The widow goes with the tricks taken by the temporary partners, and if they win, the player who picked up the widow collects chips from two of the opponents, while his partner collects from only one. If all pass, the game is played at "least" with the player scores the fewest points collecting from each of the three others. The untouched widow goes with the last trick.

Substantially, the rules are those of the three-handed game, with the provisions simply making it two players against three, instead of one against two. However, a variation may be played without a widow by adding sixes and fives to the pack, making forty cards in all. Each player is dealt eight cards, and whoever holds the ♣ Q calls for the player with the ♠ Q as his partner; or with both the ♣ Q and ♠ Q he calls for a nontrump ace, and so on. Those two then play the three others, with the ♣ Q player settling with two others and his partner settling with one.

SHIFTING SANDS: A form of *Mexican Stud,* page 255.

SHIMMY: A nickname for *Chemin-de-Fer.* See page 63.

SHOTGUN: *Draw Poker* with extra betting rounds. See page 266.

SHOVE 'EM ALONG: Another term for *Take It or Leave It,* page 270. See *Push Poker,* page 261.

SHOWDOWN POKER: *Straight Poker,* page 269, without the draw. See *Showdown Poker,* page 267.

SIR GARNET: This is *Napoleon,* page 163, with the addition of a five-card "widow." Bidding is as usual, but in making the limit bid of five for "Nap," a player can add the widow to his hand, discard five, and play those that remain. He collects the usual ten chips from each opponent if he wins; but if he loses with the widow, he must pay each ten instead of only five, as with an ordinary bid of "Nap." Additional bids of "Wellington" or "Blucher" are not allowed in this game.

SIX-BID SOLO: Based on the old German game of "heart solo," which belongs to the skat family, six-bid solo gains its name from the fact that six different types of bids are allowed. Known in some localities simply as "solo," it is a three-player game in which a fourth may participate as dealer, utilizing a thirty-six-card pack, in which each suit ranks **A, 10, K, Q, J, 9, 8, 7, 6.** Each player is dealt eleven cards, preferably in rounds of four, three, four, with a three-card "widow" being dealt at the end of the second round.

Bidding then begins with the player at the dealer's left, who may pass or bid at any of the following levels, each ranking higher than the one before and having its own special rules:

Solo: The bidder names any suit trumps except hearts and must take more than 60 points during play, such points consisting of aces, 11 each; tens, 10; kings, 4; queens, 3; jacks, 2, as in skat. Regardless of who gained the bid, the player at dealer's left leads to the first trick. Others follow suit if they can; if not, they must play trump if possible, but they are not required to go higher. Otherwise, a player simply discards from a side suit. The widow is not taken up by the bidder, but is added to the tricks the bidder takes. Bidder does not name a trump unless or until he gains the bid.

For winning "solo," the bidder collects two chips from each active opponent for each point over 60. For losing, he pays them two chips for each point under 60.

Heart Solo: Here, the bidder must name hearts as his intended trump when he makes his bid. Play is exactly as in solo. For winning or losing, bidder collects or pays three chips instead of two.

Misere: There is no trump in this form of play. The bidder must avoid taking any counters in order to win; otherwise, he loses. The widow is not used; its counters (if any) are simply ignored. For winning, the bidder collects thirty chips from each active opponent; for losing, he pays them thirty chips each.

Guarantee, or *Guarantee Solo,* is played like solo, but the bidder must take 80 points to win, unless he names hearts as trump, when he requires only 74. For winning, he collects forty chips each; for losing, he pays forty chips each.

Spread or *Spread Misere:* Exactly like "misere," but the bidder spreads his hand face up and the player to his left leads to the first trick. Since the opponents gain a great advantage by seeing the bidder's hand, he collects 60 chips each if he wins; and pays 60 each if he loses.

Call Solo: Like "guarantee solo," but the bidder must take all 120 points, those in the widow being added to his score. Since this is very difficult, he may precede play by calling for any card that he needs or wants to improve his hand, and the player holding it must give it to him, receiving some useless card from the bidder in return. If the called card is in the widow, it simply stays there.

For winning, the bidder receives 100 chips from each opponent, unless he names hearts as trump, when he receives 150. For losing, he pays 100 chips each, or 150 with hearts trump.

Note: Originally, call solo required that the bidder take *every trick,* not just all the "counters" (♠ A, 10, K, Q, J), which made the bid still more difficult. But since such counters are the points of contention at every other bidding level, it is more consistent and therefore preferable to limit call solo to the taking of all 120 points, any in the widow going to the bidder as in all solo bids.

With a fourth player in the game, a question arises regarding the dealer's participation in the payoff. Here, there are three options, one of which should be agreed upon in advance:

(1) The dealer does not have to pay if the bidder wins, but collects like the two other players if the bidder loses.

(2) The above rule applies to bids of solo and heart solo,

but at higher levels, the dealer must pay or collect like an active player.

(3) The bidder collects or loses at all levels. Of the three options, this has the merit of being the simplest.

SIX-CARD STUD: *Poker.* See page 211.

SIX-SPOT RED DOG: Another name for *Slippery Sam* (page 319).

SIXTH CARD OPTIONAL: *Poker.* See page 267.

SIXTY-FOUR-CARD PINOCHLE: A two-handed game, using a bezique pack, running **A, A, 10, 10, K, K, Q, Q, J, J, 9, 9, 8, 8, 7, 7.** Each player is dealt sixteen cards and the rules of two-handed pinochle are followed, but the seven of trump becomes the dix instead of the nine. See *Pinochle,* page 174.

SIXTY-SIX: An abbreviated, fast-moving game similar to two-handed pinochle, using a half-pack of twenty-four cards, ranking in order **A, 10, K, Q, J, 9** in each suit. Six cards are dealt to each player—by twos or threes—and the next is turned up for trump, the pack being laid face down across it. Opponent leads to the first trick with any card, and the dealer also plays any card he wants. High card of suit led takes the trick, unless a plain suit lead is trumped. Winner of the trick draws the top card from the pack, adding it to his hand; and the loser draws the next card. Winner then leads to the next trick.

When all cards have been drawn, ending with the turned-up trump, play is "closed," and a player must follow suit if he can. If not, he can either discard from another suit or take the trick with a trump. If trump is led, he does not have to play a higher trump. (This differs from two-handed pinochle, in which a player must trump an opposing lead when he can and must go higher, if possible, when trump is led.) Cards taken in play are valued as follows: Each ace, 11; each ten, 10; each king, 4; each queen, 3; each jack, 2; last trick, 10. This makes a total count of 130, hence the first player to reach 66 wins the hand and scores 1 point (or more) toward a game of 7 points, each deal alternating between the players.

A player holding or drawing the nine of trump may exchange it for the turned-up trump (as with the dix in pinochle) provided he has already taken a trick, but there is no count for this. However:

A player may meld a royal marriage (K and Q of trump) for a count of 40, or an ordinary marriage (K and Q of a plain suit) for a count of 20, by simply leading one card of the pair and showing the other. This may be done at any time, even after play is "closed" and the last six tricks are being played out. He does not have to take the trick to score the marriage. However, if the opponent declares a marriage on the opening play of the hand, he must take a trick before it can be counted.

At any time, a player may announce that he has reached sixty-six, whereupon play is ended. The counters that he took in tricks are added, plus his count in melds; and he is allowed to meld one additional marriage—if he has it in his hand—by simply showing the king and queen, without playing either. If the announcer's count totals 66 or more, he wins the hand and scores 1 point toward game. If the loser's count, including any meld, comes to less than 33, it is a "schneider," and the winner scores 2 points toward game. If the loser fails to take a single trick, it is a "schwarz" and the winner scores 3 points. In contrast, if the announcer's count falls short of 66, his adversary scores 2 points toward game.

As an adjunct toward announcing sixty-six, a player is allowed to close the play before making a lead, by simply turning down the face-up trump. This means that no more cards are to be drawn from the pack, with play continuing on a "closed" basis until both hands are played out, unless one player announces sixty-six before then. Either way, there is no count of 10 for "last trick," as the play does not continue until the pack is exhausted.

A player who closes the play scores the usual point or points if his count reaches 66 or more. If he fails to make 66, his adversary scores 2 points. If he should close the play before his adversary has taken a trick, and then fail to reach 66, his adversary scores 3 points toward game.

Whenever the pack is played completely through, with neither player announcing sixty-six, each adds up his counters, and if only one player has reached 66, he scores 1 or 2 points toward game, according to his adversary's count. If both reach 66, as frequently happens, neither scores; but the player winning the next hand is given a bonus, or "carry-over," of 1 point. Occasionally, when there are no melds, the players finish in a tie of 65 points each. In that case, neither scores.

Three-handed Sixty-six: This is the two-handed game with three players, each taking his turn at dealing to the two others. The dealer scores the same number of points as the player who wins the hand, but he can not score a seventh point for game except during a hand in which he is an active player. If two active players tie at 65, or both make 66 or more, neither scores, but the dealer is given 1 point toward game.

Four-handed Sixty-six involves a thirty-two-card pack, which includes eights and sevens. Players seated opposite are partners and eight cards are dealt clockwise to each player, usually by threes, then two. The final card is shown to represent trump and then goes into the dealer's hand. Lead is made by the player at the dealer's left.

Each player must follow suit and play a higher card if possible. If out of suit, he must trump the trick if he can and overtrump any trump already played. Otherwise, a player may discard from a side suit. This is more like old-time pinochle than sixty-six, except that there is no melding whatever. Counters are valued as usual with a count of 10 for the last trick.

Partners pool their counters, and the team making 66 scores 1 point toward game; making more than 99 scores 2 points; taking every trick scores 3 points. Game is 7 points. With ties of 65 each, the game point is carried over to the next deal, made by the player on the dealer's left.

Auction Sixty-six is a four-handed partnership game in which players beginning at the dealer's left bid for the privilege of naming trump. The minimum bid is 60, but a player may pass if he chooses, re-entering the bidding only if his partner makes an intervening bid. Play begins at the dealer's left and partners pool their counters, which in this case are regarded as points toward game, which is 666 points. If a team makes its bid, it scores all such points taken in play. If it falls short, the other team scores the amount of the bid, plus all the points that it takes in play. Highest possible bid is 130 and a team making it scores 260; otherwise the defending team scores 260. Further deals follow and scores are added until one team reaches the required 666.

In play, instead of requiring players to play higher on each trick and to trump when out of suit, the rules used in the two-handed game are generally followed; namely: If out of the suit led, a player may trump or discard as he pleases; and in no case is he required to "head the trick" by playing a higher card than one played earlier.

SIXTY-THREE: A form of *Cinch* with additional trump points making a total of 63, and with unlimited bidding allowed. See *Cinch,* page 65.

SKAT: A three-handed game of German origin in which the participants are designated as *V* for Vorhand, the leader; *M* for Mittlehand, or middle hand; and *H* for Hinterhand, the last man, who serves as dealer. Skat is unique in that it actually constitutes a group of games, or variations; and from these, a successful bidder, termed the Player, can choose the one he wants for that particular hand. In the play that follows, the two opponents act as partners in an effort to defeat the successful bidder, or player.

The pack consists of thirty-two cards, the sevens being the lowest. The trump suit is always headed by the ♣ J, ♠ J, ♡ J, ◇ J, in that exact order, followed by the A, 10, K, Q, 9, 8, 7 of the suit named. The other suits run A, 10, K, Q, 9, 8, 7. But in certain games, the jacks, which are known as wenzels, form a trump suit of their own in the order given. This fifth suit is called "grand" to distinguish it from the side suits of clubs, spades, hearts, and diamonds.

Ten cards are dealt to each player, usually in two rounds of three and one of four. After the first round, two cards are dealt aside, face down, to form a widow, which in this game is called the skat. Players then bid for the privilege of naming the type of game to be played, as well as the trump.

Instead of opening the bidding, *V* allows *M* to bid from a minimum of 10 points up. *H* has no say in the bidding as long as *V* is willing to match any bid that *M* makes. But if either passes, *H* can make a higher bid, which must be matched by the remaining bidder, either *V* or *M,* as the case may be. Otherwise *H*'s bid stands.

Regardless of who is bidder, Vorhand starts the play by leading to the first trick. The others follow suit if possible; if not, they may discard or play trump. The highest card of suit led wins the trick unless it is trumped; if trumped twice, the higher trump wins.

The purpose of the Player (or bidder) is to take in counter cards, valued as follows: ace, 11; ten, 10; king, 4; queen, 3; jack, 2. If he takes a total of 61 or more, he scores 1 point for "game"; a total of 91 or more, 1 additional point for "schneider"; for taking every trick, 1 point more for "schwarz." A counter in the skat goes toward the Player's total. The nonbidders, operating as partners, pool any counters that they take in an effort to thwart the Player's aim.

In addition, the Player scores 1 point or more for "matadores," which consist of a sequence of trumps running from the highest (♣ J) down without interruption. If these are in the Player's hand, he is said to be playing "with" that number of matadores. For example, with spades trump, if the Player holds ♣ J, ♠ J, ♡ J, ◇ J, ♠ A, ♠ 10, ♠ 8, he is playing "with six" matadores, as the top six trumps are in sequence.

However, if the matadores are in the opposing hands, they still count for the Player (or bidder), the only difference being that he is playing "without" matadores, since he does not hold them. For example, with hearts trump, a Player holding ♡ **10 Q 9 7** would be "without five," as all the wenzels and the ♡ **A** are in the other hands, forming a five-card trump sequence down to the Player's ♡ **10.**

In short, the Player always scores for matadores, either *with* or *without.* He is sure of scoring at least 1 such point; and since there are eleven trumps (counting the wenzels) he can score as high as 11 points, as the cards in the skat are regarded as belonging to his hand. By keeping those factors in mind, the matter of the matadores becomes quite simple.

Suits also have special point values, which vary in different types of games, so those must be considered in the bidding. In all cases, the suit points are multiplied by the total of all other points, in order to determine the Player's score. To clarify this, the various forms of skat will be described in order:

Tournee: Upon gaining the bid, the Player looks at either card of the skat, and if he wants its suit for trump, he shows the face of the card and adds it to his hand, then adds the other skat card without showing it. He then discards any two cards face down to replace the skat, which goes along with any tricks he takes.

Play proceeds as already described, and if the Player takes 61 counters or more, he adds his points (for game, schneider, schwarz, and matadores) and multiplies their total by the value of the trump suit. These values run: diamonds **(D),** 5; hearts **(H),** 6; spades **(S),** 7; clubs **(C),** 8. If this comes to more than his bid, he scores whatever points he makes; if he falls short, either in counters or points, he loses the amount of his bid, which is charged against his score.

Example: A player holding ♣ **J,** ♠ **J,** ♡ **J,** ◇ **J,** ♡ **A 9** turns up the ♡ **7** and takes 98 counters in play. He scores the following points: game, 1; schneider, 1; with (matadores), 5, multiplied by 6 for hearts gives him a total of 42 points $(1+1+5=7\times6=42)$.

Passt Mir Nicht: This is tournee with a "second turn," which means that, if the Player does not want the trump represented by the first card he takes from the skat, he can put that card in his hand without showing it and turn up the other skat card for trump. Play proceeds as in tournee, and if he makes his bid, he scores his points as usual; but if he fails to make it, he is set back double the amount of the bid.

Tournee Grand: Although jacks, as wenzels, are the top cards of any trump suit, if the Player turns up a jack—on either his first or second turn—he can name its suit as trump, and often does. However, if he prefers, he can name "grand" as trump, thus playing with a fifth suit consisting of wenzels in their usual order (♣ J, ♠ J, ♡ J, ◇ J) as trump. Grand, as trump, has a multiple value of 12 points when the hand is played as in tournee or passt mir nicht.

Gucki Grand: If a Player wants grand for trump without turning up the skat, he can declare "gucki grand" by simply picking up the skat cards and adding them to his hand, then making a regular discard. Play is exactly as in tournee grand, but the trump (grand) has a multiple value of 16 points; and if the Player fails to make his bid, he is set back double.

Solo: A bidder with only one long, strong suit can seldom afford the risk of turning up the wrong card for trump, so his recourse is to play "solo," by naming the trump "out of hand" and ignoring the skat until play is ended. Then, its cards are added to the Player's tricks, so that any counters of matadores it may contain can be considered in the final reckoning. Values of trump suits in solo are: diamonds (D), 9; hearts (H), 10; spades (S), 11; clubs (C), 12. These serve as multipliers, as usual.

Grand Solo: This is solo with "grand" as trump, its value being 20 points. It is riskier than gucki grand, as the Player has no chance to discard high counters from his hand.

Grand Ouvert: With a very strong hand—indeed, one that is all but invincible—the Player can ignore the skat and lay his hand face up, playing grand solo "openly," as the name implies, but with the understanding that he must take every trick, as in schwarz. The multiple value of grand in this game is 24 points.

Schneider Announced: In any solo game, the Player may

announce beforehand that he will schneider his opponents by taking tricks containing 91 counters or more. If successful, he scores 1 point extra; if not, he loses the amount bid.

Schwarz Announced: In solo, the Player may also announce schwarz beforehand, and by taking every trick he scores 1 point extra (plus the point for schneider announced). Otherwise, he loses his bid. Note that with grand ouvert these announcements are automatic.

Ramsch: When all three players pass, the leader, Vorhand, declares a special game in which grand is trump and each player is on his own, the purpose being to take the fewest counters. The skat is ignored until the play is finished, when it is given (with its counters) to the player who took the last trick. The only score in ramsch is 10 points for smallest count, which is doubled to 20 if the winner takes no tricks at all. However, if one player takes every trick, it is regarded as a lost game and 30 points are charged against him, with no score for the other players. If two players tie for low count, the one who took a later trick is the loser; if all three tie, Vorhand is the winner.

Nullo: In this different type of game, the bidder must lose every trick. There is no trump and cards of all suits rank **A, K, Q, J, 10, 9, 8, 7.** There are no matadores and the skat is not used. Any bid up to 20 allows a declaration of nullo, as the Player scores 20 points if he makes his bid and has 20 charged against him if he fails.

Nullo Ouvert: This is nullo with the Player laying his cards face up to start. Being more difficult than nullo, it scores 40 points, plus or minus, according to whether he wins or loses. Often, a player with a good nullo hand may have to bid higher than 20, in which case, nullo ouvert is his only recourse.

In skat, each individual hand is regarded as a game, and settlement is usually made on that basis. A cumulative score may be kept during an extended session, with the player scoring the most points over a specified period becoming the winner.

SLAM: An old-time form of *Whist,* page 375.

SLAPJACK: A childish game with a pack divided among two or more players, who hold their packets face down and deal cards face up to the center of the table, in regular rotation. When a jack appears, each player slaps a hand upon the center pile; and the first to land wins it. The winner puts those cards face down beneath his packet, and play resumes on the same jack-slapping terms until one player gains all the cards and wins the game. For a large group, an additional pack or packs may be used.

SLIPPERY ELMER: Form of five-card stud. See page 267.

SLIPPERY SAM: Also termed *Six-Spot Red Dog,* this is played with a fifty-two-card pack, with suits ranking from ace down to two, as in *Red Dog,* page 289. Players form a pool, with equal contributions of chips; and three cards are dealt to each, face down; these remain untouched. The dealer then turns up cards from the top of the pack until he comes to one with six spots or less (as the ◊ 4). Each player bets in turn up to the size of the pool, then turns his hand face up. If he has a higher card of the suit turned up by dealer, he takes the amount bet from the pool. If not, he pays the pool. All bet against the same turned-up card, unless one player wins the entire pot, which calls for a new pool and a new deal. Players may also be required to add chips to the pool before each deal.

SLOBBERHANNES: A game of the *Hearts* family, page 140, but more like *Polignac,* page 283, as it uses the same thirty-two-card pack, ranking **A, K, Q, J, 10, 9, 8, 7.** With four players, each is dealt eight cards, and the first player leads any card he wants, while the rest must follow suit if possible. The winner of each trick leads to the next until all have been played. There are no trumps in this game, and each player's

purpose is to avoid taking the first trick, the last trick, or the
♣ Q, as each counts 1 point against him. Taking all those points
is "slobberhannes" and counts 1 point more. A revoke (playing
the wrong suit) is usually counted as 1 point against the player,
as it could affect the entire hand. The player who first reaches
a total of 10 adverse points loses the game and must pay the
others the difference between his points and theirs.

Since each player is on his own, the game can also be
played with three, five, or six players; but on such occasions,
the ♠ 7 and ♣ 7 must be removed from the pack so the cards
will deal evenly.

SLOUGH: Also termed *Sluff,* this is a form of *Frog.* See page
125.

SMUDGE: A name frequently applied to *Auction Pitch,* when
the "smudge bid" is incorporated into the rules. See *Pitch,*
page 214.

SNIP SNAP SNOREM: Exactly like *Earl of Coventry,* page
105, in play but somewhat faster, as the players, when matching a face-up card, simply say, "Snip," then "Snap," and
finally, "Snorem" in that order, instead of making rhyming
statements.

SNOOZER: A name very often applied to *Dom Pedro,* when
the joker, or "snoozer," is included in the game. This dis-
tinguishes it from the earlier form of *Dom Pedro,* with only
the "Dom" as a special counter. See *Pedro,* page 172.

SOLITAIRE: The term "solitaire" applies to any card game
played by one person who usually deals out cards and then
assembles them in special groups according to established rules.
A standard pack of fifty-two cards is generally used, with more
elaborate forms requiring two packs or even more.

Cards are ranked in *ascending sequence,* **A, 2, 3, 4, 5, 6,**

7, 8, 9, 10, J, Q, K, or in *descending sequence,* **K, Q, J, 10, 9, 8, 7, 6, 5, 4, 3, 2, A.** Either way, the ace is low and the king high, unless otherwise specified. The suits, ♢ ♣ ♡ ♠, play a part in most games of solitaire; and the *colors, red* and *black,* also figure in certain games.

Generally, the player first deals a group or groups of cards to form a *layout,* or *tableau,* always face up, unless otherwise stipulated. These may be dealt in *piles,* with only the top card visible; or in *columns,* from top to bottom, or in *rows,* running crosswise. Columns and rows are sometimes dealt in overlapping fashion, so that only the final card is fully seen. The same applies to *fans* or *clusters,* which are used in a few games.

These final cards are *free* or *available* for transfer to other groups, under conditions pertaining to individual games. In most instances, the ultimate object is to establish *bases* or *foundations,* upon which available cards can be *built* in *sequence* according to their *values* and also their *suits,* if so specified. With aces as bases, builds are made in ascending sequence up to kings; with kings as bases, in descending sequence down to aces. With double packs, both types of builds are occasionally used.

In many games, when an available card cannot be used in a build, it may be transferred to another group in the layout proper, being placed in sequence on the available card that is showing there. The cards on which such temporary builds are made are termed *auxiliary* cards; and generally, the rules for building on *auxiliaries* are more liberal than those that apply to builds on bases, always specifying whether such auxiliary sequences must be done by suits, alternating colors or simply by value.

In older games, only the available card could be moved to an auxiliary, but in more modern solitaires, moves are made with entire sequences. Thus, if a vertical column shows a descending sequence in alternating colors, as ♡ **7,** ♣ **6,** ♡ **5,** ♠ **4,** the four cards would be transferred as a group to the ♠ **8,** but only the ♠ **4** would still be available for building on a base. Here, again, rules vary in different forms of solitaire. In some, the single available card may also be moved on its own without the sequence; in others, partial sequences may be moved.

In games where cards are originally dealt face down, with face-up cards upon them, as soon as the face-up cards are transferred to other piles or built upon bases, the top card of each face-down group is turned face up, thereby becoming available for further play. This continues until all the cards in a pile or column have been turned up and moved, leaving a *space* or *vacancy,* which in most games may be filled by an available card, subject to certain restrictions. In a few games, however, spaces must be left empty, and this has an important bearing on the play.

In solitaires where only part of the pack is dealt an extra group or pile is sometimes dealt to one side as a *reserve,* from which cards may be played within certain limitations; hence the reserve, when used, is technically a part of the layout, but it figures in only a very few games. In the great majority of games, any cards left over from the layout are retained as a *pack,* or *stock,* from which cards are dealt when no further play is possible from the layout, which is said to be *blocked.* Usually, the pack is held face down, with each card being turned face up when dealt from the top.

If such cards can be built on bases or auxiliaries, they are used accordingly; otherwise, they go into a *discard* or *waste pile,* which is usually kept face up, with its top card—the one just discarded—still available, like the top card of a layout pile. Once played, it reveals another face-up card, which is also freed for use, so sometimes it is possible to bring back several discards in succession. In some games, after the entire pack has been dealt out, it is allowable to turn the discard pile face down and deal through it again, as with the original pack. Another *redeal* is sometimes allowed, making three deals in all.

Since solitaire is basically a one-person game, a player may introduce minor rules of his own, which accounts for many variants that have come into vogue. Individual solitaires will be found under the following heads:

ACCORDION: A simple form of solitaire in which the entire pack is first dealt in one long face-up row. Any card may then be placed on the card to its left if it matches it in suit or value; thus the ◇ 6 could be placed on any diamond or any six. The rule also applies to the third card on the left, the player being allowed to jump the two cards in between to make a match. As piles are formed, they are matched in the same way, the top card representing the suit and value of the entire pile.

The object of the game is to gather the entire pack in one big fifty-two-card pile at the extreme left. To save space, which is often limited, many players go by the rule that piles can be formed as the deal progresses, usually after the first dozen cards or so. From then on, a player keeps moving or jumping to the left and dealing to the right as he sees fit.

In a more difficult variant, *Idle Year,* moves and jumps are compulsory, beginning with the deal of the second card, the only choice being when the chance for either a move or a jump occurs. Example: Deal begins with ♠ 8, ♣ J, ♡ 3, ◇ J, ♡ 4, ♠ K, ♠ J. Here, the player can either move the ♠ J onto the ♠ K or jump the ♠ J onto the ◇ J. The jump is preferable, as the pile thus formed, being topped by the ♠ J, could then be jumped onto the ♠ 8.

ACES UP: A simple solitaire in which cards rank A, K, Q, J, 10, 9, 8, 7, 6, 5, 4, 3, 2 in descending order. Four cards are dealt in a face-up row, as ♡ 8, ♠ J, ♡ 10, ◇ 5. If two of the same suit are dealt, the lower one is discarded, in this case, the ♡ 8. Four more cards are dealt face up on those, including the space if there is one. Again, the lower card or cards of a duplicated suit are discarded. As this is repeated in succeeding deals, the elimination of a card may mean the uncovering of another that can also be discarded.

As piles increase in size, their top cards must also be moved into spaces prior to the next deal, and this often aids in further discards. The aim of the game is to finish with only the four aces in the layout, as elimination of all other cards constitutes a win. This game is also appropriately known under the name of *Idiot's Delight*.

AULD LANG SYNE: A simple solitaire that is easy to play but very hard to beat. The four aces are placed face up in a row to serve as bases; below that, the player deals a row of four face-up cards and builds any that he can on the aces, as 2 on A, 3 on 2, and so on, in ascending sequence, regardless of suits. Another four cards are dealt on the same row, covering the cards already there and filling any spaces; this is followed by further builds if possible. Four more are dealt in the same fashion, and this continues through the entire pack.

Since key cards are easily buried, this game is often blocked before the bases can be built to kings, so pauses should be allowed during the deal if there is a chance to build a card already showing on a pile. Example: A base has been built up to ◇ 5. The ♠ 7 is showing on the third pile. The player deals the ♣ 6 on the second pile. He pauses and builds ♣ 6 on ◇ 5 and ♠ 7 on ♣ 6, before finishing the four-card deal; otherwise, the ♠ 7 might be buried forever. Even with that privilege, the game is so difficult that the real object is to see how many cards can be built before play is finally blocked, rather than trying to build up the entire pack.

Tam o' Shanter is a tougher version of *Auld Lang Syne*, in which the entire pack is shuffled and then dealt by fours, so that aces aren't available until they crop up in the deal. Easier variants are known under a variety of titles that are not worth listing, because so many better and brighter solitaires are willing, waiting, and wanting for whosoever would like to play them.

AUXILIARY SEQUENCES: See *Storehouse* (page 348).

BELEAGUERED CASTLE: A solitaire in which the four aces are dealt in a face-up column to serve as bases. Then, more columns are dealt face up, alternating left and right, to form eight cross-rows of six cards each, alternating outward. The outermost cards are available for building on the aces in ascending order up to kings, according to their suits. When—and if!—the entire pack is so built, the game is won.

To aid that aim, an available card may be moved to the outermost card of another row, but in descending order, as ♣ J on ♠ Q, ♣ 7 on ♡ 8, without any regard to suits. Cards may only be moved singly, never in groups; but whenever a space occurs, any available card may be placed therein. Hence it is possible to wangle cards back and forth from one row to another in order to get at those needed for builds, making the game both intriguing and ingenious, though often difficult to win.

In the variant called *Citadel,* the entire pack is shuffled to start, and the side columns are dealt as already described. Whenever an ace appears it is dealt between the rows as a base; and as the deal continues, other cards of that suit can be built upon it if they appear in ascending sequence, **2, 3, 4,** etc., putting the player that far ahead when the deal is finished, particularly when it reduces the number of cards in certain rows, which is helpful toward gaining a space.

Another variant, *Streets and Alleys,* is simply *Beleaguered Castle* with the aces shuffled into the pack, which is then dealt in the usual rows but with seven cards in the four rows on the left. A central space is kept clear for placement of the aces as they become available for bases.

BETROTHAL: A solitaire similar to *Accordion,* page 323. The king and queen of any suit are removed from a pack, which is then shuffled and the king placed on the bottom, the queen on the top. Cards are then dealt in a face-up row from left to right. Anytime one or two cards are flanked by two of the same suit or rank, they are discarded and the space is closed. Example: Deal runs ♡ Q, ♠ 7, ◇ 6, ♠ 9, ♣ 6, ◇ 7, ♣ 10, ♠ Q.

Discard ◇ 6 (between two spades), the ♠ 9, and ♣ 6

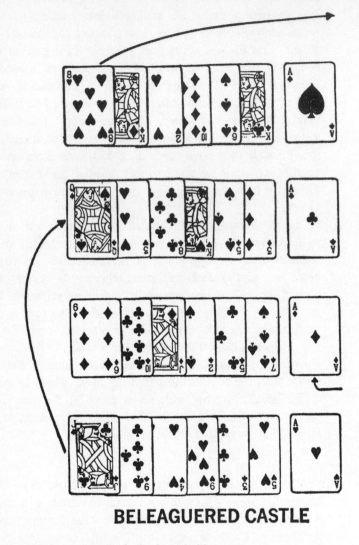

BELEAGUERED CASTLE

Layout for Beleaguered Castle, indicating suitable moves.

(between two sevens), the ◇ **7** and ♣ **10** (between two spades), the ♠ **7** (between two queens). The object is to eliminate all cards except the ♡ **Q** and ♡ **K**, bringing them together at the finish. This game is also called *Coquette* or *Royal Marriage*.

BIG FORTY: See *Lucas,* page 339.

BISLEY: A novel form of solitaire, in which the four aces are dealt in a row to serve as bases, followed by nine face-up cards. Below that, the entire pack is dealt in three cross-rows of thirteen cards each and a fourth of nine cards, to form overlapping columns. The card at the foot of each column is available for building on an ace in upward sequence toward a king, according to suit, which frees the next card for similar play.

However, when a king becomes available, it may be placed below the layout to serve as a base on which cards may be built in downward sequence toward an ace. There is no limit to the extent of either type of build, up or down, the player's purpose simply being to build all his cards. Moves may also be made from one auxiliary column to another, card by card, either up or down, according to suit, with any number of transfers allowable. Thus the ♡ **9** could be put on the ♡ **10** and later removed and put on the ♡ **8**. But once a column has been cleared, the space is dead and no card can be moved into it.

This game must be studied well ahead to see if there are any automatic blocks that will prevent its completion; if so, it should be abandoned therewith. The great hazard is that of blocking your own builds by trapping cards in layout columns, so they cannot be built in the needed direction. A few trials will make this evident.

CALCULATION: A simple but intriguing solitaire in which suits are disregarded and values alone are counted, with ace =1; jack=11; queen=12; king=13; all other cards according to the number of spots. Any ace is first dealt face up, next to it any two, then any three and any four. These serve as bases, representing 1, 2, 3, 4 respectively.

The remainder of the pack is shuffled, and from this stock the player turns up cards one by one, placing each on a base if he can, the builds running in ascending values, but according to the following progressions:

On Pile 1: 1, 2, 3, 4, 5, 6, 7, 8, 9, 10, 11, 12, 13.
On Pile 2: 2, 4, 6, 8, 10, 12, 1, 3, 5, 7, 9, 11, 13.
On Pile 3: 3, 6, 9, 12, 2, 5, 8, 11, 1, 4, 7, 10, 13.
On Pile 4: 4, 8, 12, 3, 7, 11, 2, 6, 10, 1, 5, 9, 13.

Any cards that cannot be built are placed face up in discard piles below the bases. These are four such piles and the player may place his discards as he chooses, though he cannot transfer them from one such pile to another. However, the uppermost card of each discard pile can always be built on a base, should such an opportunity occur.

The object is to build the entire pack onto the bases, which requires studied placement of the discards; hence the player may spread a discard pile when he needs to check back on it; but only the uppermost card is buildable.

CANFIELD: A popular name for the most popular of solitaires, originally known as *Klondike* and described under that head. See page 338.

CITADEL: See *Beleaguered Castle*, page 324.

COQUETTE: See *Betrothal*, page 325.

DEMON: See *Fascination*, below.

FASCINATION: This solitaire, which is simply a development of *Storehouse*, page 348, was frequently played at Canfield's gambling casino, at the time when another solitaire, *Klondike*, page 338, sprang to popularity. The two became confused in

BISLEY

Sample layout used in Bisley, indicating suitable moves.

the public mind, so that *Klondike* gained the name of "Canfield" and has been called that ever since, though some authorities claim, with good reason, that the title properly belongs to *Fascination*, which is here described under that head, strictly as itself.

Thirteen cards are dealt face down and squared into a pile that is turned face up to be used as a reserve, as in storehouse. The next card is dealt face up, slightly above and to the right, as a simple base on which cards are to be built in ascending order, according to suit. Thus, if the ◇ 8 should be turned up as a base, the building sequence would run ◇ 8, 9, 10, J, Q, K, A, 2, 3, 4, 5, 6, 7. Any other base cards—in this case, eights—that become available during play are promptly placed alongside the sample, so that they too can be built up according to their respective suits.

Next, four cards are dealt in a face-up row to the right of the reserve, as auxiliary piles, on which descending sequences may be built in alternating colors, red and black, as ♡ 3 on ♠ 4; ♣ 2 on ♡ 3; ◇ A on ♣ 2; ♠ K on ◇ A; ♡ Q on ♠ K; and so on down. Such sequences can be moved only in their entirety, never in sections or as single cards; this is also a rule in Klondike. Thus the sequence ♠ 4, ♡ 3, ♣ 2, ◇ A, ♠ K, ♡ Q would have to be placed on the ♡ 5 or ◇ 5.

Whenever a space occurs in the layout, it must be filled by the top card of the reserve, never from another auxiliary pile; this is a rule held over from storehouse. The top card of the reserve may also be built directly onto a base; and cards from an auxiliary pile are built in the same way. Thus in the sequence just shown, the ♡ Q would be available for building on the ♡ J; and that would free the ♠ K for building on the ♠ Q; and that would free the ◇ A for building on the ◇ K; and so on.

When play is blocked, the pack comes into action. Holding it face down, the player deals a cluster of three cards face up as a discard pile; and the card showing there is available for building on a base or placing on an auxiliary sequence, just as if it came from the reserve. The card then showing on the discard pile automatically becomes available for play. The same deal is continued by threes, through the entire pack, with the top card of the discard pile always available; after that, the discard pile is turned face down and again is dealt through by threes, as a pack. This may be continued as many times as desired.

However, a space in the layout cannot be filled by a card from the pack until after the reserve pile is exhausted, then it becomes allowable, but with this difference: Where a layout space must be filled from the reserve, the player does not have to fill it from the pack after the reserve is used up. This may enable him to keep dealing through until he comes to a more suitable card; and the rule applies to any other plays from the pack. None are mandatory.

No cards can be placed on the reserve, nor returned there. Similarly, no card can be taken back into the pack. Auxiliary sequences must remain as formed; and once a card has been built upon a base, it cannot be recalled for use in an auxiliary sequence, even though it may be badly needed there.

In a variation of this game called *Demon,* when the pack is down to less than six cards, the player is allowed to deal through them one by one. This is a good rule, which many players apply to fascination as though it were part of the standard game. In another variant, *Grand Demon,* the player is allowed to bring back one card that he has built upon a base, if needed for an auxiliary sequence. Some players liberalize this to the extent that any number of cards may be brought back from their bases. In the final analysis, choice in this matter should be up to the individual player, since he is the person most concerned; in fact, usually the only one concerned.

Actually, a strict interpretation of the rules of Fascination suggest an innovation that has been almost entirely overlooked and is therefore worthy of consideration by solitaire addicts who dislike repeated frustration. The rule says to "deal through the pack by threes," so whenever the deal finishes with an odd card, it is regarded as a final trio; and the same applies if two cards are left over. But this rule can also be interpreted to mean that one or two extras are not part of the "deal by threes" and therefore should be laid aside face down and placed upon the pack after it is turned over. Then, the next "deal by threes" is apt to bring up cards that would otherwise be hopelessly buried, putting new life in the game.

By using the "old deal" until the game is finally blocked, a player can follow the accepted pattern of fascination to the limit; then, rather than give up, he can switch to the "new deal" and see how far it will carry him, resorting to it whenever the deal comes out unevenly.

FLOWER GARDEN: An excellent one-pack solitaire in which all the cards are dealt in a face-up layout as follows:

Shuffle the pack and deal thirty-six cards in six overlapping columns of six cards each. These represent the "garden," and the final or bottom card of each column is available for play. Deal the remaining sixteen cards in a face-up row below the columns to serve as a reserve, termed the "bouquet," and all of its cards are constantly available.

In play, as aces become available, they are placed in a row above the layout, and cards are built on them in ascending value according to suits. Available cards may also be placed on the bottom of auxiliary columns in descending value, according to suits. When a column becomes vacant, any available card may be moved into the space to renew the column.

This is important, because cards can only be moved singly, so spaces are needed to dismantle downward sequences that have been placed on auxiliary columns, in order to release cards for builds.

FORTY THIEVES: See *Lucus,* page 339.

GRAND DEMON: See *Fascination,* page 329.

HOUSE IN THE WOODS: The same as *La Belle Lucie* (described under *Trefoil* (page 348) but played with a double pack of 104 cards. Each of the eight aces serves as a base when released.

HOUSE ON THE HILL: A two-pack solitaire similar to *House in the Woods*, but using only four aces, each of a different suit, as bases, which are built up in the usual ascending order. The other four bases consist of kings, each of a different suit, which are built downward in descending order.

IDIOT'S DELIGHT: See *Aces Up*, page 323.

IDLE YEAR: See *Accordion*, page 323.

KING ALBERT: A highly intriguing solitaire of the Canfield-Klondike type. The entire pack is dealt face up, beginning with nine cards in a cross-row; then, starting with the second column, eight in a cross-row; then, starting with the third column, seven in a cross-row, and so on, each row overlapping the one above. The result is nine such columns of from one to nine cards, or forty-five in all. The remaining seven cards are placed in a face-up row to serve as a reserve. The final card at the foot of each column is available for immediate play, as are all the reserve cards.

The aim is to place aces as bases and build them up to kings by suits. Available cards may be moved from one column to another, and each must be placed on a card of the next higher value of the opposite color, as red jack on black queen, black ten on red jack, etc., but all must be moved singly, never as a sequence. Reserve cards can be built on bases or placed on auxiliary columns, but no card can be returned to the reserve. A space may be filled with any available card, but it is wise to keep them open in order to transfer sequences from one column to another, card by card, a great feature of the game.

Often, the game is totally blocked in its early stage, but once that is past, new opportunities frequently arise, making it possible to build up the entire pack quite rapidly. To aid this worthy cause, some players include a special rule, allowing a card already built on a base to be brought back to a column, but never to the reserve.

FLOWER GARDEN

Typical layout in Flower Garden.
Bottom row represents bouquet.

KLONDIKE : More generally but incorrectly known as *Canfield* (see *Fascination,* page 329, for explanation), this is far and away the most popular of American solitaires, almost to the exclusion of all others. It is played as follows:

A card is dealt face up, with a row of six face down to the right of it. On the second card, a card is dealt face up, with five more to the right. On the third, a face-up card, with four more to the right; and so on, resulting in a twenty-eight-card layout such as:

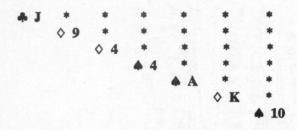

Any aces are taken from the layout and used as bases to be built upward in each suit, 2, 3, 4, to J, Q, K. Cards may be shifted from one layout column to another, to form descending sequences in alternating colors (red-black or vice versa). Such sequences can only be shifted in their entirety. This removal of a face-up card (or cards) allows a face-down card to be turned up on its column, thus becoming available for play. When a column is completely cleared, a king may be moved into the space thus left.

Example, with the layout shown: Build ♠ A and turn up a card, as ♣ Q. Move ♣ Q onto ◇ K and turn up ♣ 9. Move ◇ 9 onto ♠ 10 and turn up ♣ A. Build ♣ A. Move ◇ K–♣ Q into the space and turn up ♣ 2. Build ♣ 2 on ♣ A and turn up ♠ 6.

When play is blocked, as it now is in the example, the top card of the remaining pack (or "stock") is turned up and built or added to a sequence if possible. (Example: ♡ 8 could be placed on ♣ 9.) Otherwise, it is laid aside face up to form a discard pile. The next card of the pack is then turned up; and so on. Always, the top card of the discard or "waste pile" is available for play; and may uncover a previous discard that may also become available.

In the original game, a player can deal out the pack only once, so to build as many as ten cards is better than average. A popular procedure is to turn the discard pile face down and again turn up cards one by one, repeating this a third time if necessary before abandoning the game. Another way is to begin by turning up three cards in a group and continuing thus through the pack, time after time. Each play from the discard pile will bring other cards into view the next time through. As an added rule: When dealing by threes, if the pack gets down to six cards or less, they may be gone through singly indefinitely.

LA BELLE LUCIE: See *Trefoil*, pages 348–50.

LOUIS NAPOLEON: See *Napoleon's Favorite*, page 344.

LUCAS: A standard two-pack solitaire that forms a pattern for several others. The eight aces are removed from two fifty-two-card packs and placed in a row as bases. The packs are shuffled and thirteen columns of three cards each are dealt face up below the bases. For example:

♡ A ♡ A ◇ A ◇ A ♠ A ♠ A ♣ A ♣ A

♡ 5 ♡ 6 ♠ 8 ◇ 3 ♣ 5 ◇ 10 ♠ 6 ♣ 9 ◇ 2 ◇ J ♡ 9 ♡ 6 ♠ 3
♣ 7 ◇ Q ◇ J ♡ Q ♠ 7 ♡ 4 ♠ 2 ♡ K ♠ 6 ♡ 10 ◇ 5 ♠ 9 ♡ 3
♣ 10 ♡ 2 ♣ K ◇ 8 ◇ 7 ♠ 8 ♠ 4 ♠ K ♠ 10 ◇ 4 ♣ J ♣ 8 ♠ Q

Only the lowermost row is available, so it is best to overlap the columns. To play, build upward on the bases by suits; and downward on the auxiliary columns, also by suits. Example: Build ♡ 2. Put ♣ 10 on ♣ J, ♣ 7 on ♣ 8, ◇ 7 on ◇ 8, ♠ 7 on ♠ 8, ♠ Q on ♠ K. Build ♡ 3. Put ♠ 3 on ♠ 4. This leaves a space at the extreme right, which can be filled by any available card. By putting ◇ Q in that empty column ♡ 5 can be put on ♡ 6, leaving a space at the extreme left.

KING ALBERT

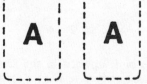

Play is now blocked, so the player must deal from the pack, turning cards face up and placing them in discard pile if not usable. Assuming that the ♣ 6 turns up, he could put it on the ♣ 7 and put the ♣ 5 on the ♣ 6, giving him two spaces. He would put the ♠ 7 in one, the ♠ 8 in the other, freeing the ♡ 4 so it could be built on the ♡ 3, followed by ♡ 5 and ♡ 6. Putting the ♣ 7 on the ♣ 8 would again give him two spaces for further moves.

Naturally, more deals are necessary to produce needed cards like aces for new bases, but always the top card of the discard pile is available, so with reasonable luck, it is possible to bring back the entire discard pile and thus achieve the ultimate aim of building all eight bases from aces up to kings. This adds zest to all solitaires of this type, which include the following:

Big Forty, in which the entire two packs are shuffled, aces included, and then dealt in ten columns of four cards each. Play proceeds as in *Lucas,* with the aces being placed as bases when they become available. All this makes the game more difficult and therefore more popular with advanced players, who also refer to it as *Forty Thieves* and *Napoleon at St. Helena.*

Other offshoots are known under titles too numerous even to mention, differing only in number of cards or columns, whether certain rows should be face down instead of face up, or the formation of auxiliary sequences in alternating colors instead of suits. These are points that players could decide for themselves if they so chose, naming games to suit their own fancy.

MISS MILLIGAN: A two-pack solitaire that begins with a deal of eight cards in a face-up row, such as:

◇ 3   ◇ K   ♣ 7   ♣ J   ♠ A   ♡ 6   ♣ 9   ♠ 2

Any aces are removed and can be built upward in the same suit, so in this case this ♠ A is placed aside as a base and the ♠ 2 would be put on it. Cards can also be moved in the layout, to form descending sequences in alternating colors, so the

♡ 6 would be placed on the ♣ 7, partly overlapping it. The row would then stand:

◇ 3   ◇ K   ♣ 7   ♣ J   *   *   ♣ 9   *
♡ 6

A second new row of eight cards is dealt face up, filling spaces and going on cards already there, slightly overlapping them. Only these are available for builds or layout moves, but as soon as they are played, the cards they partly covered again become available. When play becomes blocked, a third row of eight is dealt in the same overlapping fashion; and so on until thirteen deals have been completed. As descending sequences are formed on layout piles, they can be moved in whole or in part, as well as card by card, provided they are formed by alternating colors.

Following the thirteenth deal, play simply continues until all builds are completed up to kings, which is very difficult if too many key cards have been buried. So the player is allowed to "waive" a card by removing it from the foot of the column, to get at the next card. The waived card is kept aside until it can be played, then another may be waived. The game can be further liberalized by allowing an entire sequence to be waived and later played back, card by card or as a unit.

MONTE CARLO: A fast-moving solitaire dependent on values only, suits being of no consequence. A row of five cards is dealt from left to right, a second row below that, a third below that, and a fourth below that, making a layout of twenty cards. For example:

8	K	8	J	2
K	9	7	J	5
3	10	10	A	7
5	Q	6	6	A

If two cards of the same value are touching, either horizontally, vertically, or diagonally, they are removed from the layout. In the sample, the cards thus eliminated would be **K–K, J–J, 10–10, A–A, 6–6**. Cards are then moved up to fill the spaces, so the sample would become:

$$8 \quad 8 \quad 2 \quad 9 \quad 7$$
$$5 \quad 3 \quad 7 \quad 5 \quad Q$$

More cards are then dealt in the usual order to restore the required total of twenty, and the elimination procedure is repeated. This continues with further deals, the aim being to pair up the entire pack as described. Only pairs may be removed; if three cards of the same value are adjacent to one another, the player must choose two and leave the third until later.

NAPOLEON AT ST. HELENA: See *Lucas,* page 339.

NAPOLEON'S FAVORITE: A two-pack solitaire in which four kings and four aces are placed face up in separate rows to serve as bases. From the shuffled double pack, a layout is then dealt face up as follows:

Four cards in a row, left to right, above the kings. (Positions 1, 2, 3, 4.) Two cards down the right. (Positions 5, 6.) Four cards right to left below the aces. (Positions 7, 8, 9, 10.) Two cards up the left. (Positions 11, 12.) Continue thus until the entire pack has been dealt into twelve face-up piles of eight cards each. The layout then appears:

```
        (1)   (2)   (3)   (4)
(12)     K     K     K     K    (5)
(11)     A     A     A     A    (6)
        (10)   (9)   (8)   (7)
```

Top row cards (1, 2, 3, 4) can be built in downward sequence, according to suits, upon the kings. Bottom row cards (7, 8, 9, 10) can be built in upward sequence, according to suits, upon the aces. Side row cards (5, 6, 11, 12) can be built either way.

Cards may be moved from one layout pile to another as long as they are placed in sequence, either up or down, as jack on queen, or queen on jack; five on six, or six on five. A player can switch from one to the other and suits do not matter in such placements.

When play is blocked, bases are left as they stand, and the layout piles are gathered, shuffled, and redealt so that play can continue. A second redeal is allowed, making three deals in all. The game is won when the entire pack is built down to aces and up to kings.

In the variant called *Napoleon's Square,* the center is left empty and only four cards are dealt in each of the twelve face-up piles, making forty-eight in all. Any available aces are placed in the center and built in ascending sequence, according to suits. Cards may be moved from one layout pile to another, but only in descending sequence, and they must be the same in suit. When spaces occur, they may be filled by any available card. As sequences are formed, they may be moved in whole or in part, as well as card by card. Cards may also be dealt singly from the remaining pack of fifty-six cards and built on bases or layout piles. If not usable, these go into a face-up discard pile, with its top card always available.

Another variant, *Louis Napoleon,* uses kings and aces as bases, as in the parent game, but single cards are dealt in the face-up layout. These may be built onto bases, downward on kings, upward on aces, always following suit, but with no restriction as to which piles they come from. Layout cards can also be moved onto one another in immediate sequence, either up or down, as with *Napoleon's Favorite,* but in this game they must be of the same suit, as ♡ 8 on ♡ 7, or ♡ 7 on ♡ 8. When spaces occur in the layout, cards are dealt from the hand to fill them. If play becomes blocked, the entire pack is dealt face up, card by card, around the square without pause, and play proceeds from there. If play is again blocked, all layout piles are gathered, shuffled, and the entire pack is dealt in rotation, with all cards face up, and play again proceeds. If a block occurs again, another redeal is permitted.

NAPOLEON'S SQUARE: See *Napoleon's Favorite* (above).

NESTOR: A fast, card-matching solitaire in which values alone count, suits playing no part whatever. Deal six columns of eight cards, face up, from top to bottom, overlapping them as you do, but if any value is duplicated in the same column, bury one of the cards in the pack and deal another in its place. The result will be eight columns, each composed of different values, plus four extra cards, which are laid aside, face up, as a reserve.

The game now is to pair cards of the same value, the final card at the foot of each column being available for that purpose. Thus if a jack appears at the foot of Column 3 and another at the foot of Column 7, both would be removed and turned face down. That makes the next card of each column available for pairing with those at the foot of every other column. So the player simply keeps working up, pair by pair, hoping to clear the columns entirely. The four reserve cards may also be used for pairing with the column cards, often coming in very handily when play would otherwise be blocked.

Although eight cards are constantly available with four extras in the early stages, the pairing process is far more difficult than it would seem, and many deals may be required before clearing the board completely, so it is better simply to aim for as high a score as possible, which makes a good competitive game when several players are involved.

ROYAL MARRIAGE: See *Betrothal*, page 325.

SHAMROCKS: A variant of *Trefoil*, page 348, played in the usual way, but with two special rules: (1) In moving cards from one cluster to another in descending sequence, the cards *do not* have to be of the same suit. This makes the game easier. But: (2) At *no time* can a cluster contain *more* than three cards. This makes the game harder, as a card must first be built on a base in order to reduce a cluster to two cards. Hence one rule counterbalances the other.

SPIDER: An intriguing two-pack solitaire in which there are no actual bases and no discard pile. Shuffle two packs together and deal ten face-down piles, each with the number of cards indicated here:

6 5 5 5 6
6 5 5 5 6

Turn up the top cards and move cards from pile to pile, forming descending sequences, which can be of mixed suits, turning up a new card after each move. Suppose the original top cards are:

♠ J   ◇ 2   ♡ J   ◇ 4   ♡ 10
♡ 9   ♣ 9   ♠ A   ♠ 6   ◇ 7

You would put ♠ A on ◇ 2; ♠ 6 on ◇ 7; following that, ♡ 10 on ♡ J and ♡ 9 on ♡ 10. This is preferable to putting ♡ 10 on ♠ J and ♣ 9 on ♠ 10, for two specific reasons:

A sequence composed of the same suit, as ♡ J, 10, 9, can be moved as a unit, whereas mixed sequences, as ♠ J, ♡ 10, ♣ 9, can only be shifted card by card. Thus, if the ♠ Q and ♣ K should be turned up, the ♠ Q could be put on the ♣ K and the three-card sequence ♡ J, 10, 9, could be placed on the ♠ Q.

The other reason is that the ultimate aim is to form complete sequences of individual suits, as ◇ from K down to A. These can be removed from the layout and placed aside, until the entire pack has been so treated and the game is won.

When all cards of a pile have been turned up and moved, the space can be filled by any available card or sequence in the same suit. Whenever play is blocked, *ten cards* are dealt face up from the pack, one for each pile; these go on the cards already showing there, and play is then continued.

STOREHOUSE: An old-time solitaire with elements of modern *Canfield.* The four twos are placed face up in a row to serve as bases, which are to be built in ascending sequence; 2, 3, 4, 5, 6, 7, 8, 9, 10, J, Q, K, A, according to suit. Next, thirteen cards are dealt in a face-down pile, which is squared and turned face up, below and to the left of the bases, where it serves as the storehouse, or, more properly, the reserve. Four cards are then dealt face up below the bases to form a layout of auxiliary piles.

Play proceeds as follows: The top card of the reserve or an auxiliary pile may be built on a base. Any space resulting in the layout is immediately filled by the top card of the reserve. A card may be moved from one auxiliary pile to another, to form a descending sequence, according to suit, as ♡ K on ♡ A, ♠ 10 on ♠ J, ♣ 3 on ♣ 4, etc. The top card of the reserve is also available for placement on an auxiliary pile.

When play is blocked, the top card of the pack is turned up and may be built on a base or placed on an auxiliary pile, by the same rule. If no play is possible, the card is put in a face-up discard pile, from which the top card is always available for play. But a space in the layout cannot be filled from the pack or the discard pile until the original reserve is exhausted. After the entire pack has been dealt, one card at a time, the discard pile is turned face down and is again dealt through, singly, as a pack. Another such redeal is permitted, making three deals in all.

In an early form of this game called *Auxiliary Sequences,* aces were used as bases. For a later and more popular development, see *Fascination,* page 329.

STREETS AND ALLEYS: See *Beleaguered Castle,* page 324.

TREFOIL: A unique form of solitaire in which the four aces are placed face up as bases and the remainder of the pack is dealt face up in fans or clusters of three cards each, resembling clover leaves, making sixteen in all. (See samples in the accompanying diagram.) The uppermost card of each cluster

BASES

STOREHOUSE
RESERVE

AUXILIARY PILES

PACK   DISCARD

STOREHOUSE

can be built in upward sequence on a base of the same suit, as
♠ 2 on ♠ A, ♠ 3 on ♠ 2, continuing up to ♠ K. To get at
buried cards, the player may also move the top card of one
cluster to another, but in descending sequence in the same suit,
as ◊ 9 on ◊ 10, ♣ 4 on ♣ 5. It is not wise, however, to move
the last or lowest card of a cluster, as in this game a space cannot be filled, but must remain vacant.

When play is blocked, the cards left in the layout are gathered, shuffled, and redealt into new groups as far as they will
go, with one or two odd cards being treated as an abbreviated
cluster, playable like the rest. The builds are left as they are, so
the game resumes, and if blocked again, another redeal of the
layout cards is permitted, making three deals in all. On the
final deal, if a king blocks a lower card of the same suit, as
♠ K over ♠ 9, the player is allowed to move the king beneath
the other card; otherwise it would be impossible to complete

the game. Even with that privilege, this solitaire is often hard to win.

In the newer game of *La Belle Lucie,* the rules are the same, except that the entire pack, aces included, is dealt in clusters, making seventeen of three cards each, with a single card for the final cluster. Aces must be freed in play in order to serve as bases. The game is also called *Midnight Oil.*

TREFOIL

WASHINGTON'S FAVORITE: Another name for *Napoleon's Favorite,* page 344.

WEDDINGS: *Solitaire*. Another name for *Monte Carlo*, page 343.

WESTCLIFFE: *Solitaire*. A variant of *Lucas*, page 339.

WHISTLER: A type of solitaire played exactly like *Canfield* or *Klondike* but without the rule of using alternating colors when forming descending sequences on the auxiliary piles in the layout. Aces are still built upward by suits, but the layout is concerned with values only, making the game much faster and easier. See *Klondike*, page 338.

WHITEHEAD: An adaptation of *Canfield* or *Klondike*, page 338, in which the entire layout is dealt face up instead of face down. In its simplest form, builds and layout moves follow the pattern of the parent game, but as descending sequences are formed on auxiliary columns, the cards composing them can be moved either singly or as a group; and whenever a space occurs, it can be filled by any available card or sequence. As a variant, bases may be built upward in alternating colors; while auxiliary columns are formed in descending sequences of the individual suits.

WHITE PASS: *Solitaire:* A variant of *Yukon*, below.

YUKON: A solitaire in which the first twenty-eight cards are dealt exactly as in *Canfield* or *Klondike*, page 338, and, following that, the remaining twenty-four are dealt in six columns of four cards each, which are overlapped face up upon all the original columns except the first (see diagram, see pages 354–55).

If the final card of any column (including the first) is an ace, it is immediately placed as a base above the layout; and any final cards are available for building on such bases, in ascending sequence according to suits, as ◇ **2** on ◇ **A,** ◇ **3** on ◇ **2,** and so on up to ◇ **K.** When all such builds are completed, the game is won.

Meanwhile, the final card of any column serves as an auxiliary, on which any face-up card in the entire layout may be placed in descending sequence, alternating in color, as ♡ **Q** on ♣ **K**, ♠ **J** or ♣ **J** on ♡ **Q**, and so on down. In placing such a card, all those that overlap it are lifted with it, as a group, thus increasing the length of the auxiliary column.

When all the face-up cards are lifted from a column, the face-down card thus freed is turned face up and becomes available for building or auxiliary use. When an entire column is completely cleared, any king may be placed in the space, along with all the cards that overlap it. Play continues in the usual manner.

White Pass is a novel extension of *Yukon,* which follows the regular rules until play is completely blocked. The player may then square up any column and turn it completely over, so that its face-up cards are face down and a whole new set of face-up cards are available for play, which proceeds until another block necessitates another turnover.

SOLO: A name applied to various games related to *Skat,* page 314, the chief form being *Six-Bid Solo,* page 309, described under that head. The simpler game of *Frog,* page 125, is also sometimes termed "solo"; and the name has been applied to *Ombre,* page 166, in its modern form. *Heart Solo,* page 309, is also a type of bid, described under *Six-Bid Solo,* along with lesser variants.

SOLO WHIST: This is a modern development of *Boston,* page 38, and other obsolescent games derived from *Whist,* with the usual fifty-two-card pack ranking **A, K, Q, J, 10, 9, 8, 7, 6, 5, 4, 3, 2** in descending order. Cards are dealt singly to four players, and the last is turned up as a prospective trump, and later taken into the dealer's hand. The type of game to be played is decided upon by bidding; and each player is on his own, except at the lowest bidding level, when two act as temporary partners. Bids and their values are as follows:

Proposal, to win at least eight tricks, subject to *Acceptance* by a subsequent bidder, the two being partners for that deal, with turned-up card as trump. . . . .

5 points.

Solo, to win at least five tricks playing alone with turned-up trump. . . . . 10 points.

Nullo (originally *Misere*), to take no tricks, playing alone without a trump. . . . . 15 points.

Abundance, to win at least nine tricks alone, but with a trump of the bidder's choice (other than the one turned up). . . . . 20 points.

Abundance in Trumps is the same, but with turned-up trump. . . . . 20 points.

Spread (or *Open Misere*), to take no tricks, alone and without trump, but with bidder's hand spread face up. . . . .

30 points.

Declared Abundance, or *Slam,* to win all tricks alone, but with bidder's privilege of naming the trump and leading to the first trick. . . . . 40 points.

If a player passes, he cannot re-enter the bidding, except to declare "acceptance" to another's "proposal." Any bid is ruled out by a bid in a higher bracket; and a bidder overcalled by another can make a higher bid in his next turn, until all but the final bidder have passed. If all pass at the outset, the deal either moves along or:

By previous agreement, *Grand* may be declared and played. This is simply a hand with no trump, and the player who takes the last trick loses to each of the three others, at the "solo" value of 10 points.

Play is almost identical with *Whist,* with the high card of suit led winning the trick, all players following suit if they can. A trump may be played when a player is out the suit led, and the highest trump takes the trick; or a player can simply discard from a side suit. This does not apply in cases where there is no trump; then, players simply follow suit if possible. In all cases, the winner of each trick leads to the next.

In all declarations except "slam," the player at dealer's left leads to the first trick, but in "spread," the bidder does not have

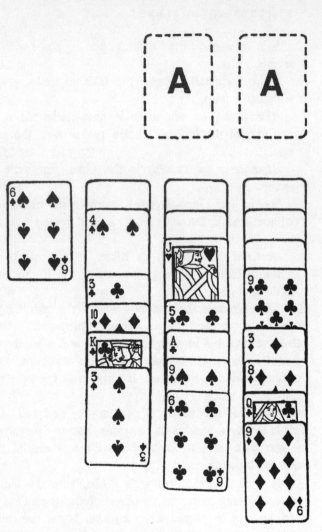

YUKON

to show his hand until after the first trick has been played and taken. In "slam," the dealer leads to the first trick and can name any suit as trump, including the one originally turned up.

Each deal is a game, and for convenience, instead of marking scores plus (+) or minus (−), they can be paid with chips or counters. In "proposal and acceptance" each partner collects or pays 5 points to one other player, according to whether the hand was won or lost. In all other bids, the lone player wins or loses points to each opponent according to the schedule. For each extra trick, over his bid, a player collects one chip; for each extra trick under, he pays one. This does not apply with nullo, spread, or slam.

SPADE CASSINO: In this high-scoring version of *Cassino*, page 57, the single point usually given to the player taking the most spades goes instead to the player who takes the ♠ J. Also, *any* spade taken by a player counts 1 point in its own right. This produces the following scoring table:

Cards: For the most cards taken	3 points
Spades: For taking the ♠ J	1 point
Big Cassino: For taking the ◇ 10	2 points
Little Cassino: For taking the ♠ 2	1 point
Each Ace: 1 point. Total	4 points
Each Spade: 1 point	13 points
Total (not counting sweeps)	24 points

Note that the ♠ J, ♠ 2, ♠ A each count *two* points, one in their own right, the other for being a spade.

This game may be played with a cribbage board, pegging points as scored, except for "cards," which must be counted at the end of a hand. The first player to peg 61 points (as in cribbage) is the winner. If he pegs 61 before his opponent pegs 31, the margin of victory is doubled.

SPADES ROYAL: This is a combination of *Spade Cassino*, above, and *Royal Cassino*, played exactly like royal cassino, but with the same scoring as in spade cassino. If a sixty-card pack is used (including 11's and 12's, 2 more points are scored for ♠ 11 and ♠ 12, making 26 points in all. Otherwise, the rules are identical.

SPIDER: A form of *Solitaire.* See page 347.

SPIN or SPINADO: A special feature dating from early forms of *Boodle,* page 38, now used in games like *Michigan,* page 161, *New Market,* page 164, and *Saratoga,* page 301, thus gaining recognition of its own. The rules of any such games are followed in *Spinado,* but one card, the ◊ A—termed "spin" or "spinado"—can be used to end any sequence that its holder happens to be playing. That enables him to switch to another suit in which he can play a "boodle card" or block some other player's chance at cashing one. Since the ◊ A is "wild," the ◊ K becomes the highest card of its suit, unless a joker is used as spinado, so that the ◊ A can function normally. The game can be stepped up by using two jokers, each as a spinado.

SPITE AND MALICE: An ultramodern development of *Double Solitaire,* page 104, with two players utilizing two packs of cards: One, the "payoff pack," containing the standard fifty-two cards running from ace up to king in value; the other, the "mutual pack," with the usual fifty-two cards plus four "wild" jokers, making fifty-six in all. Values alone count, suits being disregarded in this game.

The payoff pack is shuffled, and twenty-six cards are dealt face down to each player, to serve as his payoff pile. Each lays his pile to his right and turns up its top card. If the same in value—as two nines—they are turned down, and each pile is shuffled separately so another card can be turned up. Whoever finally has a higher card becomes Player *X* and plays first, his adversary being Player *Y.*

Prior to play, the mutual pack of fifty-six cards is shuffled and laid face down in the center of the table as a "stock." Player *X* draws five cards from this stock, keeping the faces toward him as a playing hand, then Player Y draws five in the same way. Play then proceeds thus:

If X has an ace showing on his payoff pile, he must put it face up near the center of the table as a base. If he is holding any aces in his hand, he can use them to form bases if he chooses. If an ace has been played and a two is showing on X's payoff pile, he must build it on the ace. If he has a two in his hand, he can build it if he chooses. Anything higher than a two does not have to be built at all, except as a matter of choice. Having finished his builds—if any—Player X lays a card face up in front of him to begin a discard pile. He then draws one or more cards from the stock to give his hand its original quota of five cards, putting him in readiness for his next turn.

Player Y does the same, either starting new bases from his payoff pile and hand, or building on any started by Player X. Play continues alternately from then on, but with new factors to be considered; namely: In discarding to end his turn, a player can start a new discard pile, but with a limit of four such piles. Or he can discard a card of the same value as the card showing there, as placing an eight on an eight. Or he can discard in descending sequence on a card showing there, as putting a seven on an eight.

As play proceeds, a player can extend his turn by building from a discard pile directly onto a center pile, exactly as from his payoff pile or his hand. However, it is often better to build from the hand, as that enables him to draw an extra card at the end of his turn. Best of all is a build from the player's payoff pile, as his main purpose is to play out his entire payoff pile and thereby win the game.

Two important points should be noted: If a player manages to play all five cards from his hand before discarding, he can draw five more from the stock and continue with his turn. Also, when the stock is reduced to less than a dozen cards, play stops until the players gather all the center piles that have been built up to the king. These are shuffled along with the stock, which again becomes a sizable mutual pile from which the players draw. If the stock runs out before any center piles have been built up to the king, all center piles are gathered and shuffled as a new stock. The fact that the two original packs ("payoff" and "mutual") become mixed during play does not in any way affect the game.

In building, a player may use a wild joker by calling it any value he wants; and it remains as such until its center pile has been shuffled into the stock, when it becomes wild for whichever player draws it. A player may also discard a joker to end his turn, by simply placing it on any of his discard piles, without naming its value until a later turn. Thus, if he discards a joker on his jack, in his next turn he could call the joker a jack and discard either a jack or a ten on it.

Instead, he could call the joker a ten and discard a nine on it. Better still, he could discard a joker on a joker, calling them as he deems best. Example: Starting with a jack, player discards one joker, then another joker. When ready for his next discard, he can term them "jack, jack, jack"—"jack, jack, ten"—"jack, ten, ten"—or "jack, ten, nine." Also, when a joker is uppermost on a discard pile, a player can build it onto a center pile, calling it any value he wants, as in building a joker is always wild.

When a player can neither build nor discard, his hand becomes "frozen" and his adversary takes over, sometimes continuing through several turns until the frozen player is free to play again. However, a player may freeze his hand purposely by refusing to build or discard until he feels that it is advantageous, which is a fine point of the game. However, a player must always use an ace from his payoff pile, or a two from either his payoff pile or a discard pile, provided there is a center ace on which he can play it. A player does not have to build an ace or two from his concealed hand unless both players become frozen. In that case, each may demand that the other build an ace or two from his hand if able to do so. At no time, however, is a player forced to build or discard a joker. He can get out of that by simply declaring the wild joker to be a card of some unplayable value.

As already stated, the player's object is to get rid of his payoff pile by building all of its twenty-six cards into center builds.

He then becomes the winner, and the other player's payoff pile is then counted to determine the margin of victory, the winner scoring 1 point for each of the loser's remaining cards.

Whenever both hands become frozen, stopping all further play, the payoff piles are left as they stand; and all the other cards are gathered, shuffled, and formed into a new mutual pack. From this stock, each player in turn draws five cards, as if starting a new game. This, to a marked degree, offsets any freezing on the part of either player by turning such tactics into part of the over-all strategy.

SPIT IN THE OCEAN: One of the most popular forms of wild-card *Poker* from which others have been derived and used in *Dealer's Choice*. See pages 268–69.

SPOIL FIVE: A famous old trump game with unique ranking of the suits and some odd rules of play that add intriguing complexities to an otherwise simple procedure.

The Pack: The standard fifty-two cards, with the complete rank of suits listed on the opposite page, showing exactly how they vary according to which suit is trump.

A trump suit ranks **5, J,** then ♡ **A** (which is always the third-highest trump), **A, K, Q,** followed by spots in descending order (from **10** down, skipping the **5**) if trump is a *red* suit; but in ascending order (from **2** up, skipping the **5**) if trump is a *black* suit.

Ordinary suits rank **K, Q, J,** then from **10** downward in *red* suits, clear to **A** in diamonds, but only to **2** in hearts, as the ♡ **A** belongs to whichever suit is trump. The cards rank **K, Q, J,** then **A** up to **10** in ordinary *black* suits.

The order of the spot cards can be remembered by the saying, "Highest in red, lowest in black." As for the ♡ **A,** it can be regarded as a simple form of joker, as it functions much like one, but the game dates back to a period before jokers came into common use.

Number of Players: From two to ten, each on his own, but three, four, or five are the most suitable numbers.

The Deal: Five cards to each player, usually by threes, then twos, in clockwise order. The next card is turned face up on the pack to designate the trump suit. If it is the ace, the dealer can take it into his hand and discard another card, face down under the pack. If another value is turned up as trump, any player holding the ace of that suit can take up the trump card from the pack and make a face-down discard in its place. He must do this before his turn to play; and if he wishes, he can reject the turned-up card by turning it down, but in either case, he must show his ace.

Playing the Hand: Any card is led by the player at the dealer's left. Others may follow suit, or play a trump even if they are able to follow suit. If out of the suit led, they can trump or discard from another suit. The highest card of suit led wins the trick unless trumped, in which case the highest trump wins. The winner of each trick leads to the next.

When a trump is led, other players must follow suit, except with the three highest trumps (5, J of trump, or ♡ A). A player can renege, or hold back any of those cards, unless a higher trump is led. Example: With spades trump, if the ♠ 5 is led, a player would have to follow with the ♠ J or ♡ A if he had no other trump; or if the ♠ J should be led, he would have to play the ♡ A if he had no other trump. But leads of lower trumps can be ignored.

Purpose of Play: Each player's main aim is to win a majority of the tricks, that is, at least three, and if possible all five. Since that is often difficult and sometimes impossible with a poor hand, he may resort to the immediate purpose of spoiling some stronger player's chances, by taking at least one trick that his adversary needs; hence the expression "spoil five."

Thus a hand is generally played defensively throughout, with weaker players letting one another take tricks, rather than waste two winning cards on the same play; yet at the same time watching for any break that may enable one of them to gain a surprise win. A stronger player may often feign defensive tactics for that same purpose, rather than overplay his hand at the start.

Scoring the Game: The usual procedure is for each player to contribute one chip or token to a common pool, which is taken by anyone winning the hand. If the hand is spoiled, the deal moves on, with the new dealer contributing an extra token. This continues until a hand is won, then a new pool is formed.

The Jink Option: As soon as a player has taken three tricks, the hand is finished, unless those happen to be the first three tricks and the winner decides to go for two more. This is called "jinking," and, to announce his intention, the player simply leads to the next trick instead of throwing in his hand and collecting the pool. If he takes all five tricks, he collects an additional token from each player for the jink. If he fails, the pool remains intact and the deal moves on, with the new dealer contributing the customary chip.

SPOT HEARTS: A variant of *Hearts,* page 140, in which each heart counts against anyone taking it according to the number of its spots: **2, 3, 4,** and so on up to jack, 11; queen, 12; king, 13; ace, 14.

STEALING BUNDLES: A juvenile form of *Cassino,* page 57, for two players, in which all cards are treated as face cards and can therefore be taken only by a card of their own value, as ♣ J taking ♠ J; ♡ 3 taking ♣ 3; and so on. In short, no "builds" are allowed, though a player may lay a card like an eight on an eight showing on the board, announcing that he intends to take them with another eight, which he also has in his hand.

The deal is the same as in cassino: Four to the opponent, four to the dealer, and four more cards face up on the table as a layout. After taking in cards, or discarding odd cards on the layout, four more are dealt to each; and play continues. However, each player must keep all the cards he matches in a face-up pile in front of him, in the exact order taken. If the other player can match the top card of the packet, he can add the entire "bundle" to his own, hence the name of the game.

Often, bundles pass back and forth with rapidity and hilarity.

Whoever takes in the last "match" from the layout also takes any odd cards left there. Players then count their bundles, and the one with the most cards wins. A player should be compelled to take in any card that he can match; otherwise, once his bundle has the fourth card of its kind on top, he could keep discarding to the layout, making the game pointless.

HOW CARDS ARE RANKED IN
SPOIL FIVE

When Hearts Are Trumps

Trump ♡ 5, J, A, K, Q, 10, 9, 8, 7, 6, 4, 3, 2

Other Suits
- ◇ K, Q, J, 10, 9, 8, 7, 6, 5, 4, 3, 2, A
- ♠ K, Q, J, A, 2, 3, 4, 5, 6, 7, 8, 9, 10
- ♣ K, Q, J, A, 2, 3, 4, 5, 6, 7, 8, 9, 10

When Diamonds Are Trumps

Trump ◇ 5, J, ♡ A, ◇ A, K, Q, 10, 9, 8, 7, 6, 4, 3, 2

Other Suits
- ♡ K, Q, J, 10, 9, 8, 7, 6, 5, 4, 3, 2
- ♠ K, Q, J, A, 2, 3, 4, 5, 6, 7, 8, 9, 10
- ♣ K, Q, J, A, 2, 3, 4, 5, 6, 7, 8, 9, 10

When Spades Are Trumps

Trump ♠ 5, J, ♡ A, ♠ A, K, Q, 2, 3, 4, 6, 7, 8, 9, 10

Other Suits
- ♣ K, Q, J, A, 2, 3, 4, 5, 6, 7, 8, 9, 10
- ◇ K, Q, J, 10, 9, 8, 7, 6, 5, 4, 3, 2, A
- ♡ K, Q, J, 10, 9, 8, 7, 6, 5, 4, 3, 2

When Clubs Are Trumps

Trump ♣ 5, J, ♡ A, ♣ A, K, Q, 2, 3, 4, 6, 7, 8, 9, 10

Other Suits
- ♠ K, Q, J, A, 2, 3, 4, 5, 6, 7, 8, 9, 10
- ◇ K, Q, J, 10, 9, 8, 7, 6, 5, 4, 3, 2, A
- ♡ K, Q, J, 10, 9, 8, 7, 6, 5, 4, 3, 2

Players follow suit when trump is led, but may renege with the three highest trumps (5 or J of trump, or ♡ A) unless a higher trump is led.

STOPS: Any form of game in the general category of *Eights, Fan-Tan, Michigan,* etc., in which cards are played in sequence until blocked by missing cards or those withheld by other players, thus acting as "stops" to immediate play.

STOREHOUSE: A type of *Solitaire*. See page 348.

STORMY WEATHER: *Poker*. See page 269.

STRAIGHT POKER: See page 269.

STREETS AND ALLEYS: A variant of *Beleaguered Castle Solitaire*. See pages 324–25.

STRIPPED PACK: *Poker*. See page 269.

STUD POKER: See pages 228, 270.

STUD WITH SPIT: *Poker*. See page 270.

STUSS: *Faro,* page 116, reduced to simplest terms. Players place bets on a layout showing cards ranging in value from ace up to king, or merely state their choices. From a fifty-two-card face-down pack, the dealer turns up one and places it to the right as his card and collects all bets made on that value. He turns up the next card and places it to the left as the player's card, paying any who bet on that value. All bets are even money, but the dealer has an "edge" because he wins whenever two cards of the same value are dealt in the same turn. The deal ends after twenty-four turns (or forty-eight cards), with no play on the remaining cards, as is customary in faro.

SUDDEN DEATH: *Poker*. See page 270.

SUIT VALUE WHIST: Standard *Whist,* page 375, but with a special scoring system. Tricks vary in value according to the suit turned up as trump: Each trick 1, with spades trump; 2 with clubs; 3 with diamonds; 4 with hearts. Each team scores whatever it wins, and the first to reach 10 points wins game, with 10 points bonus for rubber. Honors are not counted.

SUPER CONTRACT BRIDGE: Almost identical with *Contract Bridge,* page 72, but with a joker added to the pack to represent the highest card in whatever suit the holder calls it, provided he has not discarded to that suit. The joker also rates as an honor in either trump or no-trump, and a player holding all honors scores 300 points. In the deal, the fifty-third card is turned face up, and the declarer may openly exchange any card in his hand for it; hence if the joker is dealt as the odd card, it is sure to be in play. All other rules follow those of contract bridge.

SWEDISH RUMMY: A game similar to *Eights*, page 106.

TABLE STAKES: A form of *Poker* in which a player's bets are limited to the amount of chips he has on the table. See page 270.

TAKE-ALL HEARTS: A form of *Hearts* in which a bonus is given for taking all the cards of that suit. Often incorporated as a special rule in *Omnibus Hearts*, it is described under *Take-All Hearts*, page 143.

TAKE IT OR LEAVE IT: Also called *Shove 'Em Along*. A form of "dealer's choice" in which cards are passed from one player to another. See *Push Poker*, page 261.

TAM O' SHANTER: A variant of *Auld Lang Syne*, page 324.

TAMPA: An outgrowth of *Canasta*, page 43, using three packs —162 cards including six jokers—with wild-card melds allowed and a wild canasta counting 2000 points as in *Uruguayan Canasta*, page 372. Beyond that, however, the rules of *Samba*, page 300, take over, but with one important exception; namely, the sequence melds, or escaleras, are not allowed. Thus Tampa can be simply defined as "samba without the samba," but with wild canastas allowable instead.

TAP OUT: *Poker*. See page 270.

TAROC or TAROK: An ancient game played with the seventy-eight-card tarot pack (usually used for fortunes), with twenty-two trump cards and four suits of fourteen cards each. It is still played in modified form in a few parts of Egypt, and its modern developments are games of the *Skat* type, page 314, where certain cards serve as permanent trumps.

TENNESSEE: A variant of *Cincinnati.* See *Tennessee,* page 270.

TENNESSEE JED: A variant of *Tennessee.*

TEXAS TECH: An elaboration of *Shotgun.* See *Texas Tech,* page 271.

THIRTY-FIVE: See *Trenta-cinque,* page 367.

THIRTY-ONE: Half-a-dozen players are each dealt three cards from a fifty-two-card pack; and three are dealt face up as a "widow." Beginning at dealer's left, each may take one card from the widow and discard another face up in its place, the purpose being to form a total as near thirty-one as possible, in a *single suit,* an ace counting 11; face cards (**K, Q, J**) 10 each; others according to their spots. (Examples: ♡ **K, 8, 7**=25; ♣ **A, Q, 10**=31.) Or a player may assemble three cards of one rank (as ♠ **6,** ♡ **6,** ◊ **6**), which has a special value of 30½. In case of two such trios, the higher takes precedence, cards ranking **A, K, Q, J, 10** down to **2.** Drawing and discarding continues around the table until one player knocks, thinking his hand is best. The rest have one more chance to draw and discard; hands are then shown, and the highest wins a pool to which all contributed. In case of a tie, the pool is split. Often, a fairly high hand, as ◊ **J, 8, 5**=23, is worth a quick knock rather than allow opponents time to form a higher total or a trio.

THREE-CARD MONTE: A game with a queen and two spot cards, which are thrown face down on a table, the dealer offering odds of two to one that a player cannot pick the queen. Also known as *Find the Lady,* the game is often used by deft sharpers to trim unwary victims, as a skilled thrower can easily confuse an onlooker.

THREE-CARD POKER: Also termed *Monte,* this is an abridged form of *Poker.* See page 271.

THREE FORTY-FIVE: A form of wild-card *Poker,* page 272.

THREE-HANDED GAMES: As *Bridge, Canasta, Cassino, Cribbage, Euchre, Five Hundred, Pinochle,* and others, these will be found under their general heads.

TIGER: Another name for *Blind Opening,* page 245.

TOWIE: A well-developed but little played form of *Three-Handed Bridge.* See page 90.

TREFOIL: A form of *Solitaire,* page 348.

TREIZE: A variant of the *Consolation* round in *Five in One* or *Garbage.* Thirteen cards are dealt face up (instead of only ten) with the dealer counting ace as 1, and so on up to 11, 12, 13 for jack, queen, and king. If he hits a number, he collects that many chips from each opponent; if he misses completely, he pays seven chips to each. See *Five in One,* page 122.

TRENTA-CINQUE: A fast Italian game requiring a forty-card pack (no eights, nines, or tens) with four players, each on his own. Nine cards are dealt to each with four as a face-down "widow." Each player puts five chips in a pool and after looking at his hand may pass or bid up to five chips for the privilege of staying on the chance of having the highest count in a single suit, with an ace as 1, spots according to their number, and face cards (**J, Q, K**) at 10 each. Two or more may "stay" on a bid of five, and whichever has the highest count wins the bid, puts five chips in the pool, and takes up the widow. If he can then hit a total of 35 or more, he wins the pool; otherwise it stays to the next deal. Any player who "stays" and shows an original hand without a face card, or a hand with the **K, Q, J** of a single suit, immediately collects two chips from each of his opponents.

TRENTE ET QUARANTE: In English, *Thirty and Forty,* this game is also called *Rouge et Noir,* or *Red and Black.* It is played in gambling casinos such as Monte Carlo and requires a special layout, where players place bets of two types. The first and more important go on diamond-shaped spaces representing "red" and "black," which function as follows:

A dealer shuffles six fifty-two-card packs into one big batch and deals a face-up row, which he designates as "black." Only the values are counted in ascending order: ace for 1, others according to their spots, with face cards **(J, Q, K)** at 10 each. He keeps on dealing until the row totals more than 30, but not more than 40. He then deals a row for "red" on the same basis. The row that totals closest to 31 is winner. Example:

   Black: 8–4–J–3–4–5=34
     Red: Q–A–2–2–5–6–K=36

In this case, black wins, and the dealer pays the amounts wagered to players who chose black, while taking in all bets that were placed on red.

The layout also has a square marked "color" and a triangle for "inverse." Even-money bets can be placed on color, on the following terms: If the very first card dealt is black—as the ♣ 8 or ♠ 8—the player wins if the black row wins; but if it is red—as ♡ 8 or ◇ 8—he wins if the red row wins. With inverse, it is just the opposite; the player wins if the color loses. If both rows add up to the same total, bets are off, unless it is exactly 31, when the bank takes half of the amount wagered.

TRESETTE: A game of Italian origin, with four players, opposites paired as partners, using a forty-card pack with the unique ranking of **3, 2, A, K, J, Q, 7, 6, 5, 4.** Each player is dealt ten cards, and the first player leads any card he wants, others following suit if they can, or else playing from a side suit, as there is no trump in this game. The highest card of the suit led wins the trick, and the winner leads to the next.

However: In leading, a player may order his partner either to play his best card in that suit, or to play the ace if he has it. Also, a player, in following a lead, may tell how many cards he has in that suit. In addition, in leading or playing, he can state that he has a blank, singleton, or doubleton in some other suit, though he is not allowed to name it. These clues help materially in partnership play.

If a player holds a high-card sequence; namely, 3–2–A of the same suit, he can announce it as a "meld" after playing all three cards. Similarly, he can meld a set of three or four high cards (as 3–3–3; 2–2–2–2; A–A–A–A). Every card so melded counts as 1 point toward the team's score. For every three high cards or face cards taken during play, a team scores 1 point, any extras not being counted. The last trick counts 1 point for the team taking it in play. Game is 31 points.

The deal moves on after each hand, but in this game it customarily goes to the right instead of the left, with play starting on the dealer's right and continuing in that direction.

TRIANGLE CONTRACT: A three-handed game with the dealer and player opposite as partners. They bid and play as in *Contract Bridge* against a single player on the dealer's right, who is dealt two hands, a face-up dummy and his own, so he can bid and play both. See page 72.

TRIOMPHE, TRIUMPH, or TRUMP: An early trump game from which *Écarté,* page 105, *Euchre,* page 107, *Napoleon,* page 163, and others were derived. Also called *French Whist.*

TRIONFETTI: A game very similar to *Gile* or *Gilet.* See page 130.

TRIPOLI: A modern form of *Pochen,* page 218, using the same layout but with one suit—as hearts—designated for payoffs, and with a fixed sequence in another suit, as ♠ 7 8 9. A fifty-two-card pack is used and dealt equally among four to seven players, with at least six cards left for a dead hand. Thus, four players would have 11 cards each; five, nine each; six, seven each; seven, six each.

In the first phase, players collect for payoff cards as in pochen; for ♡ A, K, Q, J, 10; heart marriage; or ♠ 7 8 9 sequence. Each then shows his best five cards as a modern poker hand, including straights, flushes, full houses, and straight flushes, for the second phase, the winner taking a pot to which all contributed, as in pochen. The third phase is a game of "stops," beginning at the dealer's left, with each player using his entire hand and with the dead hand left on the table, as in *New Market,* page 164. There are no "boodle" cards, however; first player to go out collects one chip per card from each of the others, according to their individual holdings. Any chips remaining on layout cards go to the winner of a final hand that is specified as such.

TUNK: A cross between *Gin,* page 130, and *Knock Rummy,* page 154, with "wild deuces" representing any needed card. From two to four players are each dealt seven cards, and the next is turned up beside the pack. Each player in turn draws from the pack or takes the upcard and then discards as in knock rummy, but cannot knock until the count of his unmatched cards is down to 5 points, as in gin. He then lays down his hand, using deuces when needed to meld sequences of three or more cards in one suit; or sets of three or four of a kind, which must have two "natural" cards (as J–J–2 or 9–9–2–2). After the knocker has discarded, each player has one chance to draw, meld, and lay off on the knocker's hand, unless he has matched it entirely. Each player's unmatched cards are scored against him; and if anyone undercuts the knocker, the knocker's count is doubled. Deals continue in the usual order, and as each player reaches 100, he is eliminated until only one remains and is the winner. With five or more players, a double pack of 104 cards is used, with eight wild deuces.

TWENTY-FIVE: A simplified form of *Forty-five* with game limited to 25 points. See page 123.

TWENTY-NINE: A simple but fast-moving game with a fifty-two-card pack in which cards are valued numerically; face cards and aces one each, others according to their spots. There are four players, with those seated opposite teamed as partners. Each is dealt thirteen cards; play begins at dealer's left. First player lays a card face up; next adds one to it; and so on, until a player makes the total exactly 29 and wins the trick for his team. The player on his left leads to the next trick and play continues. If unable to play without going over 29, a player must pass his turn. The team taking the most cards wins the game. If the last trick fails to total 29, its cards are disregarded.

TWENTY-ONE: Another term for *Blackjack,* page 32, particularly the game as played in gambling casinos, which have their own dealers and house rules as to when the dealer must "stay" or "draw," and special payoffs on stipulated bonus hands.

TWIN BEDS: An elaborated form of *Cincinnati.* See *Twin Beds,* page 273.

TWO-CARD POKER or TWO-CARD HIGH-LOW: A two-card game based on *Poker* and described thereunder. Also known as *Hurricane.* See *Two-Card Poker,* page 273.

TWO-HANDED GAMES: As *Bridge, Five Hundred, Pinochle,* and others appear under their general heads.

TWO-MELD RUMMY: See page 293.

UNLIMITED LOO: A form of *Loo,* page 156, in which players who are "looed" must put up an amount equal to the pool, which sometimes pyramids to fantastic proportions. A game to be avoided. See *Unlimited Loo,* page 158.

UP AND DOWN THE RIVER: A name frequently applied to *Put and Take* (page 285), but sometimes played on the basis that a player pays or collects an amount equal to the spots on the matched cards, with face cards rating at ten chips each. See page 273.

URUGUAYAN CANASTA or URUGUAY: Regular *Canasta,* page 43, but with wild-card melds of three to seven cards allowed. A "wild canasta" (of seven cards) scores 2000 points. The pot, or discard pile, is always frozen in this game.

UTAH: Another name for *Cincinnati.* See *Utah,* page 273.

VAN JOHN: A corruption of the French term *Vingt-un,* hence a popular name for that game. See below.

VARIETY: Another name for *Five in One.* See page 122.

VINGT-ET-UN or VINGT-UN: The original form of *Twenty-one,* page 371, as played in France, the words *Vingt-et-un* being French for "twenty-one." In its early form, the game had several variations now seldom played. From it developed the highly popular game of *Blackjack,* page 32.

VINT: A Russian antecedent of *Auction Bridge,* page 18, with a similar mode of bidding. The player at high bidder's left leads to the first trick, but play is more like that of *Whist,* page 375, as there is no dummy. A fifty-two-card pack is used, ranking **A** down to **2;** and thirteen cards are dealt to each of four players, as opposing teams. The dealer opens the bidding, which runs from "one" up to "seven," according to the number of tricks over "book," suits rating in ascending order: ♠, ♣, ◇, ♡, no-trump. However, in scoring: With a bid of one, each team scores 10 points for every trick it takes; with "two," 20 points; and so on up to "seven," which scores 70 points per trick. These are entered "below the line," as in bridge, and the first team to reach 500 wins the game, declaring "out" in course of play, though the hand is finished to register additional scores.

Bonus points go "above the line" as follows: For winning game, 1000 points; winning rubber (two games), 2000; for taking twelve tricks (small slam), 1000+5000 if "six" was bid; for thirteen tricks (grand slam), 2000+5000 if "six" was bid, or 10,000 if "seven" was bid. If a team fails to make its bid, opponents score 100 times the trick value for each trick short of it. Honors consist of A, K, Q, J, 10 of trump, and a team holding the most scores ten times the value of a trick for each, the loser's honors being disregarded. The four aces are honors in no-trump, at twenty-five times the value of a trick; and if each team holds two aces, the team taking the most tricks scores its pair. If one player holds three aces, or a three-card sequence in any suit (as ♠ J 10 9), he scores 500 points for a "coronet." A fourth ace, or any extra cards in sequence, counts 500 in addition. A trump sequence doubles in value; and when playing at no-trump, all coronets—aces or sequences in any suit—are doubled, rating the original trio at 1000+1000 for each extra. All are scored above the line. Final settlements are made as in bridge.

VIVE L'AMOUR: An old-time game in which a pack is dealt equally among four players, who simultaneously pass cards face down to the next player in rotation. This continues until one player acquires all the cards of a single suit and announces himself as winner.

WAR: Primarily a two-player game, preferably for juveniles, with a fifty-two-card pack ranking A, K, Q, J, 10, 9, 8, 7, 6, 5, 4, 3, 2 with suits disregarded. Each is dealt twenty-six cards face down, and each turns his top card face up. The higher value takes the lower and the cards are placed face down beneath the winner's packet. This continues indefinitely, until one player has won all the other's cards. If two cards happen to be tied—as two tens—they are laid aside and go to the winner of the next turnup. The player who gathers in all the cards wins the game.

As an added rule, after a tie, each player lays a card face down before turning up another; and these cards also go to the winner of the next turnup. This may enable a player to capture an opposing ace when he has none of his own. The game can be played with three or more players, each on his own, utilizing a double pack if desired. If two are tied for high, any player turning up a lower card is included in the tie and has a chance of winning them all with the next turnup. A player drops out when his cards are gone, and others continue until one player wins. This game is also called *Everlasting,* due to its duration.

WASHINGTON'S FAVORITE: *Solitaire.* See page 350.

WEDDINGS: Another name for *Monte Carlo Solitaire,* page 343.

WELLINGTON: *Napoleon* with an extra bid. See page 163.

WESTCLIFFE: A variant of *Lucas Solitaire,* page 339.

WHANGDOODLES: *Poker.* See page 274.

WHISK: A former name for *Whist.* See page 375.

WHISKEY POKER: Though a distinctive game of its own, this can be played as a form of "dealer's choice." Players contribute equally to a pool and five cards are dealt to each, with an extra hand as a "widow," face down. First player may take up the widow and lay his own hand face up in its place; or he may simply refuse it. In that case, the option moves around the table, and if nobody takes the widow, the dealer spreads it face up. Once a hand is thus disclosed, the next player may exchange his entire hand for it or draw just one card from it, discarding one of his own cards face up in the widow. This continues around until some player knocks the table, signifying that he is satisfied with his hand. The remaining players each have one more chance to draw as before or to stand with what they have. There are no bets or raises; hands are simply shown and the highest takes the pot, according to standard poker hands.

Note: Whiskey poker was originally played with hands of three cards each, as an outgrowth of *Commerce,* page 69, using the evaluations common to that game.

WHIST: This is the game that made Hoyle famous, or vice versa, since both have left indelible impressions upon the real silent majority, the card-playing public, whist being the forerunner of *Bridge,* page 18, and Hoyle the all-time authority who triggered it. Whist is a four-player game, with those opposite as partners; and the standard fifty-two-card deck is used, each suit ranking **A, K, Q, J, 10, 9, 8, 7, 6, 5, 4, 3, 2.**

The entire pack is dealt, one card at a time, in clockwise rotation, the last card being turned up to designate trump. The dealer adds it to his hand before making his first play. The player at dealer's left leads to the first trick, and the others must follow suit if possible; otherwise they can play from a side suit or trump the trick if an ordinary suit is led. Highest card of suit led wins unless trumped, when the highest trump wins. Winner of each trick leads to the next.

Six tricks are termed a "book," and a team scores 1 point for each trick taken beyond that. The deal moves around the table, and the first team to reach 7 points wins the game, according to American rules. The loser's score is deducted from the winner's to establish the margin of victory; and it is usual to play out the final hand, so the winners may add extra points to their score. In official or serious play, 7 is the limit. The English mode of scoring is more complex and is described under *English Whist,* page 376.

Whist has many conventional plays, such as always leading a trump when holding five or more; leading the fourth highest of the longest suit; showing a holding of **A–K** by leading the **K;** playing "low" in second hand and "high" in third hand. Many of these have been inherited by bridge and elaborated in that game.

In *Bid Whist,* instead of turning up trump, each player can announce the number of tricks, plus the trump honors **(A, K, Q, J)** that he thinks his team can take during play, with the understanding that he decides on the trump suit and leads to the first trick. Since there are thirteen tricks and four honors, the possible points total 17. Usually, players are permitted to keep raising bids until three pass in succession; and in that generally accepted form, the game is technically known as *Auction Bid Whist*.

If the bidder is successful, his team's points are counted and the opposing team's points are deducted to determine the winning margin, each deal constituting a game. For example, a player on Team *A* bids "eleven" and his team takes nine tricks and three honors (A Q J) for a total of 12 points, while Team *B* takes four tricks and one honor (Q) for a total of 5. The bidder's team thereby wins by 5 points. However, if a bidder fails, his team scores 0 and the opponents score what they make. Thus in the example cited, if Team *A* takes only eight tricks and two honors (A J) while Team *B* takes five tricks and two honors (K Q), Team *B* would win by its full score of 7 points.

This game has several variations: In one, honors are credited to the team holding them, not to the team taking them; in another, honors are totally disregarded, so there are only thirteen tricks. In scoring, sometimes only the tricks over "book" are counted, making 7 possible points (plus four honors if used). In a continuous game, this can be played as *Setback Bid Whist*, a losing bid being deducted from a team's existing score, while the nonbidding team always scores whatever points it makes.

English Whist: This long-established form of whist differs from the American version chiefly in the mode of scoring, which runs as follows: Game is 5 points. Each trick over six counts 1 point for the team taking it. After tricks are scored, either team may score for holding a majority of the honor cards, consisting of ace, king, queen, jack of trump. All four honors count 4 points; any three honors, 2 points. Therefore:

Assuming that team scores stand *A–C,* 2 points; *B–D,* 3 points. *A–C* takes eight tricks, scoring 2 points for a total of 4; but *B–D* holds three honors, thereby scoring 2 points for a total of 5 and winning game. However, if *A–C* takes nine tricks, scoring 3 points for a total of 2+3=5, *A–C* thereby wins game, as the honors held by *B–D* do not count.

A team with a standing score of 4 cannot count honor points, but must score 1 trick or more to win game. Example: Scores stand *A–C,* 2; *B–D,* 4. *A–C* takes eight tricks, scoring 2 points to reach 4; while *B,* holding three honors, cannot score, so the teams stand 4-all. However, if *A–C* had held those three honors, *A–C* would have scored 2 points for tricks and 2 for honors, which, added to the standing score, would win game (2+2+2=6).

A team winning two games wins "rubber," which is the ultimate aim. A team is credited with a "treble," or 3 game points, for winning a game by a score of 5 (or more) to 0. It gains a "double," or 2 game points, for winning by 5 (or more) to 1 or 2. It gains a "single," or 1 game point, for winning by 5 (or more) to 3 or 4. A team that wins rubber adds 2 "rubber points" to its score. The highest possible score is two trebles and a rubber, 3+3+2=8 against an opposing 0. The lowest possible is two singles and a rubber, 1+1+2=4 against an opposing treble of 3, giving the winning team a victory by 1 point.

WHISTLER: A form of *Solitaire.* See page 351.

WHITEHEAD: A form of *Solitaire.* See page 351.

WHITE PASS: A variant of *Yukon.* See *Solitaire,* page 351.

WIDOW CINCH: Six-handed cinch with three teams of partners seated opposite. Each player is dealt eight cards, and the remaining four are set aside as a "widow" that goes to the highest bidder, before he names trump. All hands then discard down to four cards each, and play follows as in *Cinch.* See page 65.

WIDOW NAP: A form of *Napoleon,* page 163, with an extra five-card hand dealt as a face-down "widow" that goes to a player bidding "Nap." This enables him to improve his hand by choosing the five best cards from his own hand and the widow, a privilege that encourages high bids. Also applicable to bids of *Wellington,* page 374, or *Blucher,* page 36.

WILD-CARD CANASTA: A development of *Uruguayan Canasta* (page 372) but with thirteen cards dealt to each player. The pot is always frozen and can be taken only by matching the upcard with a natural pair from the hand. Wild cards can be melded in sets of three or more, each joker scoring 50; each deuce, 20. A wild canasta counts 2,000 points; formed by four jokers and three deuces, 3,000; by seven deuces, 4,000. Game is 7,500 and the required opening meld is raised to 150 points at the 5,000 level.

Black threes cannot be discarded until after the first round, and a player taking a pot must weed them from it, each counting 5 points for his team; all four are weeded or melded, scoring 100. Red threes score 100 for the first; 200 each for the next two; 500 for the fourth, but these are minus if the team fails to form a canasta. This game is commonly called *Cuban Canasta,* and, as a popular variant, black threes may be treated as red threes, each forming a special set scored the same way.

Wild Card Canasta represents a transition from *Canasta* (page 43) toward still wilder games as *Bolivia,* page 37, *Samba,* page 300, *Mexicana,* page 161. For a full list, see page 55.

WILD-CARD POKER: Any form of *Poker* in which cards of certain values can represent other cards that the players decide upon. Such games are common in *Dealer's Choice,* page 241. See page 239 for *Wild-Card Poker.*

WILD-CARD RUMMY: See page 294.

WILD WIDOW: *Wild-Card Poker* in which a single card or "widow" is turned up to establish a wild-card value. See page 274.

WOOLWORTH: A form of *Poker* described on page 274.

X MARKS THE SPOT: Similar to *Crisscross* or *Cross Widow,* but with five cards dealt to form an X, giving them special usage. See page 275.

YASS: Another name for *Jass*, page 148.

YERLASH: Another term for *Vint*, page 372.

YUKON: A form of *Solitaire*, page 351.

ZEBRA POKER: A form of *Dealer's Choice*. See page 275.

ZIGINETTE: A modern and highly popular form of *Lans-quenet*, page 155, using a forty-card pack (no eights, nines, or tens) from which two cards of different value are dealt face up, each as a player's card. Another value is dealt face up as the dealer's card. Players place bets on the first two, and more cards are turned up, with each new value open for bets as a player's card. But if a card turns up to match a player's card, the dealer wins all wagers on that card; and when he matches his own card, he pays off all existing bets, and the deal moves on. If the dealer wins all bets before matching his own card, he can retain the deal. If any of the first three cards match, there is no play, and the same dealer deals again.

ZIONCHECK: The original form of *Contract Rummy*, page 91, in which only the first five types of "deals" are required, instead of all seven.

ZOMBIE: A form of *Dealer's Choice*.

GLOSSARY-INDEX

(Games are italicized.)

Abandon: Give up a hand or deal.

Above the line: Premium score in *Bridge.*

Abundance: Type of bid in *Solo Whist.*

Acceptance: Agreement to a proposed bid.

Accordion (Solitaire): 323

Ace: A card with one spot.

Ace high: *Poker* hand with ace as highest card.

Ace in the hole: An ace as down-card in *Stud Poker.*

Ace kicker: An odd ace retained with a pair of another value in *Draw Poker.*

Acepots: 241

Aces Up (Solitaire): 323

Aces up: A hand with two pair including aces. *Poker.*

Active player: One participating in bidding, betting, or actual play.

Adversary: An opponent.

Age or edge: Player at dealer's left.

Agreement: Acceptance of specified options in any game.

Airplane: 13

Albany lead: In *Whist,* a lead indicating that a player holds four trumps.

All Fives: 13

All Fours: 13

Alone: Playing without a partner's aid as in *Euchre.*

Alsos: 15

Alternate straight: A term for a Dutch straight in *Poker.*

Ambigu: 15

American Brag: 40

American leads: Special leads in *Whist* showing length of trump suit.

American Pinochle: 16

American Skat: 16

American Whist: 16, 375

Anaconda (Poker): 241

Anaconda with Pass Along (Poker): 241

Animals: 16

Announce: To name a trump or a game.

Ante: A preliminary bet or a pool of such bets.

Ante up: To make a preliminary bet.

Any Card Wild (Poker): 242

Any Suit Wild (Poker): 242

Anything Opens (Poker): 242

Any Value Wild (Poker): 242

Approach bid: In *Bridge,* an early bid of an informative type.

Apres: Term denoting a tie in *Trente et Quarante.*

Arlington: 16

Army and Navy Pinochle: 204

Around the corner: A sequence of cards in which an ace links the lowest with the highest, as 3–2–A–K–Q.

Around the World (Poker): 242

As or *As Nas:* 18

Ask: To make a legitimate inquiry in games like *Canasta* or *Skat.*

Asking bid: In *Contract Bridge,* a bid seeking a response that may lead to a slam.

Assist: To order up trump in *Euchre.*

Auction: Continuous bidding toward making a trump.

Auction Bid Whist: 376

Auction Bridge: 18

Auction Cinch: 67

Auction Euchre: 113

Auction Forty-five: 123

Auction Hearts: 20

Auction High Five: 67

Auction Pinochle: 177, 181, 184, 185

Auction Pinochle with Partners: 193

Auction Pitch: 214

Auction Sheepshead: 306

Auction Sixty-six: 313

Auld Lang Syne (Solitaire): 324

Australian Poker: 245

Authors: 20

Automatic Lowball (Poker): 243

Auxiliary Sequences (Solitaire): 348

Baccara or *Baccarat:* 21

Back in: To bet after having checked in *Poker.*

Back to back: A hole card and up-card of same value in *Stud Poker*.

Bait: Another term for bate.

Balk: In *Cribbage*, giving cards to the crib that may be useless to the dealer.

Bango: 22

Banker and Broker: 22

Banker or bank: Player who takes all bets or buys and sells chips to others.

Bank Night (Poker): 243

Barnyard: 22

Baseball (Poker): 243

Basset: 23

Basta: The third highest trump, ♣A, in *Ombre*, or the ♠Q in a more modern version sometimes termed *German Solo*.

Bate or bete: Failure to win a bid in *Pinochle*.

Battle Royal: 23

Beast: 23

Beat Your Neighbor (Poker): 243

Bedsprings (Poker): 243

Beer Play: 23

Beg: In *All Fours*, a proposal by first player that each be dealt three more cards and a new trump be turned up.

Beggar My Neighbor: 23

Beleaguered Castle (Solitaire): 324, 326

Belotte: 24

Below the line: Entries of trick scores in *Bridge*.

Best bower: The joker as highest trump in *Euchre* or *Five Hundred*.

Best Flush (Poker): 244

Bet: A stake placed on a coming play or showdown.

Bete: Same as bate.

Bet or Drop (Poker): 244

Betrothal (Solitaire): 325

Bet the pot: To make a wager equal to the amount in the pot or kitty.

Betty Hutton (Poker): 244

Bezique: 24

Bezique: The ♠Q and ◇J (or similar combination) in the game of *Bezique*.

Bicycle: 5, 4, 3, 2, A, the lowest hand in *Lowball*.

Bid: To agree to take a certain number of tricks or points in a hand. Common to many games.

Bidder: Any player making a bid, but, more specifically, the highest bidder after bidding is concluded and play begins.

Bid Euchre: 32

Bid Whist: 375

Bierspiel: 32

Big cassino: The ◇10 in *Cassino*.

Big cat: A freak poker hand, ranging from king down to eight.

Big dog: A freak poker hand, ranging from ace down to nine.

Big Forty (Solitaire): 342

Big tiger: Another term for the big cat.

Bimbo (Poker): 244

Binage: A term for the ♠Q and ◇J in a half-pack variant of *Bezique*.

Binochle: 32

Binochle: Another term for *Pinochle*, now practically obsolete.

Bisley (Solitaire): 328, 330

Black Jack: 32

Black Jack: In *Hearts*, the ♠J when used as a penalty card instead of the ♠Q.

Blackjack: 32

Black Lady: 35

Black Lady: The ♠Q, particularly as a 13-point penalty card in *Hearts*.

Black Maria or *Black Widow:* 36

Black Maria: Another name for Black Lady.

Blackout: 36

Black Queens Partnership: In *Sheepshead*, a rule making holders of the black queens (♣Q and ♠Q) partners for that deal.

Blackwood Convention: In *Bridge*, a method of using cue bids to reach a slam.

Blank suit: A suit totally absent from a player's hand; a void.

Blaze: In *Poker*, a special hand consisting entirely of face cards.

Blind: A preliminary ante; also another term for widow.

Blind All Fours: 36

Blind and Straddle (Poker): 245

Blind Cinch: 67

Blind Euchre: 113

Blind Hookey: 22

Blind Opening (Poker): 245

Blind Stud (Poker): 245

Blind Tiger (Poker): 245

Block: Anything that prevents one or more players from continuing to play the hand.

Block Rummy: 293

Blucher: 36

Blucher: An additional bid in *Napoleon*.

Bluff: 36

Bluff: Betting a weak *Poker* hand as if

it were a strong one; also an early term for the game itself.

Boathouse Rummy: 37, 293

Bobtail flush: In *Poker,* four cards of a single suit.

Bobtail Opener (Poker): 245

Bobtail straight: In *Poker,* four cards of mixed suits in a sequence, excluding an ace.

Bobtail Stud (Poker): 245

Bolivia: 37

Bonus cards: In *Hearts,* cards (as the ◊ J) that deduct points.

Bonus melds: In *Pinochle,* special melds in games with extra packs.

Boodle: 38

Boodle cards: Payoff cards in games of the *Boodle* type.

Book: In *Whist* or *Bridge,* the quota of six tricks that a team must win before it can score.

Boost: In *Poker,* to raise a bet.

Borrow: In some forms of *Rummy,* the privilege of moving a card from one meld to another.

Boston: 38

Boston de Fontainebleau: 38

Bouillotte: 38

Bourre: 39

Bourre (pronounced "boor"; sometimes misspelled "bouré"—pronounced "booray").

Bower: In *Euchre,* each jack of the same color, providing that one of their suits is trump.

Box: A won hand in *Gin Rummy.*

Box the pack: Inadvertently gather face-up cards with face-down cards before or during shuffling.

Boys from Brooklyn: In *Pinochle,* a nickname for a meld of four jacks.

Brag: 39

Brazilian Canasta: 38

Brelan: 40

Bridge: See *Auction Bridge:* 18; and *Contract Bridge:* 72

Bridge Whist: 40

Brisque: An ace and a ten in *Bezique.*

Buck: An object used in *Poker* to designate the dealer.

Buck the tiger: Play against a *Faro* bank.

Bug: The joker, when used in *Poker* as an extra ace or a wild card with a flush or straight.

Build: Adding a card to one on the table, as in *Cassino.*

Build-Up: 40

Bullet: An ace.

Bump: To raise, as in *Poker.*

Bumper: A score of 8 points, the largest possible in *English Whist.*

Bunch: To give up a deal by mixing the hands together.

Burn: To put a card on the bottom of the pack, usually face up.

Bury: To put a card deep in the pack.

Bust: To overdraw in *Blackjack* or similar games; also, a worthless hand in any game.

Butcher Boy (Poker): 245

Buy: To draw or call for cards; to pay for a privilege such as the right to deal in certain games.

Bye: To pass a chance to bet or bid.

Calabrasella: 40

Calabrella: 41

Calculation (Solitaire): 328

California Jack: 41

California Loo: 41

California Lowball (Poker): 42

Call: Equalize a bet, as in *Poker;* make a bid in *Bridge;* demand a certain card.

Call-Ace Euchre: 113

Call Rummy: 293

Call the turn: Name the order of the last three cards in a *Faro* game.

Canadian Stud (Poker): 246

Canasta: 43

Canasta: In *Canasta,* seven or more cards of one value.

Cancellation Hearts: 55

Canfield (Solitaire): 338

Cans: 55

Capot: In *Piquet,* a bonus scored by player winning all the tricks.

Captain: Player having final say in certain partnerships.

Card Dominoes: 55

Cards: A 3-point score for having most cards in *Cassino.*

Carousel: 55

Carte blanche: A hand with no face cards, as in *Piquet.*

Case card: The only card of any specific value still to be dealt or played.

Cash: To lead a winning card; to turn in chips.

Cassino: 57

Cat: A freak poker hand. *See* Big cat and Little cat.

Catch: Draw a needed card in *Poker;* or find such a card in a widow.

Catch the Ten: 62

Cat-hop: Term denoting that two of the last three cards in a *Faro* deal are the same denomination.

Cayenne or *Cayenne Whist:* 62

Cedarhurst: 63
Cent: 63
Chase the Ace: 288
Check: To pass the bet to the next player in *Poker;* also a chip or counter used for scoring.
Check Pinochle: 199
Chemin-de-Fer: 63
Chicago: 64
Chicago (Four-Deal Bridge): 124
Chicago (Poker): 246
Chicane: Another term for carte blanche.
Chile or *Chilean Canasta:* 64
Chinese Bezique: 29
Chinese Bridge (Solitaire): 64
Chinese Fan-Tan: 64
Chinese Whist: 65
Chip: A token or counter used in scoring games.
Chip in: To put chips in the pot.
Chouette: 65
Cientos: 65
Cinch: 65
Cinch hand: An unbeatable hand in *Poker.*
Cincinnati (Poker): 246
Cincinnati Liz (Poker): 246
Cinq Cent: 68
Citadel (Solitaire): 325
Clabber or *Clob, Clobber, Clobberyash, Clubby:* 68
Clear: Drive out adverse cards of a suit.
Clob or Clobber: Terms for *Klaberjass.*
Close: To end the privilege of drawing from the pack in certain games.
Closed Poker: 246
Closed poker: Any form of *Poker* in which no cards are disclosed until the showdown; particularly *Draw Poker.*
Clubs: A suit of playing cards.
Coffee housing: Using unethical practices in a card game.
Cold Hands or *Cold-Hand Poker:* 246
Cold hands: *Poker* hands when dealt face up. Also a form of *Draw Poker.*
Cold Hands with Draw (Poker): 246
Color: Red or black cards; also a special suit in *Solo.*
Column: *Solitaire.* Cards arranged in vertical order.
Combination: Cards with special value as a group.
Combine: Taking cards by adding their values in *Cassino.*
Come in: To enter the betting in *Poker.*

Comet or *Commit:* 68
Command: Holding the best card in a game where tricks are taken.
Commerce: 69
Commercial Pitch: 303
Commit: Another name for *Comet.*
Common marriage: King and queen of a nontrump suit in *Pinochle.*
Complete hand: A *Poker* hand containing its full quota of cards.
Complete or completed trick: One to which everybody has played.
Concealed hand: One that goes out "all at once" in *Canasta* or *Rummy.*
Concede: Give up a hand without playing it.
Concentration: 70
Conditions: Certain card combinations in the game of *Panguingue.*
Condone: To ignore an infraction of the rules in any card game.
Conquian: 71
Consolation: 72
Consolation: The final hand in *Five in One;* also a term used in *Ombre.*
Contest: Any type of card game.
Contestant: A player, team, or participant.
Continental Rummy: 72
Contract: Number of tricks needed to make good a bid. Also, a short name for *Contract Bridge.*
Contract Bridge: 72
Contract Pinochle: 210
Contract Rummy: 91
Contract Whist: 94
Convention: A bid or play according to a system, especially in *Bridge.*
Coon Can: 94
Copper: To bet on a card to lose in *Faro.*
Coquette (Solitaire): 328
Couleur: A bet involving color in *Trente et Quarante.*
Count: Value given to specific cards when bidding or playing.
Counter: Card with a special point value; also a chip or token.
Count out: To keep score of points or tricks when going for game.
Coup: A term for a bet or deal in certain games.
Court card: Any king, queen, or jack.
Cover: Play a higher card of a suit on a trick.
Crapette: 94
Crazy Aces: 95
Crazy Eights: 95
Crazy Jacks: 95

Crazy joker: The joker when a wild card.

Crib: An extra hand formed from discards in *Cribbage*.

Cribbage: 95

Cribbidge: Original name for *Cribbage*.

Crisscross (Poker): 247

Cross: In *Euchre*, naming a new trump opposite in color to the original.

Cross Over (Poker): 247

Crossruff: To trump alternating leads back and forth in *Bridge* or *Whist*.

Cross Widow (Poker): 247

Cuban Canasta: 378

Cuckoo: 101

Cue bid: In *Bridge*, a bid showing the bidder's control of a suit.

Cut: Placing the lower portion of the pack on the upper.

Cutthroat: A game with more than two players in which each plays for himself.

Cutthroat Bridge: 90

Cutthroat Euchre: 110

Darda: 101

Dead card: One that has been played, discarded, or made unavailable.

Dead hand: One that is out of play.

Dead man's hand: In *Poker*, two pair consisting of aces over nines.

Deadwood: Cards left over in a hand, especially in *Rummy;* or discards in other games.

Deal: Distribution of cards, often as hands to players; also the play that follows.

Dealer: The person who deals the cards, whether a player or not.

Dealer's Choice (Poker): 241

Deal out: Exclude a player from a deal.

Deck: A pack of cards.

Declare: To name a trump, make a meld or some other announcement.

Declare out: Announcement during play that a player or his team has sufficient score to win the hand or game.

Declarer: In *Bridge*, the player originally naming the suit (or no-trump) that his team finally decides to play.

Deece: A popular term for dix.

Defenders: In *Bridge*, the team opposing the declarer.

Defensive bid: A bid made to bluff opponents into bidding higher.

Demand bid: In *Bridge*, a bid calling for a response by bidder's partner.

Demon (Solitaire): 333

Denomination: Rank or value of a card.

Deuce: A two-spot.

Deuces and Jokers (Poker): 247

Deuces and Joker Wild (Poker): 247

Deuces and One-eyed Jacks Wild (Poker): 247

Deuces and Pothooks Wild (Poker): 248

Deuces and Treys Wild (Poker): 247

Deuces Wild (Poker): 239

Deuces Wilder (Poker): 247

Diamond jack: A bonus card ($\Diamond$ J) in *Hearts*.

Discard: Dispose of unwanted cards, often in exchange for others; or, in trump games, to play from an odd suit.

Discard Hearts: 102

Discard pile: In *Canasta* and *Rummy*, a face-up pile where players place unwanted cards, or from which they draw desired cards. A similar term applies in various *Solitaires*.

Distribution: Division of cards in a player's hand, by suits.

Division Loo: 102

Dix: A nine of trump in *Pinochle*, or seven of trump in *Bezique*.

Doctor Pepper (Poker): 248

Dog: A freak poker hand. *See* Big dog and Little dog.

Dom: The three of trump in *Dom Pedro*.

Domino Hearts: 102

Domino Whist: 102

Dom Pedro: 172

Donkey: 102

Double: In *Bridge*, a bid that may add to trick values or penalties; also, to play a hand at double value in various games.

Double-Barreled Shotgun (Poker): 271

Double bate: Penalty for losing bid if the hand is played out in *Auction Pinochle*.

Double Dummy Bridge: 103

Double-Handed High-Low (Poker): 248

Double Hasenpfeffer: 103

Double Hearts: 104

Double-Pack Pinochle: 204

Double pairs royal: In *Cribbage*, four cards of the same rank.

Double Pedro: 65

Double pinochle: A meld of $\Diamond$ J J and ♠ Q Q.

Double Rum: 94

Double run: In *Cribbage*, a sequence with one card duplicated, as **10, 10, 9, 8**; in *Pinochle*, a double sequence.

Double sequence: In *Pinochle*, the A, A, 10, 10, K, K, Q, Q, J, J.

Double Solitaire: 104

Doubleton: In *Whist* or *Bridge*, a holding of only two cards of a suit.

Double up: To be twice as much as before.

Down the board: Pegging scores toward the far end of a cribbage board.

Down the River (Poker): 229

Draw: To take cards from the pack; in *Poker*, to be dealt cards to replace some in the original hand.

Draw Cassino: 104

Draw game: Any type of game in which neither player or team wins.

Draw Hearts: 55, 104

Draw Poker: 226

Dummy: In *Bridge* or *Whist*, the declarer's partner, or his hand, which he lays face up so the declarer can play it. In other games, an extra hand, which is sometimes played.

Dummy whist: Form of *Whist* with dealer's partner serving as dummy.

Duplicate *Bridge* or *Whist*: Games in which identical hands are dealt to different teams so the results can be compared in tournament play. Applicable to other games as well.

Dutch Bank: 22

Dutch straight: A freak hand in *Poker*; same as skip straight.

Dynamite (Poker): 248

Eagles: A fifth suit once included in packs of playing cards, with green eagles as symbols. Similar to *Royals.*

Earl of Coventry: 105

Écarté: 105

Echo: In *Whist* or *Bridge*, a play of a high card followed by a low in the same suit as a signal for the partner's next lead.

Edge: An advantage in the play of a hand, usually held by player at dealer's left.

Eight-Card Stud (Poker): 230

Eights: 106

Eighty-eight (Poker): 248

Eighty kings: A meld of four kings for 80 points in *Pinochle.*

Eldest hand: Player at dealer's left.

End game: In *Bridge*, plays made with the last few cards.

Endhand: The last player to be dealt cards in *Skat.*

Enflé: 106

English Poker: 245

English Stud: 248

English Whist: 376

Enter: To join in bidding or play.

Entry: In trump games, a card strong enough to bring the lead into the player's hand.

Escalera: A seven-card sequence in *Bolivia* and other forms of *Canasta.*

Establish: To gain full control of a suit.

Euchre: 107

Everlasting: 374

Exposed card: Any card shown accidentally or illegally during play.

Exposed hand: A hand played face up for a bonus score in certain games, or as a dummy in *Bridge.*

Face cards: Kings, queens, and jacks.

Faced card: One turned face upward.

False openers: In *Draw Poker*, an insufficient combination on which a player falsely opens the pot, as anything less than a pair of jacks, when a pair of jacks or better is required.

Fan: A spread of face-up cards. To spread cards fanwise.

Fan-Tan: 115

Farm or *Farmer:* 115

Faro: 116

Fascination (Solitaire): 329

Fatten: To throw counter cards on a trick; also to put more chips in a pool.

Feed: To contribute to a pool, pot, or kitty.

Felsos: 116

Fiery Cross (Poker): 249

Fifteen: 286

Fifteen: Cards adding to fifteen in *Cribbage.*

File: A vertical row of cards, especially in *Solitaire.*

Fill: In *Poker*, to draw or be dealt cards that "fill" the hand by completing a desired combination.

Find the Lady: 366

Finesse: In partnership play, particularly in *Whist* or *Bridge*, an attempt to win a trick with the lower of two cards, when an opponent is holding one or more of intervening value.

Firehouse Pinochle: 197

First hand: Either the hand at dealer's left or the hand that leads to a trick during the course of play.

Fish: 117

Fishhook: A nickname for a seven-spot.

Five and Dime (Poker): 249

Five and Dime, or Five and Ten: A freak *Poker* hand ten high, five low, with no pair, as **10–9–8–6–5.**

Five and Ten: 117

Five-Card Final (Poker): 249

Five-Card Loo: 158

Five Cards or *Five Fingers:* 117

Five-Card Stud (Poker): 228, 249

Five-Card Stud, Last Up or Down (Poker): 249

Five-Card Stud with Replacement (Poker): 249

Five Hundred: 117

Five Hundred Rummy: 295

Five in One: 122

Five of a kind: Highest combination in *Deuces Wild,* in which **Q–Q–Q–2–2** would represent **Q–Q–Q–Q–Q.** The same applies to other types of wild-card *Poker.*

Five or Nine: 122

Five-suit pack: A special sixty-five-card pack with an extra suit—either eagles or royals—that enjoyed brief popularity.

Five-suit poker: Played with a five-suit pack, with five of a kind the highest hand.

Flash: A hand containing a card of each suit in a game of *Five-Suit Poker.*

Flip (Poker): 255

Flip Stud (Poker): 250

Flop: In *Poker,* a group of common up-cards. *See Hold 'Em.*

Flower Garden (Solitaire): 334, 336

Flush: In *Poker,* a hand with all cards of the same suit; in *Pinochle,* a trump sequence (A–10–K–Q–J).

Fold: To turn down a hand in *Stud Poker.*

Follow suit: To play a card of the suit led in games where tricks are taken.

Football (Poker): 250

Forcing bid: In *Contract Bridge,* a conventional bid that automatically calls upon a partner to respond. *See* Demand bid.

Forcing play: To make an opponent use a trump to win a trick; in *Canasta,* a discard that an opponent is forced to take.

Forehand: The first player to dealer's left in *Skat.*

Forty-five: 123

Forty jacks: In *Pinochle,* a meld of four jacks for 40 points.

Forty Thieves (Solitaire): 342

Foul hand: A *Poker* hand that is short of the proper number of cards.

Four-Card Poker: 250

Four-Deal Bridge: 124

Four flush: *Poker* hand with four cards of one suit and odd card of another.

Four-Flush Opener (Poker): 250

Four-Flush Poker: 124

Four-Flush Stud (Poker): 250

Four Forty-four (Poker): 250

Four Forty-two (Poker): 250

Four Jacks: 284

Four of a kind: In *Poker,* a holding of four cards of the same value, as **A–A–A–A** or **10–10–10–10.**

Four straight: 283

Frage: 125

Freak hand: Any very unusual hand, particularly in a trump game.

Freak hands: Special combinations allowable in some *Poker* games.

Freak Hands (Poker): 251

Free ride: In *Poker,* staying in a pot without betting, after other players have checked.

Free trip: Same as Free ride.

Free Wheeling (Poker): 260

Freezeout (Poker): 251

Freeze the pack: To discard a wild card in *Canasta,* making it more difficult to take up the discard pile.

French Boston: 124

French Euchre: 125

French Ruff: 125

French Whist: 303

Frog: 125

Full hand: In *Poker,* the same as a full house.

Full house: A *Poker* hand consisting of three cards of one value and two of another, as **Q–Q–Q–6–6** or **5–5–5–9–9.**

Full pack: A regulation pack of fifty-two cards.

Gaigel: 125

Game: Any card game or the points or tricks required to win it. In *Pitch,* a scoring point dependent on taking counter cards, or, in some variants, the ten or trump.

Garbage: 122

Gentlemen's Agreement: 127

German Skat: 127

German Solo: 127

German Whist: 129

Gift: In *All Fours,* a point given to the opponent by the dealer, when the latter is allowed to name the trump and does so.

Gile or *Gilet:* 130

Gin: Short for *Gin Rummy.* Also, a gin

rummy hand melded without dead-wood.

Gin Rummy: 130

Gleek: 135

Go: A chance to score one or two special points in *Cribbage.*

Go Boom: 135

Go down: In trump games, failure to make a bid, with the corresponding loss in score; in *Rummy,* to place leftover cards from the hand face up on the table.

Go Fish: 135

Go out: In many games, to take enough tricks or points to win. In *Rummy* and *Canasta,* to meld or lay down all the cards still in a hand.

Go over: To make a higher bid or play a higher card.

Go rummy: To meld an entire *Rummy* hand all at once.

Goulash: A nickname for *Sixty-four Card Pinochle.*

Grand: 136

Grand Demond (Solitaire): 333

Grand pinochle: The ♠K Q ◊J when scored as 80 points in *Pinochle.*

Grand slam: Taking all thirteen tricks in *Bridge.*

Group: In *Rummy,* three or four cards of the same value.

Gruesome Twosome (Poker): 251

Guarantee: One of the bids in *Six-Bid Solo.*

Guards: In *Bridge,* low cards protecting those of higher value.

Gucki: A type of bid in *Skat.*

Gucki grand: A type of bid in *Skat.*

Guts (Poker): 251

Half-Pot Limit (Poker): 251

Hand: Cards dealt to a player; or the player himself. Also used as the equivalent of "deal."

Hands as games: Scoring each hand as a game in *Pinochle* and in other games.

Hasenpfeffer: 139

Hearts: 140

Heartsette: 144

Heart Solo: 144

Hearts triple: In *Pinochle,* a special rule giving triple value to a bid in hearts.

Heinz (Poker): 251

Help: Any bid that enables a partner to bid higher; or any hand that provides needed strength for a partner's play.

High: In *Pitch,* the highest card dealt; also, a point scored for holding it. In many games, the highest card played on a trick. In *Poker,* the highest hand.

High card: In *Poker,* the highest card in a hand that contains no pair or anything better.

High Five: 65

High, Low, Jack and Game: 144

High-Low, Jack (All Fours): 13

High-Low Draw (Poker): 232

High-Low Five-Card Stud (Poker): 233

High-Low Jack (Pitch): 144

High-Low Poker: 232

High-Low Rummy: 293

High-Low Seven-Card Stud (Poker): 234

High-Low Six-Card Stud (Poker): 234

High Poker: 251

High Spade Split (Poker): 251

Hilo (Poker): 252

Hilo Picolo (Poker): 252

His heels: A jack turned up as "starter" in *Cribbage.*

His nobs: The jack of the same suit as the "starter" in *Cribbage.*

Hit: To deal a player another card in *Blackjack.*

Hit the Moon: 145

Hoc or Hock: 145

Hock: Term for the final card in a *Faro* deal.

Hoggenheimer: 145

Hokum (Poker): 252

Hold 'Em (Poker): 252

Holding: The cards composing a player's hand.

Hole card: Any card dealt face down in *Stud Poker.*

Hole-Card Stud (Poker): 252

Hollywood (Poker): 253

Hollywood Canasta: 146

Hollywood Gin: 132

Honest John: 22

Honeymoon Bridge: 146

Honors: The top five trumps (A K Q J 10) in *Whist;* the same in *Bridge,* but including the four aces in no-trump.

Honor tricks: Special combinations of high cards used in evaluating a hand in *Bridge.*

House in the Woods (Solitaire): 334

House on the Hill (Solitaire): 335

House rules: Special rules applying to games as played in gambling houses.

Howell settlement: A way of scoring in *Hearts.* Each player counts the hearts he has taken, multiplies it by the number of opponents, and puts that many chips into a pool. He then subtracts his hearts from thirteen and takes back that many chips.

Hoyle: A standard reference work on card games.

Hundred aces: A *Pinochle* meld of 100 points for four aces of different suits.

Hurricane (Poker): 273

Idiot's Delight: 147
Idiot's Delight (Solitaire): 324
Idle Year (Solitaire): 323
I Doubt It: 147
Immortal hand: An unbeatable hand.
Imperial: 148
Improve: To better a hand by a draw in *Poker.*

Incorrect pack: Any pack that is short of necessary cards or that contains any extra cards.

Index: The corner of a playing card that shows value and suit.

Indifferent card: A card that is of no use to a hand.

Informatory double: In *Bridge,* a false double that notifies the partner as to the bidder's holding.

Initial bid: An opening bid.

Inside straight: A *Poker* hand containing four cards toward a straight, but with an in-between value missing, as 10–8–7–6, which needs a 9 for a straight.

Insufficient bid: Any bid lower than a previous bid.

In the hole: A minus score, particularly when so indicated by drawing a circle around it as a "hole." Also, in *Stud Poker,* any card dealt face downward.

Invitation bid: A bid in *Bridge* that encourages but does not compel partner to bid higher.

Invite: To lead a low card of the longest suit in *Bridge.*

Irish Loo: 158

Irregularity: A slight or careless infraction of the rules of a game, often condoned by other players.

Irregular lead: Any lead at variance with formal procedure, as in certain trump games.

Italian Canasta: 52

Jack: A face card, usually outranked by the king and queen but given a higher rating in certain games. In

Pitch, a point scored for taking the jack of trump during play.

Jackpots (Poker): 253
Jacks Back or *Jackson (Poker):* 253
Jacks High (Poker): 253
Jambone: 114
Jamboree: 114
Jass: 148
Jeux de règle: Hands that give mathematical advantages in *Écarté.*
Jig: 149
Joker: An extra card added to the pack of fifty-two and given special rating, often as the highest trump, and termed the "best bower" in *Five Hundred.* Two or more jokers are used in some games.
Joker Euchre: 113
Joker Hearts: 149
Joker Poker: 239
Joker Rummy: 149
Jump bid: A bid going beyond conventional requirements in *Bridge.*

Kaloochi or *Kaluki:* 149
Kankakee (Poker): 253
Kibitzer: An onlooker during a card game.
Kicker: In *Poker,* an odd or unneeded card kept in the hand while making a draw, often as a bluff.
Kilter: A freak *Poker* hand with cards ranging from 9 down to 2. Also the lowest skip.
King: In most games, the highest face card; and usually the highest card in games where aces are ranked as low.
King Albert (Solitaire): 335, 341
King Rummy: 150
Kings Back or *Kingston (Poker):* 253
Kings in the Corners: 150
Kitty: A pool or part of it; also a term for widow.
Klaberjass or *Klob:* 151
Klob: A term for *Klaberjass.*
Klondike (Solitaire): 329, 338
Knave: British term for a jack.
Knock: To end a hand or make an announcement by knocking on the table.
Knock Poker: 153
Knock Rummy: 154
Kontraspiel: 154
Kreutz-Mariage: 155

La Belle Lucie (Solitaire): 350
Lalapalooza (Poker): 254
Lamebrain Pete (Poker): 246
Lamebrains (Poker): 246

Lansquenet: 155
Lanterloo: 156
Laps: 114, 155
Laps: A form of *Euchre;* also a mode of scoring in other games.
Last: Score for the last point in *Cribbage.*
Last In: 155
Last trick: A special 10-point score in *Pinochle.*
Last turn: A bet on the order of the last three cards in a *Faro* deal.
Lay away: To make discards in a crib in *Cribbage;* or in a widow in *Pinochle.*
Lay down: Make a meld or reveal a winning hand.
Lay off: To dispose of cards by placing them on an opponent's meld in *Rummy.*
Layout: Arrangement of cards on table in *Solitaire* and games like *Russian Bank* or *Spite and Malice.* Also extra cards placed on a table to indicate payoffs in *Faro* and *Michigan.*
Lazy Edna or *Lazy Lucy (Poker):* 156
Lead: Play a card from the hand face up as the start to a trick.
Least: An option to take the fewest points in *Schafkopf.*
Left bower: In games of the *Euchre* type, the jack of the same color as the jack of trump, or right bower.
Left pedro: In *Cinch,* the five of the same color as the five of trump, or right pedro.
Lefty Louie (Poker): 254
Leg in Pot (Poker): 254
Lift Smoke: 156
Light: Drawing chips from the pot in *Poker* to show how many the player owes when out of chips himself.
Limit: The ceiling placed on bets, particularly in *Poker.*
Little cassino: the ♠2, valued as a point in *Cassino.*
Little cat: Freak hand in *Poker,* with eight high and three low, but no pair, as **8 7 6 5 3** not of the same suit.
Little dog: Freak hand in *Poker,* with seven high and two low, as **7 6 5 3 2** not of the same suit.
Little slam: Taking twelve of the thirteen tricks in *Bridge.*
Little tiger: Same as "little cat."
Liverpool Rummy: 156
Lone hand: A player who plays on his own against two or more opponents.
Long game: Any in which the entire pack is dealt to start.

Long stud: A *Stud Poker* game in which a player is dealt more than five cards.
Long suit: Predominant suit in hand, or any exceeding length.
Long Whist: See English Whist: 372
Loo or *Lanterloo:* 156
Looed: To be penalized for failing to take any tricks in *Loo.*
Louis Napoleon (Solitaire): 345
Low: Any low card or hand; in *Pitch,* the lowest card in play; also a point scored for holding or taking it.
Lowball (Poker): 237
Low Card Wild (Poker): 254
Low English Stud (Poker): 254
Lowest hand: In standard *Poker,* five cards with values 7–5–4–3–2.
Lowest with swinging ace: In *High-Low Poker,* the following: 6–4–3–2–A.
Low Hole Card Wild (Poker): 254
Low Poker: 255
Lucas (Solitaire): 339
Lurched: To be beaten before reaching half the score for game; a player so defeated is left "in the lurch."

Macao: 159
Ma Ferguson (Poker): 255, 266
Major suits: Spades and hearts in *Bridge.*
Make: Name a trump; also, to win an amount bid.
Manilla: The seven of trump in *Solo;* in a few other games, the second highest trump.
Manille: Similar to Manilla.
March: To win all five tricks in *Euchre.*
Marker: A token or chip.
Marriage: 159
Marriage: The meld of a king and queen of the same suit, in *Bezique* and *Pinochle;* in *Solitaire,* an auxiliary build.
Matadors: Unbroken sequence of highest trumps in *Skat.*
Matched cards: Those forming a set in *Rummy.*
Match 'Em (Poker): 255
Matrimony: 159
Maw: 160
Mediator: 160
Meld: To lay combinations of cards face up and score their value.
Memory: 160
Menagerie: 160
Menel: The nine of trump in *Klob* and *Jass.*
Mexicana or *Mexican Canasta:* 161
Mexican Low Card (Poker): 255

Mexican Stud (Poker): 255

Mexican Stud with Low Card Wild (Poker): 255

Mexican Wild (Poker): 256

Michigan: 161

Michigan Rummy: 294

Middlehand: Second of three players in *Skat.*

Midnight Oil (Solitaire): Nickname for *La Belle Lucie,* 350.

Mike (Poker): 256

Minor suits: Diamonds and clubs in *Bridge.*

Misdeal: To deal cards incorrectly, usually requiring a new deal.

Misere (Poker): 256

Misere: The same as "nullo."

Misery: A term applied to variants of standard games in which players try to lose tricks instead of taking them.

Miss: Unsuccessful attempt to improve a hand in *Draw Poker.* Also the "widow" in *Loo.*

Miss Milligan (Solitaire): 342

Mistigris (Poker): 256

Mittelhand: Same as Middlehand.

Mixed canasta: A meld of seven or more cards consisting of both wild and natural cards.

Monte (Poker): 271

Monte Bank: 162

Monte Carlo (Solitaire): 343

Mort: French term for a dummy hand in *Whist.*

Mortgage (Poker): 256

Mouth bet: Promise to contribute to the pot in *Poker.*

Muggins: 163

Multiple Klondike: Klondike played by three or more persons, who can add to builds of opposing players, as in *Double Solitaire,* 104.

Mustached jacks: The ♠J, ◇J, and ♡J.

Mustached Jacks Wild (Poker): 256

Mustached kings: All the kings except the ♡K.

Mustached Kings Wild (Poker): 256

My Bird Sings: 163

My Ship Sails: 163

Nap: A nickname for *Napoleon.*

Napoleon: 163

Napoleon at St. Helena (Solitaire): 342

Napoleon's Favorite (Solitaire): 344

Napoleon's Square (Solitaire): 345

Natural: A *Poker* combination made without wild cards.

Natural canasta: Seven or eight cards of the same rank, with no wild cards included.

Nestor (Solitaire): 346

New Guinea Stud (Poker): 256

New Market: 164

New York Stud (Poker): 257

Nine-Card Stud (Poker): 257

Ninety-nine (Poker): 257

Noddy: 165

No Draw (Poker): 257

No Limit (Poker): 257

No Low Cards (Poker): 257

Norwegian Whist: 165

No-trump: In a trump game, a hand played without a trump.

Nullo: A hand or game in which a player tries to lose all tricks or points instead of winning them.

Odd trick: One that gives a player or team a majority.

Oh, Hell!: 165

Oklahoma: 16

Oklahoma Gin: 134

Old Maid: 166

Old Sledge: 13

Omaha (Poker): 257

Ombre: 166

Omnibus Hearts: 140

Once around: A *Cribbage* game for 61 points instead of 121.

One-Card Poker: 258

One-eyed jacks: The ♠J and ♡J.

One-Eyed Jacks Wild (Poker): 258

One-eyed king: The ◇K.

One-Eyed King Wild (Poker): 258

One-Meld Rummy: 293

One pair: The lowest *Poker* combination, as J–J or 8–8.

Open: To make the first bet or first bid; also the first lead.

Open-end straight: In *Poker,* a bobtail straight, or four cards in sequence, as 10–9–8–7, but not of the same suit.

Openers: Cards needed to open a *Poker* pot, as a pair of jacks or better.

Open Gin: 168

Opening bid: First bid in any auction game.

Opening lead: The first lead after hands are dealt.

Open Poker: 258

Open poker: Any type of *Poker* in which cards are dealt face up; chiefly *Stud Poker.*

Opponent: An opposing dealer; particularly the nondealer in a two-handed game.

Option (Poker): 233, 258

Option: A form of *High-Low Five-Card Stud Poker.*

Order it up: In *Euchre,* the nondealer's acceptance of the turned-up card as trump, said card going to dealer.

Ordinary suit: Any nontrump suit.

Original bidder: The player making the first bid, or the first bid for his team.

Original hand: A hand as first dealt.

Overbid: Bid too high to win.

Overcall: Bid higher than the previous bid.

Overhand shuffle: To draw off groups of cards with one hand and throw the rest on top with the other, like a series of rapid cuts.

Overruff: The same as overtrump.

Overtrick: One more than needed to win, particularly in *Bridge.*

Overtrump: To play a higher trump on a trick already trumped.

Pack: All the cards used in a game.

Packet: A portion of the pack.

Pa Ferguson (Poker): 258, 266

Paint: To force a heart on an opponent in *Hearts.*

Pair: Two cards of the same value, especially in *Poker.*

Pairs royal: Three cards of the same value in *Cribbage.*

Pam: The ♣J in *Loo.*

Pam-Loo: 168

Pan: A popular term for *Panguingue.*

Panguingue or *Pan:* 169

Papillon: 171

Parliament: 171

Partner: A member of a team of two and sometimes more players.

Partnership Games: 171

Pass: To refuse to bid, also to exchange cards with another player.

Pass Along (Poker): 259

Pass and Back In (Poker): 259

Pass and back in: In *Poker,* the privilege of passing and coming back in the game later.

Pass on Hearts: 171

Pass Out (Poker): 171

Pass out: To pass and drop from the betting in *Poker.*

Pass the Garbage or *Pass the Trash (Poker):* 259

Pat hand: A *Poker* hand that cannot be improved by a draw.

Patience: 172

Pedro (Pitch): 172

Pedro (Poker): 259

Pedro: The five of trump in *Pedro.*

Pedro Sancho: 172

Peep Poker: 259

Peep and Turn (Poker): 259

Peep Nap: 173

Peg: To score points on a *Cribbage* board.

Pelter: The same as kilter; also an occasional term for skeet.

Penchant: 173

Pennies from Heaven: 173

Penny Ante (Poker): 259

Penny ante: A *Poker* game with a one-cent limit.

Persian Pasha: 173

Persian Rummy: 295

Picture card: A face card.

Pig: 173

Pig in Poke (Poker): 259

Pink Lady: 142

Pink lady: The ♡Q when given special penalty value in *Hearts.*

Pinochle: 174

Pinochle: A meld of ◇J and ♠Q for 40 points.

Pinochle Poker: 259

Pinochle Rummy: 295

Pip: A spot on a playing card.

Piquet: 211

Pirate Bridge: 214

Pisha Pasha: 214

Pistol, Pistol Pete, Pistol Stud (Poker): 260

Pitch: 214

Pivot Bridge: 217

Place and Show (Poker): 260

Place Poker: 260

Plafond: 217

Plain suit: Any nontrump suit.

Play: Put a card on a trick.

Player: Active participant in a card game.

Play off: Preventing an opponent from scoring in *Cribbage.*

Play on: Inviting an opponent to score in *Cribbage* in hope of going him one better.

Play or Pay: 217

Plus or Minus: 217

Pochen: 218

Point: Scoring unit in various games.

Point count: A system of evaluating bids in *Bridge.*

Point value: The number of points a counter card is worth.

Poker: 219

Poker Gin: 130

Poker Rum: 154

Poker Solitaire (Poker): 260

Polignac: 283

Polish Bezique: 284

Polish Rummy: 294

Pone: Nondealer in a two-handed game; the dealer's opponent.

Pontoon: A nickname for *Twenty-one.*

Pool: Common fund of chips or tokens.

Pope Joan: 284

Post-mortem: Analysis of a hand or deal after it has been played.

Pot: A term for a pool, consisting of chips or tokens. In *Canasta,* the "pozo" or discard pile.

Pothooks Wild (*Poker*): 260

Pot Limit (*Poker*): 260

Pounce: 284

Poverty Poker: 260

Pozo: The discard pile in *Canasta.*

Pre-empt: To bid so high that the opponents are unable to overbid, particularly in *Bridge.*

Pre-emptive bid: One preventing the opposing team from bidding.

Preference: 284

Premium: A bonus paid to high winning hands; in *Bridge,* any scores registered above the line.

Primero (*Poker*): 260

Prize pot: A canasta discard pile containing a wild card.

Procter and Gamble (*Poker*): 261

Progressive Bridge: 285

Progressive Jackpots (*Poker*): 261

Progressive Rummy: 285

Prussian Whist: A variant of *Whist* in which a card is cut from another pack to establish trump.

Psychic bid: An unconventional bid in *Contract Bridge,* intended to deceive the opposing team.

Punto: The fourth highest card, when a red ace in *Ombre* or *Quadrille.*

Push Poker: 261

Push Poker: A common term for *Take It or Leave It.*

Pussy Cat (*Poker*): 262

Put and Take: 285

Quadrille: 286

Quatre Valets: 284

Queen: Next highest card to a king in most games, but of special importance in certain games, as described under those heads.

Queen City Poker: 262

Queen City Rum: 286

Quick trick: A high card holding in *Bridge,* promising a fast win.

Quinella: 286

Quinola: 286

Quint: A sequence of five cards in *Piquet.*

Quinze: 286

Racehorse: 13

Railroad Euchre: 113

Raise: Bid higher or add chips to a pot.

Rake-off: A share of pots taken by a gambling house or a dealer.

Rams: 287

Ramsch: A term for "nullo" in *Skat.*

Rana: 288

Rangdoodles (*Poker*): 262

Rank: Relative value of a card.

Ranter-Go-Round: 288

Rap Poker: 288

Razzle Dazzle: 67

Rebid: A new bid by a former bidder.

Red and Black: 288

Red and Black (*Trente et Quarante*): 368

Red Dog: 289

Redeal: A hand dealt over again by the same dealer. In *Solitaires,* dealing through the discard pile as a new pack; or gathering cards from the layout and dealing them in new order.

Red or Black: 289

Redouble: To double a double in *Bridge.*

Re-entrant: Player who comes back into a game to replace a loser.

Re-entry: A card used by a player to regain the lead in *Bridge.*

Reject: A form of "nullo" in *Dutch Whist.*

Renege: Failure to follow suit or play a required card.

Renounce: Discard on the suit led.

Reserve: A special pile of cards dealt in some forms of *Solitaire.*

Response: Support for a partner's bid in *Bridge.*

Reversi: 289

Revoke: The same as renege.

Rickey de Laet (*Poker*): 262

Ride along: Keep calling bets in *Poker.*

Riffle: A shuffle in which the ends of the pack are interlaced.

Right bower: The jack of trumps, when highest trump, as in *Euchre.*

Rob: Exchange a card for a turned-up trump.

Rob the pack: To take cards from the pack to replace those in the hand.

Rolling Stone: 106

Roodles (*Poker*): 262

Roodles: A round of *Poker* hands with stakes increased by agreement.

Rothschild (*Poker*): 262

Rouge et Noir: 368

Rounce: 290

Round: A series of hands in which everybody deals.

Round game: A game without partners and with a variable number of players.

Roundhouse: Meld of four kings and four queens in *Pinochle* for 240 points.

Round of Jacks (*Poker*): 262

Round the Corner (*Poker*): 263

Round the Corner Gin: 290

Round the Corner Rummy: 293

Round the corner straight: An optional *Poker* hand in which an ace is both low and high in a sequence, a 2–A–K–Q–J.

Round the World (*Poker*): 263

Round trip: Same as roundhouse in *Pinochle.*

Row Cards dealt side by side in *Solitaire.*

Royal Cassino: 290

Royal Draw Cassino: 291

Royale: A holding of K, Q, J of one suit in *Trenta-Cinque.*

Royal flush: the A–K–Q–J–10 of the same suit, an unbeatable hand in standard *Poker* when wild cards are barred.

Royal Marriage (*Solitaire*): 328

Royal marriage: King and queen of trump in *Pinochle,* scoring 40 points.

Royals: A fifth suit in special packs of cards, with crowns as symbols. Similar to eagles.

Royal sequence: A trump sequence, A–10–K–Q–J in *Pinochle.*

Royal Spade Cassino: 291

Royal straight flush: Same as a royal flush in *Poker.*

Royalton: 291

Rubber: Best of three games in *Bridge* or *Whist.*

Rubicon: To be beaten before reaching a required score; similar to lurch.

Rubicon Bezique: 26

Rubicon Piquet: 291

Ruff: To trump a lead from another suit.

Ruffs and Honors: 291

Rule of eleven: A mathematical rule that if a player leads his fourth highest card, in *Bridge* or *Whist,* subtraction of its value from eleven reveals the number of cards of that suit in the remaining hands. Example: Player leads the ♡7. He will have three higher hearts; the other players will have four higher hearts among them.

Rule of fourth highest: A customary lead from the longest suit in a *Bridge* hand.

Rummy: 291

Rummy: Dispose of the final card in a *Rummy* hand; also to lay down a matched hand all at once.

Run: A sequence of three or more cards in *Cribbage* or *Rummy;* or a trump sequence in *Pinochle.*

Run the cards: To deal three extra cards to each player in *Seven Up.*

Russian Bank: 296

Samba: 300

Saratoga: 301

Schafkopf: 301

Schmear: A defensive play in *Pinochle.*

Schmeiss: Agreement to abandon a deal in *Klob.*

Schneider: To fall short of half the needed points in *Skat.*

Schwarz: Failure to take any tricks in *Skat.*

Schwellen: 106

Scoop: 301

Scopa: 301

Scopone: 302

Score: Total tricks or points won by player or team.

Scotch Whist: 302

Screwy Louie (*Poker*): 263

Second Hand Low (*Poker*): 263

See: To call a bet in *Poker.*

Sellout: 303

Serve: A type of deal.

Set: Lose a bid; also, a meld of three or more cards in *Rummy.*

Setback: 214

Set back: Lose a score or go in the hole.

Setback Bid Whist: 376

Setback Euchre: 303

Settlement: Balancing up of scores, particularly with chips involved.

Seven and a Half: 303

Seven-Card Flip (*Poker*): 263

Seven-Card Flip, Modern Form (*Poker*): 263

Seven-Card Hokum (*Poker*): 264

Seven-Card Mutual (*Poker*): 264

Seven-Card Pete (*Poker*): 264

Seven-Card Reverse (*Poker*): 264

Seven-Card Stud (*Poker*): 229, 231

Sevens: 304

Shamrocks (*Solitaire*): 346

Shanghai Rummy: 304

Shasta Sam: 304

Sheepshead: 304

Shimmy: 308

Short game: A game in which only part of the pack is dealt.

Short suit: Any suit in a hand with less than an average number of cards; particularly, the shortest suit.

Short Whist: A game of *Whist* played for only 5 points.

Show: Meld or lay down cards often for scoring purposes.

Showdown: Disclosure of all hands, particularly in *Poker*.

Shuffle: Mix the cards of a pack.

Shutout: Keep opponents from scoring. In *Bridge*, to pre-empt.

Shy: Owing chips to a pot.

Side: A team.

Side bets: Private bets among individual players, particularly in *Poker*.

Side card: Highest card not forming part of a combination in a *Poker* hand. Example: J-J-A-7-3 would be a pair of jacks with an ace as side card, defeating J-J-K-Q-9, with only a king as side card. Also any card of an ordinary suit in a trump game.

Side pot: A special pot in *Table Stakes*.

Side strength: High cards other than trumps.

Side suit: Any suit except the trump suit.

Signal: Conventional bid or play in partnership game.

Simple game: One played at the lowest bidding level, particularly in *Skat*.

Singleton: In *Whist* or *Bridge*, a lone card of a suit in the hand as originally dealt.

Sixty queens: Four queens in *Pinochle*, scoring 60 points.

Skeet: A freak *Poker* hand, containing 9-5-2 with two other values between.

Skip or skip straight: A freak *Poker* hand with alternating values, as K-J-9-7-5.

Skunked: Badly defeated, particularly when held scoreless.

Slam: Taking twelve or thirteen tricks in *Bridge*.

Smear: Same as *schmear*.

Space: An opening gained by removal of a pile of cards from a *Solitaire* layout.

Spades: A score of 1 point for making the most spades in *Cassino*.

Spades double: A popular rule giving a spade bid double value in *Pinochle*.

Spadilla: The highest trump ♣Q in *German Solo.*

Spadille: The highest trump ♠A in *Ombre.*

Spider (Solitaire): 347

Spin or *Spinado:* 357

Spin: Short for "spinado."

Spit (Poker): 268

Spit, No Card Wild (Poker): 269

Spit, Other Variants *(Poker):* 269

Spite and Malice: 357

Spit in the Ocean (Poker): 268

Split: In *Blackjack,* to separate two cards of equal value and play each as an individual hand.

Split openers: To discard part of an opening combination in *Draw Poker,* usually one of a pair. Example: Holding **K–Q–J–J–10,** a player would discard one jack, hoping to fill a straight, consisting of **A–K–Q–J–10** or **K–Q–J–10–9.**

Spoil Five: 360, 363

Spot card: Any card other than an ace or a face card; an ace, when ranked as low, may be regarded as a spot.

Spot Hearts: 362

Spread: To spread out cards on the table, either as a meld or as a showdown, or to prove that the hand is a sure winner.

Squeeze: A series of plays in *Bridge* that force an opponent to discard a winning card.

Squeezers: Modern playing cards, with an index at each upper left corner.

Stack: A pile of chips or counters.

Stake: The amount of chips that a player is willing or able to expend during a game.

Stand: To agree upon a turned-up card as trump; or to play out a deal or put required chips in a pot.

Standard pack: Fifty-two cards in the majority of games; varying numbers in others.

Stand pat: To play a hand as dealt in *Draw Poker,* without drawing any cards.

Stay: To call in *Poker.*

Stealing Bundles: 362

Stock: Portion of pack not yet dealt.

Stop: Interruption of play in certain games.

Stop cards: Black threes and wild cards in *Canasta* that prevent the next player from taking up the discard pile.

Stopper: A card high enough to keep an opponent from winning an entire

suit in *Bridge* and some other games.

Stops: 363

Storehouse (Solitaire): 348, 349

Stormy Weather (Poker): 269

Straddle: In *Poker,* to follow a blind bet with a blind raise.

Straight: In *Poker,* a sequence of mixed suits, as **Q–J–10–9–8.**

Straight flush: A *Poker* sequence in one suit, as ♡ **9–8–7–6–5.**

Straight Poker: 269

Streets and Alleys (Solitaire): 325

Striped straight: A freak *Poker* hand with cards alternating red and black when arranged in descending order, as ♡ **J** ♠ **7** ◇ **6** ♠ **4** ◇ **2.**

Stripped Pack (Poker): 269

Stripped pack: A pack with some of the low cards removed, used in *Poker* games to produce stronger hands when the game is short of players.

Stud Poker: 228, 270

Stud with Spit (Poker): 270

Stuss: 364

Sudden Death (Poker): 270

Suits: The four distinctive groups of a standard pack: ♠ ♡ ◇ ♣.

Suit Value Whist: 364

Super Contract Bridge: 364

Swedish Rummy: 365

Sweep: To take 1 point in *Cassino* by clearing the board.

Sweeten: To add a new ante or put extra chips in a pot.

System: Any recognized or established bidding method in *Bridge* and certain other games.

Tableau: An old term for a *Solitaire* layout.

Table Stakes (Poker): 270

Take: To agree to play with the turned-up trump in *Klob.*

Take-All Hearts: 143

Take in: To win a trick. In *Cassino,* to gather the leftover cards.

Take It or Leave It (Poker): 270

Takeout: In *Bridge,* to make a bid at variance with a partner's bid.

Takeout double: An informatory double in *Bridge.*

Take up: The dealer's privilege of exchanging a card for the trump card turned up in *Euchre;* also to pick up the discard pile in *Canasta* and certain forms of *Rummy.*

Tam o' Shanter (Solitaire): 324

Tampa: 365

Tap: To announce an intention by tapping on the table, such as forgoing the privilege of cutting the pack, or passing a chance to bid. In *Poker*, a player taps when he bets all his remaining chips in *Table Stakes*.

Tap Out (*Poker*): 270

Taroc or *Tarok:* 365

Team: A partnership.

Tenace: In *Bridge* or *Whist*, honor cards with a gap between, as **A–Q** (major) or **K–J** (minor).

Ten-Card Stud (*Poker*): 270

Tennessee (*Poker*): 270

Tennessee Jed (*Poker*): 271

Tens High (*Poker*): 271

Tenth card: A card counting for 10 in *Cribbage;* namely, **K, Q, J, 10.**

Texas Tech (*Poker*): 271

Third Hand High (*Poker*): 271

Third hand high: A customary procedure in *Whist*, where the third player puts his highest card on a trick. Applicable to other games.

Thirty and Forty: 368

Thirty-five: See *Trenta-Cinque:* 366

Thirty-one: 366

Three-Card Monte: 366

Three-Card Monte (*Poker*): 271

Three-Card Poker: 271

Three Forty-Five (*Poker*): 272

Three-Handed Games: 367

Three of a kind: In *Poker*, a holding of three cards of the same value.

Three Out of Five (*Poker*): 272

Three Pair High (*Poker*): 272

Three-Toed Pete (*Poker*): 272

Throw Away Two (*Poker*): 272

Throw in: To throw a hand face down as unplayable, particularly in *Draw Poker*.

Throw off: To make a discard.

Tierce: A three-card sequence in *Piquet*.

Tiger (*Poker*): 367

Tiger: A freak *Poker* hand, the same as *cat;* also a symbol used to advertise a *Faro* game.

TNT (*Poker*): 272

Touching: In *Bridge*, two suits next to each other in value.

Towie: 367

Trail: To lay down an odd card in *Cassino*.

Trash: Worthless cards.

Trefoil (*Solitaire*): 348, 350

Treize: 367

Trenta-Cinque: 367

Trente et Quarante: 368

Tresette: 368

Trey: A three-spot.

Triangle Contract: 369

Trick: Cards played singly by each player, forming a group that one player wins.

Trick score: Points for tricks bid and won in *Bridge*, going below the line on the scoresheet.

Tricon: French term for three of a kind.

Triomphe, Triumph or *Trump:* 369

Trionfetti: 369

Tripleton: Only three cards of a suit in a *Bridge* hand as originally dealt.

Triplets: Three of a kind.

Tripoli: 369

Tlips: Nickname for "triplets."

Trump: 369

Trump: Modern name for *Triomphe*.

Trump: Card of a special suit that ranks higher than the others; also, to play a trump card on another suit.

Trump suit: The suit named as trump.

Tunk: 370

Twenty-five: 371

Twenty-nine: 371

Twenty-one: 371

Twice around: A *Cribbage* game of 121 points as scored on a special board.

Twin Beds (*Poker*): 273

Twin Beds Wild (*Poker*): 273

Twist: To draw or substitute added cards at the end of a *Poker* hand, in hope of improving holdings before the showdown.

Two-Card Poker or *Two-Card High-Low:* 273

Two-Handed Games: 371

Two-Meld Rummy: 293

Two pair: A *Poker* hand with two pairs of different values, with an odd card, as **K–K–4–4–8.**

Two suiter: A hand in any long game (in which the entire pack is dealt) composed chiefly of two suits of about the same length.

Uncle Doc: A nickname for *Five-Card Stud* with a spit.

Undercut: To finish a hand of *Gin Rummy* with a count lower than the knocker's.

Underplay: Temporarily retain a high card by playing one of lower rank.

Under the guns: The player to the left of the dealer.

Undertrick: Each trick below a bidder's required contract in *Bridge*.

Unlimited Loo: 158, 371

Unlimited Poker: A term applied to any

Poker game where players may bet as high as they want.

Unload: To get rid of high-count cards in *Rummy*.

Unmatched: Any leftover card in *Rummy*.

Up: To raise a *Poker* bid, also, the higher of two pair, as example, a hand containing 9–9–5–5 would be termed "nines up."

Up and Down the River: 273, 371

Upcard: A card dealt face up in *Stud Poker;* also the top card of the discard pile in *Rummy* and *Canasta*.

Uruguay: Short for *Uruguayan Canasta.*

Uruguayan Canasta or *Uruguay:* 372

Utah (Poker): 273

Vacancy: A space in a *Solitaire* layout.

Valet: French term for a jack in certain games.

Valle: Term for "value" in *Panguingue,* the threes, fives, and sevens being known as "valle cards."

Value: The rank or denomination of a card.

Van John: 372

Variety: 122

Vice President (Poker): 273

Vigorish: Percentage taken by a gambling casino.

Vingt-et-un or *Vingt-un:* 372

Vint: 372

Vive l'Amour: 373

Void: A blank suit, particularly in *Bridge.*

Vole: Term for winning all five tricks in *Écarté.*

Vorhand: Forehand in *Skat.*

Vulnerable: A team with one game toward rubber in *Contract Bridge.*

War: 373

Washington's Favorite (Solitaire): 350

Waste-pile: Discard pile in *Solitaire.*

Weddings (Solitaire): 351

Wellington: 374

Wenzel: A jack of trump in early *Skat.*

Wescliffe (Solitaire): 351

Whangdoodles (Poker): 274

Wheel: Any 5–4–3–2–A in *Lowball.*

Whisk: 374

Whiskey Poker: 374

Whist: 375

Whist de Gand: Another name for *Solo Whist.*

Whistler (Solitaire): 351

Whitehead (Solitaire): 351

White Pass (Solitaire): 351

Wide cards: A *Cribbage* term for two cards spaced at least two values apart, as 9 and 6, 8 and 4, 7 and 2, etc.

Widow: A special deal of extra cards, which a player may later pick up. Similar to blind, kitty, skat, talon, equivalent terms used in different games.

Widow Cinch: 67, 377

Widow Nap: 377

Wild card: A card representing any other.

Wild-Card Canasta: 378

Wild-Card Poker: 239

Wild-Card Rummy: 294

Wild Court Cards (Poker): 274

Wild Face Cards (Poker): 274

Wild Suit (Poker): 274

Wild Widow (Poker): 274

Wired: Cards "back to back" in *Stud Poker.*

With: To hold a certain number of matadors in *Skat.*

Without: To be without a certain number of matadors in *Skat.*

Woolworth (Poker): 274

X Marks the Spot (Poker): 275

Yarborough: A *Whist* hand with nothing higher than a nine. Bets of 1000 to 1 have been offered against holding it, but the actual odds have been calculated at 1827 to 1. The term is sometimes applied to *Bridge* hands.

Yass: 379

Yerlash: 379

You Roll Two (Poker): 275

Yukon (Solitaire): 351, 354

Zebra: Same as striped straight in *Poker.*

Zebra Poker: 275

Ziginette: 379

Zioncheck: 379

Zombie (Poker): 275

Zsa Zsa: A very lovely hand.